Acclaim for Russell Shorto's

THE ISLAND AT THE CENTER OF THE WORLD

"Wonderful. . . . This is one o   s in the picked-over field of
colonial history, a whole new pi   hrown-open window. . . . With his
full-blooded resurrection of an unfamiliar American patriot, Russell
Shorto has made a real contribution."   —*The New York Observer*

"Deserves to be a bestseller . . . narratively irresistible, intellectually pro-
vocative, historically invaluable."   —*The Guardian*

"[An] absorbing, sensual, sometimes bawdy narrative featuring whores, pirates, explorers and scholars. With clarity and panache, Shorto briskly
conveys the complex history of the age of exploration."

—*Times Literary Supplement*

"As Russell Shorto demonstrates in this mesmerizing volume, the story we
don't know is even more fascinating than the one we do. . . . Historians
must now seriously rethink what they previously understood about New
York's origins."   —*New York Post*

"Russell Shorto fires a powerful salvo in the war of words over America's
origins . . . he mounts a convincing case [that], in Shorto's words, 'Manhattan is where America began.' Readers . . . find themselves absorbed in
what can only be described as a plot, revolving around two strong men
with conflicting visions of the future of Dutch North America."

—Joyce Goodfriend, *America: The National Catholic Weekly*

"Fascinating. . . . A richly nuanced portrait set against events on the world
stage."   —*Time Out New York*

"Shorto brings this . . . deeply influential chapter in the city's history to vivid, breathtaking life [with] a talent for enlivening meticulous research and painting on a broad canvas. . . . In elegant, erudite prose, he manages to capture the lives of disparate historical characters, from kings to prostitutes."
                                                                    —*Pittsburgh Post-Gazette*

"Remarkable. . . . [C]ompulsively interesting. . . . Shorto argues that during the brief decades of its Dutch colonial existence Manhattan had already found, once and for all, its tumultuously eclectic soul."   —*New Statesman*

"Shorto delineates the characters in this nonfiction drama convincingly and compellingly."   —*Fort Worth Star-Telegram*

"A spry, informative history. . . . Shorto supplies lucid, comprehensive contexts in which to see the colony's promise and turmoil. . . . [D]elivers the goods with clarity, color and zest."   —*The Seattle Times*

"Shorto's book makes a convincing case that the Dutch did not merely influence the relatively open, tolerant and multicultural society that became the United States; they made the first and most significant contribution."
                                                                    —*American History*

"Shorto's prose is deliciously rich and witty, and the story he tells—drawing heavily on sources that have only recently come to light—brings one surprise after another. His rediscovery of Adriaen van der Donck, Peter Stuyvesant's nemesis, is fascinating."   —Edward G. Burrows, coauthor of *Gotham: A History of New York City to 1898*, winner of the Pulitzer Prize in History

"A landmark work. . . . Shorto paints the emotions and attitudes of his characters with a sure hand, and bestows on each a believable, living presence."   —*The Times* (London)

"A triumph of scholarship and a rollicking narrative . . . an exciting drama about the roots of America's freedoms."
                                    —Walter Isaacson, author of *Benjamin Franklin: An American Life*

Russell Shorto is an American author, historian and journalist. His books have been published in nine languages and he is the contributing writer at the *New York Times Magazine* and the director of the John Adams Institute in Amsterdam.

BY RUSSELL SHORTO

Descartes' Bones

The Island at the Center of the World

Saints and Madmen

Gospel Truth

Amsterdam

THE
ISLAND
AT THE
CENTER
OF THE
WORLD

The Epic Story of Dutch Manhattan and
the Forgotten Colony That Shaped America

RUSSELL SHORTO

ABACUS

First published in the United States in 2004 by Doubleday
First published by Abacus as an ebook in 2013
This paperback edition published in 2014 by Abacus

3 5 7 9 10 8 6 4

A CIP catalogue record for this book
is available from the British Library.

ISBN 978-0-349-14020-9

Book design by Fritz Metsch

Printed and bound in Great Britain by
Clays Ltd, St Ives plc

Papers used by Abacus are from well-managed forests
and other responsible sources.

MIX
Paper from
responsible sources
FSC
www.fsc.org   FSC® C104740

Abacus
An imprint of
Little, Brown Book Group
Carmelite House
50 Victoria Embankment
London EC4Y 0DZ

An Hachette UK Company
www.hachette.co.uk

www.littlebrown.co.uk

For my father

CONTENTS

ACKNOWLEDGMENTS XI
PROLOGUE: THE MISSING FLOOR 1

PART I. "A CERTAIN ISLAND NAMED MANATHANS"

1. *The Measure of Things* 13
2. *The Pollinator* 25
3. *The Island* 37
4. *The King, the Surgeon, the Turk, and the Whore* 67

PART II. CLASH OF WILLS

5. *The Lawman* 93
6. *The Council of Blood* 110
7. *The Cause* 129
8. *The One-Legged Man* 146
9. *The General and the* Princess 167
10. *The People's Champion* 191
11. *An American in Europe* 209
12. *A Dangerous Man* 233

PART III. THE INHERITANCE

13. *Booming* 257
14. *New York* 284
15. *Inherited Features* 301

EPILOGUE: THE PAPER TRAIL 319
NOTES 326
BIBLIOGRAPHY 352
INDEX 373

ACKNOWLEDGMENTS

This book would not exist without the work of Charles Gehring, who, as director of the New Netherland Project, has devoted thirty years to translating the manuscript Dutch records of the New Netherland colony. But published translations aside, for more than two years he has welcomed me into his workspace, opened his files to me, offered advice, made introductions, and helped in dozens of other ways. Over Vietnamese lunches and pints of microbrew beer, on the Albany waterfront and along the canals of Amsterdam, he has been my guide. My greatest thanks to you, Charly.

I also owe a debt of gratitude to Janny Venema of the New Netherland Project, for similar help mixed with friendship. She spent days transcribing as-yet-unpublished manuscripts for me. She gave me a primer in how to read seventeenth-century Dutch handwriting. She made the town of Beverwyck, long since swallowed up by the city of Albany, come alive for me.

Of the many others who helped me, I would like to thank Jeremy Bangs and Carola de Muralt of the American Pilgrim Museum in Leiden, the Netherlands, who gave me a sense of the texture of seventeenth-century Dutch life and a magnificent afternoon-long tour of their one-of-a-kind museum. Patricia Bonomi, professor emeritus of history at New York University, offered guidance as I set out on the project and encouragement as I approached the end. Peter Christoph of the New York State Library shared with me his reminiscences about his discovery of the Dutch manuscripts and efforts to get them translated. Diane Dallal, archaeologist with New York Unearthed and the South Street Seaport Museum, helped me to visualize New Amsterdam amid the canyons of lower Manhattan. Firth Fabend, historian and author, helped on many fronts, especially in understanding how "Dutchness" changed in North America from the seventeenth century onward, and in assessing the colony's legacy. The Friends of New Netherland invited me to speak at their annual meeting in 2003, thus providing me a chance to air some of my ideas about the Dutch colony. Willem Frijhoff of the Free University of Amsterdam, distinguished historian and authority on New Netherland and its people, is a man of great generosity who offered brilliant, timely advice and encouraged me in my focus on Adriaen van der Donck. Elisabeth Paling Funk, Dutch-born scholar and authority on Washington Irving, helped me to disentangle history from myth, and translated some seventeenth-century poetry for me. Wayne Furman of the New York Public Library, as well as the staff of the library's New York History and Genealogy division, accommodated me throughout my research. I'm grateful to Joyce Goodfriend of the University of Denver, authority on early New York, for good conversation on history and historians, for advice and pointers, and for introducing me to Jack's Oyster House in Albany. Anne Halpern of the National Gallery of Art assisted with research on the portrait of Adriaen van der Donck. Leo Hershkowitz, professor of history at Queens College, who has written with equal elegance about both the Jews of New Amsterdam and Boss Tweed, knows New York history as few people on earth do, and gave me the benefit of his perspective. Maria Holden, conservator at the New York State Archives, gave me a primer on the Dutch documents as artifacts: on paper, ink, and methods of preservation.

On a sun-dazzled Fourth of July morning on the terrace of the Stadscafe in the city of Leiden, Jaap Jacobs of the University of Amsterdam broadened my view of seventeenth-century American colonial history, helping me to see it not merely as foreshadowing later American history but as part of European history and the global power struggle between England and the Dutch Republic; I am also grateful for his elegant writings on New Netherland and on the concept of tolerance in the seventeenth century, and for conversation on the prickly figure of Peter Stuyvesant, a biography of whom he is currently at work on. My thanks to Joep de Koning, probably the world's foremost collector of maps of New Netherland, for conversation, for insights, and for giving me a chance to roam among his one-of-a-kind collection; to Dennis Maika of Fox Lane High School, Bedford, New York, whose dissertation on and insights into the significance of the 1653 municipal charter and the subsequent boom in the colony were instrumental in shaping my own thoughts; to Simon Middleton of the University of East Anglia, for pointers on early modern Republicanism in the Netherlands and for his encouragement as a fellow Van der Donck enthusiast; to Peter Neil, director of the South Street Seaport Museum; to Chip Reynolds, skipper of the *Half Moon,* for taking me aboard and giving me a feel of the ship; to Peter Rose, authority on seventeenth-century Dutch food, for culinary assistance; to Thomas Rosenbaum of the Rockefeller Archives, Pocantico Hills, New York, who afforded me access to that institution's remarkable collection of seventeenth-century Dutch notarial records; to Ada Louise Van Gastel, for her work on Adriaen van der Donck and her encouragement; to Hanny Veenendaal of the Netherlands Center in New York City, for giving me a grounding in the Dutch language and for assisting in translations and in reading old Dutch documents; to Greta Wagle, who welcomed me into the family of New Netherland aficionados, put me in touch with people, and has been generally delightful to know; to Gerald de Weerdt, curator of 't Behouden Huys Museum, Terschelling, the Netherlands, for sharing insights on Dutch seafaring; to Laurie Weinstein, Western Connecticut State University, who helped in my attempts to understand Dutch-English-Indian interactions; and to Thomas Wysmuller for discussions on Dutch history and for enthusiastic support.

A separate thank you to Firth Fabend, Charly Gehring, Leo Hershkowitz, Joep de Koning, Tim Paulson, Janny Venema, and Mark Zwonitzer for reading the manuscript and offering excellent comments and critiques. The book is greatly improved by their input, though of course any errors remain my own doing.

My thanks also to Coen Blaauw; José Brandão, Western Michigan University; Marilyn Douglas, New York State Library; Howard Funk; Dietrich Gehring; April Hatfield, Texas A&M University; L. J. Krizner, the New York Historical Society; Karen Ordahl Kupperman, New York University; Hubert de Leeuw; Harry Macy, editor of *The New York Genealogical and Biographical Record*; Richard Mooney, *New York Times* editorial board, retired; the staff of the New York State Library and Archives; Hennie Newhouse, Friends of New Netherland; Don Rittner; Martha Shattuck; Amanda Sutphin, New York City Landmarks Preservation Commission; Martine Julia van Ittersum, Harvard University; Cynthia van Zandt, University of New Hampshire; Loet Velmans; David William Voorhees, of The Holland Society of New York and managing editor of *de Halve Maen*; Charles Wendell, Friends of New Netherland; and James Homer Williams, Middle Tennessee State University.

Thanks also to my team. Anne Edelstein, my agent and friend, plucked the rabbit of an idea out of my brain and made this all happen. Laura Williams gave advice in the early going, and Emilie Stewart assisted in the endgame. Anne Hollister and Elisabeth King fact checked the manuscript with scrupulosity and style. Tim Paulson listened to my initial rambling, inchoate idea, pushed me to carry it forward, and was there along the way with smart counsel. Bill Thomas, my editor at Doubleday, championed the project from the beginning and managed throughout to support it with the excellent combination of overflowing enthusiasm and sharp critical judgment. Thanks also to Kendra Harpster, John Fontana, and Christine Pride of Doubleday. In London, Marianne Velmans, my editor at Transworld, brought her Anglo-Dutch perspective to bear, and critiqued the manuscript with great insight.

Finally, my wife, Marnie Henricksson, endured the years of this project, shared the good times of it with me and saw me through what were some definite not-so-good times. She is the love of my life and I owe her everything.

So much for the living. From time to time during the course of my work on this book I've had the flickering sense that the spirits of Adriaen van der Donck and Peter Stuyvesant were hovering somewhere nearby, the first, perhaps, interested at the notion of being plucked from historical oblivion, the second maybe at potentially being rescued from the status of historical cartoon. There is one other spirit I've felt as well, a less obvious one. I would like to express my gratitude to the late Barbara W. Tuchman: for providing a model of a writer committed to history and narrative both; for being among the first popular historians to recognize, in her final book, *The First Salute,* the overlooked contribution of the Dutch to early American history; and finally and perhaps most importantly to me, for making a bequest to the New York Public Library in honor of her father, which resulted in the establishment of the Wertheim Study Room, where much of this book was researched.

THE ISLAND

AT THE CENTER

OF THE WORLD

Prologue

THE MISSING FLOOR

If you were to step inside an elevator in the lobby of the New York State Library in Albany, you would discover that, although the building has eleven floors, there is no button marked eight. To get to the eighth floor, which is closed to the public, you ride to seven, walk through a security door, state your business to a librarian at the desk, then go into another elevator and ride up one more flight.

As you pass shelves of quietly moldering books and periodicals—the budgets of the state of Kansas going back to 1923, the Australian census, the complete bound series of *Northern Miner*—you may be greeted by the sound of German opera coming from a small room at the southeast corner. Peering around the doorway, you would probably find a rather bearish-looking man hunched over a desk, perhaps squinting through an antique jeweler's loupe. The hiddenness of the location is an apt metaphor for the work going on here. What Dr. Charles Gehring is studying with such attention may be one of several thousand artifacts in his care—artifacts that, once they give up their secrets through his efforts, breathe life into a moment of history that has been largely ignored for three centuries.

This book tells the story of that moment in time. It is a story of high adventure set during the age of exploration—when Francis Drake, Henry Hudson, and Captain John Smith were expanding the boundaries of the world, and Shakespeare, Rembrandt, Galileo, Descartes, Mercator, Vermeer, Harvey, and Bacon were revolutionizing human thought and expression. It is a distinctly European tale, but also a vital piece of America's beginnings. It is the story of one of the original European colonies on America's shores, a colony that was eventually swallowed up by the others.

At the book's center is an island—a slender wilderness island at the edge of the known world. As the European powers sent off their navies and adventurer-businessmen to roam the seas in history's first truly global era, this island would become a fulcrum in the international power struggle, the key to control of a continent and a new world. This account encompasses the kings and generals who plotted for control of this piece of property, but at the story's heart is a humbler assemblage: a band of explorers, entrepreneurs, pirates, prostitutes, and assorted scalawags from different parts of Europe who sought riches on this wilderness island. Together, this unlikely group formed a new society. They were the first New Yorkers, the original European inhabitants of the island of Manhattan.

We are used to thinking of American beginnings as involving thirteen English colonies—to thinking of American history as an English root onto which, over time, the cultures of many other nations were grafted to create a new species of society that has become a multiethnic model for progressive societies around the world. But that isn't true. To talk of the thirteen original English colonies is to ignore another European colony, the one centered on Manhattan, which predated New York and whose history was all but erased when the English took it over.

The settlement in question occupied the area between the newly forming English territories of Virginia and New England. It extended roughly from present-day Albany, New York, in the north to Delaware Bay in the south, comprising all or parts of what became New York, New Jersey, Connecticut, Pennsylvania, and Delaware. It was founded by the Dutch, who called it New Netherland, but half of its residents were from elsewhere. Its capital was a tiny collection of rough buildings perched on the edge of a limitless wilderness, but its muddy lanes and waterfront were prowled by a Babel of peoples—Norwegians, Germans, Italians, Jews, Africans (slaves and free), Walloons, Bohemians, Munsees, Montauks, Mohawks, and many others— all living on the rim of empire, struggling to find a way of being together, searching for a balance between chaos and order, liberty and oppression. Pirates, prostitutes, smugglers, and business sharks held sway in it. It was *Manhattan,* in other words, right from the start: a place unlike any other, either in the North American colonies or anywhere else.

Because of its geography, its population, and the fact that it was under the control of the Dutch (even then its parent city, Amsterdam, was the most liberal in Europe), this island city would become the first multiethnic, upwardly mobile society on America's shores, a prototype of the kind of society that would be duplicated throughout the country and around the world. It was no coincidence that on September 11, 2001, those who wished to make a symbolic attack on the center of American power chose the World Trade Center as their target. If what made America great was its ingenious openness to different cultures, then the small triangle of land at the southern tip of Manhattan Island is the New World birthplace of that idea, the spot where it first took shape. Many people—whether they live in the heartland or on Fifth Avenue—like to think of New York City as so wild and extreme in its cultural fusion that it's an anomaly in the United States, almost a foreign entity. This book offers an alternative view: that beneath the level of myth and politics and high ideals, down where real people live and interact, Manhattan is where America began.

The original European colony centered on Manhattan came to an end when England took it over in 1664, renaming it New York after James, the Duke of York, brother of King Charles II, and folding it into its other American colonies. As far as the earliest American historians were concerned, that date marked the true beginning of the history of the region. The Dutch-led colony was almost immediately considered inconsequential. When the time came to memorialize national origins, the English Pilgrims and Puritans of New England provided a better model. The Pilgrims' story was simpler, less messy, and had fewer pirates and prostitutes to explain away. It was easy enough to overlook the fact that the Puritans' flight to American shores to escape religious persecution led them, once established, to institute a brutally intolerant regime, a grim theocratic monoculture about as far removed as one can imagine from what the country was to become.

The few early books written about the Dutch settlement had a brackish odor—appropriately, since even their authors viewed the colony as a backwater, cut off from the main current of history. Washington Irving's "Knickerbocker" history of New York—a historical burlesque never intended by its author to be taken as fact—muddied any attempt to understand what had actually gone on in the Manhattan-based settlement. The colony was reduced by popular culture to a few random, floating facts: that it was once ruled by an ornery peg-legged governor and, most infamously, that the Dutch bought the island from the Indians for twenty-four-dollars' worth of household goods. Anyone who wondered about it beyond that may have surmised that the colony was too inept to keep records. As one historian put it, "Original sources of information concerning the early Dutch settlers of Manhattan Island are neither many nor rich [for] . . . the Dutch wrote very little, and on the whole their records are meager."

Skip ahead, then, to a day in 1973, when a thirty-five-year-old scholar named Charles Gehring is led into a vault in the New York State Library in Albany and shown something that delights his eye as fully as a chest of emeralds would a pirate's. Gehring, a specialist in the Dutch language of the seventeenth century (an obscure topic in anyone's estimation), had just completed his doctoral dissertation. He was casting about for a relevant job, which he knew wouldn't be easy to find, when fate smiled on him. Some years earlier, Peter Christoph, curator of historical manuscripts at the library, had come across a vast collection of charred, mold-stippled papers stored in the archives. He knew what they were and that they comprised a vast resource for American prehistory. They had survived wars, fire, flooding, and centuries of neglect. Remarkably, he doubted he would be able to bring them into the light of day. There was little interest in what was still considered an odd backroad of history. He couldn't come up with funds to hire a translator. Besides that, few people in the world could decipher the writings.

Two influential Americans of Dutch descent—an investment banker named Ralph L. DeGroff and a retired brigadier general named Cortlandt van Rensselaer Schuyler—then stepped into the picture. Gen. Schuyler had recently overseen the building in Albany of Empire State Plaza, the central state government complex, for his friend Governor Nelson Rockefeller. The two men independently put in calls to Rockefeller, who was by now out of office and about to be tapped by Gerald Ford as his vice president. When DeGroff suggested that the amount needed to launch the translation project was $25,000, Rockefeller's reply was, "I thought you were talking about real money." Rockefeller made the funds available, and Christoph called Gehring to tell him he had a job. So it was that while the nation was recovering from the midlife crisis of Watergate a window onto the period of its birth began to open.

What Charles Gehring received into his care in 1974 was twelve thousand sheets of rag paper covered with the crabbed, loopy script of seventeenth-

century Dutch, which to the untutored eye looks something like a cross
between our Roman letters and Arabic or Thai—writing largely indecipher-
able today even to modern Dutch speakers. On these pages, in words
written three hundred and fifty years ago in ink that has now partially faded
into the brown of the decaying paper, an improbable gathering of Dutch,
French, German, Swedish, Jewish, Polish, Danish, African, American Indian, and English characters comes to life. This repository of letters, deeds,
wills, journal entries, council minutes, and court proceedings comprises the
official records of the settlement that grew up following Henry Hudson's
1609 voyage up the river that bears his name. Here, in their own words, were
the first Manhattanites. Deciphering and translating the documents, making
them available to history, Dr. Gehring knew, was the task of a lifetime.

Twenty-six years later, Charles Gehring, now a sixty-one-year-old grandfather with a wry grin and a soothing, carmelly baritone, was still at it when I
met him in 2000. With the support of the Holland Society of New York, he
had produced sixteen volumes of translation, and had several more to go.
For a long time he had labored in isolation, the "missing floor" of the state
library building where he works serving as a nice metaphor for the way history has overlooked the Dutch period. But within the past several years, Dr.
Gehring and his collection of translations have become the center of a modest renaissance of scholarly interest in this colony. As I write, historians are
drafting doctoral dissertations on the material and educational organiza-
tions are creating teaching guides for bringing the Dutch settlement into accounts of American colonial history.

Dr. Gehring is not the first to have attempted a translation of this archive.
In fact, the long, bedraggled history of the records of the colony mirrors history's treatment of the colony itself. From early on, people recognized the importance of these documents. In 1801 a committee headed by none other
than Aaron Burr declared that "measures ought to be taken to procure a
translation," but none were. In the 1820s a half-blind Dutchman with a shaky
command of English came up with a massively flawed longhand translation—which then burned up in a 1911 fire that destroyed the state library. In
the early twentieth century a highly skilled translator undertook to translate
the whole corpus only to see two years' worth of labor burn up in the same
fire. He suffered a nervous breakdown and eventually abandoned the task.

Many of the more significant political documents of the colony were translated in the nineteenth century. These became part of the historical record, but without the rest—the letters and journals and court cases about marital strife, business failures, cutlass fights, traders loading sloops with tobacco and furs, neighbors stealing each others' pigs—in short, without the stuff from which social history is written, this veneer of political documentation only reinforced the image of the colony as wobbly and inconsequential. Dr. Gehring's work corrects that image, and changes the picture of American beginnings. Thanks to his work, historians are now realizing that, by the last two decades of its existence, the Dutch colony centered on Manhattan had become a vibrant, viable society—so much so that when the English took over Manhattan they kept its unusually free-form structures, ensuring that the features of the earlier settlement would live on.

The idea of a Dutch contribution to American history seems novel at first, but that is because early American history was written by Englishmen, who, throughout the seventeenth century, were locked in mortal combat with the Dutch. Looked at another way, however, the connection makes perfectly good sense. It has long been recognized that the Dutch Republic in the 1600s was the most progressive and culturally diverse society in Europe. As Bertrand Russell once wrote, regarding its impact on intellectual history, "It is impossible to exaggerate the importance of Holland in the seventeenth century, as the one country where there was freedom of speculation." The Netherlands of this time was the melting pot of Europe. The Dutch Republic's policy of tolerance made it a haven for everyone from Descartes and John Locke to exiled English royalty to peasants from across Europe. When this society founded a colony based on Manhattan Island, that colony had the same features of tolerance, openness, and free trade that existed in the home country. Those features helped make New York unique, and, in time, influenced America in some elemental ways. How that happened is what this book is about.

*

I CAME TO this subject more or less by walking into it. I was living in the East Village of Manhattan, a neighborhood that has long been known as an artistic and countercultural center, a place famous for its nightlife and ethnic restaurants. But three hundred and fifty years earlier it was an important part of the unkempt Atlantic Rim port of New Amsterdam. I often took my young daughter around the corner from our apartment building to the church of St. Mark's-in-the-Bowery, where she would run around under the sycamores in the churchyard and I would study the faded faces of the tombstones of some of the city's earliest families. The most notable tomb in the yard—actually it is built into the side of the church—is that of Peter Stuyvesant, the Dutch colony's most famous resident. In the mid-seventeenth century this area was forest and meadow being cleared and planted as Bouwerie (or farm) Number One: the largest homestead on the island, and the one Stuyvesant claimed for himself. St. Mark's is built near the site of his family chapel, in which he was buried. Throughout the nineteenth century New Yorkers insisted that the church was haunted by the old man's ghost—that at night you could hear the echoed clopping of his wooden leg as he paced its aisles, eternally ill at ease from having to relinquish his settlement to the English. I never heard the clopping, but over time I began to wonder, not so much about Stuyvesant, who seemed too forbidding for such a verb, but about the original settlement. I wanted to know the island that those first Europeans found.

Eventually, I got in touch with Charles Gehring. I learned about the extraordinary documents in his keeping, and about the organization, the New Netherland Project, he had founded to promote interest in this neglected period of history. In the fall of 2000, I attended a seminar he sponsored on the topic and encountered dozens of specialists who were exploring this forgotten world, unearthing pieces of it that hadn't seen the light of day in centuries. They were digging into archives from Boston to Antwerp and turning up hitherto forgotten journals, voyage diaries, and account books. Our understanding of the age of exploration was expanding under this new examination. In my interviews with Dr. Gehring and others, I realized that historians were fashioning a new perspective on American prehistory, and also that no one was attempting to bring all the disparate elements, characters, and legacies into a single narrative. In short, no one was telling the story of the first Manhattanites.

It turns out to be two stories. There is the small, ironic story that originally attracted me, of men and women hacking out an existence in a remote wilderness that is today one of the most famously urban landscapes in the world, who would shoulder their muskets and go on hunting expeditions into the thick forests of what is now the skyscrapered wilderness of midtown Manhattan. But going deeper into the material, you begin to appreciate the broader story. The origins of New York are not like those of other American cities. Those first settlers were not isolated pioneers but characters playing parts in a drama of global sweep—a struggle for empire that would range across the seventeenth century and around the globe, and which, for better or worse, would create the structure of the modern world.

Moving back and forth from the individual struggles detailed in the records to the geopolitical events of the day, you can sense the dawning of the idea that would lead to the transformation of Manhattan into the centerpiece of the most powerful city in the world. Of all the newly claimed regions whose exploitation was rapidly changing Europe—from the teeming cod fisheries off Newfoundland to the limitless extent of North America to the sugar fields of Brazil—this one slender island, sitting in the greatest natural harbor on the coast of a vast new wilderness and at the mouth of the river that would become the vital highway into that continent, would prove the most valuable of all. Its location and topography—"like a great natural pier ready to receive the commerce of the world," is how one early writer described it—would make it the gate through which Europeans could reach the unimaginable vastness of the North American land mass. Possess it, and you controlled passage up the Hudson River, then west along the Mohawk River Valley into the Great Lakes, and into the very heart of the continent. Later migration patterns proved this to a T; the Erie Canal, which linked the Hudson and the Great Lakes, resulted in the explosive growth of the Midwest and cemented New York's role as the most powerful city in the nation. In the seventeenth century that was still far in the future, but one by one, in various ways, the major players in this story sensed the island's importance. They smelled its value. Thus Richard Nicolls, the British colonel who led a gunboat flotilla into New York Harbor in August 1664 and wrested control of the island from Peter Stuyvesant, instantly termed it "best of all His Majties Townes in America."

So the story of Manhattan's beginnings is also the story of European exploration and conquest in the 1600s. And at the heart of the material I found a much smaller story: a very personal struggle between two men over the fate of a colony and the meaning and value of individual liberty. Their personal battle helped to ensure that New York City, under the English and then as an American city, would develop into a unique place that would foster an intense stew of cultures and a wildly fertile intellectual, artistic, and business environment.

One of the protagonists in this struggle, Peter Stuyvesant, has been portrayed by history as almost a cartoon character: peg-legged, cantankerous, a figure of comic relief who would do his routine, draw a few laughs, and then exit the stage so that the real substance of American history could begin. But much of what was known about Stuyvesant before came from records of the New England colonies. To New England, the Dutch colony centered on New Amsterdam was the enemy, and so history has accepted the portrait of Stuyvesant drawn by his greatest detractors. In the New Netherland records, by contrast, Stuyvesant comes across as full blooded and complex: a genuine tyrant; a doting father and husband; a statesman who exhibits steel nerves and bold military intuition while holding almost no cards and being surrounded by enemies (English, Indians, Swedes, foes from within his own colony, even, in a sense, the directors of his company in Amsterdam). He is a man who abhors unfairness—who publicly punishes Dutch colonists who cheat the Indians in business deals—but who, with the harshness of a hard-line Calvinist minister's son, tries to block Jews from settling in New Amsterdam. He is a tragic figure, undone by his own best quality, his steadfastness. But Stuyvesant didn't act in isolation. The colony's legacy revolves around another figure of the period, a man named Adriaen van der Donck, who has been forgotten by history but who emerges as the hero of the story and who, I think, deserves to be ranked as an early American prophet, a forerunner of the Revolutionary generation.

But if the colony's end points forward to the American society that was to come, its beginning is dominated by another figure—willful, brooding, tortured—who hearkens back to an earlier era. Henry Hudson was a man of the Renaissance, and Manhattan's birth thus becomes a kind of bridge between these two worlds. So the story begins far from the American wilderness, in the heart of late Renaissance Europe.

All that said, what originally captivated me about the Dutch documents—that they offered a way to reimagine New York City as a wilderness—stayed alive throughout my research. More than anything, then, this book invites you to do the impossible: to strip from your mental image of Manhattan Island all associations of power, concrete, and glass; to put time into full reverse, unfill the massive landfills, and undo the extensive leveling programs that flattened hills and filled gullies; to return streams from the underground sewers they were forced into, back to their original rushing or meandering course. To witness the return of waterfalls, to watch freshwater ponds form in place of asphalt intersections; to let buildings vanish and watch stands of pin oak, sweetgum, basswood, and hawthorne take their place. To imagine the return of salt marshes, mudflats, grasslands, of leopard frogs, grebes, cormorants, and bitterns; to discover newly pure estuaries encrusting themselves with scallops, lamp mussels, oysters, quahogs, and clams. To see maple-ringed meadows become numbered with deer and the higher elevations ruled by wolves.

And then to stop the time machine, let it hover a moment on the southmost tip of an island poised between the Atlantic Ocean and the civilization of Europe on one side and a virgin continent on the other; to let that moment swell, hearing the screech of gulls and the slap of waves and imagining these same sounds, waves and birds, waves and birds, with regular interruptions by wracking storms, unchanged for dozens of centuries.

And then let time start forward once again as something comes into view on the horizon. Sails.

PART I

"A CERTAIN

ISLAND NAMED

MANATHANS"

Chapter 1

THE MEASURE OF THINGS

On a late summer's day in the year 1608, a gentleman of London made his way across that city. He was a man of ambition, intellect, arrogance, and drive—in short, a man of his age. Like our own, his was an era of expanding horizons and a rapidly shrinking world, in which the pursuit of individual dreams led to new discoveries, which in turn led to newer and bigger dreams. His complicated personality—including periodic fits of brooding passivity that all but incapacitated him—was built around an impressive self-confidence, and at this moment he was almost certainly convinced that the meeting he was headed toward would be of historic importance.

He walked west, in the direction of St. Paul's Cathedral, which then, as now, dominated the skyline. But the structure in the distance was not the St. Paul's of today, the serene, imperial building that signifies order and human reason, with the spirit of the Renaissance and the Enlightenment shining from its proud dome. His St. Paul's had a hunkering tower in place of a dome (the steeple that had originally risen from the tower had been struck by lightning almost half a century before and hadn't been replaced); it was a dark, medieval church, which suited the medieval market town that London still was in the early seventeenth century. The streets through which he walked were narrow, shadowy, claustrophobic, sloping toward central sewer ditches. The houses that lined them were built of timber and walled with wattle and daub—it was a city made chiefly of wood.

Since we know his destination and have some notion of the whereabouts of his house, it is possible to trace a likely route that Henry Hudson, ship's captain, would have taken on that summer day, on his way to meet with the directors of the Muscovy Company, funders of voyages of exploration and discovery. The widest thoroughfare from Tower Street Ward toward Cordwainer Street Ward was Tower Street. He would have passed first through a neighborhood that, despite being within sight of the scaffold and gallows of the Tower itself, was an area of relatively new, "divers fair and large houses," as John Stow, a contemporary chronicler, described, several of them owned by prominent noblemen.

On his left then came the dominating church of St. Dunstan in the East, and a reminder of his heritage. The Muscovy Company had not only funded at least two of Henry Hudson's previous sea voyages; going back through its history of half a century, it contained several Hudsons on its rolls. Among its charter members in 1555 was another Henry Hudson, who rose from a humble "skinner," or tanner, to become a wealthy member of society and an alderman of the City of London, and who may have been the explorer's grandfather. So our Henry Hudson was presumably born to the sea and to the company both, and inside the church he was now passing, his Muscovy Company namesake lay, beneath a gilded alabaster stone inscribed:

HERE LYETH HENRY HEARDSONS CORPS,
WITHIN THIS TOMBE OF STONE:
HIS SOULE (THROUGH FAITH IN CHRIST'S DEATH,)
TO GOD IN HEAVEN IS GONE.
WHILES THAT HE LIVED AN ALDERMAN,
AND SKINNER WAS HIS STATE:
TO VERTUE BARE HEE ALL HIS LOVE,
TO VICE HE BARE HIS HATE.

If in his walk the seaman chose to detour down the hill past the church, he would have come to the open expanse of the Thames, where the view west downriver was dominated by the span of London Bridge with its twenty stone arches, houses perched precariously along both sides of its course. Directly across the river, beckoning lowly and enticingly, lay Southwark, a wild outland and thus also the entertainment district, with brothels tucked into its alleys and, visible from here, the "bear bayting" arena, which provided one of the most popular distractions for the masses. Beyond it stood the rounded wooden structure of the Globe Theater in its original incarnation. Indeed, somewhere over on the Southwark side at this very moment, amid the tradesmen, whores, "sturdye Beggers," and "Common Players in Enterludes" that populated the borough, Shakespeare himself—at forty-four a near-exact contemporary of Hudson, then at the height of his powers and fame as the leading dramatist of the day—was likely going about his business, sleeping off a night of sack at the Mermaid with his actor friends Richard Burbage and John Heminge, maybe, or brooding over the foolscap sheets of *Coriolanus,* which was written about this time and which, coming on the heels of the great tragedies, may have felt a bit hollow.

Tower Street became Little Eastcheap, which in turn merged into Candlewick and then Budge Row. Hudson's business lay here, in an imposing building called Muscovy House, home of the Muscovy Company. The medieval look of the London of 1608 belied the fact that England's rise to global empire was under way, and one of the forces behind that rise lay through these doors. From the bravado of its formal name—the "Merchants Adventurers of England for the Discovery of Lands, Territories, Iles, Dominions, and Seigniories Unknown"—one might be excused for thinking it had been founded out of sheer, unstoppable exuberance. The original band of merchants and aristocrats who had formed it more than half a century earlier included many of the most distinguished men in London in the middle of the sixteenth century—the Lord High Treasurer, the Steward of the Queen's Household, the Keeper of the Privy Seal, the Lord High Admiral— as well as sundry other knights and gentlemen. But while global exploration, the great intellectual and business opportunity of the day, had brought them all together, no one considered the undertaking a swashbuckling adventure. It was desperation that drove them toward new horizons. The England of the 1540s had been a backwater, economically depressed, inward-looking, deep in the shadows of the great maritime empires of Spain and Portugal. Wool was the country's chief commodity, but English traders had been blocked from access to major European markets for more than a century. Economic stagnation was bound up with intellectual stagnation: while the Renaissance was in full flower on the Continent, English interest in the wider world was slim, and the few long voyages of exploration England had mounted were mostly led by foreigners, such as the Venetian

John Cabot (né Giovanni Cabotto). When it came to sea voyages, the English declined.

History traditionally links the rise of England in the period with the elevation of Queen Elizabeth to the throne in 1558. But one could trace it to 1547, when an intellectually voracious twenty-year-old named John Dee did something countless students since have done: spent his summer abroad and returned flush with new knowledge and insights. After an academic career at Cambridge in which he proved to be something of a mathematical genius, Dee traveled to the University of Louvain in what is today Belgium. The rich summer sun of the Brabant region might have been revelation enough, but Dee soon found himself in a lecture hall gazing at an object that was, to him, transcendent. The teacher was Gemma Frisius, a Flemish mathematician and charter of the heavens, and what Dee saw was a map astonishing in its level of detail, in the new lands it portrayed, even in its lettering. The Low Countries, he discovered, were miles ahead of his island in new learning.

Dee spent long candle-lit nights poring over Frisius's maps with a Flemish scholar named Gerhard Kremer. Kremer, an engraver by training, had, under the academic pen name of Mercator, begun to make a name for himself ten years earlier by creating a map of Palestine that rendered the Holy Land with greater accuracy than had ever been achieved. Mercator was a genuine Renaissance man—a master cartographer, an engineer of telescopes, sextants, surveying equipment, and other highly sensitive measuring devices, the author of a gospel concordance, promoter of the new italic typeface that made map print more legible—and in him Dee found a soul mate. In 1569, Mercator would publish the map that would give him his immortality, which rendered latitude and longitude as straight lines, the meridians of longitude evenly spaced and the distance between the parallels of latitude increasing in size as one approached the poles. It would solve a cumbersome problem of navigating at sea because with it sailors could plot and follow a straight course rather than have to constantly recalculate their position. (The Mercator projection is still a feature of navigational maps, although, even at that time, some mariners were as confused as later generations of schoolchildren would be by the distortions in size it caused.)

In a nice foreshadowing of the complicated intermingling between the Low Countries and the British Isles that would shape the next century, when Dee returned to London he brought with him maps, measuring instruments, and globes, created by Mercator and Frisius, that would help spark England's rise to global prominence. What Dee's English colleagues found most intriguing about the maps and globes was an area most people would ignore: the top, the Arctic Circle. Frisius's map, oriented as if looking down from the north star, showed a distinct open channel cutting across the Arctic, which was self-confidently labeled in Latin *Fretum trium fratrum*. The sight of the boldly indicated Strait of the Three Brothers must have made Dee's English friends gasp. The Holy Grail for all learned and adventuresome minds was the discovery of a short passage to the riches of Asia. Finding it would repay investors many times over; for the English, it would vault their economy out of the Middle Ages and into the European vanguard. The legend of the Strait of the Three Brothers was confused even at that time, but it appears to have been based on the adventures of the Corte Real brothers, Portuguese mariners who explored the area around Newfoundland at the beginning of the sixteenth century, and who, in the minds of some, sighted, or perhaps even sailed, the fabled passage to Asia before two of them vanished into Arctic oblivion. (Ironically, the Spanish also had a theory about this mythical strait, only they called it the Englishmen's Strait.) Now there it was on Frisius's map, thanks apparently to Frisius's contacts with Portuguese mariners. It was on Mercator's globe as well, labeled simply *fretum arcticum,* arctic strait. As with most people in any endeavor, seeing the thing in print, seeing its coasts and coves delicately but decisively rendered, confirmed its reality.

Fate, it seemed, had brought together the men, the means, and the time. The solution to England's twin crises of economy and spirit was *out there.* So the nation's leaders formed a business circle, chipping in twenty-five pounds per share and raising a total of six thousand pounds.

With the principals lined up and funds ready, it only remained to choose the likeliest route—either the one indicated on Frisius's map or one of several others that were now being put forth with equal confidence. The point was to find a northern passage both because such a shortcut would render obsolete the Spanish and Portuguese monopoly on the Southern Hemisphere and because any northern peoples encountered along the way would be more likely buyers for English wool. That an Arctic sea route existed was beyond anyone's doubt. The universal belief among the intelligentsia in something we know to be a physical impossibility in wooden sailing vessels rested on several arguments, such as the one put forth by the Dutch minister and geographer Peter Plancius that "near the pole the sun shines for five months continually; and although his rays are weak, yet on account of the long time they continue, they have sufficient strength to warm the ground, to render it temperate, to accommodate it for the habitation of men, and to produce grass for the nourishment of animals."

The name by which the company became known gives away what happened on the first voyage it financed. A doughty mariner named Richard Chancellor took the northeast route, and while he failed to discover a passage to the Orient, he became the first Englishman of the era to make landfall at Russia. The so-called Muscovy trade that ensued—in which the English found a ready market for their wool, and imported hemp, sperm oil, and furs from the realm of Ivan the Terrible—was so profitable that the search for a northern route to Asia was largely abandoned.

The company expanded, and the nation with it. Elizabeth ascended to the throne; Drake circumnavigated the globe; Shakespeare wrote. When, in 1588, Philip II of Spain launched an invasion fleet toward England, intending to bring the island into his empire and win its people back to Roman Catholicism, the undersized English navy shocked the world by crushing the Armada. The aftermath of the victory was one of those moments when a nation suddenly realizes it has entered a new era. Theirs wasn't a dark and chilly island after all, the English public was informed by their great poet, but a "precious stone set in the silver sea."

By the early 1600s, however, the wheel had taken another turn. The queen was dead, and the Russia trade had fallen off. Faced once again with financial crisis, the company's directors made a decision to return to their original purpose. They would resurrect the Renaissance dream, commit themselves anew to discovering a northern passage to Asia.

The man they now turned to to renew the quest is not the protagonist of this story, but the forerunner, the one who would make it possible. In the ranks of legendary explorers, Henry Hudson has been slighted: not celebrated in his time by the English public as Francis Drake or Martin Frobisher or John Cabot had been, not given nearly the amount of ink that history has devoted to Columbus or Magellan. There is a logic of personality in this: Drake had defined manhood for an era, and the Italian Cabot had a feckless charm (he was in the habit, after his celebrated return from the New World, of promising people he met in taverns that he would name islands for them), but when we come to Henry Hudson it is a dark and moody figure hovering behind the records, one seemingly more comfortable in the shadows of history. A new appreciation for the Dutch colony in North America, however, compels a reappraisal of the man whose fitful decision-making rerouted the flow of history.

Nothing is known of his early career, but the fact that he was a ship's captain indicates that he had had a lengthy one by the time we encounter him in 1608. It's reasonable to assume that he had served in the defeat of the Armada twenty years earlier, though we have no information on this. The Muscovy Company tended to start apprentices as boys and have them work through one or more aspects of the business: bureaucrat, "factor" (i.e., agent), or sailor. Thus, one Christopher Hudson, who rose to the position of governor of the company from 1601 to 1607 and whom some historians have thought was most likely Henry Hudson's uncle, had worked his way up in the sales and marketing line, serving as a company representative in Germany in his youth. Henry Hudson was in his forties when he stepped into the light of history, a seasoned mariner, a man with a strong and resourceful wife and three sons, a man born and raised not only to the sea but to the quest for a northern passage to Asia, who, weaned from infancy on the legends of his predecessors, probably couldn't help but be obsessed by it.

The fire of obsession was fanned, in him as it was in the country, by a compatriot named Richard Hakluyt. Hakluyt was a consultant to the Muscovy Company, but more importantly he was a unique figure in his day: part journalist, part popularizer, part lionizer, above all a zealot for the internationalist cause in England. In the 1580s he began gathering log books, journals, and other records of voyages, and he published the whole lot of them in repeated waves—the main body under the title *The Principle Navigations Voyages Traffiques and Discoveries of the English Nation,* which came out, with impeccable timing, shortly after the defeat of the Armada—creating a steadily building crescendo of popular enthusiasm for English adventures at sea. The result was to make England aware of itself in an international context, to see the European nations casting outward in a new age, an age of discovery. Hakluyt exhorted his countrymen to be proud that they were living in "an age wherein God hath raised so general a desire in the youth of this realm to discover all parts of the face of the earth."

Thanks to Hakluyt, mariners now saw themselves in historical terms. Because of Hakluyt, Hudson—a determined and self-possessed man to begin with—openly hungered for a place on the list that included Columbus, Magellan, Cabot, Cortés, and Da Gama. And for Hudson there was only one brand of glory. He would be the one to locate at last—after the failures (glorious failures, but failures still) of Columbus, Cabot, Chancellor, Frobisher, Cartier, Verrazzano—the fabled ribbon of icy blue water, sail through it, emerge into the nutmeg-scented air of Cathay, and singlehandedly open the planet wide. He believed he would be the one.

He would be wrong in this. And yet, fate being what it is, his dream of achievement would come true—bounteously, far more strangely than he could have imagined. Fate would make him not just the somewhat ironic patron saint of a grand city that would rise in the future to the presumptuous title of capital of the world, but, along with it, of a society that would become a model for the world of a distant century. A wavering but unbroken chain would stretch from him to a far-off hodgepodge: of skyscrapers and bodegas, dim sum and hip-hop, supers and subways, limos and egg creams and finance and fashion—the messy catalogue of ingredients that, stewed together over time, would comprise a global capital, twenty-first-century style. To the extent any individual could, he would be a fulcrum on which history would turn: from a world of wood and steel to one of silicon and plastic.

*

HIS FIRST VOYAGE was pure madness. While geographers debated whether the elusive passage to Asia lay to the northwest, via Canada, or the northeast, around Russia, what Hudson attempted in his first command was something fantastically bolder and far more ridiculous than either of these, something that no human being had ever tried: to go straight up, over the top of the world. He was relying on an "established" theory, first proposed eighty years before by Robert Thorne, a merchant-adventurer who argued that in addition to finding the ice melt away as one neared the pole, that the lucky sailor who ventured across the top of the world would benefit from the "perpetual clearness of the day without any darkness of the night." Daylight may be handy, but to purposely steer a seventy-foot wooden boat, manned by a crew of twelve and powered only by wind, straight north on a direct course for the top of the world, defying the six-million-square-mile Arctic ice shelf, proposing to slice straight across it and come careening down the other side of the planet—the nerve of it beggars the imagination. No wonder that on the morning of April 19, 1607, Hudson and his tiny crew, including his young son John, whom he was probably in the process of training just as he had been trained, stepped out of the weak spring sunlight, shuffled into the dark ancient interior of the Church of St. Ethelburga just inside Bishopsgate (apparently successfully ignoring the tap houses crowding around the door of the church: the Angel, the Four Swans, the Green Dragon, the Black Bull), took their places among the congregation, and beseeched the God of their forefathers to bless their endeavor.

Even more remarkable than Hudson's decision to attempt such a voyage was that he survived it. Slicing through fog and ice, living on bear and seal (at one point the crew fell sick from rotten bear meat), surviving vicious storms and the horror of a whale attempting to surface under the keel of their ship, they made it above eighty degrees latitude, within six hundred miles of the North Pole, before Hudson noted drily, "This morning we saw that we were compassed in with Ice in abundance. . . . And this I can assure at present . . . by this way there is no passage."

By any normal measure the voyage would have been considered a failure, but normalcy was out the window—it was now the seventeenth century, a vast new world was out there. Entrepreneurs and ships' captains knew that crossing one false path off the list was a form of progress. Far from considering his attempt a failure (for one thing, Hudson's report of "many whales" off Spitzbergen Island led to a massive and lucrative whaling enterprise there in the following years, and, predictably, the decimation of the whale population), the company, immediately on his return in September 1607, signed him up to attack the problem again the next season.

Hudson spent the winter at his London home, plunging into his charts and letters from fellow mariners and geographers, warming himself at his own hearth and in the company of his family, laying plans, perhaps meeting with Hakluyt himself—the two had by now become friends—to discuss options. The following season sees him setting off straightaway—April 22, 1608—in the same Muscovy Company ship, the *Hopewell,* this time with a crew of fourteen, sitting in his closetlike captain's cabin, carefully putting pen to the page of his logbook as they pull away from the Thames-side docks, heart thrumming with the high adrenaline of setting-forth, as he records dutifully: "We set sayle at Saint Katherines, and fell downe to Blacke wall."

He had a new course this time: northeast. It had been attempted by others, including his Muscovy Company predecessors, but the directors were still of the belief that to the north of Russia lay the best chance for reaching Asia. Hudson himself may have been doubtful—he had reason to believe the northwest was more likely—but he was willing to follow their wishes. Or so it seemed. The failure of his second voyage is less interesting than what happened on July 6, after he had concluded it was impossible to continue (on entering the strait that he had pinned his hopes on he writes with awe, "it is so full of ice that you will hardly thinke it"). Unable to find a way around the islands of Nova Zembla (today Novaya Zemlya in the Russian Arctic), he was now "out of hope to find passage by the North-east," and so proposed to alter course completely, tear up the mission directive from the company, and have a go at the northwest. After slaving for ten weeks against the raw elements of the Arctic, his crew, with good sense, balked at the idea of taking a detour straight across the Atlantic and into a wholly new wilderness. A near mutiny ensued; Hudson was forced to remove his gaze from the distant horizon of his obsession and focus instead on the human beings in front of him on the deck. He backed down. They returned to London.

No sooner did he arrive than he was busy readying himself for his next foray. He had momentum now: two voyages in two successive seasons; two routes down, and one to go. He was convinced that he was zeroing in on the passage, that the puzzle that had occupied Europe for the length of the Renaissance was about to be solved. The answer, it now seemed certain, lay in the misty, all-but-unknown region that was only recently being labeled on maps as America.

At around this time—possibly before the 1608 voyage—he received letters from his friend and fellow explorer, the considerably larger-than-life John Smith, who had fought in Hungary against the Turks, was captured and sold into slavery in Istanbul, won the heart of his female captor, escaped to Transylvania via Russia, and trekked across North Africa—all before his twenty-fifth birthday. Not content with such a résumé, in 1607, Smith spearheaded the founding of a colony in Virginia—what would be the first permanent European settlement on the North American coast (Walter Raleigh's Roanoke colony, which broke ground in 1587, had vanished by the time relief forces arrived in 1590), where he and his comrades were now living out a hell on earth (only thirty-eight of the one hundred and fifty original colonists survived the first winter). Smith sent Hudson maps of the North American coast, together with certain theories he had been developing. These were precisely what Hudson wanted to hear; they conformed with his own theories: that a sea or river somewhere to the north of Virginia gave out onto the Sea of Cathay. (Smith's information seems to have come from Indians who talked of a great ocean accessible via the Hudson River—presumably the Great Lakes, reachable via portage through the Mohawk River valley.)

Thus we find Hudson where we met him at the beginning of this chapter, shortly after landfall in late August or early September 1608, about to step into Muscovy House—in starched ruff collar and embroidered jerkin, perhaps, clothing suitable for a formal interview—for his obligatory meeting with the company directors. His mind was apparently in a swirl. On the one hand, Smith's information buttressed his belief that he was homing in on his goal. Then again, Samuel Purchas, a director of the company and like Hakluyt a popularizer of England's sea ventures (it is from him that most of our knowledge of Hudson's voyages comes), on meeting up with Hudson one day immediately after his return, found him "sunk into the lowest depths of the Humour of Melancholy, from which no man could rouse him. It mattered not that his Perseverance and Industry had made England the richer by his maps of the North. I told him he had created Fame that would endure for all time, but he would not listen to me." This was completely within character: Hudson seems to have typified the figure of the man of energy and obsession wracked by periods of despair. As he entered Muscovy House, the reality of recent failure and the possibility of imminent glory must have hammered at his brain from opposite sides. He seems to have thrived on such tensions, such contradictions: seeking to expand human civilization by immersing himself in the void of nature; strolling in the easy center of culture and society while the too-wild tang of rotten bear meat still lay on his tongue.

We can't follow him inside. The building itself, along with all the records of the Muscovy Company, was destroyed in the Great Fire. If there was a corporate record of the meeting, of who voted against funding him again and why, it is lost. We can only imagine his shock, then, when they rejected him, gave up on the great quest, and abandoned one of their own. Maybe they had grown leery of his monomania and propensity for sparking mutiny. Possibly the Muscovy Company was running out of steam (it would soon be subject to the seventeenth-century version of a corporate takeover by the younger and more vigorous East India Company).

But he had barely enough time to sink into the depression to which a psychologist might have diagnosed him as susceptible before a new, unexpected avenue stretched open before him. Shortly after stepping out of the company's mansion into the glare of a summer day, he found himself accosted by a courtly, discreet, seventy-two-year-old gentleman. Emanuel van Meteren had been born in Antwerp, but when he was fifteen his family moved to London, where he had lived ever since, acquiring an English education and an English sense of refinement, but remaining elementally Dutch. For the last thirty years he had served as the Dutch consul in London, and was on intimate terms with many of the prominent businessmen, aristocrats, and explorers in both countries. He had learned that the Muscovy Company was dropping Hudson—with his closeness to the directors of the company, he may have known before Hudson did.

The moment Van Meteren put his dignified presence before Hudson, he revealed the true scope of interest in the mariner's obsession. It wasn't a matter of one ship's captain and the company he worked for. Hudson's quest was tied into the historic current washing over the powers of Europe, the self-conscious need to blast out of the Mediterranean paradigm that had held them through the Middle Ages and to reach around the globe: to discover, exploit, expand, do business. Van Meteren spoke on behalf of certain Dutch merchants, who were desirous, seeing that his own countrymen had lost faith, of abetting Hudson's ambition. In short, they wanted to hire him.

The mariner apparently suffered no pangs of disloyalty, either to the country of his birth or the company that had nurtured him. Delaying only to attend the christening, in mid-September, of a granddaughter (Alice, child of his son Oliver), Hudson boarded a ship to cross the channel, having no idea that his contribution to history would come not from discovering the passage to the Orient but as a result of this very twist of fate, this kink in his chain of bold, brilliant, and majestically misguided voyages.

Chapter 2

THE POLLINATOR

In the seventeenth century, to enter Amsterdam was to be softly assaulted in the senses. There was the squeal of caroming sea birds and the slap of oars; a stew of smells: cabbage, frying pancakes, the miasma of the canals. There was the sensation, on entering the ultramarine opacity of the canal grid, of gliding into an orderly enclosed space. The slender-bricked houses made an elegant but modest statement, their gabled tops framing and taming the sky. The cobbled quaysides were alive with workers wheeling barrows or wobbling under the strain of sacks being loaded into lighters. Women with billowing skirted bottoms scrubbed stoops and sprinkled them with fat handfuls of sand; everywhere there were dogs and horses and children.

As Henry Hudson arrived in Amsterdam in the autumn of 1608, the world around him was turning. The Spanish and Portuguese empires that had had their way with South America and the East Indies for more than a century were in decline, and two new powers were rising in tandem. The Dutch were growing in might right alongside the English, and would peak sooner, giving the world Rembrandt, Vermeer, the microscope, the tulip, the stock exchange, and the modern notion of home as a private, intimate place.

The Dutch, of course, were of the sea; keeping it back was a way of life. Consequently, water was their orientation; they were the continent's shipbuilders, sailors, pilots, and traffickers, and this was their key to empire. When the union of Spain and Portugal in 1580 closed to Dutch traders the port of Lisbon (where they had long received Asian goods for resale throughout Europe), the Dutch merchants took the drastic step of stocking their vessels with gunpowder and cannonballs and going directly to the

Iberian supply source, the islands of the East Indies, more than a year's journey away by the southern route. They arrived with guns blazing at the Portuguese military-trading posts there, and took them, converting Java, Sumatra, and the Malaysian peninsula into outposts of a new empire. When the first successful convoy returned home in 1599, its hulls packed with six hundred thousand pounds of pepper and an equal amount of nutmeg, cloves, and other spices, Amsterdammers were stunned at the plenitude. Churchbells throughout the city rang, and the rise to world power began.

Geography shapes character, and the character of the city Hudson entered was vastly different from the one he had just left. This single point helps to explain why Manhattan, which owes its originating contours to Hudson, would become such a different place from, say, Boston or Philadelphia. One difference between England and the Dutch Republic was contained in the abstract and to our ears wan-sounding noun *tolerance.* England was on the verge of a century of religious wars that would see royal heads roll and crowds of ordinary citizens flee. The Dutch—traders and sailors, whose focus was always *out there:* on other lands, other peoples, and their products—had always had to put up with differences. Just as foreign goods moved in and out of their ports, foreign ideas, and for that matter, foreign people, did as well. To talk about "celebrating diversity" is to be wildly anachronistic, but in the Europe of the time the Dutch stood out for their relative acceptance of foreignness, of religious differences, of odd sorts. One example of this could be found in Hudson's new employers, the men who made up the Amsterdam Chamber of the East India Company: Catholics and Protestants, many of them refugees from persecution in the south or elsewhere. They had come here, wedged themselves into society, and worked their way up. Over the course of the seventeenth century, the Dutch Republic would give intellectual or religious haven to Descartes, John Locke, and the English Pilgrims, the latter of whom lived in Leiden for twelve years before setting out to found a new Jerusalem in New England. The philosopher Baruch Spinoza was a product of Amsterdam's vigorous Jewish community. To this day, Amsterdammers' proud slang term for their city is *Mokum,* the centuries-old Jewish name for it. (For that matter, Amsterdam slang for "see you later" is the Yiddishism *de mazzel.*)

Landscape has a political dimension, too, and the low-lying provinces—the Netherlands is really one vast river delta—were always an easy target for invaders. The French expanded into them in the 1300s, then in 1495, three years after Columbus's voyage, Spain added the low countries to its empire. As Hudson entered Amsterdam, the United Provinces of the Netherlands had been fighting for independence from their Spanish overlords for nearly four decades, and the long war had toughened them, focused them, made them militarily and economically stronger. Before, they had been scattered, each province tending to go its own way. The Catholic tyranny of Spain—complete with bloody Inquisition tactics to force Protestants to return to the fold—united them. It gave them a Father of the Country in the person of Willem I, the Prince of Orange, known to history as William the Silent. The assassination of this heroic military leader gave Groningen farmers, Frisian horse traders, Zeeland shipwrights, and the cosmopolitan artists and merchants of Amsterdam a common focal point. They also had their own Minutemen, called the Sea Beggars, a scrappy, Robin Hood–like band of sailors who against all odds defeated the precision-drilled Spanish regulars who held the coastal town of Briel, taking the town and giving the Dutch their first hope of throwing off the foreign yoke.

Maybe the most striking difference between the Netherlands and England was that the new government the seven united Dutch provinces formed during their struggle was something utterly anomalous in Europe: in the midst of the great age of monarchies, stretching from Elizabeth Tudor to Louis XIV, the Dutch carved out a republic. It wasn't a republic in the full Enlightenment-era sense—it wasn't of the idealistic, self-righteously stubborn, "we hold these truths to be self-evident" model that gave rise to the American republic, but rather had come into being in a piecemeal way, as towns joined together to protect their interests. But it was a bottom-up system: it came from the people. The French had their intricately intertwined systems of fashion and protocol, the Spanish court its tottering "magnificent fountain" of patronage, and the English their class system, with an aristocracy rooted into the nation's soul. The Dutch of the seventeenth century distinguished themselves by being Regular Guys. They had a cultural distaste for monarchy and ostentation—as one writer of the time put it, a "strenuous spirit of opposition to a sovereign concentrated in one head." They believed in hard work, in earning an honest guilder, in personal modesty. They thought the English preoccupation with witches was paranoia.

The Dutch dressed so simply that foreigners complained that on the streets of Amsterdam it was impossible to tell the difference between a city magistrate and a simple shopkeeper. In the early part of the century Amsterdam had few grand houses; the homes that lined the Herengracht and Brouwersgracht were still modest, single-family affairs. Fantastically for the time, the Dutch didn't believe in keeping fleets of servants: a wealthy family might have one or two. A French naval commander, boarding a Dutch frigate, was appalled to find its captain sweeping his own cabin. There were noble families, but they had nothing like the power held by other European aristocrats. Instead, power went to those who made things happen: businessmen and local magistrates. Over time, human nature being what it is, these men would create a kind of merchant nobility, sometimes even buying titles from cash-poor foreigners, but this in itself underscores the point. Upward mobility was part of the Dutch character: if you worked hard and were smart, you rose in stature. Today that is a byword of a healthy society; in the seventeenth century it was weird.

The whole package—the Founding Father, the young and vibrant republic, the war for independence, the hard-nosed, practical populace that disdains monarchies and maintains a frank acceptance of differences—has a ring of familiarity to it, which was not lost on the American founding fathers of the next century. As John Adams, in his capacity as the first American ambassador to the Netherlands, wrote in 1782: "The Originals of the two Republics are so much alike, that the History of one seems but a Transcript from that of the other; so that every Dutchman instructed in the subject, must pronounce the American revolution just and necessary, or pass a Censure upon the greatest Actions of his immortal Ancestors." Some of those similarities are inevitable (don't all rebellions have heroes and martyrs?), but the most elemental one—a cultural sensibility that included a frank acceptance of differences and a belief that individual achievement matters more than birthright—is, as I hope this book will show, at least in part the result of a kind of genetic transfer from the one culture to the other, a planting of Dutch notions in one vital region of the future United States, from which they would be taken up into the American character. And the unlikely and unwitting carrier of this cultural gene was here, this man, in this place.

As with the English, the Dutch had had a long-standing interest in finding a northern route to Asia. Fifteen years earlier, the Dutch explorer Willem Barents had made three attempts at a northeast passage. That he froze to death on his last voyage didn't dull local enthusiasm for the project. The Dutch East India Company had sprung into being from the recent, extravagantly successful voyages to Southeast Asia, and would soon deploy a vast fleet with no fewer than five thousand sailors. It was better organized and had more money at its disposal than the Muscovy Company. If, as the company's intelligence reports had it, Hudson was on the verge of discovering the long-sought northern passage to Asian markets, they wanted Hudson.

But they weren't the only ones who wanted him. Hudson arrived in the Dutch Republic at a decisive moment, when all of Europe was focused on these low-lying provinces. Two years before, in a thicket of masts and gunpowder discharge and carnage, Dutch ships under Jacob van Heemskerck had blasted their way through the Spanish fleet as it lay moored off Gibraltar. This provided a coda to England's defeat of the Armada twenty years earlier, and finally brought the Spanish king, Philip III, to the bargaining table. While Hudson was sitting down to negotiate a contract with the Dutch merchants, representatives from all the nations of Europe were gathered thirty-five miles away at The Hague to hammer out a truce that all had a stake in. If a truce could be worked out, it would be tantamount to recognition of the United Provinces as a nation in its own right.

Hudson was comfortable in Holland; he may even have spent an earlier portion of his life in the country. He had friends here. Joost de Hondt was an engraver and mapmaker who acted as Hudson's interpreter in the contract negotiations; Hudson stayed at his house in The Hague through the winter. Another friend was the geographer Peter Plancius (he of the polar sun-power theory), with whom Hudson spent long evenings that winter, poring over maps and stray bits of information or hearsay. Plancius had the greatest knowledge of the shape of the world of any man in the Dutch provinces. He was one of those who believed that the route to Asia lay to the northeast, but Hudson was adamant that the most likely passage was to the northwest. He got further support for this belief from an item Plancius somehow had gotten his hands on and now furnished Hudson with: the journal of the Englishman George Weymouth, who had made detailed observations of his own attempt at the northwest route seven years earlier.

While Hudson sat at East India House overlooking the still, green water of the Gelderse Kade and negotiated with the Dutch merchants, spies from delegations to the truce negotiations at The Hague were listening in, for the two things were connected. The main issue of the conference was a truce, but the subtext was the rising Dutch power. The Spanish and Portuguese representatives were still fuming at the Dutch inroads in Asia and wanted these rolled back as a condition of peace. England felt the same. James I, the bookish and ungainly Scotsman who had replaced Elizabeth on the throne, had directed his representatives at The Hague negotiations to push for an end to Dutch trading in the East.

The VOC—as the Dutch East India Company would become known worldwide, the initials of its Dutch name, *de Verenigde Oostindische Compagnie,* emblazoned on ships in all ports of the world—had a charter that gave it a monopoly on Asian trade carried out via the southern route only. So if someone were to discover a northern back door to Asia, the company's rise to power would be halted. Hence the eagerness to get to Hudson. But before the VOC reached an agreement, others made a play for him. Pierre Jeannin, who headed the French delegation at the negotiations, dashed off a missive to King Henri IV, informing him of a development that had ramifications for the "present negotiations to obtain a truce for the States General." There was word, Jeannin reported, the Dutch were about to close a deal with the English mariner Hudson, who was on the verge of discovering a short route to Asia. (Perpetuating the Plancius myth, Jeannin gossiped that Hudson "has found that the more northwards he went, the less cold it became.") Jeannin put forth the plan of a renegade Dutch merchant named Isaac le Maire, who proposed stealing Hudson away from the VOC and signing him to a pact with a French-led consortium, and added, "there are also many rich merchants who will gladly join in."

By now the English were angry that they had let go of Hudson. The Dutch merchants, meanwhile, got wind of the French activity, and it speeded them to sign a contract with the mariner. This frenzy of activity among the major European players heightens the notion of Hudson as a fulcrum: they all sensed this sailor was going somewhere—the future lay in his direction, and they wanted to follow him.

*

To SEA THEN, launching from near the squat brick tower called the Schreierstoren, where the city walls fronted the water and where generations of Dutch women had stood gazing nervously out, waiting for their men to return. Hudson made it by spring, in time for the sailing season of 1609. He had a new ship, the eighty-five-foot *Halve Maen* ("Half Moon"), and a crew of sixteen, half English and half Dutch. He had orders, too: to find a north*eastern* route. He must have pushed strongly for the northwest, for they pushed back; in the accompanying instructions the Dutch merchants warned him "to think of discovering no other routes or passages" than the northeast. In his best fashion, he disobeyed them utterly. After taking a flier along the coast of Norway in the general direction of Russia, he went along with a gale blowing westward and then kept going. He was about to voyage three thousand miles in the opposite direction from what he had promised: inconceivable in another ship's captain; for him, pretty standard. Thus, his historic journey was truly of his own doing, even if its result was something beyond his intention.

Having convinced his crew to reverse course in mid-ocean, he had two options: to follow George Weymouth's journal, which suggested a true northwest passage, navigating the islands and ice floes of what is today northern Canada; or John Smith's notes, indicating that the passage was in fact not northwest at all, but southwest, straight through the North American continent. He followed Smith. After approaching Newfoundland, he hugged the coast southward for six weeks, until he came within ten miles of the Jamestown settlement of Virginia, and his friend. Then, abruptly, he stopped. He knew perfectly well where he was, for his English first mate recorded in his journal, "This is the entrance into the Kings River in Virginia, where our English-men are." They were at the mouth of the Chesapeake, where the Chesapeake Bay Bridge now crosses. Hudson was aware that he was sailing for a Dutch concern, and likely wouldn't have felt welcome or comfortable sailing into the English settlement. He had probably sailed here to orient himself. After swinging farther south to Cape Hatteras Island, he headed north, and on August 28 came into Delaware Bay, the first European ever to do so. No sooner had he entered the bay than the crew sighted treacherous shoals and sand bars. The captain quickly determined that this river could not be the wide, deep channel that led to Cathay.

And so they continued north: misty mornings, bloody sunsets, a stretch of coast like a long smooth cut; surf eternally pounding the belt of sand;

wild silence beyond. They were aware that they were shouldering a new world, impossibly dark, utterly unknown, of imponderable dimension, and with no clear means of access.

And then they felt something happening. Rounding a hooked point, they were startled at what they perceived to be three rivers; cliffs rose up—the land "very pleasant and high, and bold to fall withal." They were in the outer reaches of New York Harbor, riding along the coast of Staten Island. Fish streamed thickly around them: salmon, mullet, wraith-like rays. They anchored and went ashore, marveling at primordial oaks and "an abundance of blue plums."

Then, just like that, people appeared. They came at them frankly, dressed in skins, peaceable, and with an air of dignity, offering corn bread and green tobacco. In 1801 the Moravian missionary John Heckewelder interviewed a Long Island Indian and published an account of Hudson's arrival from the Indian perspective. The story, supposedly handed down through generations of Delaware Indians, gibes with the account by Hudson's mate Robert Juet of the first encounter: peaceable, wary, curious. The Indian told of sighting "a large house of various colors" floating on the water (Dutch ships were indeed vividly painted with geometric motifs). As in Juet's version, the Indian story has the first meeting taking place on land, with several of the visitors, including their leader, rowing ashore. The Indian story adds that the leader of the newcomers is dressed in a "red coat all glittering with gold lace"—a nice and by no means incongruous addition to the portrait of Hudson.

Out came the products. Hemp, dried currants, oysters, beans. Knives, hatchets, and beads. Over the next three days, as the ship explored an intricate mesh of islands, bays, and rivers, making the rounds of Brooklyn, Staten Island, and coastal New Jersey, there would be two violent encounters with Indians, which Juet claims were initiated by the Indians. People died. It's ironic that immediately upon entering the watery perimeter of what would become New York City, these two things take place: trade and violence.

Hudson then sailed his small, three-masted wooden vessel into the coliseum-like interior of the harbor—"a very good harbor for all windes." From his perch on the high poop-deck, looking down on his crew, he gave the order to proceed upriver. His heart must have quickened as the vista unfolded before him. "The River is a mile broad: there is very high Land on both sides," wrote Juet—as likely a channel into the other side of the world as one could hope for. Upriver, they encountered more natives: "a very loving people . . . and we were well taken care of." Hudson went ashore with them, visiting their circular house made of bark. "The land is the finest for cultivation that I ever in my life set foot upon," he wrote. He and his men noted more offerings from the locals: furs.

Then it ended. The river grew narrow and shallow: no ship could pass through; Asia did not lie over there. They turned south again: more skirmishes with the Indians of the southern reaches of the river. It's not certain if Hudson was aware that the land they "rode quietly" past one rainy night was an island—in the first written record of the name, Juet refers to "the side of the river called *Manna-hata*." In any case, while Hudson dutifully noted the possibilities for trade—the grandness of the harbor and the river, the toehold they would provide onto the continent—his own gaze never left the horizon of his obsession. He headed for home, empty-handed.

Strangely, Hudson did not sail straight to Amsterdam but put into port at Dartmouth, in England. He may have done so to disembark some of his English crew—once again there had been loud grumbling on the voyage; once again a crew had bickered among themselves while the captain kept his head in the clouds. At any rate, an international skirmish ensued on arrival. His contractual obligation was to submit all charts, logbooks, and notes to his employers in Amsterdam, but the English authorities tried to stop him; they detained Hudson bodily and got a look at at least some of his records. International spies were still following him. "Juan Hudson," a Spanish spy wrote to Philip III less than a month after the *Halve Maen* pulled into Dartmouth, "has . . . arrived here in England and did not give a full report to his employers." Eventually, Hudson managed to pass his log to Van Meteren, who sent it, along with a report, to Amsterdam.

The news of Hudson's river voyage passed through the sieve of Dutch political and business interests. To the sea-minded merchants on the Zandhoek and the Buitekant, Amsterdam's harborfront, monitoring the offloading of lighters packed with Spanish taffeta, German porcelain, Swedish copper, and East Indies spices while looking for the next business opportunity, hopes of a newfound passage to Asia were forgotten as they studied Van Meteren's report (published as an announcement to the world that the discovery was

Dutch). There they learned of the discovery and charting of a water highway into the unexplored continent that was "as fine a river as can be found, wide and deep, with good anchoring ground on both sides." It was a bonus that it was lightly inhabited by a "friendly and polite people." What jumped out at them, however, were other words, sharp, money-laden nouns—*"Vellen . . . Pelterijen . . . Maertens . . . Vossen . . ."*—the report making a frank promise of "many skins and peltries, martins, foxes, and many other commodities."

And so the story comes back to the founding, half a century earlier, of the English fur trade with Russia. It had dwindled in part because the Russian slaughter had outstripped the beavers' sexual abilities. North America held a fresh, seemingly limitless supply. For some time, Dutch traders had tried unsuccessfully to insinuate themselves into the French fur trade farther north in Canada. That would no longer be necessary: they had their own foothold on the continent. The Dutch staked their claim to the territory Hudson had sailed and which the subsequent explorer Adriaen Block would chart—a swath encompassing three river systems, which would eventually become the Delaware, the Hudson, and the Connecticut, occupying a position on the eastern seaboard of North America to the north of the English territory that Walter Raleigh had named in honor of his virgin queen—and promptly forgot about the mariner himself.

Which was fine because, after his prodigal return, the English wanted Hudson back. He kept his eyes on his prize, now tacking away from the epicenter of history. His obsession was unyielding, making him, finally, a man of the past: of the Renaissance dream of a voyage to far Cathay. He conned three fantastically wealthy young aristocrats into believing in the imminence of his discovery. Having ruled out John Smith's route, he now laid everything on Weymouth's indication of a passage to the icy north, through what was known as "the Furious Overfall" (the channel into Hudson Bay, now called Hudson Strait). The three funded him forthwith, he raised a crew and set off, without skipping a beat, the following spring. His calculations and his hunch pointed to it as inevitable: the passage had to be there.* He wouldn't take no for an answer. The world would have to kill him to stop him.

Which is what happened. Hudson hadn't reckoned that his crew might

---

*For the record, Hudson was right. Roald Amundsen finally achieved the northwest passage in 1906, but by then it was a matter of personal adventure, the commercial possibilities of a northern route to Asia having been largely extinguished by the brutal realities of the voyage.

not share his conviction and would do whatever necessary to save themselves. His arrogance was so supreme that he didn't see his end coming. Even as he was being lowered from the deck of his ship into the shallop, hands bound behind his back, dressed in "a motley gown" as one of the mutineers would later testify (for they took him at daybreak, as he stepped out of his cabin), he remained clueless. "What do you mean by this?" he asked in bewilderment, as they bound him and told him that he would soon find out. He had egged and cajoled and lashed the twenty-two men onward, month upon month, as they fought a losing battle against the pack ice, as the shrouds and sails froze above them, as the food ran out and the sightings of bears and seals out on the white strip of the horizon stopped, as they were reduced to clambering ashore and scavenging moss for sustenance. First their gums bled, then their teeth loosened. Toe by toe, frostbite ate its way into their flesh, so that many could no longer stand, their pallets crowding every available space on board. Finally, they could take it no more.

Besides him, the small party loaded into the shallop comprised the most desperately sick and those that had remained loyal to him, including his son John, still a boy. At some point after they were set adrift—after the ship had moved away from them into open water, her topsails fattening in a fresh wind; after he had watched her hull evaporate into the white hoar of early morning, leaving their small vessel to the elements, without food, water, or source of fire, and three hundred thousand square miles of ice-choked sea around them—his iron will must have finally caved in. And he would have been left, then, before the cold ate its way into his blood and heart, to endure what must be any man's twin nightmares: watching his innocent child suffer and die because of his own folly, and contemplating the utter destruction of his life's ambition. At some point before his mind closed down, he would have acknowledged that his dream of discovery was to die here, as he would die.

The irony of his end came when the surviving mutineers limped back to London, stood trial for mutiny and murder, and then were exonerated based on their outrageous but ingenious claim that, in fact, Hudson *had* found the northwest passage, and that *they* knew where it was. Rather than being hanged, then, the survivors found themselves inaugurated by King James, along with some of the most prominent men in London, as members of a new company, the "Company of the Merchants Discoverers of the North-

West Passage," with a charter to proceed through their newfound strait to commence trade "to the great kingdoms of Tartaria, China, Japan, Solomons Islands, Chili, the Philippins and other countrys . . . "

The wave of history, which Hudson had ridden so effortlessly for a short while, rapidly engulfed him. He was destined to serve as a pollinator, to bring the spores of a culture not his own to new soil. Even before he froze to death in the southern reaches of what became Hudson Bay, on the Amsterdam waterfront a young man named Arnout Vogels was in a whirl of activity. Vogels, a thirty-year-old of adventure and drive, had been born in Antwerp to the south, and was one of those who fled troubles elsewhere in Europe to the safe haven of Amsterdam, in his case after Spanish forces invaded his hometown in 1585. He threw himself into business with the zest of one who has grown up amid war and knows how short life can be. He apprenticed in the fur business in the service of a trading company, but longed to strike out on his own. When the report of Hudson's discoveries spread through the dockside offices of Amsterdam's traders, Vogels moved fast. On July 26, 1610, as Hudson was making his way through the massive icy bay where he would meet his end, Vogels shook hands with Captain Sijmen Lambertsz Mau on a deal to trade in the new, virgin territory. The destination was vague still to most European minds, and so on the contract it was stated rather broadly: "West Indies, and nearby lands and places." The term "West Indies" was still being applied to all American regions.

Overnight, times had changed. The idea of a shortcut to Asia, once the height of fashion, suddenly seemed antique and retro to men of Vogels's generation. The future was nearer: just across the Atlantic. The Englishman Hudson had scouted it for enterprising Dutchmen to follow. There was no concern at this date of a competing claim from England: the English had established a shaky beachhead at Virginia, but their New England settlements were still years in the future. Hudson's venture on behalf of the Dutch predated the Pilgrims' landing by more than a decade. So the field was clear, and the refrains must have repeated in the minds of the Dutch traders: "skins and peltries, martins, foxes," "a very good harbor for all windes." And they had an image to summon in their minds as a goal, a key, a way into the heart of a virgin continent: "as fine a river as can be found . . . a mile broad"—a glistening highway to pure possibility.

Chapter 3

THE ISLAND

Catalina Trico, a French-speaking teenager. Joris Rapalje, a Flemish textile worker. Bastiaen Krol, a lay minister from the farming province of Friesland. By tens and twenties they came in the years 1624 and 1625, pitching on the inhuman waves in yachts, galiots, ketches, pinks, and pinnaces, well-crafted but still frightfully vulnerable wooden vessels, banging around in the narrow and rheumatic below-decks, with pigs rooting and sheep bleating hollowly at every slamming swell, with the animal reek and their own odors of sickness and sour filth, each clutching his or her satchel of elixirs to ward off the plague, the devil, shipwreck, and "the bloody flux." The very names of their ships—*Fortune, Abraham's Sacrifice*—signaled the two poles of hope and fear that governed them.

Three months it took to follow Hudson, four if the winds failed. From Amsterdam the ships made their way across the wide inland sea called the IJ, with its treacherous shoals, to the windswept island of Texel, and then set off into the white hoar of the North Sea. They gave the Portuguese coast a wide berth and skirted the Canary Islands off North Africa, their captains with skill and luck avoiding predatory privateers and pirates (or not: some ships were taken by both). Then, riding the trades, they beat a long, forbidding arc southwest across the blue-gray wilderness of the Atlantic, swinging upward again north of the Bahamas and along the coast of the new land, the new world, keeping a sharp eye for the hooked peninsula that Hudson noted, and so into the enveloping embrace of the great harbor.

There still lingered, fifteen years after Hudson's trip, and ten years after Shakespeare penned *The Tempest* based on accounts of a voyage to America shipwrecked on a supposedly bewitched isle (Bermuda), the notion that this might be the gateway to the riches of the sultry, pagan, exotically civilized East. It was possible, as far as they knew, that the western shore, which in fifty years' time would be christened New Jersey, was in fact the backdoor of China, that India, with its steamy profusion of gods and curries, lay just beyond those bluffs. But these were not explorers but settlers, and their immediate focus was here: the river, this new home. In the decade and a half since Hudson's find, scouts and traders had made good contacts with the Indians of what the Dutch were now calling the River Mauritius, after Maurits of Nassau, son of the assassinated hero William the Silent and now leader of the rebellion against Spain (though another name had already sprung up: as early as 1614, fur traders were paying homage to their forerunner by referring to "de rivière Hudson"). In their lean and silent canoes the "River Indians" (as the traders called them: they were variously of the Mahican and Lenni Lenape tribes) came to them from the north, the east, the west, from far out in the unknown vastness, bringing excellent furs in remarkable quantities. There was indeed business to be had, the traders reported. And so a consortium of smaller interests was formed to exploit it in a systematic way.

The truce negotiated between Spain and the Dutch Republic during the year of Hudson's voyage was to last for twelve years. It ended promptly in 1621, and immediately the spear-rattling began among Dutch right-wingers. A patriot-businessman named Willem Usselincx, a birdlike man roiling with religious zeal, had for years championed the idea of Dutch provinces in the New World that would be driven by both commerce and Calvinist fire. "It is obvious," Usselincx argued in the series of meetings that led to the establishment of the West India Company, "that if one wants to get money, something has to be proposed to the people which will move them to invest. To this end the glory of God will help with some, harm to Spain with others, with some the welfare of the Fatherland; but the principal and most powerful inducement will be the profit that each can make for himself. . . ." The new lands, he stressed, were inhabited not by wild-eyed savages, but by intelligent natives among whom the Dutch could plant a colony. There were natural products there to be exploited, maybe gold and silver, as well as raw materials "which are the sinews of war."

The renewal of war with Spain fit in with this scheme: Dutch frigates of a privately owned company could be equipped with guns and carry out raids on Spanish ships in Caribbean and South American waters while also conducting trade in New World ports. Privateering—government-authorized piracy on enemy ships—was an accepted wartime activity.

Merchants and politicians were suddenly interested. Wealthy businessmen organized themselves into five regional chambers, each of which contributed startup funds. The States General, the governing body of the country, added a modest amount, and by October 1623 the West India Company was as flush as any new company in history, with more than seven million guilders in its coffers. The East India Company had exploited Asia to fabulous result; now its new colleague would encompass the Atlantic Rim—its monopoly extending to West Africa, the Caribbean islands, and the coast of North America. It was to be a creature of war as well as trade, and its network of merchants, skippers, sailors, accountants, carpenters, armourers, and soldiers infiltrated the new sphere of interest with remarkable speed. By 1626 an inventory of the company's property, addressed to the directors, included:

12 ships and yachts destined for the African trade in Guinea, Benin, Angola, Greyn, and Quaqua coasts, with the exported cargoes and expected returns . . .

1 ship of Dordrecht to Cape Verd, with cargo . . .

1 ship destined for the trade of the Amazon and the Coast of Guiana . . .

1 ship of about 130 lasts, 1 yacht well equipped, destined for the trade and colonization of New Netherland . . .

33 ships . . . which the Company hath still lying here in port, provided with metal and iron guns, and all sorts of supplies of ammunition of war, powder, muskets, arms, sabres, and whatever may be necessary for the equipment, which can be fitted for sea . . .

Moneys . . . which being in the Treasury, will be applied to keep the foregoing ships at sea, not only to injure the King of Spain, but also by God's blessing to do your High Mightinesses and the Company much service, and the Partners good profit.

The North American territory would play an economic role in this scheme. The company would exploit it for furs and timber, and also use it as a transportation hub, with ships cycling from Europe to South America and the Caribbean, and then to the North American harbor and so back home. Of course, settlers were required, and raising them proved to be one of the hardest aspects of the whole complex business of creating an Atlantic empire. Times were good in the homeland; the future looked even better. And Amsterdam was probably the best place in the world to be poor (its almshouses, wrote an English consul with some exaggeration, were "more like princes' palaces than lodgings for poor people"). To get people to sign on for a passage to what was now being called New Netherland, they had to find those who were ignorant or desperate or poor enough to leave the deeply civilized bosom of Amsterdam—with its paved streets, its scrubbed floors, its wheels of cheese and tankards of excellent beer, its fluffy pillows and blue-and-white-tiled hearths and cozy peat fires—and venture to the back of beyond, to an absolute and unforgiving wilderness.

But, as always, the country was loaded with refugees, and, by promising land in exchange for six years of service, the company managed to round up a handful of hale young Walloons—French-speaking exiles from what is today Belgium—made sure, like Noah, that they had a female for every male, and hustled them into the Amsterdam council chamber, where they swore an oath of allegiance to the company and the government.

The councillor who administered the oath, Claes Peterszen, was a renowned physician and surgeon, so renowned that while we know him from Rembrandt's viscerally famous painting *The Anatomy Lesson of Dr. Tulp* ("Tulp," or "tulip," being a nickname, from the flower painted above his front door), at the time it was the doctor who, in agreeing to the portrait, helped make the artist famous. We have a nice mental image, then, of the black-dressed, dignified, austere physician-magistrate with his sharp black V of facial hair, representative of the Dutch political and scientific establishment, and before him, in their rough country attire, the young men and women, shifting and twitching with nerves and exuberant raw youth, who were about to start a new society in a wilderness called Manhattan.

There was lots of raw youth: four couples were actually married at sea, the ship's captain, Cornelis May (for whom, incidentally, Cape May, New Jersey, is named), doing the honors. Another pair—the ones named at the top of this chapter, Catalina Trico and Joris Rapalje—were smarter. Maybe they knew what conditions would be like on board, and didn't relish the idea of

consummating a marriage there. They agreed to take part in the wildly hazardous enterprise on the condition that the company first marry them in a
hastier-than-normal ceremony, which took place four days before their ship
left Amsterdam on January 25, 1624. "Espousé le 21 de Janvier," the clerk
of the Walloon Church of Amsterdam recorded, without wasting too much
time getting the names right, "Joris Raporbie de Valencenne, et Caterine
triko." Being illiterate, both made their marks on the page. He was nineteen,
she was eighteen; neither had parents sign the registry, which suggests that
both were either alone in the world or alone in that part of the world, which
amounted to the same thing. Like many who were to follow, they had nothing
to lose.

Considering the stupendous dangers awaiting them, first at sea and
then on arrival, it wasn't a union a betting man would likely lay money on.
And yet, sixty years later, when the English colonies of Pennsylvania and
Maryland were embroiled in a border dispute and needed evidence of
"Christian" occupation of certain lands along the eastern seaboard, the representatives of William Penn found an old woman to testify who was known
to have been among the first European settlers. Catalina Trico, now in her
eighties, was a widow, but she and Joris had had a long and fruitful marriage. The records of New Netherland show them among the first buyers of
land in the wilderness of southern Manhattan, building two houses on Pearl
Street steps away from the fort, obtaining a milk cow, borrowing money
from the provincial government, moving their homestead to a large tract of
farmland across the river in the new village of Breuckelen, and giving birth
to and baptizing eleven children. Their first, Sarah, was considered the first
European born in what would become New York (in 1656, at the age of
thirty, she proclaimed herself "first born christian daughter of New Netherland"). She was born in 1625, and the same records duly show her marriage
in 1639, to the overseer of a tobacco plantation in what would become
Greenwich Village, and, in turn, the birth of her eight children. Over the
course of the brief life of New Netherland and into the history of New York
the Rapalje children and their offspring would spread across the region. In
the 1770s, John Rapalje would serve as a member of the New York State Assembly (he rejected revolution and became a Loyalist). Their descendants
have been estimated at upwards of one million, and in the Hudson Valley
town of Fishkill, New York, a lane called Rapalje Road is a quiet suburban

testament to the endurance of a long-ago slapdash wedding of two young nobodies on the Amsterdam waterfront, which, as much as any political event, marked the beginning of the immigrant, stake-your-claim civilization not only of Manhattan but of America.

As the sea-battered ships finally entered the harbor, the passengers gazed out onto a wholly new landscape, stranger and more complex than the flat land they had left. In contemporary scientific terms, the region that would be their new home comprised an intersection of three physiographic provinces: sandy coastal plain, rolling upland hills, and craggy metamorphic ridges, much of which was slashed and gouged by the glaciers of the last ice age, leaving a stippling of streambeds, jumbled moraine, and glacial lakes. Sailing silently into the inner harbor, approaching the southern tip of Manhattan Island, the ships glided into a reedy, marshy expanse of tidal wetland (the Mohawk name for Manhattan—*Gänóno*—translates as "reeds" or "place of reeds"), a complicated crossover region of freshwater and marine species, where bay, swamp forest, and serpentine barrens bred skying, cawing shore birds—plovers, sandpipers, dowitchers, yellowlegs—as well as thick populations of homebody mallards, and also drew migrating flocks of oldsquaws, mergansers, and wigeons that blackened the gray November sky. Mussels, conchs, clams, and periwinkles encrusted the estuaries, and most of all oysters, some of which, a settler wrote, are "quite large and occasionally containing a small pearl," while others were tiny and sweet and another variety was "fine for stewing and frying. As each one fills a big spoon they make a good bite." Rising up above the island's reedy shoreline were oak and chestnut forests and hills populated by wolves, mountain lions, and black bear. The best guess on the origin of the Indian name that would stick is the Delaware *mannahata,* "hilly island," though some have suggested that simply "the island" or "the small island" is a more accurate translation.

Putting foot to solid ground, the settlers decided they liked what they saw. "We were much gratified on arriving in this country," one wrote home. "Here we found beautiful rivers, bubbling fountains flowing down into the valleys; basins of running waters in the flatlands, agreeable fruits in the woods, such as strawberries, pigeon berries, walnuts, and also . . . wild grapes. The woods abound with acorns for feeding hogs, and with venison. There is considerable fish in the rivers; good tillage land; here is especially free coming and going, without fear of the naked natives of the country. Had we cows, hogs, and other cattle fit for food (which we daily expect in the first ships) we would not wish to return to Holland, for whatever we desire in the paradise of Holland, is here to be found." In Europe, newspapers as such didn't yet exist, but periodical pamphlets were a major source of news, and no sooner did the first settlers of New Netherland begin writing home than an Amsterdam physician named Nicolaes van Wassenaer started to publish a semiannual pamphlet of the doings in the far-off land. "It is very pleasant, all products being in abundance, though wild," he wrote in December 1624. "Grapes are of very good flavor, but will be henceforward better cultivated by our people. Cherries are not found there. There are all sorts of fowls, both in the water and in the air. Swans, geese, ducks, bitterns, abound."

At first the company sprinkled its few settlers over a wide area. In the Dutch understanding, laying claim to a patch of territory required inhabiting it (for the English, as would later become an issue, all that was required was having an official representative set foot on a patch of soil not previously claimed by Christians). Also in the Dutch understanding, water was the key to any piece of land. Thus, the company set about dividing its few colonists among the three principal waterways of their territory. What under the English would become the Delaware River, which Hudson had considered exploring but quickly ruled out as a route to Asia due to its shoaly bay, the Dutch called the South River, for the good reason that it formed the southern limit of their territory. For most of their time in North America they called the Hudson the North River (mariners, famously conservative and resistant to change, call it that to this day). The other main waterway—what would become the Connecticut River, which bisects that state—the Dutch called the Fresh River.

These were the highways of the region, the places to which Indians brought pelts, and the means of exploring the interior. The company sent a few settlers to form a small camp on each—literally a few. Two families and six single men were shipped east to the Fresh River. Two families and eight men sailed down the coast to the South River. Eight men stayed on a small island in the harbor. The rest of the families sailed a further hundred and fifty miles up the North River, through the mud-colored tidal chop, by majestic palisades of rock along the western shore, then passing on both shores the undulating humps of the highlands, to the place the traders reported was the key junction of Indian traffic. Here the east-flowing Mohawk River, after traveling all the way from the Great Lakes region, careened over seventy-foot falls before emptying into the North River. Here the newcomers disembarked and stood defenseless before the towering pines. For shelter initially they dug square pits in the ground, lined them with wood, and covered them with bark roofs (a minister who arrived a few years later, when proper houses were being built, sneered at the "hovels and holes" in which the first arrivals "huddled rather than dwelt").

Catalina and Joris were in the party initially shipped upriver from Manhattan to the falls, where a fort-trading post was to be constructed. The natives of the country appeared soon after the settlers stumbled ashore, exchanged presents, and made other gestures of friendship with the ship's captain. It was disorienting for the newcomers, but the sun had the warmth of spring in it, and the crumbly black earth seemed to cry out to be impregnated with seed. The Rapaljes and the other couples stayed two years at the location, in autumn harvesting grain "as high as a man," the next spring whispering prayers of thanks when three company ships arrived whose names—*The Cow, The Sheep, The Horse*—betrayed their cargo. During the whole time the Indians "were all quiet as lambs," as Catalina remembered in old age, coming regularly and trading freely with the settlers.

The initial plan was for an island on the South River, a hundred-odd miles from Manhattan, to become the capital of the new province. This was based on the decidedly mistaken belief that the climate of what would become southern New Jersey approximated that which the Spanish had found in Florida. The balminess of those reports sounded good to the Dutch, who wouldn't have to deal with the extreme bother of a harbor freezing up in the winter, bringing trade and communication to a halt. The first settlers to arrive there were dismayed to find no palm trees. Worse, the bay did indeed freeze over that first winter and in subsequent ones, too, so that attention shifted to the bay to the north, which, thanks to geographic peculiarities, rarely froze despite its latitude.

The knots of colonists scattered over two hundred and fifty miles got to work—cleared ground, felled trees, constructed palisade defenses, sowed grain. Ships arrived. The colonists made deals with the Indians and established a system for trade: in 1625 they bought 5,295 beaver pelts and 463 otter skins, which they loaded onto the ships to be sent back home. The ships in turn brought news. In England, James I, Elizabeth's successor, had died. He had been an awkward monarch—he tended to drool and was given to crude mannerisms—and was never revered as Elizabeth had been. He had unsuccessfully resisted the Dutch rise to power, attempting to ally with Spain at a time when English hatred of Catholicism was at a fever pitch. (Then again, he had, however, also overseen the creation of the King James Bible, one of the world's great literary works.) The nation breathed a sigh of relief when his son Charles—handsome, chaste, dignified—took the throne, not knowing that in time hopes would be dashed in the most violent way, for him and for the nation, and with great consequences for this far-off Dutch province.

In the United Provinces, too, power had passed, from brother to brother. Maurits, Prince of Orange, the stadtholder or chief nobleman of the country, had led the fight against Spain since the death of his father, William the Silent, in 1584. But he had grown weak in recent years, and he had fatally compromised his legitimacy six years earlier by resolving a power struggle with the great statesman Jan van Oldenbarnevelt by having the man's head cut off. Maurits's brother, Frederik Hendrik, who at age forty-one was seventeen years his junior, was a brilliant diplomat and military tactician; he would continue the revolt and bring the nation to the verge of final recognition of independence. Under these new leaders the Dutch and the English, united in their common Protestantism, had signed a treaty of cooperation against Catholic Spain, their joint enemy. This treaty provided that each nation would have access to the other's ports, including provincial ports.

The New Netherland settlers, chests heaving and faces streaked with sweat, would have had to pause in their labors to digest this information. They knew perfectly well that a group of English religious pilgrims had settled to their north a few years earlier—"Brownists" they were called at the time, after the Separatist preacher Robert Browne—and they hoped for good relations. In fact, they expected good relations. Remarkably, most of the Walloons who made up the majority of the Dutch colony's early population had come from asylum in the university town of Leiden (spelled Leyden at the time), the same place that had harbored the English Pilgrims. In their flight from persecution in England, the Pilgrims had spent twelve years there as guests of the Dutch before leaving to found a virgin theocracy in the New World.

Events soon derailed the initial settlement strategy in the Dutch province. Joris Rapalje, his wife Catalina, and the other settlers at what was now called Fort Orange (which under the English would become Albany) saw their hard work come to a sudden, grisly end in the spring of 1626. Their settlement on the riverbank was on former hunting grounds of the Mahicans, who had welcomed them. To the north and west stretched the territory of the Mohawks. These two tribes—the first, one of the Algonquin-speaking nations, the second, one of the five tribes of the Iroquois League—had very different backgrounds and beliefs. Their languages were as distinct as English and Russian; they had different customs and little respect for one another. For decades they had been fighting an intermittent war, and the appearance of European traders in their midst stirred the conflict to a new level. In addition, after more than a decade of contact with Europeans, these tribes were reorienting their lives around the acquisition of foreign products: fishing hooks, axes, kettles, glassware, needles, pots, knives, and duffel (the rough wool cloth that originated in the Flemish town of Duffel and which gives us the term "duffel bag"). Later, of course, guns and liquor would be added to the list. Mahicans were even relocating their villages to be closer to the Dutch, in an attempt to form a trade and defensive alliance. Call it friendship or self-interest, by 1626 the Mahicans and Dutch had established a closeness.

This closeness was probably what led Daniel van Crieckenbeeck, the commander of the fort, to ignore explicit orders forbidding interference in intertribal affairs, with results that would redound to the present. One spring day in 1626, a Mahican party of more than two dozen men—like the Dutch "in figure, build and share," as one writer described, their hair "jet-black, quite sleek and uncurled, and almost as coarse as a horse's tail," and probably, given the period and the time of year, wearing deer skins loosely about their bodies and tied at the waist—came into the palisade of rough-cut logs and asked Van Crieckenbeeck for Dutch aid in their fight against the Mohawks. The man who asked this favor was most likely a tribal leader named Monemin. Van Crieckenbeeck had his orders; the West India Company had clearly instructed Willem Verhulst, head of the province, that "he shall be very careful not lightly to embroil himself in [the Indians'] quarrels or wars, or to take sides, but to remain neutral . . ." On the other hand, Van

Crieckenbeeck surely felt responsible for the well-being of the handful of young couples, including a number of pregnant women and perhaps some infants, in the midst of the forest thousands of miles from home. It stood to reason that helping the Mahicans now would yield a firm ally in the future. So he agreed. The Mahicans led the way, and he and six of his men followed, disappearing into the pines.

Three miles from the fort, they were inundated by a storm of arrows. In one swift, bloody assault, a band of ambushing Mohawks put an end to the Dutch-Mahican alliance and, by the way, altered the history of the world. Van Crieckenbeeck, three of his men, and twenty-four Mahicans, including Monemin, took fatal hits. The Mohawks made a show of their victory, and nicely capped the terror they had caused by roasting and eating one especially unfortunate Dutchman named Tymen Bouwensz.

Meanwhile, the other settlement on the North River was also in turmoil. It had been decided that the settlement in the harbor would be on a tiny, teardrop-shaped island that the colonists called Noten (Nut) Island, after the walnut and chestnut trees they found there. The first settlers who arrived camped here, and their cattle were sent to pasture five hundred yards across the bay, on Manhattan Island. The colony's provisional director, Willem Verhulst, began causing problems from the start. He meted out harsh and inconsistent punishment, infuriating the colonists. He and his wife may also have misappropriated funds or—an even worse offense—cheated Indians. Both because of the colony's Calvinist sense of propriety and out of a practical awareness that it was not a good idea to upset the natives who were surrounding you, the West India Company had sent Verhulst explicit instructions on dealing with the Indians: "He shall also see that no one do the Indians any harm or violence, deceive, mock, or contemn them in any way, but that in addition to good treatment they be shown honesty, faithfulness, and sincerity in all contracts, dealings, and intercourse, without being deceived by shortage of measure, weight or number, and that throughout friendly relations with them be maintained . . ." Whatever the exact offenses, Verhulst and his wife had set the colonists howling; they wanted him gone.

At the moment this crisis was boiling over, a ship arrived from the upriver settlement with news of the Indian attack. The colony was barely a year old and already it was in turmoil, in danger of collapse. It needed a leader, and one stepped forward.

He had grown up speaking German and Dutch was his second language, but his ancestry was French, so his name was pronounced in the French way—"Min-wee." He is one of those figures of history for whom everything we know about him makes us wish we knew more. He had had no military training, but he was an individualistic, take-charge sort who would affect the course of history in more ways than one. His father had taken part in the northward migration of Protestants fleeing Spanish troops and inquisitors, and settled in the small German town of Wesel, near the Dutch border, and it was here that Peter Minuit grew up. He would turn out to be a scrappy businessman with no fixed loyalties and a great drive to get ahead, and, in good upwardly mobile fashion, he made his first smart move in life by marrying the daughter of the mayor of the nearby town of Kleve. He and his wife then moved seventy-five miles west to the larger Dutch city of Utrecht, where Minuit trained to become a diamond-cutter. He found that a dull occupation, though, and heard of the formation of the West India Company. Through French-speaking circles, he learned further that a party of Walloons was signing on as pioneers in a venture to the New World. He appeared at the stately mansion of West India House on Amsterdam's Brouwersgracht (Brewers' Canal) one day in 1624, asking for a posting to New Netherland, apparently not as a settler or company official but as a private "volunteer" businessman scouting trade opportunities. The directors must have been impressed by his energy. Minuit appears to have shipped out with one of the first groups of settlers, for the company's initial instructions to Verhulst say that "He shall have Pierre Minuyt, as volunteer, and others whom he deems competent thereto sail up the river as far as they can in any way do so, in order to inspect the condition of the land . . ."

Minuit might thus have been among the party of Catalina Trico and Joris Rapalje when they sailed upriver, and he seems, during this early period, to have gathered a good deal of information about the new land. He then apparently returned to Amsterdam for a time, perhaps to deliver the "samples of dyes, drugs, gums, herbs, plants, trees and flowers" the instructions asked him to supply, for the records show him leaving the Dutch Republic once again in January of 1626 and returning to New Netherland on May 4. So he had spent time in the colony, enough time to impress the settlers with his abilities, and then returned to Europe; now he was coming back. Not long after his ship, the *Sea-Mew*, passed through the narrows between *Staten*

Eylandt (named in honor of the States General of the United Provinces) and *Lange Eylandt* (named for obvious reasons), and dropped anchor in the harbor, he would have been inundated with the bad news.

A newly formed council of settlers met. They put Verhulst on trial and voted to banish him and his wife from the province. Verhulst did not go gently; he was furious and vindictive. He vowed to return someday at the head of a foreign army and make use of his knowledge of the territory and its fortifications—an interesting threat in light of what not he but Minuit would do twelve years later.

The colonists then voted Minuit their new commander. Minuit acted quickly once his role had changed from private scout to officer of the province. The first decision he seems to have made is the one that would have the most profound consequences. The leaders in Amsterdam had tried to supervise the settlement from afar, which was awkward and ineffective, and Verhulst, their man on the scene, hadn't been able to see the obvious problems. Too few settlers were spread out across the hundreds of miles of territory; the news from Fort Orange convinced Minuit that safety was a major concern. Nut Island (today Governor's Island) may have been useful as an initial staging area, but it was too small for a settlement of any size. The South River did not live up to its tropical billing. To anyone with a practical and logistical mind it was clear that the island of Manhattan, separated from Nut Island by a channel "a gunshot wide," answered every need. It was large enough to support a population, small enough that a fort located on its southernmost tip could be defended. Its forests were rich in game; it had flatlands that could be farmed and freshwater streams. It was situated at the mouth of the river to which Indian fur-traders came from hundreds of miles around, and which connected to other waterways that penetrated deep into the interior. It was also at the entrance to the bay, located in a wide and inviting harbor that seemed not to freeze over in winter. It was, in short, a natural fulcrum between the densely civilized continent of Europe and the tantalizingly wild continent of North America. It was the perfect island.

*

So HE BOUGHT it. Everyone knows that. Peter Minuit purchased Manhattan Island from a group of local Indians for sixty guilders worth of goods, or as the nineteenth-century historian Edmund O'Callaghan calculated it, twenty-four dollars. From the seventeenth through the early twentieth century thousands of real estate transactions occurred in which native Americans sold parcels—ranging in size from a town lot to a midwestern state—to English, Dutch, French, Spanish, and other European settlers. But only one sale is legend; only one is known by everyone. Only one has had the durability to be riffed on in Broadway song ("Give It Back to the Indians," from the 1939 Rodgers and Hart musical *Too Many Girls*), and, at the end of the twentieth century, to do service as a punchline in a column by humorist Dave Barry (". . . which the Dutch settler Peter Minuit purchased from the Manhattan Indians for $24, plus $167,000 a month in maintenance fees").

It's pretty clear why this particular sale lodged in the cultural memory, why it became legend: the extreme incongruity, the exquisitely absurd price. It is the most dramatic illustration of the whole long process of stripping the natives of their land. The idea that the center of world commerce, an island packed with trillions of dollars' worth of real estate, was once bought from supposedly hapless Stone Age innocents for twenty-four dollars' worth of household goods is too delicious to let slip. It speaks to our sense of early American history as the history of savvy, ruthless Europeans conniving, tricking, enslaving, and bludgeoning innocent and guileless natives out of their land and their lives. It's a neatly packed symbol of the entire conquest of the continent that was to come.

Beyond that, the purchase snippet is notable because it is virtually the only thing about the Manhattan colony that *has* become a part of history. For this reason, too, it deserves exploring.

So, who were the Indians who agreed to this transaction, and what did they think it meant? The ancestors of the people whom European settlers took to calling Indians (after Columbus, who at first thought he had arrived at the outer reaches of India) traveled the land bridge from Siberia to Alaska that existed during the last ice age, more than twelve thousand years ago, then spread slowly through the Americas. They came from Asia; their genetic makeup is a close match with Siberians and Mongolians. They spread out thinly across the incomprehensible vastness of the American continents to create a linguistic richness unparalleled in human history: it has been estimated that at the moment Columbus arrived in the New World twenty-five percent of all human languages were North American Indian.

There are two rival, hardened stereotypes that get in the way of understanding these people: the one that arose from the long cultural dismissing of American Indians as "primitive," and the modern dogma that sees them as Noble and Defenseless. Both are cartoon images. Recent work in genetics, archaeology, anthropology, and linguistics makes plain what should be obvious: that the Mahican, Mohawk, Lenape, Montauk, Housatonic, and other peoples occupying the lands that for a time were called New Netherland, as well as the Massachusett, Wampanoag, Sokoki, Pennacook, Abenaki, Oneida, Onondaga, Susquehannock, Nanticoke, and others who inhabited other parts of what became the states of New York, Massachusetts, Pennsylvania, Connecticut, Vermont, New Hampshire, Maine, Delaware, Maryland, and New Jersey, were biologically, genetically, intellectually, all but identical to the Dutch, English, French, Swedish, and others who came into contact with them in the beginning of the seventeenth century. The Indians were as skilled, as duplicitous, as capable of theological rumination and technological cunning, as smart and as pig-headed, and as curious and as cruel as the Europeans who met them. The members of the Manhattan-based colony who knew them—who spent time among them in their villages, hunted and traded with them, learned their languages—knew this perfectly well. It was later, after the two had separated into rival camps, that the stereotypes set. The early seventeenth century was a much more interesting time than the Wild West era, a time when Indians and Europeans were something like equal participants, dealing with one another as allies, competitors, partners.

But if the Indians were so smart and in a strong position, why would they sell their land, the most precious thing they owned? Putting the question that way raises a point familiar to every middle school student: the Indians had a different idea of land ownership from the Europeans. With no concept of permanent property transfer, Indians of the Northeast saw a real estate deal as a combination of a rental agreement and a treaty or alliance between two groups. Indian nations were divided and subdivided into tribes, villages, and other communities. They were often at war or in fear of attack from other groups, and often entered into defensive alliances with one another, which involved sharing certain tribal lands in exchange for the strength of numbers. This colored the way the Indians saw their land deals with the Dutch and English. They would give the newcomers use of some of their land, and in exchange they would get blankets, knives, kettles, and other extremely useful goods, and also a military ally. That this was how they viewed land deals is illustrated neatly by several cases—such as one in South Carolina in the 1750s between the colonial governor and Cherokee leaders—in which the Indians refused any payment at all for the land. As they saw it, the protective alliance was payment enough.

This was probably what the Mahican Monemin had in mind when he approached the unfortunate Daniel van Crieckenbeeck: he was asking the Dutch to fulfill what he understood to be part of the bargain in the land deal at Fort Orange, to help him in a battle with his enemies. Van Crieckenbeeck may have understood this was a part of the Mahican notion of property transfer and tried to do what was expected of him, in defiance of his orders.

Thus the situation of the Indians. As to the Dutch, the neatness and compactness of the legend of Manhattan's purchase has to do with the lack of attention paid to the Dutch colony by historians and with what they perceived to be a shortage of information about the settlement. For those hoping to understand the history of the Manhattan-based colony, the great disaster took place in 1821, when the government of the Netherlands, in a truly unfortunate fit of housekeeping (the Dutch have always been fastidious cleaners), sold for scrap paper what remained of the archives of the Dutch East and West India Companies prior to 1700. Eighteen years later, an American agent named John Romeyn Brodhead, working on behalf of New York State, went to the Netherlands in search of documentary material on the Dutch colony, and found to his "surprise, mortification, and regret" that all of it—eighty thousand pounds of records—had vanished.

Fortunately, we have another great mass of relevant documents: the official records of the province, twelve thousand pages strong. As outlined at the beginning of this book, the bulk of these records are only now, after centuries of neglect, being translated by Dr. Charles Gehring of the New Netherland Project, and it is upon these that much of this book relies. These records miraculously survived wars, fires, mold, and rodents. But they begin in 1638. None of the province's records prior to that year have survived, possibly because when, like Verhulst, the early governors of the province were dismissed from service, they likely took the records of their administration back to Amsterdam with them to aid in their defense. We are left then with a gaping hole at the earliest period of New York's prehistory, which nineteenth-century historians filled in as best they could. They knew the name Peter Minuit, knew that he was an early director of the province, and they had a tantalizing scrap of paper suggesting that the island had been purchased from the *"Wilden"* (Indians) for "the value of 60 guilders."

We know more now and are able to paint a more detailed picture of what went on in the spring of 1626. In Amsterdam in the year 1910, a sheaf of papers showed up at a rare books and manuscripts auction. A curator had labeled item No. 1795 "Documents sur la Nouvelle-Néerlande, 1624–1626." The owner was a man with the formidable name of Alexander Carel Paul George Ridder van Rappard. The antique sheets he put up for sale may have been part of the collection of his grandfather, Frans Alexander Ridder van Rappard, a noted collector. It was years before the papers were bought by another collector (the American railroad tycoon Henry E. Huntington), were translated, published, and made available to scholars.* The documents—which had once been a part of the West India Company archives and had somehow escaped the wholesale destruction—comprised five letters and sets of instructions dating from the colony's beginnings. Much of the information in this chapter comes from these papers, which have provided a new perspective on what the Dutch thought they were doing with their New World colony. One long-held belief, for example, was that the colony from the beginning was an unorganized, ad hoc settlement, not so much mismanaged as allowed to grow in a state of near anarchy, that was generally a mess until the English came in and began to make it function. The so-called Van Rappard documents prove this wrong. They show that a great deal of care was devoted to the colony and to the welfare of the inhabitants. It is from these documents that we know that there was a leader before Minuit, the hapless Willem Verhulst. Before he left the Dutch Republic, Verhulst was given explicit instructions to "carefully note all places where there is any appearance of tillable or pasture land, timber of any kind, minerals, or other things," to do test drillings of the soil, to denote every waterfall, stream, and place for sawmills, to note "inlets, depths, shallows, rocks, and width of the rivers," and indicate the best places for forts, "keeping in mind that the fittest place is where the river is narrow, where it cannot be fired upon from higher ground, where large ships cannot come too close,

*In 1924, A. J. F. van Laer, Charles Gehring's predecessor as translator of the Dutch archives, produced a limited edition publication of these records, *Documents Relating to New Netherland, 1624–1626*, in the Henry E. Huntington Library.

where there is a distant view unobstructed by trees or hills, where it is possible to have water in the moat, and where there is no sand, but clay or other firm earth." The instructions note elaborate preparations for farming: " . . . divers trees, vines, and all sorts of seeds are being sent over . . . and of each sort of fruit he shall successively send us samples. . . . And with regard to the aniseed and cuminseed which is sent over to make a trial with, he shall sow the same at different times and places, observing at what time and in which place it grows best and yields most."

Thanks to this cache of documents, we have a revised picture: of a well-organized Dutch effort and of Minuit as a competent leader wrapping his mind around the problem of establishing a colony. Another figure emerges from these documents. In July of 1626, Isaack de Rasière, a thirty-year-old merchant's son with a taste for adventure, stepped off the *Arms of Amsterdam* and onto the Manhattan shore, ready to begin his duties as secretary of the province. The Van Rappard documents include letters that de Rasière wrote to his bosses in Holland. In one, he reported that the island was home to a small group of natives whom he called the Manhatesen: "they are about 200 to 300 strong, women and men, under different chiefs, whom they call *Sackimas*." It was presumably this small band—probably a northern branch of the Lenni Lenape Indians—with whom Peter Minuit consummated a real estate transaction.

It's true no deed is on file anywhere to prove that the sale took place, but many other important records of the period have failed to survive the centuries. We also have an account from the 1670s that makes reference to the deed to Manhattan, so it existed at that time. Most interestingly, we have an excellent, evocative account of the purchase, by someone who had no interest in deceiving. When the *Arms of Amsterdam,* which had brought Isaack de Rasière to New Netherland, left Manhattan on its return voyage, it carried a neat collection of items and individuals associated with this pivotal moment in history: first, the banished Verhulst himself, along with his wife, returning in disgrace and anger (but mollified somewhat by some of the spoils of their adventure—back in Amsterdam, he had a tabard, or cape, made of sixteen beaver pelts, while his wife had a tailor fashion a fur coat out of thirty-two otter skins); second, a chest containing the personal effects of the unfortunate Daniel van Crieckenbeeck, including an otterskin coat and a ring, which were being sent to his wife; third, a letter from de Rasière to the West India Company directors, in which he detailed the council's decision to oust Verhulst, as well as information about the purchase of Manhattan.

This information may have been the deed itself, which might thus have been among the West India Company records that were sold for scrap in 1821 and so vanished forever. Fortunately, however, Pieter Schaghen, a Dutch official who had just been appointed to represent the government on the company's board, was on the dock when the ship pulled into port. He wrote a letter to his superiors at The Hague giving a detailed description of the ship's contents and news of the province. It is one of the most famous historical documents in the Dutch language and one of the most important records of early American history. It is, in effect, New York City's birth certificate.

High and Mighty Lords
My Lords the States General
At The Hague

High and Mighty Lords:

Yesterday, arrived here the Ship the Arms of Amsterdam, which sailed from New Netherland, out of the River Mauritius, on the 23rd September. They report that our people are in good heart and live in peace there; the Women also have borne some children there. They have purchased the Island Manhattes from the Indians for the value of 60 guilders; it is 11,000 morgens in size. They had all their grain sowed by the middle of May, and reaped by the middle of August. They send thence samples of summer grain; such as wheat, rye, barley, oats, buckwheat, canary seed, beans and flax. The cargo of the aforesaid ship is

7246 Beaver skins
178½ Otter skins
675 Otter skins
48 Mink skins
36 Wildcat skins
33 Minks
34 Rat skins
Considerable Oak timber and Hickory.

Herewith,

High and Mighty Lords, be commended to the mercy of the Almighty.
In Amsterdam, The 5ᵗʰ November Ao. 1626

> *Your High Mightinesses' obedient,*
> *P. Schaghen*

Two days later, in an office within the fortress-like Binnenhof at The Hague, a clerk of the States General picked up his pen and wrote a terse memo: "Received a letter from Mr. Schaghen, written at Amsterdam, the 5ᵗʰ inst., containing advice of the arrival of a ship from New Netherland, which requires no action."

It is this letter, then, that gives us the purchase price. While it may be a useful whip for belated self-flagellation over the white takeover of the continent from the Indians, being fair to those involved in the transaction means looking at it from their perspective. We can, first of all, dismiss the twenty-four-dollar figure because it dates to the mid-nineteenth century and has no relationship to buying power two hundred years earlier. Second, Minuit paid not sixty guilders, which the Indians would have found useless, but "the value of" sixty guilders—meaning goods. What amount of goods was worth sixty guilders in 1626? Calculating relative worth is hopelessly fraught. A steel knife might be of relatively little value in Amsterdam or London, of considerable worth to a Dutch settler living in primitive conditions along the North River in America, and of enormous worth to an Indian living what anthropologists today call a "Late Woodlands" existence.

One way of putting the sale in perspective is to compare the figure with other amounts paid for parcels of wilderness. In 1630, for example, Peter Minuit, on behalf of the West India Company, bought Staten Island from the Tappans for "Duffels, Kittles, Axes, Hoes, Wampum, Drilling Awls, Jews Harps, and diverse other small wares." In 1664 three Englishmen purchased a vast tract of farmland in New Jersey from Indians for two coats, two guns, two kettles, ten bars of lead, twenty handfuls of gunpowder, four hundred fathoms of wampum and twenty fathoms of cloth. We can also look at the Manhattan sale in the context of land transfers between Dutch residents. Three years after the Manhattan transfer, the West India Company granted a Dutchman two hundred acres of what would become Greenwich Village in exchange for one-tenth of whatever he produced from the land, plus the promise to "deliver yearly at Christmas to the director a brace of capons." In 1638, Andries Hudde sold Gerrit Wolphertsen one hundred acres of land on Long Island for fifty-two guilders.

So the Manhattan purchase was roughly in line with other prices paid to Indians, and while it was considerably less, on a per-acre basis, than what the Dutch paid each other for land, it was in the same ballpark. As a reference point, a West India Company soldier earned about one hundred guilders per year—or nearly twice the price paid for Manhattan. The overriding fact was that in its wilderness state New World land was dirt cheap.

On the other side, given their idea of land ownership, the Indians who "sold" Manhattan fully intended to continue to use the land, and they did. Thanks to the comparative recentness of serious study about the Manhattan colony, new information is liable to turn up at any time and from the most unlikely places. As historians in the United States have become interested in the colony, some in the Netherlands have as well. Thus, a court case that ended in 1663, which has been slumbering since that date in the archives of the Dutch town of Arnhem but was unearthed and written about by Dutch historian Janny Venema in 2000, gives focus to the fuzzy notion of how American Indians saw real estate transactions in the seventeenth century. In 1648, Brant van Slichtenhorst was hired by the Van Rensselaers, the largest landowners in the province, to manage their vast estate. Years later, back in the Dutch Republic, he filed suit for expenses owed, and the seven-year case is packed with details about life among the Mohawks and Mahicans. On behalf of his patrons, Van Slichtenhorst bought several estates from the Indians during his time in the Dutch colony, and none of these transactions was remotely straightforward. Beginning days before the sale and continuing for years after, Van Slichtenhorst had to host as many as fifty Indians at a time, feeding them and providing a steady supply of beer and brandy for the sachems. In addition to the sellers and their retinue, in one case there was actually an Indian real estate broker who also demanded, as part of his commission, to stay "8 or 10 times" at Van Slichtenhorst's home, along with several women. There was always "great trouble and quarrels with all the Indian people," Van Slichtenhorst complained, "and great filth and stench, and everything within reach was stolen . . ."

This continued not for days or weeks but for *years* after the sale. Van Slichtenhorst would be out surveying the property and come across an encamped party of Indians. Rather than be indignant at the "trespassers," he was obliged, in accordance with their custom, to give them further presents and hospitality. "I can honestly say that the first three years we have, not even for half a day, been free from Indians," he wrote. In the long run, of course, the Europeans got their way. But the Indians were far from guileless dupes, and in the short term, which was what mattered at the time, they got considerably more out of a simple land transaction than the amount of the purchase indicates.

We can assume something similar happened with the sale of Manhattan. When Isaack de Rasière wrote to Amsterdam in 1628, two years after the purchase of the island, he used the present tense, reporting that Manhattan *is* inhabited by Manhatesen Indians, indicating that they had not gone anywhere. The Indians are a constant presence in the Dutch records of the colony. The settlers relied on them. And there was plenty of room; the island was, for the life of the colony, mostly wilderness. It is not until 1680 that the Manhattan Indians are referred to in the past tense, by which time they had, by some accounts, moved north into the Bronx.

We can only imagine, then, the scene that must have taken place somewhere on lower Manhattan in early summer 1626: Minuit, his aides, soldiers, and settlers, the Indian sachems and their retainers, the formal ceremony with the making of marks on parchment, and surrounding it, for weeks or months on end, the visits, drinking, eating, and bestowing of presents, in a deal that would satisfy both sides, each of which had its ideas about how it would pan out. And in some sort of follow-up ceremony forgotten by history, accompanied by a document subsequently lost, Minuit would have dedicated his city-in-the-making, and named it, appropriately, after its Dutch parent, some of whose culture and way of being—its openness and its swagger—the grubby little island village would inherit.

That piece of work completed, Minuit would then have boarded a company sloop and sailed upriver to deal with the crisis at Fort Orange. He ordered Catalina Trico, Joris Rapalje, and the other settlers to vacate the area; a message was sent to the South River settlers as well. Minuit was regrouping. Manhattan—New Amsterdam—would be the center of things from now on.

He then sailed back to Manhattan, arriving in port on a Friday evening, the last day of July. The next morning, he met the man who would become his valued assistant, Isaack de Rasière, whose ship had arrived while Minuit was away. De Rasière handed him letters from the directors; the two then fell to discussing who they should send north to replace Van Criekenbeeck, Minuit having decided to retain a contingent of soldiers at the fort. They decided to promote Bastiaen Krol, the Frisian lay minister who had come with Rapalje and Trico. Krol had also been at Fort Orange for two years, and he had become particularly close to the Indians, for de Rasière wrote that they chose him "because he is well acquainted with the language" of the tribe. So the man whose desire on arrival was to serve the church in the new province would instead be given a musket and a military command. No one knows with how much fear he accepted the job; he had seen what became of his predecessor.

The small party of soldiers aside, the settlers, about two hundred of them, were all together now along the flattish southeastern flank of Manhattan, looking across the narrower of the two rivers that wrapped around the island to the bluffed shore five hundred yards across the water. Under Minuit they worked quickly to progress from the state of campers to settlers. Within a year or so they had thirty wooden houses constructed along "The Strand." Minuit and de Rasière roomed together in one of these. The one stone building they erected, with a thatched roof made from river reeds, was the West India Company headquarters, where pelts brought from throughout the territory were stored until they were to be shipped home and where Isaack de Rasière made his office. At the southernmost tip, poised to catch the fullest gusts, a man named François, a millwright by profession, built two windmills: one for grinding grain, the other for sawing lumber.

Minuit also oversaw the construction of a fort. It occupied the southwestern point of the island, well positioned to defend against enemy vessels entering the harbor. The original plan was for a vast structure in which all the colonists would live, safe from the savages of the country. But the savages didn't seem so savage, and anyway it was clearly impossible, given the manpower, to do anything very grand. Minuit ordered a redesign. The man who had been sent over to lay out the town and build the fort was apparently uniquely unskilled for a Dutch engineer: the original structure was comprised mostly of heaped earth; it began to crumble even before it was finished. It would be torn down and rebuilt over the next several years; indeed, the ramshackle state of Fort Amsterdam would be an issue right up until the moment when Peter Stuyvesant, standing on its unsteady ramparts, would agree to surrender it to the English. The fort's general outlines are apparent today in the "footprint" of the old Customs House, which more or less occupies its former position, just opposite Battery Park. In one of history's ironies, this spot, which was originally intended to keep Indians out, is now the home of the Museum of the American Indian, arguably the only place on Manhattan in which signs of Indian civilization are apparent.

As the settlers explored their island, they found it wondrously varied: thick forest studded with great knuckles of protruding rock, grassy meadow, high hills rising in the center and to the north, charging and trickling streams, large reedy ponds. The Indians who traded with them doubled as guides. Wickquasgeck was the name of a tribe that inhabited portions of the mainland just to the north of the island, as well as some of the northern forests of Manhattan. The Manhattan Indians used the Wickquasgeck name for the path they took through the center of the island to these northern reaches. Coming south along it, Indians of various tribes reached the Dutch settlement at the southern end of the island. The Europeans could likewise follow it north—through stands of pin oak, chestnut, poplar, and pine, past open fields strewn with wild strawberries ("the ground in the flat land near the river is covered with strawberries," one of them noted, "which grow so plentifully in the fields, that one can lie down and eat them"), crossing the fast-running brook that flowed southeast from the highlands in the area of Fifty-ninth Street and Fifth Avenue, more or less where the Plaza Hotel stands, to empty into a small bay on the East River—to hunt in the thick forest at the island's center and to fish the inlets that penetrated the eastern coast. As it was clearly destined to be the most prominent lane on the island, when the Dutch widened the path they referred to it as the Gentlemen's Street, or the High Street, or simply the Highway. The English, of course, called it Broadway.*

---

*Broadway does not follow the precise course of the Indian trail, as some histories would have it. To follow the Wickquasgeck trail today, one would take Broadway north from the Customs House, jog eastward along Park Row, then follow the Bowery to Twenty-third Street. From there, the trail snaked up the east side of the island. It crossed westward through the top of Central Park; the paths of Broadway and the Wickquasgeck trail converge again at the top of the island. The trail continued into the Bronx; Route 9 follows it northward.

*

GOING ON IN this way, every muscle and every ounce of guile put into maintaining survival, the water's edge approaching and then inching away from their little community with every tide, the Manhattanites might scarcely have noticed what was happening over the next few years. The sails out in the harbor appeared more frequently, the skiffs ferrying in from anchored ships (there was no dock yet) bringing more faces, and more varied ones. Ebony faces from the central highlands of Angola. Arab faces creased from North African sandstorms. An Italian, a Pole, a Dane.

Something was happening that was quite unlike the unfolding of society at the two English colonies to their north, where the rigid Puritans, who arrived in 1630, and the even more rigid Pilgrims maintained, in their wide-brimmed piety, monocultures in the wild. This was a business settlement, a way station on the rising Atlantic trade circuit. News of its existence spread to places as far afield as the Amazonian thickets of Bahia and Pernambuco in Brazil, the newly founded Portuguese slave trading port of Luanda in Angola, and Stockholm, where an energetic monarch, Gustavus Adolphus, set his sights on making Sweden, long a frozen boondocks of Europe, a military and trading power to rival Spain and the rising nations of England and the Dutch Republic.

A trickle had started. In small clusters, the world began coming to North America via this island nestled in its inviting harbor. And while the West India Company had a firm Calvinist stamp to it, which it tried to impress on its colony, the makeup of the settlement—itself a result of the mix of peoples welcomed to its parent city of Amsterdam—helped to ensure a raggedness, a social looseness. It was also natural that the vanguard of private enterprise on the high seas—smugglers and pirates—would discover the place and make it a hub. All the elements that made it attractive to legitimate trade applied in their case, and in addition was the lure of its distance from civilization, the virtual absence of authority.

Days got livelier; with nightfall, the soft slap of waves along the shore was drowned out by drinking songs and angry curses. New Amsterdam was not a city with its own governance but literally a company town: its inhabitants were considered less citizens than employees, and there was no real legal system. So one was invented ad hoc. Every Thursday, in a room within the crudely walled fort, the "government" conducted business. Minuit's law enforcement officer, an Englishman from Canterbury named Jan Lampe,* oversaw the proceedings, resplendently Rembrandtesque in his official accoutrements of black plumed hat and silver rapier. Minuit, de Rasière, and a council of five heard cases and issued orders, which succeeding councils would reiterate and add to, building a body of frontier law. In 1638, for example, came a series of scolding decrees: "All seafaring persons are commanded to repair before sunset to the ship or sloop to which they are assigned and no one may remain on shore without permission." " . . . All persons [are forbidden] from selling henceforth any wines, on pain of forfeiting twenty-five guilders and the wines which shall be found in their houses." " . . . [E]ach and every one must refrain from fighting; from adulterous intercourse with heathens, blacks, or other persons; from mutiny, theft, false testimony, slanderous language and other irregularities . . . the offenders shall be corrected and punished as an example to others."

Multicultural galavanting was on the rise. Spaniard Francisco de Porte testified before the council that, yes, he was present at the home of Dutch wheelwright Claes Swits the night Englishman Thomas Beech's wife, Nanne, in the midst of a good drink-up, "notwithstanding her husband's presence, fumbled at the front of the breeches of most of all of those who were present," causing her husband to fly into a rage and attack one of the men.

Minuit may have been a capable strategist but he was no governor of men; chaos mounted. De Rasière struggled to maintain order during his tenure as secretary, which lasted until 1628, when he would go back to Amsterdam and eventually leave again to become a West India Company sugar baron in Brazil. He complained to the directors in Amsterdam of the "quite lawless" state of affairs and thought the directors should know that, with regard to the company's settlers, "if they are ordered to speak of your Honors with reverence and without using such profane words as they have heretofore been accustomed to use [they] consider that great injustice is done to them." When de Rasière caught a rough sort named Fongersz engaging in trade with the Indians on the sly, he told the man he would be forced to confiscate property and fine him, to which Fongersz replied, "I do not consider

---

*Presumably, he was born something like John Lamp; like many foreign residents of the Dutch colony, he had his name "Batavianized."

you are a big enough man for that." De Rasière added wearily, in his tattle-tale report, "The honorable gentlemen can see what regard such a person has for orders and instructions, but I do not consider it to be his fault, since I have seldom seen him sober and doubt whether he has been so during the last three or four weeks."

The directors could receive such complaints with equanimity. The times were very good for the West India Company. Its principal objective was to make money from battling the Spanish, and in 1628 they struck pay dirt. For the better part of a century the riches that Spain extracted from its South American colonies were sent to the homeland via a regular seagoing pipeline called the treasure fleet, consisting of as many as ninety vessels, traveling twice annually. In May of 1628, Piet Heyn, a small, pug-faced sea-man who had once been captured by the Spaniards and been forced to spend four years as a rower in a Spanish galley, surprised and swept down on the slow, heavily laden fleet with his thirty-one privateering gunships while lurking in the waters off Cuba. The haul was staggering: twelve mil-lion guilders' worth of silver and gold. It was an amount that instantly repaid the company's investors the capital they had risked, and it stoked the fire of the Dutch economy for years. To the people of the United Provinces of the Netherlands, who had been fighting for independence from the once-mighty Spanish empire for decades, it was a signal, as sharp as a pistol shot, of a historic change. The title of a bestselling pamphlet made it plain: *Tekel or Balance of the great monarchy of Spain; in which is discovered that she cannot do so much as she supposes herself able to do. Written on the occasion of the conquest of the Silver-Fleet by Gen. P. P. Heyn.*

Beyond the sea that stretched in front of the settlers, then, the world was turning. Heyn's deed seemed proof that the body of the Spanish Empire was in decay. Half a world away on the island of Java, Dutchman Jan Pieter-szoon Coen was undertaking an oriental version of Minuit's project: the building of a city (Batavia: the modern Jakarta) in an inhospitable wilder-ness that would be the base for Dutch trade in southeast Asia. In Frankfurt, meanwhile, William Harvey published his *Exercitatio Anatomica De Motu Cordis et Sanguinis in Animalibus,* spelling out his theories on the circula-tion of the blood, while in Italy the physician Santorio Santorio developed the trick of measuring body temperature using a thermometer. The method-ical Dutch system of communication (missives went in duplicate or triplicate on different ships) was slow but ensured that news got through; thanks to it, the Manhattanites knew of developments in the wider world and felt themselves a part of it.

To the north, the Pilgrim colony was limping along, and Minuit, feeling flush and expansive, decided it was time to establish contact. He sent letters of friendship, along with "a rundlet of sugar, and two Holland cheeses." William Bradford, governor of the struggling English colony, replied with thanks, adding that they were sorry they "must remain your debtors till another time, not having any thing to send you for the present that may be acceptable." Shortly after, Isaack de Rasière sailed to New Plymouth in person as official envoy of New Netherland, appearing in the Pilgrims' midst with "a noise of trumpets" (the Manhattanites feeling a bit of show was called for) and bringing with him "some cloth of three sorts and colours, and a chest of white sugar," as well as something the English had little acquaintance with, but which the New Amsterdam traders had become proficient in: belts of strung beads made of seashell, called *sewant* by the Algonquins, otherwise known as wampum.

At about this time, and perhaps none too soon, a man of God arrived at Manhattan. But if the settlers expected leadership and encouragement from the colony's first minister they were to be disappointed. The Reverend Jonas Michaelius might well have won a contest for the moodiest, bitchiest resident of New Amsterdam. In his bitter letters home he complained about the voyage, the settlers ("rough and unrestrained"), the climate, the natives ("entirely savage and wild, strangers to all decency, yeah, uncivil and stupid as garden poles, proficient in all wickedness and godlessness; devilish men, who serve nobody but the Devil"), and the food ("scanty and poor"). "I cannot say whether or not I shall remain here any longer after the three years [of his contract] shall have expired," he wrote home, adding, "we lead a hard and sober existence like poor people." Michaelius could be excused to some extent for his bitterness: the voyage to the new world had taken his pregnant, sickly wife, leaving him alone to care for their two young daughters.

For the time being, New Amsterdam was a free trade port. The company allowed freelance businessmen to strike deals with the Indians provided the company itself was the middle man that would resell furs in Europe. Business was being conducted in half a dozen languages; Dutch guilders, beaver skins, and Indian wampum were the common currencies. In a culture based on cheese and butter, cows were also a highly valued and tradable commodity.

But while beaver furs by the thousands were arriving at the West India Company's warehouse on the Amsterdam waterfront, the settlement was far from turning a profit. The directors wanted their North America colony to repay their investment the way Caribbean salt colonies were doing, and a split formed in the board over how to make it happen. Some of the directors argued that the colony would never work properly without a massive influx of settlers, and that the best way to get people to go there was by allowing wealthy men to establish plantations there. In return for these estates, each patron *(patroon* in Dutch) would transport a population of farmers, smiths, masons, wheelwrights, bakers, chandlers, and other workers. The directors who favored this scheme proposed themselves as patroons. The other directors thought it was a stupid idea, one that would essentially carve the colony into small fiefs and add to the difficulty of dealing with pirates and renegade traders. Peter Minuit injected himself into this argument, supporting the patroon faction. The Rev. Michaelius took the other side and fired off a raft of letters branding Minuit as a dark force who was in the process of cheating the directors. He managed to convince them that the situation was dire enough that, in 1631, they recalled both Minuit and Michaelius to Holland. They ordered Krol, the lay minister who had been left in charge of Fort Orange, to serve as provisional director of the colony.

Minuit was filled with rage as he climbed on board the ironically named *Unity,* his gall only increased by the knowledge that he would have to spend the two-month journey in close confines with Michaelius. He had gone far since leaving the little German town where he was raised, and he wasn't about to take this interruption in his career lightly. In five years he had established a rough but real outpost of European civilization on the edge of a limitless wilderness. He had made peace with the Mohawks to the north following the unfortunate Van Crieckenbeeck incident, forging an alliance that would last through the whole of the colony's existence. He had bought Manhattan and Staten islands as well as huge tracts along the Hudson River and around the bay of the South (Delaware) River from their native inhabitants while also managing to keep good relations with them. In so doing, he had outlined the perimeters of a New World province that occupied a considerable chunk of the Atlantic coast of North America, extending from the future state of Delaware in the south to the city of Albany in the north, and established a trade that sent more than fifty-two thousand furs to Amsterdam. Most important, he had pinpointed and begun to develop the colony's capital, a place whose natural strategic importance was by now apparent to him and his fellow Manhattanites, but which the West India Company directors would realize only belatedly. Even the vengeful Michaelius, for all his complaints about the place, could see this. "True," he had admitted in one of his bilious letters home, "this island is the key and principal stronghold of the country."

On a cold day in early 1632, then, Minuit stood on the deck of a ship laden with five thousand furs, fruits of the new world bound to warm the old, looking out on a sullen, wintry ocean, and plotting his defense. He had no idea of the rude detour that fate was about to deliver to him, or to the colony he had coaxed into being.

Chapter 4

THE KING, THE SURGEON, THE TURK, AND THE WHORE

Charles I, king of England, regarded horses and Dutchmen with something like equal and opposite intensity. As the famous equestrian portrait of Charles by Anthony Van Dyck and the mounted statue of him in Trafalgar Square in London suggest, he was never more at ease than when in the saddle. His devotion to racing was such that he spent a good portion of every year at Newmarket, site of the country's most important turf event. In the year 1632 he came early, leaving London in mid-February for the arduous sixty-mile journey. ("Essex miles" were said to be longer than standard, since the roads in that corner of England were in particularly bad repair.) It was a major undertaking because when the king went to Newmarket, so did everyone else: the political, military, and economic leadership of the country, as well as the king's household (his personal physician, William Harvey, did his historic work on the circulation of the blood while attending Charles at Newmarket). Charles was almost religiously devoted to splendor, and his Newmarket banquets had already become legendary, even infamous: in a single racing season, 7,000 sheep, 6,800 lambs, and 1,500 oxen would be consumed at the eighty-six tables set daily. When not viewing the heats or entertaining, he spent his days at the retreat hunting, playing tennis, or visiting his favorite horses in their stables.

As to the Dutch, he despised them. For that matter, he couldn't stand French people (never mind that he was married to one) and he considered the Scots, of whom he was one by birth, such irritants that he encouraged as many of them as possible to emigrate to Canada. But the Dutch irked him in several special ways. They were engaged in a vigorous revolt, one that they hoped would, through bloodshed, throw off a monarchy and replace it

67

with a republic. Charles passionately upheld the notion of the divine right of kings and he considered republicanism to be a form of mass hysteria. Of course he believed in freedom for his subjects, he famously explained, ". . . but I must tell you that their liberty and freedom consist in *having* government. . . . It is not their having a *share* in government; that is nothing appertaining to them." (He gave this explanation to the crowd gathered to watch his beheading.) He was now in the midst of what would become known as the Personal Rule, the eleven-year period in which, having dismissed Parliament because it quarreled with him, he governed on his own. During this time he would grow steadily isolated from his country, the court becoming more insular and the king's spending and partying progressively more lavish, as members of Parliament fumed and the masses moved toward open rebellion. It would end with his worst nightmare coming true: revolt, and his beheading.

While Charles thought the Dutch rebels mad and dangerous, there was the additional annoyance that currently, in ports around the world, Dutch merchant fleets were giving their English counterparts a thorough spanking. The Dutch were in the process of muscling the English out of the richest source of commerce, the East Indies; Dutch ships now controlled much of the world's trade in sugar, spices, and textiles. Ironically, Charles was hamstrung by his own authoritarian rule: having dismissed Parliament, he couldn't raise the funds he needed to compete.

Adding to his gall was the fact that, despite all of these irritations, Charles was forced to remain allied with the Dutch. Calvinism held sway in the Dutch provinces that were in revolt against Spain and, going back to Queen Elizabeth's time, England's policy had been to support the revolt in the name of Protestantism. But the alliance was weakening; Charles himself, the English leadership, and the masses of the English people were turning against the Dutch, beginning to see them as the new threat.

Such was the situation, then, as Charles settled in to enjoy the racing season at Newmarket in March of 1632. There was the deep thud of hooves beating the earth, the roar of the crowd, the bright flash of pennants against the sky. The king was in his element, richly dressed, with flowing chestnut hair and tapered fawn-colored beard (the original Van Dyck), casting a discerning eye over the favorites, placing bets with the Earl of Pembroke, whom everyone knew had a bit of a gambling problem. Surely the last thing on earth Charles would care for here was a distracting, importuning embassy from the upstart Dutch Republic. When Albert Joachimi, the old and dignified ambassador from the States General, rode into Newmarket, asking for an audience, Charles's first reaction was probably to recoil and send him away. But in the current international climate that would have been a political blunder; eventually he agreed to see the man.

The ambassador began the meeting blathering diplomatically and at length about the long friendship between the two nations, which he said had recently been disrupted by "the enemy" seeking "to foment some misunderstanding." Charles understood perfectly well the subtext of the man's complaint and was no doubt amused by the purposely fuzzy use of "the enemy." It was true that for decades the English had aided the Dutch in their war on Spain. But two years before, also at Newmarket, Charles had received another emissary, from the Spanish court. This one he had welcomed—in fact, eagerly anticipated, and it had altered the geopolitical landscape considerably.

Besides horses, Charles's other great and abiding love was for art. His personal collection, which included Raphaels, Titians, Tintorettos, Mantegnas, and Correggios, added both to his royal luster and, because of its staggering cost, to the simmering hatred for him among certain segments of the populace. The fact that, in his collecting, he had become amiable pen pals with the Pope, who had given him paintings from the Vatican collection, only increased Puritan suspicion of him. By now Philip IV, the king of Spain, whose resources were nearly exhausted by the Dutch revolt, wanted very much for England to end its support to the United Provinces. In a stroke of ingenuity that historians have credited to his wife, Philip chose as his emissary to persuade Charles to sign a peace treaty Peter Paul Rubens, the most famous and sought-after artist in Europe. Rubens, who was also something of a politician, considered himself a loyal Dutchman, but he came from Antwerp, in the Catholic-dominated southern provinces, which had chosen not to break with Spain. As Rubens gathered with Philip in Madrid to discuss the mission, his own hope was that if Charles were to end English hostilities with Spain the rebel Dutch provinces would give up on their ruinous rebellion, and the north and south would reunite. He agreed to the mission.

In England, Charles greeted Rubens with delight. He commissioned the artist to paint the ceiling of the Banqueting House at Whitehall Palace, newly built by Inigo Jones in the modern, forward-looking Palladian style. The central panel of the completed ceiling (today, the only work of Rubens still in its intended position) epitomized Charles's ardent monarchic beliefs: amid a swirling stew of cherubs, his father, James, divine kingship personified, rises to heaven. Proving that the English have always had a sardonic wit, Charles's subjects later executed him outside this very room.

Rubens also introduced Charles to his pupil, Anthony Van Dyck, who became Charles's court painter; it is thanks to him that we have a gallery of portraits capturing the king's every mood and manner. Charles knighted both men. He also signed a peace treaty with Spain—another step in the movement between England and the Dutch Republic away from friendship and toward confrontation. Rubens was elated and went next to visit his countryman, Ambassador Joachimi, in London, hoping to persuade him that now the best hope for a unified Dutch Republic was for the rebel government to seek terms with Spain. But Rubens seriously underestimated the resolve of the northern provinces. Joachimi was as much a rebel as those he served, and told the painter that the only way the provinces would unify would be if those in the south joined in the war. (They did not and eventually the Catholic southern provinces became the nation of Belgium.)

It was against this backdrop of England's recent peace treaty with Spain that Joachimi now approached Charles, amid the stamping and whinnying of Newmarket. In using the phrase "the enemy" in relation to both the English and the Dutch, he was implying that, recent treaties aside, Protestants still had to stick together in the face of the universal foe of Catholicism. ("We cannot perceive that his Majesty is indisposed towards us," Joachimi wrote to the States General after his audience, "because we have neither Saints nor Festivals, wherein the Spanish nation is very superstitious.") Specifically, the ambassador wanted the king to put a stop to a recent disturbing practice. Since England's treaty with Spain, Spanish ships that had been captured by Dutch privateers were being seized when they entered English ports, contrary to long-standing agreement between the two nations.

The king heard the man out, and with great decorum dodged the issue. Joachimi went away empty-handed.

Less than two weeks later, however, Charles, just returned to Whitehall, was forced to deal with the man yet again. This time Joachimi's diplomatic reserve showed signs of cracking. There had been a new development. Another ship had been seized, but this was not a Spanish ship prized by the Dutch. It was a bona fide Dutch vessel, Joachimi informed the king, bound for Amsterdam from "a certain island named Manathans." Reports indicated that it carried five thousand furs, as well as the former director of the province of New Netherland.

At that moment, two hundred miles to the southwest, Peter Minuit sat in English custody, fuming. It wasn't enough that he had been (to his mind) unreasonably removed from his post, forced to abandon the colony he had coaxed into being and make the long, hazardous voyage home to defend his conduct. After two frigid months at sea, the *Unity* had been caught in a storm off the coast of England and forced to make an emergency landfall at Plymouth. There, the courtesy of receiving a troubled ship from a friendly nation was not extended. Crowning the whole bitter turn of events that his life had taken, Minuit was taken prisoner. The only salve for him was the fact that his nemesis, the odious Reverend Michaelius, was also in English custody.

After word of the seizure reached the United Provinces, the leaders there were at first inclined to believe that, as one official wrote, "this intrigue was set on foot by the Spanish Ambassador in England." But as more information came in, they learned that the English had taken possession of the Dutch vessel on the grounds that its cargo was illegally gotten in English territory. The Dutch were confused—their traders had not intruded on the English territory to the north of the Dutch colony. Surely, Ambassador Joachimi now put it to His Majesty, there must be some mistake.

But this time Charles would leave no room for the ambassador to be hopeful. Speaking with a lawyerly mix of precision and subtlety, the king told the man he understood there was some dispute over claims to the territory in question, and that he could not release the ship until he was certain of his rights in the matter. The "answer of his Majesty," Joachimi reported to his superiors, "though expressed in polite terms and with a friendly disposition, did not please us . . ."

Joachimi surely understood what underlay the sudden chill in relations. The Dutch had gained mastery over the East Indies trade. And Charles was also aware that New World colonies represented another source of wealth, though reaping it to full advantage was further in the future. He had recently given—as repayment of a favor—a vast tract of the Virginia territory to his father's friend and advisor, George Calvert, a.k.a. Baron Baltimore, which his son named Maryland apparently in honor of Charles's wife, Henrietta Maria. And Charles himself had backed the tobacco trade in Virginia.

But the English had a particular reason for going at the Dutch territory in North America just now. The whole swirl of geopolitical doings involving the two rising powers had recently crystallized in one event—one of those small, far-off, seemingly minor occurrences that would have historical echoes all out of proportion to its size. On one of the lucrative Spice Islands of the East Indies (today part of Indonesia), the island of Amboyna or Ambon, a bloody encounter had taken place recently between the Dutch and English. The Dutch had won control of the island and its clove trade, but a colony of English merchants was allowed to live and work there. Probably in retaliation for a recent English assault on Dutch ships in the Indies, Dutch soldiers there tortured and killed ten Englishmen, as well as several Japanese mercenaries, whom they accused of plotting to take over the fort. The English survivors insisted there had been no such plot, and that the Dutch behavior had been motivated by simple barbarity.

However outraged the English authorities may actually have been by the incident, they spun it ferociously for moral and political advantage. Pamphlets and books appeared in England, with titles like *A True Relation of the Unjust, Cruel, and Barbarous Proceedings against the English at Amboyna*, containing vivid, novelistic descriptions and graphic woodcut illustrations of the varieties of torture the men had been subjected to, including both water and fire (". . . Johnson [was] brought againe to the torture," ran one breathless account, "where Beomont heard him for sometime cry aloud, then quiet again, then roare afresh. At last, after hee had beene about an houre in this second examination, hee was brought forth wailing and lamenting, all wet, and cruelly burnt in divers parts of his body . . ."). So great was the uproar over these accounts that, in addition to lamenting the seizure of the *Unity*, Joachimi complained about them as well in his audience with Charles. The ambassador wanted the king to understand that the Dutch considered these books to be slanderous, "the tendency whereof is only to excite the temper of one people against the other." But the king would do nothing to stop their dissemination, and so, entering the battle for public opinion in England, the Dutch countered with pamphlets of their own, printed in English, with which they flooded the English market, giving their side of the affair. (They denied burning the men, but admitted using water torture as "the most assured and civill" and "a thing customable throughout Europe.")

The mileage the English got out of Amboyna was astounding. For decades it fueled the English sense of the Dutch merchants as relentless, bloodless fiends. The Dutch record of atrocities was surely no better or worse than that of the English, Portuguese, or other European empire-builders, but believing it to be more barbarous helped assuage English bitterness that the tiny, water-logged nation had so outdistanced them in the global race. As late as 1691, more than six decades after the incident, John Dryden would write his play *Amboyna: A Tragedy,* employing as characters all the actors in the actual events, from the monstrous Dutch governor, Harmon ("Bring more candles, and burn him from the Wrists up to the Elbows"), to the heroic Englishman Beaumont ("Do; I'll enjoy the Flames like Scaevola; and when one's roasted, give the other hand.").

But there was also a negative result. The English succeeded so well in portraying the Dutch merchant-soldiers as inexorable that England virtually ceded the East Indies to the Dutch shippers, and refocused its energies elsewhere in Asia. Thus, one far-flung consequence of Amboyna, echoing through the coming centuries, would be the buildup of British India.

Another was New York. No such colony existed or would exist for decades, but in the thrust-and-parry of the two empires-in-the-making in the 1620s and '30s, events on one side of the globe would generate reactions on the other. By now some in England realized that the Dutch-controlled portion of North America was the linchpin to the continent, and they were determined that the Dutch not have control of both the East Indies and the vast unknown riches of North America. Legal minds went to work, and the case for overriding the Dutch claim to its territory was developed.

One month after Joachimi's second audience with the king, Charles's formal reply arrived at The Hague. The king declared he had no intention of suppressing books published in England that dealt with the Amboyna massacre (his response to Dutch anger on this score: "nothing save the balm of justice can heal ulcerated hearts"). Regarding the complaint about the seizure of the ship that had set sail from Manhattan Island, His Majesty countered it by disputing the Dutch claim to the territory. The Dutchmen and their vessel, Charles advised, came from "a certain plantation usurped by them in the north parts of Virginia, which they say was acquired from the natives of the country." There followed a flurry of attacks on the Dutch claim to Manhattan Island and the territory extending more than a hundred miles to the north and south of it, some quite novel. "[F]irst, it is denied that the Indians were *possessores bonae fidei* of those countries, so as to be able to dispose of them either by sale or donation, their residences being unsettled and uncertain . . . and in the second place, it cannot be proved, *de facto*, that all the Natives of said country had contracted with them at the said pretended sale." Moreover, the English claimed that they had true title to the land in question, which was "justified by first discovery." In this, the English were stretching then-accepted legalities to the point of absurdity—an absurdity that underlies all of the land grabs of the age of empire and exploration. The "first discovery" was that of John Cabot, who in 1497 made footfall at Newfoundland. By the logic of the concept of "discovery," when the foot of an explorer made contact with soil that had not previously been settled by humans whom Europeans regarded as having a proper civilization, that soil, and all soil stretching out from it for as far as the metaphysical aura of discovery could be made to stretch, came under the flag of the explorer's sponsoring nation. Even adherents of this magic-wand approach to extending one's domain, however, had to have marveled at the claim that because an Italian foot once touched the soil of a portion of land astride North America (Newfoundland is, after all, an island)—and never mind the fact that at the time Cabot thought he was in an uninhabited region of Asia—the entire land mass, millions of square miles extending up to the North Pole, westward to the Pacific, and south as far as the Spanish-held territories, miraculously and incontrovertibly became the property of England.

The Dutch didn't buy it. For one thing, they had a different legal basis for ownership. In their scheme, the discoverer also had to occupy and chart the land; thus the decision to send settlers, however few, to each of the three river systems in New Netherland. By May the matter was over; the ship was released. The English had pushed, and the Dutch—who were simply the more powerful nation at the time—had pushed back. Charles had served notice of England's interest in the property in question, but just now he was not in a position to back up his words.

No one recorded what Peter Minuit said when, on the third of May, he came tramping into the courtyard of the elegant West India Company head-quarters in Amsterdam, livid to the point of distraction, and heard that, on top of everything else, the English were now denying the very right to exist of the colony he had nurtured. He probably didn't feel outrage—not after the way the Dutch directors had treated him. It may be that what struck him most about the international dispute was how unsettled things were—that the colony itself was up for grabs. For at some point after the hearing into his conduct as director of New Netherland—which resulted in his formal dismissal, and which turned on the charge that not enough settlers had been shipped to the colony under his tenure (an outrage because Minuit had re-peatedly pressed for more settlers)—he met with Willem Usselincx, who had been the original booster of New Netherland, but who, like Minuit, was now disgruntled. The two of them would soon dream up a secret international colonizing scheme of their own, as audacious as it would be ridiculous.

*

TWO YEARS BEFORE it brought Peter Minuit back to Europe and sailed into an international incident, the *Unity,* shipping the other direction, had deliv-ered to the shores of Manhattan a raw, tough-minded eighteen-year-old named Harmen Myndersz van den Bogaert. He came equipped with train-ing that was certain to be of value in a frontier settlement, having undergone the two-year, hands-on apprenticeship (no book work required) to be in-ducted into the ancient and not especially venerated guild of the "barber-surgeon." In that time in the colony he apparently did more than trim the beards of New Netherland's residents, and must have impressed people with his nerves in amputations and blood-letting, because following the run-in with the English over the fate of the colony he was given the weighty responsibility of saving it from another European threat.

By now the colony had an undisputed second city—or rather village. In fact, Fort Orange, the trading post at the conjunction of the Mohawk and Hudson rivers where Joris Rapalje and Catalina Trico had spent their first two years, had become the center of the fur trade. From far out in the un-charted west, Indians came down the Mohawk Valley with their heavy loads of pelts; the traders bought them, stored them at the fort, then shipped them downriver to Manhattan. They had a strong relationship with the Mohawks now, one that would last the whole life span of the Dutch settlement, so the trade seemed secure.

It wasn't. In late 1634, fur traffic on the Mohawk suddenly dried up. The Dutch, whose worldview was based on water, knew the river and lake system of their territory, knew that far out there in the unexplored west lay a series of lakes, which were the main beaver areas hunted by the Indians who supplied them. If the Indians had stopped coming, there could only be one reason: the French, who long before had infiltrated the waterways far to the north and forged fur-trading alliances with Indians of Canada, had moved south into that territory and made new agreements with the Indians there. At this stage the fur trade was the colony's entire reason for being. For decades to come, debts on Manhattan would be paid in the interchangeable currencies of beaver pelts, Dutch guilders, and Indian wampum. While they were prized for their fur, beavers were even more sought-after for the pelt beneath the outer layer of fur, which was made into felt. Felt hats were a status-symbol-cum-necessity throughout Europe, from the Puritans' austere black bonnets to the dashing chapeaux of the Dutch officers in Rembrandt's *The Night Watch* and, later, the English top hat. The entire beaver-to-hat process had a fantastic quality to it. On the production end, hat makers used mercury to separate fur from felt, leading to routine mental illness and, perhaps, to the phrase "mad as a hatter." The hats were wildly expensive; the English diarist Samuel Pepys paid four pounds five shillings for one in 1641—about three months' wages for an average laborer. This, in turn, meant serious income for the Indian trappers, and for the French, English, and Dutch who competed to trade with them. (It also accounts for the image of the beaver still found on the seal of New York City.) The disruption in the beaver trade was serious. Within a very short time, the French outflanking maneuver would prove to be a coup de grâce. Something had to be done.

The now twenty-two-year-old Harmen van den Bogaert got the desperate commission to do what no resident had yet done: travel into the interior of the continent, seek out the Mohawks in their villages, and convince them that the Dutch were better trading partners. By sheer luck, the journal he kept on the voyage—which details one of the earliest forays by Europeans from the coast westward into the North American continent, provides an extraordinarily rare glimpse of thriving Mohawk villages, and also includes the first-ever Mohawk dictionary—survived. It was discovered in the late nineteenth century and has only recently been studied in depth. It gives a remarkably fresh and full-blooded view of the Eastern Indians, uncolored by the history that was to follow.

The situation was desperate enough that the mission couldn't wait until spring; choosing two men to accompany him, Jeronimus dela Croix and sailor Willem Thomassen, Van den Bogaert set out on the eleventh of December. They left Fort Orange in icy weather, their packs filled with food as well as knives, scissors, and other items intended as presents, in the company of five Mohawk guides.

Things started out hopefully enough, as they hiked into virgin pine forest, but it was a bad sign when, in the middle of the first night, Van den Bogaert woke up to find the guides silently preparing to leave camp without them. He and his mates threw their things together and hurried to catch up; later they discovered that the Indians' dogs had eaten the meat and cheese from their packs, leaving them with only bread. There followed days of brutal hiking through snow two and a half feet deep, with slashing winds, swirling snow, and sightings of bear and elk through the trees.

On the twentieth, chilled to the bone, they came to a stop before a stream that, Van den Bogaert wrote, was "running very hard with many large chunks of ice . . . so that we were in great danger. Had one of us fallen, it would have been the end. But the Lord God protected us and we made it across. We were soaked up to the waist." They slogged on, shivering, "with wet and frozen clothing, stockings and shoes." Then they reached a hilltop and an amazing sight: thirty-two houses set in a clearing, some of them two hundred feet long, each covered with elm bark, the whole surrounded by a picket palisade. The men had reached their goal: a Mohawk village, and a new civilization.

The series of villages they visited in the ensuing days surprised Van den Bogaert with their level of civilization. In one there were "36 houses, row on row in the manner of streets," each of which held several families. Some of the houses already bore the signs of European contact: iron hinges, bolts, chains. The men found boats and barrels made from bark. They encountered cemeteries, surrounded by palisades "so neatly made that it was a wonder," the graves painted red, white, and black. A chief's tomb they found was large enough to have an entrance and was decorated with carvings and paintings of animals. In some villages penned bears were being kept and fattened. Each longhouse had several hearths. They were welcomed at the first village and given baked pumpkin, beans, and venison. In the light of the fire that night, Van den Bogaert cut open Thomassen's leg to relieve swelling brought on by the long march, and smeared the cut with bear grease.

The people met them with curiosity or fear. Some, encountering them in the forest, dropped their belongings and ran. In one village, however, "we caused much curiosity in the young and old; indeed, we could hardly pass through the Indians here. They pushed one another into the fire to see us. It was almost midnight before they left us. We could not do anything without having them shamelessly running about us." The chief presented Van den Bogaert with a mountain lion skin, which he slept with, only to discover that "in the morning I had at least 100 lice."

There was an irony to the reception the Europeans received in some places. At one village, a chief eagerly invited them into his house, which was set away from the village proper because he feared the smallpox that was beginning to ravage the Indians of the region. No one on either side realized that the illness, which would decimate the Northeast Indians over the course of the century, was a result of the contact with Europeans, who brought diseases to which they themselves were immune but before which the Indians were helpless.

At every village, the people called to them, "Allese rondade!" or "shoot!" There was a great deal of excitement when the men obliged and fired their weapons—here, preserved in the amber of Van den Bogaert's journal, we catch that fleeting moment when Indian society was aware of firearms but hadn't yet begun to use them. On Christmas Eve, Van den Bogaert watched in awe as their shamans went to work, and recorded one of the most detailed and dramatic descriptions of an East Coast Indian healing ritual:

As soon as they arrived, they began to sing, and kindled a large fire, sealing the house all around so that no draft could enter. Then both of them put a snakeskin around their heads and washed their hands and faces. They then took the sick person and laid him before the large fire. Taking a bucket of water in which they had put some medicine, they washed a stick in it ½ ell long. They stuck it down their throats so that the end could not be seen, and vomited on the patient's head and all over his body. Then they performed many farces with shouting and rapid clapping of hands, as is their custom, with much display, first on one thing and then on the other, so that the sweat rolled off them everywhere.

Eventually, the travelers made their way to the most important village, where they would negotiate. The scene Van den Bogaert describes opens like the third act of a Western, in which the white man finally meets the Indians on their terms. The residents of the village formed two long lines outside the gate of the village, and the Europeans passed ceremonially between the columns, and through the elaborately carved entryway, to the house at the farthest end. The houses here had gables decorated with paintings. In the flickering firelight, amid much whooping and excitement, the men were fed and feted.

And then the rough business tactics began.

A secondary tribal leader berated them for not bringing adequate presents. He showed them the presents the French had given, including French shirts and coats. The atmosphere became tense. As the man kept up his verbal assault the others "sat so close to us here that we could barely sit." Van den Bogaert counted forty-six people crowded around them in the room. One of the Indians then began to scream, calling them, in Van den Bogaert's translation, "scoundrels," and his tirade reached such a fury that Willem Thomassen, a hardened sailor, burst into angry tears. Finally, Van den Bogaert hollered back.

At this, the tactic changed. The Indian laughed, suggested there had been a misunderstanding, and said, "You must not be angry. We are happy that you have come here." An old man stepped forward and put his hand against Van den Bogaert's chest to feel his heart; he announced with approval that the man was not afraid. The Dutchmen had apparently passed a test. Warily, the visitors dispensed knives, scissors, and other presents. Six leaders of the village stepped forward and presented Van den Bogaert with a beaver coat. When they sat down to discuss business, Van den Bogaert learned that these Mohawks would prefer to maintain relations with the Dutch because they feared the Hurons, with whom the French were allied. The Mohawks offered their terms: henceforth, each beaver pelt would be worth four hands of sewant and four hands of cloth (a hand of sewant, or wampum, being one string of beads stretched from outstretched thumb to little finger). When Van den Bogaert did not reply, an old chief from another of the five tribes of the Iroquois confederation, of which the Mohawks were a part, stepped forward. He required a translator because he spoke Onondaga, not Mohawk, and said, "You have not said whether we shall have four hands or not." Van den Bogaert told them he was not authorized to finalize the deal, but would return in the spring with the answer. They accepted this, but the old man cautioned him, "You must not lie, and come in the spring to us and bring us all an answer. If we receive four hands, then we shall trade our pelts with no one else."

A provisional agreement was made. The Indians began a chant, which Van den Bogaert diligently recorded. The chant turns out to contain the names of the five tribes of the Iroquois League, through some of whose lands the Dutchmen had traveled, and Van den Bogaert's documentation of it provides the earliest written record of this confederacy that would play a role in the American Revolution. A rough translation of the chant, given to me by Iroquois linguist Gunther Michelson, is: "This white man is a magician. He has leave to go around to all the Mohawk, Oneida, Onondaga, Cayuga, and Seneca, and lie down safely among them. This is a useful thing for the Iroquois League." The chant indicates how much Van den Bogaert succeeded in impressing the Iroquois. The reference to him as a magician also dates this to the period in which the East Coast Indians, still amazed by the tools of the whites, thought of them as having wondrous powers.

Following the agreement, Van den Bogaert was given a house, presents, and thick portions of bear meat. Although he doesn't mention it, he may have been given other things as well, for the detailed list of Mohawk vocabulary words he compiled includes the words and phrases for man, woman, prostitute, vagina, phallus, testicles, "to have intercourse," "very beautiful," "When shall you return?" and "I do not know."

The three travelers said their farewells and began the long journey home. They arrived back at Fort Orange in late January, where the people had feared them dead. They had traveled to Oneida Lake—nearly as far as Lake Ontario—and back, through savage weather, powered only by their own feet. It is no accident that their route was the one that generations of Americans and millions of tons of goods would follow westward in the coming centuries, once the Erie Canal was constructed. It was the natural highway connecting the Atlantic coast to the heart of the continent, the reason the Dutch had focused their attention on the Hudson River, and why, beginning with Minuit, they saw Manhattan Island as the logical hub. Van den Bogaert's trip would prove to be pioneering in the fullest sense.

In the spring, the deal with the Mohawks was indeed finalized. The furs began coming again. Van den Bogaert's impact on the colony would not end here—he would later make a final, tragicomic contribution to history. But for now he had done what was asked of him: the colony could go on.

*

WHICH, HOWEVER, BEGGED a question: why bother? While the old ambassador and the young explorer-surgeon were doing their utmost to preserve the colony, its parents, the merchant-princes who ran the West India Company, were running it into the ground. They disagreed over how to manage it, with the result that it went largely unmanaged. To replace the capable Peter Minuit they chose a young clerk in the company's Amsterdam offices with no particular set of skills to recommend him, only a dull devotion to the company and a family relation to an important man connected with the colony. Immediately upon arrival in Manhattan, Wouter van Twiller set about proving himself a drunk and a nonleader. At times he even managed to combine the two traits. Shortly after he began his duties, and on the heels of the recent trouble with England over the ship carrying his predecessor back to Europe, an English trader sailed into the harbor and anchored before the fort. Her captain made clear his intention to sail upriver and trade with the Indians: an open flaunting of Dutch sovereignty. Van Twiller dealt with the matter by boarding the vessel and proceeding to drink with the captain. He became so drunk that David de Vries, a Dutch adventurer who had spent time in the East Indies and now proposed to throw his lot in with the New Amsterdammers, and who had himself just sailed into the harbor, was embarrassed. The English captain then made the bold declaration that he had every right to sail upriver because the river and all the land around it was English. De Vries responded that New Netherland had long been settled by the Dutch, and that their claim was secure. The English captain countered that the area had been discovered by an English explorer, "David

Hutson." That was close enough for De Vries, but he countered, quite properly, that Hudson had charted the river under Dutch auspices. Van Twiller appears to have stayed out of the conversation.

After lying at anchor several days, the English ship set sail and headed upriver in defiance of the Dutch leader. Van Twiller moved quickly. He ordered a cask of wine brought to his office in the fort at once, filled bumpers for himself and the soldiers and other company employees assembled there, and cried out for those who loved the Prince of Orange and him to join him in stopping the Englishman. Whereupon, De Vries reported, "The people all began to laugh at him."

Van Twiller let the matter go, and the English ship sailed off northward. De Vries was incensed. He sat the man down and explained that it was precisely incidents like this that made or broke a colony. "I said, if it were my matter, I would have helped him away from the fort with beans from the eight-pounders, and not permitted him to sail up the river," De Vries wrote in his journal, and added that "if the English committed any excesses against us in the East Indies, we should strike back at them; otherwise one cannot control that nation, for they were of so proud a nature, that they thought everything belonged to them."

Clearly Van Twiller had some decisive weaknesses, but it should also be kept in mind that for this period of the Dutch colony's existence the official records are almost nonexistent, so that history has relied on bits and pieces, such as De Vries's journal, in order to re-create the times. Thanks to the wave of scholarship now under way, however, new evidence is emerging that complicates the picture. A letter written by Van Twiller in 1635 to the company directors, discovered recently in the Dutch National Archives in The Hague by historian Jaap Jacobs, shows Van Twiller building a fort on the Connecticut River (the earliest documentation for the settlement of what would become Hartford), holding the English at bay, and trying to deal with his unruly population—acting, in other words, like the colonial administrator he was supposed to be.

But if Van Twiller was not the outright incompetent that history has made him out to be, he was clearly not equal to the challenge of his rowdy, expanding capital. New Amsterdam now had a downtown arcade of five shops, and dozens of private houses. Ships carried bricks as ballast on the trip from Europe, and the settlers used these—the slender yellow bricks of

Holland, which still turn up occasionally in digs in lower Manhattan—in their first houses, particularly in chimney stacks. Ramparts were added to the fort. There was a boathouse and sailmaker's loft, a guardhouse and soldiers' barracks, and a church. But there were few residents with the drive, guts, and pioneering spirit of David de Vries. Many were pirates or itinerant fur traders. The most famous New Amsterdam pirate—Willem Blauvelt—used New Amsterdam as his base to plunder off the Spanish main (the waters north of South America), mixed piracy with privateering, and was a member of the community in good standing who dutifully logged his voyages with the provincial secretary. His financial backers included many of the town's leading citizens.

Piracy in turn brought another wave of residents, for the "cargo" of pilfered Spanish galleons included not only cases of indigo, chests of sugar, and sacks bulging with pieces of eight, but slaves bound for the Caribbean salt fields. As privateers brought them to Manhattan, some of the Africans became slaves in the West India Company's service; others worked for their freedom or were employed as freedmen from the outset. The very names of Manhattan's Africans—Pedro Negretto, Antony Congo, Jan Negro, Manuel de Spanje, Anthony the Portuguese, Bastiaen d'Angola—evoked their tempestuous journeys, from capture and enslavement in Africa to purchase by Portuguese traders and forced voyage westward on Spanish ships, only to be captured once again by Dutch pirates. Decades later, terms of slavery would be more or less standardized in the colonies, but at this point, on the free-form, slightly anarchic island, some of these people were among the more stable residents of the island; many would become farmers, carpenters, smiths, and barber-surgeons.

Such an unruly population required servicing. Prostitution became a mainstay (the wife of Tymen Jansen was known to "commit adultery . . . not for money, but for otters and beavers"). The island spawned taverns and breweries with remarkable speed—at one point in the early years one-quarter of its buildings were devoted to making or selling alcohol. The "bar scene" seems to have rivaled anything New York City could boast today (and, ironically enough, would occupy the same general downtown quadrant that accounts for much of today's nightlife): an enraged woman who came upon her husband in a tap room later wondered in court "what he was doing with another man's wife . . . touching her breasts and putting his mouth on them." A man named Simon Root had part of his ear cut off "with a cutlass" and petitioned the court to get a certificate clarifying that it happened in a fairly routine barroom brawl and should not be confused with the standard punishment for thievery. The records are rife with murderous assaults, and the leaders favored extreme forms of punishment—branding, pillorying, whipping, beating with rods, garroting, hanging—in an effort to instill order. Visible punishment of all sorts—removing an ear, boring a hole in the ear or tongue with a redhot poker, "riding the horse," which involved shackling the evildoer to a wooden horse, often for days at a time, with heavy weights attached to his arms and legs—was prized for its deterrent effect.

Harsh as punishment often was, there was a certain flexibility in carrying it out: people were occasionally let off at the last minute, sometimes in novel ways. On a cold January day in 1641, eight African slaves were brought into the fort, accused of murdering another slave, Jan Premero, "in the woods near their houses" (an area north of the town set aside for slave quarters—today it is where the United Nations resides). The men admitted to the crime "without torture or shackles." But it couldn't be determined which one did the deed, so the court, in its wisdom, decided they would draw lots to see who would be put to death, thus letting "God designate the culprit." God chose Manuel Gerrit, a.k.a. "The Giant." A week later, a crowd gathered near the shore for the entertainment of a public hanging. In theory, drawing lots may have satisfied the law; in reality, hanging a possibly innocent man may have been distasteful to the colony's leaders, or maybe they saw it as a senseless waste of a good slave. There is no proof of tampering in what followed, but the results are suspicious. The executioner fastened "two good ropes" around the man's neck and pushed him off the ladder, whereupon, to the gasps of the spectators, both ropes broke and the man tumbled to the ground unharmed. The crowd clamored for mercy, and the court granted it. The Giant went free; the system worked.

A scene that appears in the court records from a few years later nicely sums up the atmosphere of casual mayhem, of violence erupting in the midst of ordinary life, that reigned in this period:

Piere Malenfant, of Riennes [i.e., Rennes], in Brittany, 35 years of age, declares that yesterday evening about nine o'clock, as it was getting dark, he came from the farm in company with Paulus Heyman and his wife, he carrying the child on his arm and the woman the gun. Near Damen's house, the sentry, named Andries Tummelyn, called out, 'Who goes there?' He answered, 'A friend.' Paulus Heyman said, 'Good evening, Jonker Nobleman,' to which the sentry replied, 'What do you want, Merchant?' Heyman retorted, 'Lick my ass.'

At this, the Frenchman and the sentry fell on one another with swords, Malenfant was stabbed through the arm and thigh, and came limping into court seeking compensation.

Clearly, the New Netherland settlers were quite unlike their fellow pioneers to the north, the pious English Pilgrims and the Puritans who were struggling to establish their "new Jerusalem," governed by godly morality. Whether the Pilgrims, via the Thanksgiving celebration, or the Puritans made truly worthy role models for the nation that was in the distant future is another matter; throughout this period the Puritans were busy massacring the Pequot Indians in the name of God and persecuting internal "heretics" (i.e., anyone who didn't subscribe to their brand of Puritanism). One might say the English and Dutch colonies represented the extreme conservative and liberal wings of the seventeenth-century social spectrum. Technically, hard-line Calvinism was the moral force at work in the Manhattan colony, but in the records of the colony expressions of piety are overwhelmed by accounts like that of a woman who, while her husband dozed on a nearby chair, "dishonorably manipulated the male member" of a certain Irishman while two other men looked on. Excessive rigidity (of the moral kind) was not the sin of New Amsterdam's residents.

There was a kind of duke and duchess of this era of New Amsterdam, who outdid their neighbors for sheer rabble-rousing. Back in Europe, Griet Reyniers had worked as a barmaid at the tavern of Pieter de Winter in Amsterdam. In fact, she practiced two professions at once—the mistress of the tavern once spotted her in a back room, "her petticoat upon her knees," sexually servicing a party of soldiers. It's impossible to say whether the young Wouter van Twiller wandered into her establishment one evening and became enamored of her. All we know is that when he set sail for Manhattan on *de Zoutberg* ("Salt Mountain"), Griet was on board, too, ready to seek her fortune in a new land. It was a hazardous crossing: the ship was nearly captured by "Turks," and then it turned the tables and took the prize of a Spanish bark whose hulls were crammed with sugar. Griet was unfazed by the goings-on, and plied her trade at sea—passengers noticed her pulling "the shirts of some of the sailors out of their breeches." Landing at Manhattan and finding it, so to speak, virgin territory, she set up shop. She took to walking the Strand, hiking her petticoats to display her wares for the sailors. If she had come as Van Twiller's mistress, it may have been as a result of his finally dismissing her that she was observed marching into the fort one day crying out, "I have long enough been the whore of the nobility. From now on I shall be the whore of the rabble!" She had a knack for attention-getting publicity stunts; her trademark was to measure the penises of her customers on a broomstick.

Anthony van Salee was known as The Turk; he was a pirate from Morocco, the son of a Dutch seaman-turned-pirate who became the admiral of the Sultan's fleet and married a Moroccan woman. Anthony was brawny, dark-featured, and a one-man criminal class. From the time of his arrival on Manhattan in the early 1630s, he made trouble: he threatened people with loaded pistols; he roamed the village drunk and cursing; he was accused of stealing. When Hendrick the tailor called him "a Turk, a rascal and a horned beast," his anger apparently spoke for many. Even Anthony's dog was trouble: once a black townsman named Anthony the Portuguese filed suit, claiming that the man's dog had "damaged" his hog. He won.

Perhaps it was inevitable that Griet and Anthony would come together. They married, and had children, though, since she kept at her work, it wasn't always clear who the father was. From the supine position of childbirth she once asked the midwife who the newly delivered baby looked like. The woman replied, "If you do not know who the father is, how should I know? However, the child is somewhat brown." The couple became fairly notorious in New Amsterdam, but the point is they were not especially out of the ordinary. In fact, the view that American history has of the Dutch colony centered around Manhattan fits it fairly well to this point: a colorful collection of losers and scalawags, inconsequential and meandering, waiting around for the winds of fate to blow them off the map. The Dutch had succeeded in obtaining a piece of real estate of inestimable value, but while they were experts at turning that to advantage in other parts of the world, here—

the efforts of Van den Bogaert and Ambassador Joachimi notwithstanding—
they let it languish.

By now, however, others had recognized the value of the land between
the thirty-ninth and forty-second parallels on the Atlantic Coast, and were
making plays for it. Van Twiller wrote to the English in Massachusetts of his
hope that "as good neighbors wee might live in these heathenishe coun-
tryes," but they ignored him—English settlers were already drifting southward into territory claimed by the Dutch. The Fresh River (the Connecticut
River) was irresistible, and in 1636 a preacher named Thomas Hooker led
the first group of English religious pioneers south from the Massachusetts
Bay colony to set up a community on the river. They called it Hartford.

Then there was an internal play made for a portion of the colony. Kiliaen
van Rensselaer was an Amsterdam diamond merchant with interests in land
reclamation (a popular and profitable undertaking in the United Provinces)
and agricultural innovations. He was also one of the founding directors of
the West India Company, and one of the ardent advocates for setting up private plantations, or patroonships, to settle New Netherland. Through indominable drive, he got his own planned settlement approved by the board
and began the arduous task of gathering colonists to inhabit it. He chose the
manager of his estate shrewdly. Bastiaen Krol, the young man who had come
over with Joris Rapalje and Catalina Trico, intending to make a career as a
minister, had had his plans waylaid several times now. First, Minuit had put
him in charge of Fort Orange after Daniel van Crieckenbeeck's death in an
Indian ambush. Then, when Minuit was recalled, Krol found himself given
the job of interim director of the colony. When that stint was over, he returned to the Dutch Republic. Van Rensselaer met him then, realized the
depth of experience he had gained, and offered him a job. Krol carried out
his first task brilliantly. Returning to New Netherland, he purchased from
the Mahicans the land surrounding Fort Orange, stretching along both sides
of the river. Van Rensselaer exaggerated somewhat when he wrote shortly
after that his property extended west from the river "indifinitely," but it did
run about nine miles along the river and "two days' journey" inland. In
other words, the entrepreneur had taken a vital chunk out of New Netherland, and it was his intention to treat his colony-within-a-colony as a sovereign fiefdom.

But for sheer bravura, nothing beat the return of Peter Minuit to New Netherland. It happened that just before Minuit was recalled from his duties and shipped back on the ill-fated *Unity*, the king of Sweden, Gustavus Adolphus—a Lutheran warrior who was in the midst of massive participation in the Protestant-versus-Catholic Thirty Years' War in Germany—was looking for new worlds to conquer. Sweden was in the midst of its own Golden Age, and Gustavus was tired of watching as France, Spain, England, and the Dutch Republic exerted their will around the globe. As it happened, Gustavus would die in battle just when Minuit made it back to Amsterdam following his ordeal in England. The crown descended, then, to the head of his six-year-old daughter, Christina, who would grow up to become one of the most cosmopolitan and intellectually nimble monarchs in European history, but for the time being affairs were left in the hands of the chancellor, Axel Oxenstierna, who continued Gustavus's policies.

The Dutch had long been the major traders in Sweden, delivering the goods of the world to Stockholm. Oxenstierna came into contact with a Dutch merchant named Samuel Blommaert who was involved in the copper trade in Sweden. This Blommaert was, like Kiliaen Van Rensselaer, a director of the West India Company, and one of those angry over what he realized was a missed opportunity in the North American colony. Van Rensselaer's way of getting around the corporate bureaucracy was to finance his own subcolony; Blommaert's idea was slightly zanier: to defy his own company and country and establish a Swedish colony somewhere within the New Netherland territory. He met secretly with Minuit, and a plan took form. Minuit probably knew the Dutch colony better than anyone alive, and knew in particular that its choice South River territory was all but unguarded.

Thus it happened that sometime in the middle of March 1638, one of the strangest invasion fleets ever to approach American shores sailed between capes May and Henlopen, into what would eventually become Delaware Bay, and made anchor at a rocky point on a tributary called the Minquas Kill. Outfitted in battle armor, with the blue-and-yellow flag of Sweden flying from the mainmast of his ship, the *Kalmar Nyckel*, and looking for all the world like some latter-day medieval knight set to conquer, Peter Minuit was returning to North America—a German native of French extraction and recent Dutch ties, proclaiming a colony on behalf of Sweden in the wilderness that would become the state of Delaware. In the absence of a Dutch resistance force, Minuit was set to make his second imprint on America. Ranged about him on the decks of the two-ship squadron were several dozen Dutch sailors and Swedish soldiers, pikes and muskets at the ready, plumed helmets glinting sunlight. To this day, in gritty, industrial-era homage to that odd arrival, the road that connects the warehouses along the waterfront in Wilmington—the city that grew up around Minuit's landing spot—is called Swedes' Landing.

Dying from within and attacked from without, the Manhattan colony, circa 1640, was thus firmly on the road to extinction. It wasn't even a proper political entity: it had no government; its inhabitants were less citizens of a republic than serfs working at the behest of a multinational company. True, it sat on the verge of a vast continent that Europeans were soon to penetrate, motivated by the zeal to expand their horizons in the wake of men like Galileo, Harvey, Drake, and Hudson, and also by the desire to flee decades of religion-fueled war at home. As the geographic key to unlocking the continent, this region would one day help shift the global center of power. One could argue that it would become the point on which Western civilization itself would pivot as it shifted from the Renaissance era to the modern world, from Eurocentrism to a global perspective. But, for all that promise, it was little more than a place of chaos and slop, of barroom knife fights, soldiers fornicating with Indian women while on guard duty, and a steady stream of wayward newcomers: hard men hoisting themselves out of skiffs and hitting the packed soil of the Strand, purses strung around their necks heavy with Carolus guilders or Spanish pieces of eight, ready to smuggle, drink, trade, whore, and be gone. Henry Hudson had ensured that the settlement was under Dutch auspices, but so far the vaunted characteristic of Dutch society—as a pluralistic, tolerant republic—was in evidence only in a negative way. It might as well have been any nation's dregs clinging to the southern tip of the wilderness island called Manhattan. It was as if the world, having dimly identified this piece of land and water on the edge of the New World as a fulcrum, wasn't yet ready for it, and so let it disintegrate.

It was a community, in other words, sure to die out, one that history could safely forget.

The "parent" cities that together would give birth to New York: top, London, circa 1616; bottom, Amsterdam in the sixteenth century. *(Library of Congress; Amsterdams Historisch Museum)*

Henry Hudson
(New York Public Library Picture Collection)

John Farrer's map of "Virginia" shows a view of North America that was still commonly held years after Hudson's voyage. It is oriented with the south to the left and the north to the right. By traveling up the Hudson River, at the far right (north), an adventurer expected to reach "The Sea of China and the Indies." *(Library of Congress)*

The 1626 letter in which Peter Schaghen, a Dutch government official, wrote to his superiors that colonists had "purchased the Island Manhattes from the Indians for the value of 60 guilders." *(National Archives, The Hague) t' Fort nieuw Amsterdam op de Manhatans*

The earliest view of Dutch Manhattan, dated to two years after Peter Minuit's purchase, shows the fort, windmill, a cluster of dwellings, and Indians as a regular presence. *(New York State Library)*

In 1630, the West India Company published this pamphlet advertising for settlers in the New Netherland colony, depicting it as a grand and lucrative adventure. *(National Library of the Netherlands)*

Leiden University in the seventeenth century.

Hugo de Groot, a.k.a. Grotius, the father of international law and the guiding light of Adriaen van der Donck's generation of legal scholars. *(Collection of the Historical Museum, Rotterdam, on loan from the Van der Mandele Foundation)*

David Pietersz de Vries, Dutch adventurer, tried to talk Willem Kieft out of his disastrous plan to make war on the Indians around Manhattan. *(New York State Library)*

een Mahakuaes Indiaen, met hun Steden en woningen

A Dutch depiction of a Mohawk Indian and Mohawk longhouse villages, dated from the time of Van der Donck's travels among the Mohawk.

Peter Stuyvesant
(New York Public Library Picture Collection)

Appropriately enough for a figure who has been so thoroughly ignored by history, Adriaen van der Donck's image is now a matter of dispute. The National Gallery of Art in Washington, D.C., has determined that in the early twentieth century this painting passed through a pair of art dealers who were known to forge the provenances of some works, and thus now considers the subject uncertain. *(National Gallery of Art)*

Detail of Gerard ter Borch's painting of the entrance of Adriaen Pauw into Münster for the historic peace negotiations of 1648. *(Stadtmuseum Münster)*

PART II

CLASH OF WILLS

Chapter 5

THE LAWMAN

September is a vigorous month in Holland. North Sea rains angle down out of charcoal-bottomed clouds. Broad bands of blue sky appear, and the world becomes bathed in smoky light. Suddenly the sun comes on pure and full, shocking the painted-and-varnished shutters on brick facades, threatening to pierce the green murk of the canal surface, bringing ordinary humans close to bursting out in mad spontaneous song. And there is the wind, a constant presence, like an insistent hand on the back, inviting or pushing the inhabitants: *move, make sail, go.*

In September 1638 a newcomer entered the town of Leiden, in the province of Holland.* He had come from his home in the city of Breda, forty miles to the south in the seemingly remote and largely Catholic region called Brabant, which, while part of the Dutch Republic, did not have the status of a full province. If he was like other newcomers, he couldn't help but be impressed by what he found in Leiden. In a country known for its neatness, this handsome brick village stood out in the seventeenth century, its alleys and canal sides manicured, the pavement literally scrubbed, the soaring whitewashed walls of its church interiors crisply set off by dark beams. In fact, it was not a village at all—by 1622 its population had reached forty-five thousand—but it maintained a provincial simplicity. The massive sailcloth arms of windmills framed the sky not just on the outskirts but right in the town center. The streets through which the young man walked would have swarmed with children at play—an oddity at this time in Europe. The

*Properly speaking, Holland referred not to the Dutch Republic but to its chief province, with Amsterdam as its hub; the other six provinces in the seventeenth-century state were Utrecht, Gelderland, Overijssel, Zeeland, Friesland, and Groningen.

prevailing thinking elsewhere, in this age of Puritan grimness, was that childhood was a time when chaos and devilry might sweep into the soul, and thus children should be checked, subdued, kept under sober adult submission. The Dutch thinking was the opposite; they hugged and coddled their children, ignoring the scorn of outsiders and following their own experts. "[C]hildren should not be kept on too tight a rein, but allowed to exercise their childishness, so that we do not burden their fragile nature with heavy things," advised the physician Johan van Beverwijck, the Dr. Spock/Benjamin Weil of his day, whose book *Treasure of Health* was a bestseller. So—as the boisterous street scenes of Jan Steen paintings illustrate—children ran free, and the streets echoed with their play.

A cosmopolitan intensity built as one approached the canal called the Rapenburg—taverns and music halls, curling columns of tobacco smoke. Crossing a little pedestrian bridge over the canal, the newcomer would have met up with crowds of his colleagues—other young men massing on the cobbled quayside before a handsome two-story building with leaded glass panes. The entrance was through an arch in the brick wall to the north. This was the main building of the University of Leiden, the premier academic institution in the Netherlands and a major European center of learning. Into this building the young man walked on September 24, 1638, and penned his name, Adriaen van der Donck, his age, twenty, his home province, and the degree for which he was about to begin studying: law. In seventeen years, he would be dead, in a distant land of which, at this point in his life, he may never have heard. He would cause a stir in America and Europe, but in time it would diminish. Few people in history would remember him. But he would make a mark. He would bring the seed of the best and noblest aspect of seventeenth-century European civilization to fresh soil a world away, where something remarkable would grow. He would play a decisive role in the creation of a great city and a new society.

He was young, strong, and forthright, with a deep intellectual bent balanced by a roaming hunger for adventure. His family had stature in Breda—one relative had served as a steward in the court of William the Silent, another had been high ranking in the Dutch army—and he came to the university with a certain pedigree. Four decades before, in the early days of the war against Spain, an event had occurred in his home town which by this time had become legend. Breda had been one of many towns in the hands of

Spanish occupiers. William the Silent, hero of the Dutch revolt, had recently died, and the Spanish were gaining territory as they marched through the southern reaches of the Low Countries, when a daring Trojan-horse maneuver turned the tide. A contingent of seventy Dutch soldiers concealed themselves beneath layers of turf in a peat boat and floated past the Spanish troops guarding the entrance into Breda. Once inside the gate, they led an uprising that resulted in the town's recapture. The man behind the *turfschip van Breda* was Adriaen van Bergen, grandfather and namesake of Van der Donck. Van Bergen was still remembered as a hero in Breda decades later; the family shared in the patriotic luster, and young Adriaen van der Donck wore the association as a badge of honor.

The university also had ties to the early days of the rebellion. The town of Leiden had withstood a Spanish onslaught in 1574, and as a reward for the bravery of its fighters, William the Silent chose Leiden as the site of the grand university that he believed the Dutch provinces needed if they were to become a nation. In a remarkably short time the university achieved a status equaling that of Bologna or Oxford and became just what William had envisioned: a breeding ground for the new nation's top scientists, politicians, lawyers, and religious figures.

The Dutch spirit of tolerance pervaded the town. Scientists and writers from all over Europe came to have their books published at Leiden, whose printers were cheap, highly skilled, and largely unmuzzled by authorities. Indeed, no statistic gives a better indication of the Dutch role in the intellectual life of the time than the estimate that over the course of the seventeenth century the Netherlands produced one-half of all books published worldwide.

At the time Adriaen van der Donck arrived, about one-third of Leiden's population was comprised of refugees from wars and religious persecution. In a century marked by religious war, Brownists, Baptists, Walloons, Huguenots, Fifth Monarchy Men, and Ashkenazic Jews came here, as well as to other cities in the Dutch Republic, to live and worship. When, early in the century, William Bradford and his fellow Pilgrim leaders, who had fled persecution in England, wrote asking the town whether they might settle there, the magistrates promptly wrote back: "[We] refuse no honest persons ingress to come and have their residence in this city, provided that such persons behave themselves honestly, and submit to all the laws and ordinances here." The Pilgrims moved in in 1609—the year that Henry Hudson initiated the Dutch claim to its North American territory—taking up residence in the warren of streets surrounding the massive, gothic Pieterskerk, engaging in trades and practicing their faith. They took advantage of the freedom of the press and began printing tracts attacking King Charles's religious restrictions, which they smuggled into England. When Charles's ambassador complained, the town magistrates shielded their new residents, furthering Charles's low opinion of the Dutch. Ironically, it was the Dutch tolerance of religious differences—precisely the thing that had drawn them—that eventually drove some of the Pilgrims away to the New World. They feared that living among practitioners of ungodly faiths would dissipate them. And indeed, when the first group of forty sailed to Cape Cod in 1620, several hundred more stayed behind, many eventually blending into the melting pot of Dutch society.

Tolerance was more than just an attitude in the Dutch Republic. Following the bloody religious persecution of thousands in the previous century at the hands of the Spanish, the Dutch provinces had broken new ground in writing into their 1579 de facto constitution the guarantee that "each person shall remain free, especially in his religion, and that no one shall be persecuted or investigated because of their religion." This sentence became the ground on which the culturally diverse society of the seventeenth century was built. But as in so many societies—think of the early United States, a slaveholding nation that believed itself to be rooted on the principle of freedom—the guiding rule was often broken. In the 1620s a debate on the meaning and wisdom of tolerance had raged through the Dutch provinces. At its center was a clash that had taken place here, at Leiden University, between two iconic theologians. As one component to a wider debate about Calvinist teachings, the hard-liner, Gomarus, and his followers, having surveyed a continent scarred by religious war, saw in it proof of the dangers of diversity, and argued that strength came from conformity, that repression of non-Calvinist religion was good for the soul and the state both. Gomarus's opponent, Arminius, and his camp, countered that Christian principles of charity compelled tolerance of religious differences, and forbade the persecution of those who had different views. A much quoted forerunner of Arminius named Sebastian Castellio phrased it with persuasive Christian elegance: "Many will be damned on Judgment Day because they killed innocent people, but nobody will be damned because he killed nobody." Besides, the Arminians pointed out, diversity was good for business.

Out of this struggle came an elaborate written rationale for tolerance of religious diversity. Its climax—really, a watershed in human thought—came with Arminius's follower Simon Episcopius declaring in a series of carefully reasoned arguments that the strength of a state derived not from maintaining a single, firmly held faith, as was almost universally believed in Europe, but from allowing its citizens freedom of worship and intellectual inquiry. It is impossible to imagine how revolutionary this was, how intoxicating it felt to those who championed it, and how deeply it affected Adriaen van der Donck and his generation of scholars. By Van der Donck's time at Leiden, the tolerance advocates held sway, and the staggering successes of the Golden Age only strengthened their case.

Tolerance was a boon to the university itself, giving it an advantage over other centers of learning in Europe, helping it to become a major international center in the space of a few decades. In any era scholars and scientists are drawn to freedom as fire to oxygen, and in much of seventeenth-century Europe the oxygen was growing thin. Galileo had faced the Inquisition only five years before. His *Discourses and Mathematical Demonstrations Concerning Two New Sciences,* which Isaac Newton would build upon to establish the laws of physics, was being published at Leiden, at a safe remove from Vatican censors, in 1638, just as Van der Donck arrived. Top academics from throughout Europe came to teach at Leiden, attracted by the freedom, as well as by high salaries and other incentives the university offered, such as tax exemption on the alcohol they consumed, up to a healthy forty gallons of wine a year, and a half barrel of beer per month.

As a result, Leiden in the 1630's churned with history-making activity. Van der Donck soaked up the atmosphere generated by new learning then revolutionizing the fields of medicine, physics, and mathematics, and his courses in law and politics would have been imbued with Dutch ideas about democracy, monarchy, and tolerance. The dominant intellectual spirit of the decade—at Leiden and elsewhere—was René Descartes, the Frenchman whose rationalistic method of inquiry brought philosophy and science into the modern era. Descartes had moved to Holland in 1629, seeking intellectual freedom. He lived for most of the next twenty years in an Amsterdam townhouse opposite the Westerkerk. Descartes enrolled at Leiden University in 1630 and lived there for a time, then returned in 1636, seeking a publisher for his new work, and stayed for seven years, easily becoming the most talked-about intellectual in town. The *Discourse on Method* was published at Leiden in 1637, the year before Van der Donck arrived, and it caused a sensation.

It was an epochal moment in which to begin a university education—indeed, one might say it was the moment when modern higher education was born. Scientists, philosophers, and theologians (the titles were more or less interchangeable) opened up a furious debate on the most fundamental aspects of their fields. What would it mean to follow Descartes and base reasoning not on "authority" (Aristotle or the Bible) but on the mind of the thinker and, as Descartes said, its "good sense"? The famous phrase from the *Discourse* that would resound through the centuries, influencing everything from modern science to the Enlightenment political thinking of Thomas Jefferson—*cogito ergo sum,* "I think, therefore I am"—had just been voiced. The age of the individual was at hand, and the young Adriaen van der Donck was at its epicenter.

The place vibrated with the energy of new forms of inquiry. Leiden's anatomical theater was one of the first and the most famous in the world, but the frenzy for dissections was so great that it was often overbooked and professors had to hold their anatomical classes, wrote one scholar in 1638, "in the academic Garden and elsewhere." Some conducted public dissections in their homes, which they had fitted out with "domestic amphitheaters." Dogs vanished from the streets of Leiden as medical students became obsessed with the fad for direct observation and study. Johannes de Wale cut open live dogs and pumped their veins to demonstrate the circulation of the blood—work that William Harvey relied on to refine his own theories. Human cadavers were in great demand. Reinier de Graaf became obsessed by the theory that pancreatic fluid was acidic. He was known to stimulate the pancreas of a cadaver so that it would produce fluid, and then to taste it and urge his assembled observers to taste it as well, whereupon he would ask hopefully if they detected an acidic flavor. De Graaf's greater contribution to science came when he proved, by dissecting pregnant rabbits, what was then an outlandish theory, that the ovaries had a role in reproduction. Unfortunately, his discovery was overshadowed by the near simultaneous discovery by Antoni van Leeuwenhoek, using his microscope, of spermatozoa, which gave a last gasp of life to the theory stretching back to antiquity that babies came solely from sperm and the female womb was merely a receptacle.

The university's botanical garden was also a (literal) seedbed of innovation. From it came advances in chemistry and botany, and it was here that, through crossbreeding, the Dutch frenzy for tulips began.* And in the wake of Galileo the observatory was booked up by scholars scouring the heavens for sunspots and evidence to support or refute the theory of planets revolving around the sun.

Van der Donck steeped in this intellectual ferment for three years. In law, just as in science, a revolution was taking place. The very concept of a nation was being redefined. In the aftermath of the Reformation, the medieval notion of a state as existing under the umbrella of Christendom, with its laws ultimately pointing back to the Church, had collapsed, and the modern concept of a state as an independent political entity was coming into being. The dominant legal figure of the age, who did more than anyone to set the parameters by which nations interact to this day, was the Dutch jurist Hugo de Groot, known to history as Hugo Grotius. Grotius is considered the father of international law. (As an indication of his prominence in history, a bas-relief portrait of him adorns the U.S. House of Representatives chamber, alongside those of Moses, Hammurabi, and Thomas Jefferson.) Of his two major works, *Mare Liberum* created the principle of international waters, which were to be open to all nations, while *De Jure Belli ac Pacis,* written in the midst of a century of unprecedented warfare, laid down principles on which war was justified, and how it ought to be conducted.

Grotius dominated the way law was taught at Leiden, especially among the younger, more practical-minded scholars. Judging from his later actions, Van der Donck must have avoided the "antiquarian law" favored by the older generation of purely theoretical teachers, which confined itself to examination of ancient Roman texts, and instead concentrated on what was called "elegant law," which applied the reasoning of ancient authorities to practical courtroom situations. In this regard he would have been a disciple

---

*Tulip mania reached its height just at the time Van der Donck began his studies. The year before, in exchange for a single tulip bulb, a man paid four oxen, eight pigs, twelve sheep, 160 bushels of wheat, 320 bushels of rye, four casks of butter, a thousand pounds of cheese, two oxheads of wine, a silver pitcher, and a bed. The government of the province of Holland was forced to pass laws to end the speculation before it ruined the economy.

of Grotius. Grotius's work was also broadly influential because it helped to establish the framework by which the great European powers conducted their affairs—including how England and the Dutch Republic, in their increasingly bitter rivalry over North America and other territories, conducted themselves.

Beyond this, Van der Donck would have been drawn to Grotius because he, like Descartes, based his arguments not on biblical citations but "natural law," the idea that right and wrong could be determined by applying human reason—or, as Grotius put it, that an act could be judged "from its conformity or non-conformity with rational nature itself." Traditionally, American history has shown the principles of democratic government coming out of the Enlightenment era of the eighteenth century, with origins in the writings of John Locke in the late seventeenth century. But in recent decades historians have uncovered the early modern roots of those democratic impulses. Some of Grotius's followers, building on his statement of natural law, applied the same kind of radical verve to their writings as would the generation responsible for the American Revolution. One of those disciples—Piet van der Cun, a.k.a. Cunaeus—taught a radical form of Grotius's political thought in his own career at Leiden, and a collection of young idealists formed around him and perpetuated it. Cunaeus's ideas—that a republican form of government was morally superior to a monarchy, and that enterprises like the West India Company enriched a wealthy few to the detriment of both the state and ordinary people—were in the air during Van der Donck's days at Leiden, and helped mold his generation.

For three years Van der Donck studied at Leiden alongside an international contingent of scholars, took part in debating circles organized by the law professors, maybe joined with his colleagues in complaining, as students will, about the food in the dining hall (smoked fish, hashed meat with cabbage, cheese, bread and butter, and beer). In taverns in the evenings, with smoke curling from long clay pipes and Rhenish wine flowing from pewter pitchers, the young men might have applied their debating skills to the all-consuming Galileo-versus-Aristotle and Arminius-versus-Gomarus questions. Then he emerged, in 1641, a "jurist," an authority on Roman-Dutch law.

What to do next? He was a man of law. He came from a family of renown. He was a graduate of the top university in the country, and the economy was so robust it was practically exploding. Many possibilities must have been open to him—back home in Breda, in Amsterdam, at The Hague, the center of legal and political power in the nation. Instead he opted to leave the country. And not just leave, but to go nowhere, headlong into the wilderness. His country was experiencing one of the greatest flowerings of art and science and one of the most profound economic booms of any nation in any period in history. Its streets were safe, its houses snug, its offices bustling. The cuisine was surely nothing to marvel at, but the beer was fresh and excellent; pipe tobacco was sold in every conceivable grade and form; even the boxes to store it were available in an infinity of materials and styles. Homes were decked out with rugs from Turkey, Chinese porcelain, and Delft tiles; dollhouse makers were in demand, not for child's play but by proud home owners who wanted them to create mini-replicas of their dwellings. It was one of the first societies on earth in which ordinary town-dwelling citizens had developed a worldly sophistication. English travelers were amazed to find that not just the wealthy but ordinary bakers and shopkeepers decorated the walls of their homes with paintings; an obvious sign of their outward-looking nature, the Dutch of this time were the first (as shown in Vermeer's interiors) to decorate their homes with maps. The Dutch at the beginning of the century were also among the first to separate their homes into public areas (downstairs) and private living space (upstairs). A German visiting a Dutch home was astounded that "it is not permissible to ascend the stairs or set foot in a room without first removing one's shoes." It was the Dutch of this era who invented the idea of the home as a personal, intimate space; one might say they invented coziness.

All of this had happened roughly within the span of Van der Donck's life. Fueled by its global trade, the Netherlands had become a very comfortable place. It was unthinkable that anyone with good prospects would want to leave. It's not beyond reason to suppose Van der Donck took his inspiration from Descartes. The intellectual celebrity would have made a natural model for the young man. He lived in and around Leiden through Van der Donck's time there, and, for all his personal reserve, was a polarizing presence; some professors at the university became his disciples while others bitterly opposed his "natural philosophy." He had a ruddy attractiveness—dark wavy hair, curling moustache, penetrating eyes—and was a man of action as well as intellect: he had volunteered as a soldier under Maurits, son of William the Silent, and strutted the town with a sword as part of his regular dress. His *Discourse,* which Van der Donck would likely have read while at Leiden, was remarkably chatty and autobiographical for a philosophical work, and a young man of restless and individualistic spirit would have been drawn to the passage near the front in which Descartes, in talking about his own setting-forth, declared that "as soon as my age permitted me to pass from under the control of my instructors, I entirely abandoned the study of letters, and resolved no longer to seek any other science than the knowledge of myself, or of the great book of the world."

Had Van der Donck wanted to go into overseas trade, the logical route was via the offices of the East or West India Company. But they were too regimented for his nature. As in any large corporation, promotions came slowly and steadily. Van der Donck wanted something more toothsome and wild. Perhaps through his parents, or possibly through one of the pamphlets that served as precursors to newspapers, he had learned of a New World colony-in-the-making, a raw, virgin place that was in need of help. It wasn't the West India Company's New Netherland settlement that attracted him, but the colony-within-a-colony at its northern reaches, the private fiefdom of Amsterdam diamond merchant Kiliaen van Rensselaer. He made an inquiry.

His timing was excellent. Van Rensselaer had steadily enlarged his colony in the eleven years since its founding, buying tracts from the Mahicans; it now covered several hundred thousand acres along both sides of the Hudson River, encircling the West India Company's upriver base of Fort Orange. While the company's own colony centered around Manhattan was floundering, the patroon—a micromanager of the first order—had tended his settlement with great care. He had sent farmers, carpenters, smiths, wheelwrights, and bricklayers, as well as livestock, seed, and bare root trees and vines; from his base in Amsterdam (Van Rensselaer would never live to see his domain), he gave voluminous instructions for clearing forest and planting crops. Houses went up and roads were laid. Van Rensselaer was able to write in January 1641 that "In general, the affairs of the colony are all right, God be praised," but there was a problem, which stemmed from his success. He had a genuine settlement on his hands now, and it needed a government. While technically his colony was within the boundaries of New

Netherland, Van Rensselaer considered it a semi-independent entity. That meant he had to provide his own law and order. Thefts and runaways (farmers who signed on for a specific period of years, and then fled) were on the rise.

When Van der Donck wrote to Van Rensselaer, asking to be considered for a place in the colony, the merchant must have been pleased. Getting experienced workers of any kind to cross the ocean and take up a new life in his colony was difficult: he was forced to pay substantially more than they would make in the Netherlands, and even then he complained about the quality of person he was able to attract. In the mind of a middle-class businessman who had clawed his way up, Van der Donck's credentials, as a Leiden University jurist, would have shimmered. There was no lawyer in the entire colony of New Netherland; the only university-educated man was the minister in New Amsterdam. It was simply too difficult to interest such people in the posting. Van Rensselaer fired off a letter to one of the minor shareholders in his colony, who happened to live in Leiden: "When convenient please have inquiry made through Mr de laet or some one else regarding a young man, called vander donck, from the barony of breda, who has studied law at Leyden and is desirous of attempting something connected with farming in our colony; and if there are no serious charges against his character, as one can not always get the best to go thither, we might employ him also in some other capacity."

Once the two met, Van Rensselaer knew how he would employ the young man. He needed someone who could roam the wilds of his untamed land and hunt down outlaws, and also someone with a legal mind, who could administer justice and settle disputes between colonists. He offered Van der Donck the job of *schout*, a Dutch title that combined the duties of sheriff and public prosecutor. It was a difficult posting, but the young man's credentials would give him stature not only among the colonists on his patroonship but among the tough lot in New Amsterdam as well.

To a young man whose education had come more from books than the real world, it must have seemed like a utopian adventure: to march into a raw land and create a system of justice, to be the lawbringer for a whole new community. Van der Donck accepted, and in May 1641 he boarded *Den Eyckenboom* ("The Oak Tree"), bound for the New World. In his pocket was a thick sheaf of instructions from Van Rensselaer, but however detailed they were, they couldn't begin to cover all that lay ahead.

*

IT IS EASIER today to imagine the harbor into which the ship sailed ten long weeks later than it has been at nearly any intervening time period. For more than two centuries it would be the gateway to America and a commercial hub linking North America with Europe, a traffic-choked intersection in which, through the eras, frigates, schooners, steamships, container vessels, and pleasure yachts would belly past one another in their passage into and out of the array of piers that radiated from Manhattan's shoreline like the teeth of a comb. Now there is an odd tranquillity. Sailing in the harbor today, you need only turn your back on the spiny rise of Manhattan and delete from your mind's eye the Statue of Liberty and the mute hulks on Ellis Island and Governor's Island to envision it as it once was. With the water surface rippling nicely and the sails overhead snapping and coughing as they labor, urban noise recedes. For minutes at a time you are alone out here—time to take in the undulate geography of the place, its spread of islands and, as Van der Donck would later describe, its "many and different sea havens."

We can only imagine how inviting its idyllic shelter would have been after long weeks at the mercy of the open ocean. In its breadth and depth the harbor struck Van der Donck, as it had his countrymen, as a kind of New World version of the IJ, the great island sea fronting Amsterdam, whose lanes, throughout the century, bristled with a forest of masts. These Dutch were a people who knew waterways as others knew the forest or the mountains. To them, land that was inaccessible by water was useless. Conversely, rich land that was cut by navigable rivers and incised by a commodious bay was the ultimate object. This bay was one of the things that had attracted them here; they felt the latent energy in it; they smelled its potential, how it might become a copy of their great home base across the ocean. For now it remained what it had been for millennia: a sculpted wilderness of saltwater, wind, and land. The English would call it New York Harbor. To the Dutch it was too elemental even to require that much of a name. As Van der Donck later noted with his scholar's Latin, "it is named *quasi per excellentiam,* 'The Bay.' "

The ship dropped its anchor some hundreds of yards before the southern shore of Manhattan, with its clutch of gabled houses, its windmill, and the walls of its fort clustered along it. The passengers staggered down into a waiting boat and were rowed ashore.

Van der Donck didn't record his first impression of New Amsterdam, and while by any ordinary measure the look of the place could not have been one to inspire confidence, there had been a decisive change for the better in the affairs of the town and the colony in the past year. History's simplistic reading of the Dutch colony centered around Manhattan—that it was an inconsequential gathering of nobodies until the English eventually took over and began to make a thriving settlement of it—is based on the record of the West India Company. The West India Company ran the place, and the West India Company never succeeded in making it financially viable; ergo, New Amsterdam never really took flight. But that logic overlooks a crucial turn of events. In 1640 the company gave up its monopoly on trade in the region, which had kept the place from developing in any areas except piracy and smuggling, and declared New Netherland a free trading zone. In this new free-market territory, New Amsterdam would be the "staple port," the hub through which traders' and merchants' ships would pass, where they would pay duties and be cleared for travel. The effect was electric. Small-scale entrepreneurs in Amsterdam who were willing to brave the hazards of the ocean voyage now had, in Manhattan, a hub to exploit—a base around which the circle of Atlantic trade could turn. Gillis Verbrugge formed a partnership with his son, Seth, and launched the first of what would be twenty-seven trading voyages to Manhattan. The business would make Seth a wealthy man, able to support his wife, herself the daughter of a successful businessman, in style. Dirck de Wolff set up a company that shipped manufactured goods to the colonists on Manhattan and brought back furs and tobacco; his profits from this and other international trading ventures bought him an elegant Amsterdam townhouse on the exclusive Herengracht, or Gentleman's Canal, and a vast country estate in the polders near Haarlem.

On Manhattan, meanwhile, that small change would have far-reaching results. It gave rise, within the space of a few years, to an intensively active merchant class—people who wanted to buy, sell, grow, spend. Convinced now that there was a future here, they began putting down roots. What's more, the Manhattan merchants defied categorization. The tailor also brewed beer; the baker doubled as a ship's captain. Joris Rapalje, who by the time Van der Donck arrived at Manhattan had been in the colony for eighteen years, worked for the West India Company but also did stints of entrepreneurship, selling grain on behalf of farmers at Van Rensselaer's colony, and owned and operated a tavern. The looseness of Manhattan society had its disadvantages, but it also made for greater social mobility than in Europe.

Everyone in New Amsterdam had shares in one shipment of cargo or another. "Everyone here is a trader," one resident remarked in 1650, and it was true, and unprecedented—as was the opportunity for advancement. Govert Loockermans had arrived in Manhattan seven years before Van der Donck, as a sixteen-year-old cook's mate on a West India Company vessel, desperate to get ahead. As soon as the West India Company monopoly ended, he left and signed on as agent for the Verbrugges, overseeing ships and cargo. Over the next few years he would learn to speak English as well as several Indian languages, buy a farm on the East River, and begin leasing ships and moving cargo around New Netherland and the Atlantic, several times being accused of smuggling. He had a fairly sharp mean streak: in an altercation with Raritan Indians, he became infamous when he, in the words of a witness, "tortured the chief's brother in his private parts with a piece of split wood." He would die, thirty-eight years after his youthful footfall, in the new city of New York, the wealthiest merchant in the colony, owner of one of its finest homes (which would later become the home of the pirate William Kidd and is today the site of a nondescript office building, 7 Hanover Square), one of the richest men in the New World, and one of the purest exemplars of the kind of freeform upward mobility that American culture would inherit from its forgotten colony.

In New Amsterdam itself, the opening of trade was already showing results as Van der Donck arrived. Dozens of lots were leased or bought in the months after the monopoly gave way. Houses were being built, and there was a rise in the level of creature comforts in those houses. When tobacco farmer Jacque de Vernuis died unexpectedly in October 1640, shortly after signing a ten-year lease and leaving behind a Dutch wife, Hester Simons, the inventory of his property included a gray riding coat, a riding cap, shirts, cravats, coifs, stockings and handkerchiefs, pewter dishes, silverware, iron pots, copper kettles, pine chests, curtains, pillows and pillow cases, blankets, three hogs, a fishing rod, a pair of tongs, and "one brass skimmer."

A humble enough collection, but worlds beyond the hardscrabble days of even a few years before.

On arrival, then, leather boots splashing in the East River shallows where the sloop unloaded passengers (it would be years before a proper pier was constructed), Adriaen van der Donck would have taken a turn through a chaotic, energetic, rough town that was very much in transition. There were perhaps four hundred inhabitants, and it was already one of the most multicultural places on earth; in five years' time a visiting Jesuit priest would report that eighteen languages were spoken in its few dusty lanes. In the summer of 1641 the fort was tumbledown, but there were new houses, some of wood and stone, some of brick, with steep roofs and step gables. From the shore a newcomer would cross over the new Brewer's Bridge spanning the grandly named Heere Gracht (again modeling their New World base on Amsterdam, the residents felt the town needed a "gentleman's canal"—in reality it was a stinking ditch), walk past the five stone houses that formed the shopping district, by the bakery and the midwife's house, and skirt the simple wooden church on Pearl Street ("a mean barn" David de Vries called it), with the minister's house and stable behind. The lanes of the town were riotous with free-ranging pigs and chickens, the farming principle of the period being that one's animals roamed for food, and property was fenced to keep them out, not in.

It was high summer; a Dutchman, unused to the humidity, would work up a sweat as he took in the town. Logic and custom would have him stopping at at least one of the several taverns clustered on the half dozen principle streets—perhaps in the company of Cornelis Melyn, a wealthy Flemish farmer who had made the voyage with him, and who would become instrumental in involving Van der Donck in Manhattan politics. Continuing on his way, Van der Donck might have paused to chat with a German carpenter named Juriaen, who at that moment was building a house for Frenchman Philip Geraerdy, or to observe the English carpenters John Hobson and John Morris, who were fulfilling their contract with Isaac de Forest for "a dwelling house, 30 feet long and 18 feet wide, with 2 4-light windows and 2 3-light windows, 4 beams with brackets and 2 free beams, one partition and one passage way tight inside and outside and the entire house tight all around."

If he needed evidence that there was new life pulsing through the hard-scrabble community, Van der Donck need only have watched the ship he had sailed on being unloaded of its cargo, for which various residents had put in orders from Amsterdam and which they were no doubt now at the waterfront ready to receive. For Tonis Jansen the sailmaker, the crew unloaded one bale of French canvas, two bales of sail cloth, one keg containing 200 pounds of sail yarn. Hendric Jansen, locksmith, got his order of "4 chauldrons of smith's coal, 30 bars of square iron, 60 bars of flat Swedish iron, 150 pieces of hard iron." The commissary in the West India Company's store signed off on receipt of his goods, which included casks of brandy, sack, and French wine, oil, dried beef and pork, "30 tuns of fine salt," a case of stationery, 290 pounds of candles, and "2 large crates containing 50 winnowing baskets." No sooner had the ship put into port than Arent Corssen Stam, a merchant of Haarlem, signed a contract with Gelain Cornelissen, skipper of *Den Eyckenboom,* "immediately to deliver the aforesaid ship ready for sailing, tight, well caulked and provided with anchors, ropes, tackle, sails, running and standing rigging, victuals and other necessaries thereto belonging, and to arm said ship with six cannon and other ammunition in proportion." He was to deliver a new load of cargo to the English colony of Virginia, there receive another load (probably tobacco), and "sail with the first favorable wind which God shall grant from Virginia direct to London and deliver the ship's cargo to those to whom it shall be consigned."

Finally, into the fort Van der Donck would have walked, past the lattice-work guardhouse, and to the director-general's brick house. Here he pulled out a letter of introduction and placed it before Willem Kieft, who had replaced Van Twiller three years before as the West India Company's head of the colony. It was a brief, formal meeting. Then Van der Donck was off again, headed north, one hundred and fifty miles upriver, to the remote settlement that was to be his new home.

There were maybe a hundred residents in the colony of Rensselaerswyck at the time. The few homes, barns, and other signs of human habitation were dwarfed by the staggering expanses of wilderness: the smoking, brooding mountains to the north, the stands of high pine trees, the broad river, and the endless sky. Van der Donck met a man about his own age named Arent van Curler, a nephew of Kiliaen van Rensselaer, who had been in the colony for three years and was its manager. Then he made for the small wooded island just off the western shore of the river and close to Fort Orange, which had been partially cleared for farms. He had decided to make one of these his home. Soon after, a surreal version of the classic Wild West scenario played out when, rested and ready for work, high on the thrill of adventure and still buzzing from the foreignness of it all, Van der Donck emerged from his rough, thatch-roofed dwelling into the bright August morning, and, wearing "a silver-plated rapier with baldric and a black hat with plume," the badges of his office, exhibited himself for the farmers, blacksmiths, wheelwrights, and bakers of his domain, as well as for the assorted Mohawks, Mahicans, and West India Company soldiers. As he strode purposefully up the road that ran along the river, past the palisades of Fort Orange and by the fields and workshops of the colony, the residents must have gaped. Here before them in one trim, gallant, and beplumed package was the cutting-edge quintessence of European education, circa 1640, the product of a legal system centuries old, tempered by modern notions that in one form or another, compliments of Galileo, Descartes, and Grotius, placed man at the center of things. Here was one of the Republic's best and brightest. They had a lawman.

Chapter 6

THE COUNCIL OF BLOOD

By an odd twist of fate, the tragedy that would engulf the Manhattan-based colony of New Netherland, crippling it and ensuring that it would eventually lose its struggle against its English neighbors, was also the event that brought its residents together and preserved the colony's legacy for future centuries. Fate further arranged it that the nightmare would descend in the same month that Adriaen van der Donck, the man who would lead the political struggle that would preserve that legacy, arrived to seek his fortune in the New World.

The disaster came just when things were looking most hopeful for the residents of New Amsterdam and their comrades scattered across the several hundred miles of North Atlantic coast that comprised the province. With trade thrown open, new residents were pouring in, a merchant elite was forming, families were intermarrying, putting down roots. It began with what seemed a random, minor event.

Everyone on Manhattan knew Claes Swits. He was a garrulous old man, a wheelwright by trade, who had made the voyage to the New World with his wife and two grown sons. Before boarding their ship, they had put up at the Amsterdam inn of Peter de Winter, the same establishment where Griet Reyniers had worked as barmaid and prostitute before setting her sights on Manhattan. The inn was a favorite haunt of travelers from Germany; as Swits's surname suggests, he had probably originally come from Switzerland. Like everyone else on Manhattan, he became engaged in several different occupations once he arrived. He leased a two-hundred-acre plantation, called Otterspoor, covering much of what would become Harlem, on which he grew grain and milked cows (as rent he agreed to pay the owner, Jacob van

110

Curler, annually, two hundred pounds of butter and "the just half of all the grain with which God shall bless the field"). Soon after—perhaps finding that the work was too much for a man of his years—he took on a partner. Even then, Claes didn't spend much time on the farm; he was too old, or maybe he just hungered for human contact. He bought a small piece of property on the Wickquasgeck trail, at about what is today Forty-seventh Street and Second Avenue, built a house there, and set up as a jack-of-all-trades. The trail—which diverged from what would become Broadway at about Twenty-third Street and ran up the east side, before reconnecting with it in the north of the island—was alive with traffic now: Indians of the Wickquasgeck tribe's several villages, as well as members of other tribes from farther north and across the river on Long Island, streaming to and from New Amsterdam; Europeans and Africans moving along it as their farms reached up Manhattan. The territory of New Netherland remained vast and wild, but the island at its center was rapidly succumbing to settlement. There was a place here on its east side, the old man figured, for a traveler's rest.

His house on Deutel Bay* became a popular gathering spot, where people could cluster before a homey fire of an evening, drink and sing, curse and argue, maybe step out into the semi-wilderness night and gaze at the moonlight on the C-shaped bay. It was here that Nan Beech, wife of the Englishman Thomas Beech, had "fumbled at the front of the breeches of most all of those who were present," touching off a skirmish. On another occasion, Ulrich Lupoldt, a West India company official, while drinking at Claes's house, got into a shouting match with Jan Evertsen Bout, who lived across the North River, over rumors that Bout was having his way with a certain "black wench." Claes seems to have been close friends with or related by marriage to young Harmen Myndersz van den Bogaert, who had made the journey into Mohawk country in the winter of 1634 to renegotiate fur prices; Van den Bogaert frequented the man's tavern-home, and underwrote his loans.

The wheelwright was, by several accounts, a harmless and well-liked old man. He knew many Indians by name. It wouldn't have surprised him in the least, one day in August of 1641, precisely as Adriaen van der Donck was set-

---

*The "turtle" in Turtle Bay—the neighborhood that occupies that area—is a corruption of the Dutch word *deutel*, or *dowel;* the bay—long since filled in—was so named because of its shape.

tling into his duties as *schout* of Rensselaerswyck, to find a twenty-seven-year-old Wickquasgeck Indian at his door with a few furs slung over his shoulder, who said he was interested in trading them for some duffel cloth. Claes knew the young man: he lived in a village to the northeast of the island, and had worked for a time for Claes's son. The wheelwright invited him in out of the August sun, gave him something to eat and drink. And as the old man bent over the chest in which he kept his goods for trade, the young Wickquasgeck—who is unnamed in the records, which is unfortunate since he was at the center of what would become a major event in the life of the colony—in a seemingly unpremeditated act, reached for an ax that Claes Swits had leaning against the wall, raised it high, and cut off the old man's head. Then he left.

As random as the murder was, there was an inevitability to it. The Indian had no quarrel with Swits. But fifteen years before, in 1626, around the time that Peter Minuit had purchased the island, a small group of Wickquasgeck Indians who had ventured south to trade furs were set upon by some Europeans, robbed, and murdered—all except a twelve-year-old boy, who had escaped. For fifteen years he had nursed his revenge, as the Europeans increased in numbers and spread out slowly over the island, and then it erupted, perhaps surprising even him.

The murder on the Wickquasgeck road was thus an element in the clockwork regularity of movement that governs culture clashes: an event triggers another, across space and time, which leads to greater, bloodier reprisals. The killing of Claes Swits echoed. It echoed, first and most consequentially, in the brain of Willem Kieft. Sweltering in his office in Fort Amsterdam, where he had recently greeted Van der Donck and wished well in his new position up north, the forty-four-year-old director of the colony reacted to the grim news with something like exhilaration. It was an odd reaction, but he was an odd man. He had been born and raised in Amsterdam, the son of a merchant and a politician's daughter. He had excellent family connections—Rembrandt featured his cousin, Willem van Ruytenburch, in *The Night Watch* (that's him, right of center, in the dashing yellow ensemble and holding his scabbard). But Kieft was something of a black sheep. He had pursued a business opportunity in France, and had failed at it so decisively, with such financial loss to its backers, that a picture of him was tacked over the gallows in the town of La Rochelle, and he was forced to flee. Fantastically enough, he then wound up somewhere in the Ottoman Empire, given the task of ransoming Christians who had been taken prisoner by the Sultan. But, according to a pamphlet published in Antwerp attacking his administration, Kieft turned it into a for-profit venture by buying the release only of those captives who had the smallest price on their heads, leaving the others to languish in Turkish jails, and keeping the balance of the money.

Perhaps it was this cleverness that recommended him to the directors of the West India Company as the right man to replace the hapless Wouter Van Twiller. More likely, it was family connections. He had arrived in 1638, when the province was in disorder, determined to exert the iron authority he believed was necessary to turn the settlement around—never mind that it began turning itself around shortly after his arrival, thanks to the advent of free trade. In fact, his whole problem—the problem of all the colony's directors throughout its lifetime—was the impossibility of the situation. Dutch global expansion during its century of empire was built around not settlement colonies but outposts, which explains why, even though the empire extended as far afield as India, Taiwan, and Java, the Dutch language is not spread around the globe the way English is. The English as overlords either planted settlements or, as in India, imposed elements of their own culture on a society. The Dutch preferred to set up military-trading posts at strategic spots and let the locals bring trade goods to them. The trading companies did not see themselves in the business of establishing permanent colonies.

But New Netherland refused to remain a trading post. It was unique among the way stations of the Dutch empire in that it insisted on becoming a *place*. By some estimates it had, by its end, attracted more settlers from the Dutch Republic than all of the other Dutch outposts combined. Its population wasn't wholly comprised of soldiers and company employees, but ordinary settlers as well, who liked what they found and were hoping to stay. It had streets and buildings, but beyond that, by the 1640s it had developed a style, a way of getting by, which certainly had something to do with the company that ran it but had more to do with the likes of Claes Swits, Govert Loockermans, Joris Rapalje, Catalina Trico, Griet Reyniers, and Anthony "The Turk" van Salee—people who operated around the company, not within it.

The place had a life of its own. And with that came, naturally, a need for political structure. As it was, there was no judicial system; or rather, the system was Kieft. There was no body of case law; he settled disputes however he chose. There was no appeal. Kieft and the other directors of the colony weren't given a mandate to oversee the establishment of a political and legal system; instead, the company shipped them off with a single tool: military dictatorship. It was an effective tool in the sorts of situations in which they found themselves in outposts like Batavia and Macassar, but a hindrance in what was fast becoming a full-fledged society.

But they were very slow to understand the distinction, slow to comprehend that the situation on Manhattan Island was fundamentally different from that on other exotic outposts. None of the series of West India Company employees who headed the New Netherland operation ever truly did comprehend it—except the last of them, and by the time he did it was far too late for the Dutch.

Kieft never understood it at all. He was not a politician. He arrived with a directive to turn around a failing corporate venture, and he was armed with one arrow in his quiver: total fiat, the power of life and death. Those within his jurisdiction were not constituents but subjects, serfs. It was an accepted business model in the seventeenth century. In most situations in which the East and West India Companies found themselves, it worked.

Kieft did make an initial try at satisfying the natural need among his populace to feel that they were in some way involved in the company's decision making. He appointed a council of advisors to assist him. The council consisted of two members. One was Johannes la Montagne, a benign Walloon medical doctor who was well liked and no threat to anyone, including Kieft; as a bonus, he was in debt to the company and so unlikely to go against it. The other councilor was Kieft himself. Kieft further decided that, as director, he would have two votes on the council, and La Montagne would have one vote. Decisions were made by majority rule. Thus Kieft's nod to representative government.

The next order of business was to deal with an immediate outside threat, which came from one of Kieft's predecessors. Peter Minuit, with his Swedish settlement force, had anchored at his chosen spot on a tributary of what the Dutch called the South River in the middle of March 1638, or about two weeks before Kieft stepped ashore on Manhattan. Minuit had calculated the placement of his colony with great deftness. He knew the area (today the Delaware River and lands astride it, encompassing parts of Maryland, Delaware, New Jersey, and Pennsylvania) well, and, more to the point, he had an exquisite appreciation of the claims of the Dutch and English in that part of the continent. He knew that the English still held to their right-of-first-discovery claim, by which, in their eyes, the entire coastline—indeed, the entire continent—was theirs. Practically speaking, however, the English colony of Virginia was well to the south, and thus Minuit hoped to avoid detection by them until his settlement had established itself.

As to the Dutch, while the South River territory fell under their claim by means of Hudson's voyage, Minuit knew that the West India Company had been spotty in following up on the claim by buying lands along the South River from the Indian tribes that occupied them. He knew what had been purchased and what had not; specifically, the Dutch had bought title to lands along the eastern shore of the South River (i.e., New Jersey) but not the western shore. Immediately upon landing, then, Minuit gathered the tribal chiefs of the area, held a conclave in the cabin of his flag ship, the *Kalmar Nyckel,* and got them to make their marks on a deed. The point was not, of course, to satisfy tribal notions of land ownership, nor did the Swedish government care much about executing legal transactions with natives. Minuit had his eyes on the Dutch; he wanted to forestall any legal arguments they might make by employing their own system of property transfer. Using the skills he had learned in the service of the Dutch, he purchased the land on the west side of the river, below the branching river the Dutch named the Schuylkill—i.e., the future states of Delaware and Maryland and the corner of Pennsylvania that would become Philadelphia—on behalf of the twelve-year-old Queen Christina of Sweden.

A month later, soldiers at the lone Dutch outpost on the South River spotted Minuit's ship and sent a report to Manhattan, which must have infuriated Kieft. This was a military and diplomatic challenge to Dutch sovereignty by a nation that was supposed to be an ally. And Minuit's role at the center of it must have particularly roiled him. Kieft wasted no time, but sent a communiqué aimed directly at the man who had once held his job. In May, a Dutch vessel sailed down the coast, between the capes that to this day preserve the names—Henlopen and May—given them in the Dutch period, into the bay, up the South River, into the tributary called the Minquas Kill, and made anchor before the rocky outcrop behind which Minuit's men were sweating in the spring air, digging out the perimeter of their fort. A soldier disembarked and handed a letter to the leader of New Sweden:

I, Willem Kieft, Director-General of New-Netherland, residing on the Island of the Manhattes and in Fort Amsterdam, under the authority of their High Mightinesses the Lords States-General of the United Netherlands and the Incorporated West-India Company, Chamber at Amsterdam, make known to you Peter Minuit, who style yourself Commander in the service of Her Royal Majesty of Sweden, that the whole Southriver of New-Netherland has been many years in our possession and secured by us above and below by forts and sealed with our blood, which even happened during your administration of New-Netherland and is well known to you. Now, as you intrude between our forts and begin to build a fort there to our disadvantage and prejudice, which shall never be suffered by us and we are very certain, that her Royal Majesty of Sweden has not given you any order to build fortresses on our rivers or along our coasts, Therefore, in case you proceed with the erection of fortifications and cultivation of the soil and trade in peltries or in any wise attempt to do us injury, We do hereby protest against all damages, expenses and losses, together with all mishaps, bloodsheds and disturbances, which may arise in future time therefrom and that we shall maintain our jurisdiction in such manner, as we shall deem most expedient.

Since the notice did not overtly promise a military attack, Minuit ignored it: from the beginning he had staked the venture on his belief that New Netherland would have too few soldiers to cover its territory. He finished the construction of Fort Christina, then, leaving the fort garrisoned by twenty-five men, sailed off, full of hope and dash, for Stockholm, where he intended to put together the next expedition for the New World. This one would be comprised not of soldiers but of colonists. By now Minuit's plan had expanded. He intended to gather not only Swedish Adams and Eves but also refugees from his native Rhine region whom he believed would leap at the opportunity to escape two decades of war and start a new life on new soil. Having worked so hard and diligently in his first effort as colonizer, only to see it taken away from him, had sharpened his ambition, refined it. He wasn't out for adventure any longer. He was a utopian now: he wanted to build a new society.

But Minuit never made it back to Europe. His dream died when he died, in August of 1638, in a hurricane in the Caribbean, where he had sailed to obtain a shipment of tobacco for resale in Europe. Minuit's determination and seventeenth-century-style frontier spirit would, however, have a second legacy in addition to that of Manhattan Island. The little garrison he had left behind at Fort Christina would serve as the base for what, over the course of the next seventeen years, would become a sizable Swedish colony, extending a hundred miles up the Delaware River valley and encompassing the future cities of Philadelphia and Trenton. Out of Minuit's efforts to exploit this rich, wild valley—and, eventually, the Dutch determination to expel the intruding colony—the queer, little-known sidebar to history called New Sweden would make surprising contributions to history.

As Minuit had guessed, Willem Kieft opted for the time being not to mount a serious challenge to the Swedes on his southern flank. For one thing, he had a financial crisis on his hands. The opening of trade resulted in an instantaneous boost for the people of New Netherland, but the West India Company didn't benefit. As the directors in Amsterdam saw it, they had given up the monopoly that might ensure them eventual profits, yet were saddled with administering the colony and protecting its inhabitants. The various agreements they had made with the Indians in their territory required the company to protect them, too, in the case of attack by an enemy tribe. The merchant princes put pressure on their in-country director to find a way out of this quandary.

Kieft tried. First he tackled the blossoming currency crisis. Florins, doubloons, pennies, pieces of eight, schellings, reals, stooters, daelders, oortjes, Brabant stuivers, Carolus guilders, and Flemish pounds all rattled in the tills of New Amsterdam's taverns and jangled in the purses of townspeople: the sort of currency chaos that accompanies a highly laissez-faire, free-trade economy. And coins weren't even the main means of transacting business. Pelts were offered for everything from a glass of French brandy to a town lot. But the major currency, the most common thing dropped into the plate when it came time for contributions during Sunday church service, was sewant. Wampum, as it is now more commonly known, was a much more widely used currency among the East Coast Indians than is generally realized today. For tribes from different linguistic groups, it formed a kind of universal language, a way to cap joint rituals, to seal treaties, pay homage to dignitaries. The very first Dutch traders to follow in Henry Hudson's wake seized on this medium of exchange and expanded it. They learned which variety of polished beads was most highly prized—that of a purple clamshell that came from the easternmost shores of Long Island—and not only adopted it in their dealings with Indians but became wampum speculators among tribes. With the sudden increase in freelance trade on Manhattan had come a flood of low-grade sewant, and Kieft understood that the accompanying confusion was causing financial havoc. Therefore, on one of the regular Thursday "council sessions" in which he and Dr. La Montagne sat, he issued a directive:

> Whereas at present very bad seawan is in circulation here and payments are
> made in nothing but dirty, unpolished stuff that is brought here from other
> regions where it is worth 50 percent less than here, and the good, polished
> seawan, ordinarily called Manhattan seawan, is exported and wholly disap-
> pears, which tends to the decided ruin and destruction of this country;
> therefore, in order to provide against this in time, we do hereby for the
> public good, interdict and forbid all persons, of whatever state, quality or
> condition they may be, during the coming month of May to receive or give
> out in payment any unpolished seawan except at the rate of five for one
> stiver, that is to say, strung, and thereafter six beads for one stiver. Whoever
> shall be found to have acted contrary thereto shall provisionally forfeit the
> seawan paid out by him and ten guilders to the poor, the same applying to
> the receiver as well as to the giver. The price of the well polished seawan
> shall remain as before, to wit, four beads for one stiver, provided it be
> strung.

Next, Kieft turned his attention to the Indian question. The company did indeed, at considerable expense, supply Fort Amsterdam, Fort Orange, and Fort Nassau on the South River with soldiers, who were there to protect the company's interests and servants, and who were obliged by the land treaties entered into with Indian tribes to offer protection to them as well. Since the company couldn't back out of this arrangement, Kieft hit on what he thought quite a clever notion: to ask the Indians to pay taxes for the service rendered. The idea was too rich to be denied. Thursday came around, and Kieft opened the council meeting with his directive:

Whereas the Company is put to great expense both in building fortifications and in supporting soldiers and sailors, we have therefore resolved to demand from the Indians who dwell around here and whom heretofore we have protected against their enemies, some contributions in the form of skins, maize and seawan, and if there be any nation which is not in a friendly way disposed to make such contribution it shall be urged to do so in the most suitable manner.

The residents who had been on the scene long enough to know the tribal groups in the region of New Amsterdam—the Tappans, the Hackinsacks, the Wickquasgecks, the Raritans—reacted with alarm, telling Kieft this was more or less exactly what not to do. The Indians, these residents knew, were far from simple in their understanding of the real estate transactions they had made with the Europeans. The armful of goods mentioned in each title transfer was not, in their eyes, an outright purchase price, but a token that represented the arrangement to which they were agreeing. That arrangement had them sharing the land with the "purchaser," and at the same time entering into a defensive alliance.

But while some of the European residents of the colony had surprisingly nuanced views of the natives who lived among them (an example from Van der Donck's writings: "their womenfolk have an attractive grace about them . . . and if they were instructed as our women are they would no doubt differ little from them, if at all"), Kieft was not one of these. The sum of his actions and writings shows him, in fact, as more or less set on a strategy of eventual extermination. After being rebuffed, even laughed at, by several chiefs over his demand of protection payments, he seized on a small matter—the theft of some hogs from a Dutch farm on Staten Island—as the excuse for a punitive expedition. Even without knowing the history one can almost see the chain of events unfolding from there. First there were the ironies: the thieves had apparently not been Indians at all but Dutchmen; the farm belonged to David de Vries, the trader who had tried to shame Van Twiller into behaving like a leader, who was friends with many Indians, spoke several of their dialects, and who, in dinners with Kieft at his quarters in Fort Amsterdam, tried to stop what was coming. "These savages resemble the Italians," De Vries warned, "being very revengeful."

But Kieft was inexorable. He sent a posse to the Raritan village that his information told him was the home of the thieves; several Indians were killed. On cue, then, the Raritans attacked De Vries's farm, killing four farm hands and burning down the man's house. Kieft then took his turn. He would not, he decided, be drawn into war, but rather would adopt the classic strategy of pitting his enemies against one another. Thursday came (it happened to be the fourth of July), and he delivered his edict in council:

> Whereas the Indians of the Raretangh are daily exhibiting more and more hostility . . . we have therefore considered it most expedient and advisable to induce the Indians, our allies hereabout, to take up arms . . . and in order to encourage them the more we have promised them ten fathoms of seawan for each head, and if they succeed in capturing any of the Indians who have most barbarously murdered our people on Staten Island we have promised them 20 fathoms of seawan for each head.

The offer of bribery yielded fast results. Shortly after the edict was posted, an Indian named Pacham, of a tribe that had had testy relations with the Raritans, strolled past the guardhouse and into Fort Amsterdam holding aloft—with what he presumably felt was appropriate ceremony and pride—a human hand dangling from a stick. On being admitted with his trophy into Kieft's presence, he declared that it belonged to the Raritan chief who had ordered the attack on De Vries's farm.

Kieft was mollified. He felt pleased that his plan had succeeded, and vindicated in the character of leadership he was providing. "All men are created equal" was a sentiment off in the future; in the seventeenth century, as in those before, the different races, religions, and genders were seen by one and all as occupying different rungs on the chain of being. To a mind like Kieft's—not especially distinguishable from that of Captain John Mason, who had led the English massacre of the Pequots in Connecticut four years earlier, or Nathaniel Bacon, the Jamestown colony's advocate of Indian extermination—the wild peoples of the world, on whatever continent they lived, understood power, and in the face of it they would assume their naturally subordinant rank. The Raritans showed no signs of retaliating, which proved the point.

The whole business might have ended there. But then, without immediate connection to these events, though perhaps subconsciously kindled by them, the unnamed Wickquasgeck Indian chose this moment to seek vengeance for his uncle's long-ago murder. Claes Swits's old head had barely hit the floor of his Deutel Bay home before Willem Kieft was launched on a full-scale retaliation. The natives had now shown that they could never be trusted; extermination was the only solution.

Waging war requires politicking, and Kieft moved first to gain popular support for his effort against the tribes of the area by asking that the residents nominate a council of twelve men who would assist him in deciding on a course of action. He deserves some credit for bringing into being the first popularly chosen body in what would become New York State, one of the first in the New World, though he had no notion of how this move would backfire on him. The twelve assembled themselves, and chose David de Vries as their president. Also on the council was Joris Rapalje, who, with his wife, Catalina Trico, had stuck it out in the colony, moving from youth into middle age, and had recently begun to prosper. Kieft asked the assembly three questions, which, helpfully, he numbered for them:

1. Whether it is not just to punish the barbarous murder of Claes Swits committed by an Indian and, in case the Indians refuse to surrender the murderer at our request, whether it is not justifiable to ruin the entire village to which he belongs?
2. In what manner the same ought to be put into effect and at what time?
3. By whom it may be undertaken?

To Kieft's annoyance, the twelve did not council war. They agreed that "by all means the murderer according to the proposition of the honorable director should be punished," but insisted that "two or three times more a sloop be sent by the honorable director to make a friendly request without threats, for the surrender of the murderer . . ." The twelve councilors knew they had no power, so they tried to lay roadblocks in the path of their willful leader. In the event that all-out conflict with the tribes should be called for, they declared, in what seemed a patent stalling tactic, that the colony should first send for two hundred coats of mail from the home country. Also, since by this time Kieft was developing a reputation for, as David de Vries wrote, calling for war while "being himself protected in a good fort, out of which he had not slept a single night during all the years he had been there," the council added a gentle stipulation that in the event of any military expedition "whereas we acknowledge no other commander than the director . . . therefore . . . the honorable director shall personally lead this expedition . . ."

Kieft had made it plain that the council was to be a rubber-stamp body; he was furious at its willfulness, and decided to try again, this time communing with each representative separately, in the belief that removing the security of the group would cause the simple farmers and tradesmen to give their approval to his plan. But while sailor Jacob Waltingen said he was "ready to do whatever the director and council may order," and Jacques Bentyn, a West India Company official, gave Kieft a thoroughly satisfactory reply that "it will be best to kill the Indians so as to fill them with fear," the majority still wanted to take matters slowly and pursue a course of seeking justice for the specific wrong that was done.

To add to Kieft's annoyance, the council of twelve, having failed to give the endorsement it was assembled to provide, then took it upon itself to begin advising the director on other matters. The councilors wanted certain rights for individuals, "according to the custom in Holland." They wanted a prohibition on the sale of English cattle. Most of all, they wanted themselves, or some like body, to become a permanent representative assembly, as existed in even the smallest villages in the United Provinces. Kieft responded two weeks later with a firm reply in the form of a decree:

And whereas the Commonality at our request appointed and instructed these 12 men to communicate their good counsel and advice on the subject of the murder of the late Claes Cornelissen Swits, which was committed by the Indians; this being now completed by them, we do hereby thank them for the trouble they have taken, and shall, with God's help, make use of their rendered written advice in its own time. The said Twelve men shall now, henceforth hold no further meeting, as the same tends to a dangerous consequence, and to the great injury both of the country and of our authority. We therefore, hereby forbid them calling any manner of assemblage or meeting, except by our express order, on pain of being punished as disobedient subjects. Done in fort Amsterdam, this eighth of February, 1642, in New Netherland.

The attempt at winning popular support for his military action having backfired, Kieft went ahead anyway, ordering West India Company soldiers to attack Indian villages. So began what became known as Kieft's War, a series of murderous attacks and counterattacks that would continue for several years. The ugliest assault came on the night of February 25, 1643. David de Vries had once again stayed at the director's home inside Fort Amsterdam, where he sat across the dinner table from Kieft and tried to argue him out of the attack. Kieft stated that he "had a mind to wipe the mouths of the savages," to which De Vries replied that Kieft had no right to act on his own, that "such work could not be done without the approbation of the Twelve Men; that it could not take place without my assent, who was one of the Twelve Men . . . that he should consider what profit he could derive from this business . . . But it appeared that my speaking was of no avail. He had, with his co-murderers, determined to commit the murder, deeming it a Roman deed, and to do it without warning the inhabitants in the open lands, that each one might take care of himself against the retaliation of the natives, for he could not kill all the Indians."

The two men had now finished their meal. Kieft did not reply directly, but told De Vries to go into the new great hall he had had built in the fort. There, De Vries found the soldiers massed for their attack. Two parties were formed: one to march two miles to the northwest to launch a raid on a small group of Indians camped at Corlaer's Hook (today the Lower East Side of Manhattan), the other to cross the river and attack a larger group camped in the area of the plantation called Pavonia, at what is now Jersey City, New Jersey.

De Vries found the business disgusting. These Indians, of the Wickquasgeck and Tappan tribes, had come to the Dutch seeking sanctuary from Mohawks farther north, to whom they were behind on tribute payments and who had therefore attacked them in their villages. "Let this work alone," De Vries said to Kieft. "You will also murder our own nation, for there are none of the settlers in the open country who are aware of it." But the soldiers went off on their missions. De Vries stayed in the director's quarters that night, sitting up all night by the kitchen hearth, watching the blaze, and waiting. Around midnight, "I heard a great shrieking, and I ran to the ramparts of the fort, and looked over to Pavonia. Saw nothing but firing, and heard the shrieks of the natives murdered in their sleep." Shortly after, an Indian couple, whom De Vries knew, appeared inexplicably inside the fort. They had managed to flee the massacre, which in the confusion they thought was being done by Mohawks. De Vries told them it was Dutchmen who were annihilating their makeshift village, and that Fort Amsterdam was the last place they should come for refuge. He helped them escape into the woods. In the morning, De Vries heard the returned soldiers boasting that they had "massacred or murdered eighty Indians, and considering they had done a deed of Roman valor, in murdering so many in their sleep."

De Vries then repeated in his journal an account of the massacre that later appeared in a pamphlet published in the Dutch Republic, written by anonymous inhabitants of the colony in hopes of stirring their countrymen to the abuse of power taking place in the North American colony: "[I]nfants were torn from their mother's breasts, and hacked to pieces in the presence of their parents, and the pieces thrown into the fire and in the water, and other sucklings, being bound to small boards, were cut, stuck, and pierced, and miserably massacred in a manner to move a heart of stone. Some were thrown into the river, and when the fathers and mothers endeavored to save them, the soldiers would not let them come on land but made both parents and children drown. . . . Some came to our people in the country with their hands, some with their legs cut off, and some holding their entrails in their arms, and others had such horrible cuts and gashes, that worse than they were could never happen. And these poor simple creatures, as also many of our own people, did not know any better than that they had been attacked by a party of other Indians—the Maquas. After this exploit, the soldiers were rewarded for their services, and Director Kieft thanked them by taking them by the hand and congratulating them."

The pamphlet that De Vries copied, called "Broad Advice," probably exaggerated the horrors, but its exaggerations help make the point that the colonists opposed the war against the Indians, and, in fact, were so shocked by the folly and danger of living at the whim of one man that it spurred them to press for some form of representative government. Kieft's War is fairly named. Kieft overrode the vast majority of the residents, and what is striking is that both his hard line and their instincts toward moderation fit with the times. The Dutch were constructing an empire—by definition an ugly business. Over the course of the century the Dutch trading companies, their directors, and soldiers proved themselves as bloody and inexorable as their

English, Spanish, and Portuguese counterparts. Kieft was not very different from Dutch administrators in Malacca or Macassar, the English East India Company directors in Calcutta and Madras, or the Portuguese rulers of Goa.

But the colonists who opposed bloodshed were also acting true to type. It was no innate goodness that motivated them, but a practical wisdom won over decades of strife in the Dutch provinces. In both De Vries's journal and the anti-Kieft pamphlet, the passage describing the horrors of the Pavonia attack is followed by a sentence that must have echoed in the minds of many of the colonists: "Did the Duke of Alva in the Netherlands ever do anything more cruel?" Seventy years before, with rebellion against Spanish rule simmering in the Low Countries, the Spanish regent had sent Fernando Álvarez de Toledo, the notorious Duke of Alva, to quell it and reform heretics—that is to say, Protestants. The duke went on an Inquisitional rampage of torture and murder that became known as the Council of Blood, which involved decapitating rebellious nobles and slaughtering commoners in the hundreds.

The Council of Blood became ingrained in the national psyche; it helped vault the Dutch states toward an open war of rebellion. It also reinforced the notion of tolerance as a part of what it meant to be Dutch. This had been building for some time and would continue through the seventeenth century, as more and more people from other parts of Europe came to live in the Dutch provinces. In fact, it's something of a misnomer to think of "Dutch" in this era as an ethnic signifier. The Dutch provinces in the seventeenth century were the melting pot of Europe. As English, French, German, Swedish, and Jewish immigrants came and settled, they adopted the language, "Batavianized" their names (e.g., Bridges became Van Brugge), and, in time, adopted a basic framework for looking at the world one of the main features of which was the need to accommodate others. As the "Dutch" emigrated to their New World colony, then, they brought with them not only a ready-made mix of cultures but a tolerance of differences, the prescription for a multicultural society. In its very seeding, Manhattan was a melting pot.

We should be clear, however, about the meaning of tolerance, which had nothing to do with "celebrating diversity"—a concept that would have been seen as sheer loopiness in the seventeenth century. "Putting up with" was probably closer to the mark. If that sounds wan, consider that in Germany at the time an estimated forty percent of the population died due to the unholy enmeshment of religious intolerance and politics that gave rise to the Thirty Years' War (in the city of Magdeburg alone, thirty thousand were killed in a single day). In the United Provinces, meanwhile, tolerance had developed into a cultural trait. Dutch writers openly acknowledged that knowing how to get along, fit in, accommodate, was good for business. Foreign tourists in the provinces constantly noted it, and usually found it odd, a destabilizing force, a symptom of moral laxity. As they expanded, however, the Dutch put it to use, and it revealed itself in the most mundane ways.

The ruthlessness of Kieft and other merchant warriors masks the fact that the farmers and traders who made up the colony learned Indian languages, adopted Indian farming techniques, embraced the wampum trade, and, for a time and in a great many ways, tried to coexist. Kieft's own council of blood thus led to a reaction on the part of the Manhattanites that came straight from their experiences in Europe. Colonists bemoaned the war on the most practical grounds: they were vastly outnumbered by the Indians, and what was more, the Dutch were not trappers; the fur trade, their whole reason for being here, depended on the Indians. It made better sense to get along than to fight.

Even as the attacks, counterattacks, and colonists' complaints escalated, the settlers tried to maintain their way of life. Thomas Chambers signed a contract to build a house for Jan Schepmoes. Skipper Willem Dircksen agreed to ship cargo for John Turner and Willem Holmers and deliver it safely "on the beach beyond high water, at the island of St. Christopher, in the Caribbees." Isaac Allerton filed a complaint against Anthony "The Turk" van Salee. John and Richard Ogden, of Stamford, Connecticut, contracted to build a stone church for the company within the walls of Fort Amsterdam. The company finished building a stone tavern and inn at the spot along Pearl Street where arriving sailors and passengers disembarked. Jeuriaen Hendricksz filed a complaint against Anthony "The Turk" van Salee. Jan Haes called Nicolaes Tenner "a rogue and a double rogue," and Tenner took him to court for slander. Harmen van den Bogaert, who had made the daring winter journey into Mohawk country several years earlier, received the unfortunate Claes Swits's property, having been named in the old man's will, and in turn sold it to James Smith and William Brown. Van den Bogaert later testified, along with Claes's son Adriaen and another man, that they had gotten beer at the tavern of Jan Snediger three times, the first time it was "one pint short in hardly three pints, the second time it was found to be scarcely wine measure, the third time it was found to be a gill short in three pints." Andries Hudde filed a complaint against Anthony "The Turk" van Salee. Catalina Trico and her daughter Sara testified in a custody case that the promiscuous Nan Beech had told them that "Mr. Smith" had fathered the child she was carrying. Hendrick Jansen sold Willem Adriaensen his "garden dwelling and brewhouse." Pierre Pia and Jean St. Germain testified, in the case of a shot hog, that they had seen an Englishman with a gun in the vicinity a short time before. Cornelis Hooglandt sold to Willem Tomassen his house across the river on Long Island, together with the right to operate the ferry that had recently gone into regular service to bring Manhattanites to their farmland in what was already being called Breuckelen.

But the trouble was inescapable. Kieft's action had brought about something that heretofore had been unachievable: the unification of area tribes into a confederation, one aimed at slaughtering Europeans. Attacks came without warning, in the deep of night, with a whispering hail of arrows and explosions from the muskets sold to the Indians by traders in the area around Rensselaerswyck. The plantation at Achter Col (today Newark, New Jersey) was reduced to burning heaps. Budding communities on Long Island were decimated. Small groups of Indians made sudden strikes on the outlying farms on Manhattan, hacking cattle, burning crops, killing anyone with a white face, sometimes dragging women and children away into captivity, and forcing residents to seek the safety of the fort.

In a matter of months over the course of 1642 and 1643, years of brutally hard labor—clearing and tilling fields, building by hand the mills that would saw the timber with which they then constructed successively more comfortable homes—were erased. Families huddled in hastily constructed straw huts inside the walls of the fort. Fort Amsterdam occupied approximately the position where the Old Customs House stands today. Standing outside that fortress-like building, it is surprisingly easy to summon the image of those men, women, and children, through the relentless winter months of 1643 and on into the cold spring, gathered inside the walls, here at the extreme southern rim of the island that had been their home, that had, for a time, seemed to offer itself to them, to beckon them to stay, prosper, root their families, and that now seemed ready to tip them into the bay. Refugees in their own homeland now, they huddled in the open courtyard, exposed, at the mercy of their several gods, wondering what would happen to them, but not wondering who to blame.

Chapter 7

THE CAUSE

Far to the north, meanwhile, the air still had its glorious native sweetness, complicated by pine needles and grape blossoms and lacking the dark pungency of burned homesteads. Adriaen van der Donck, the young man from Breda who had lived all of his twenty-two-odd years within a few dozen square miles of flat country that had long since been divided, channeled, poldered, and tamed by humans, spent his first months in his new land entranced by the rawness and bigness of its nature, and blissfully cut off from the horrors farther south. The mountains to the north of the colony of Rensselaerswyck loomed like a dreamscape. To one coming from a place where wood was precious, the forest beggared the imagination—"so much so," Van der Donck wrote, "that practically the whole country is covered with it, and in a manner of speaking, there is too much of it for us, and it's in our way." The river on which his small house sat was a quarter-mile broad, and yet the winters were of such ferocity that the entire expanse typically froze over every December, leaving the subjects of diamond merchant Kiliaen van Rensselaer cut off from Manhattan and points south, alone with the mountains and the snow-smothered pines, until spring.

Van der Donck decided that April and May were the finest months to explore the countryside. "The trees are then in bloom," he wrote, "and the woods are full of sweet smells. By mid-May, without fail, we have ripe strawberries, not in the gardens, because they are not planted there, but in the fields, where they grow naturally." But he found he loved autumn best in this new world: "Above the highlands, advancing northerly, the weather is colder, the fresh waters freeze, the stock is sheltered, the kitchens are provided, and all things are put in order for the winter. The fat oxen and swine are slaughtered. The wild geese, turkeys, and deer are at their best in this season, and easiest obtained." He observed the bears, "none like the gray and pale-haired bears of Muscovy and Greenland" but rather "of a shiny pitch black color," and with such an acute sense of smell that "the Indians when setting out to hunt bears . . . impart Esau's odor to their bodies and clothing, that is, they apply the scent of field and forest so that they will not be betrayed by a contrasting scent." He marveled at the "incredibly numerous" deer; he studied eagles, observed that they "soar very high in the air, beyond the vision of man" and can "strike a fish, and jerk it living from the waters." He stalked turkeys in the woods, shot quail by the dozens, admired thick populations of "woodcocks, birch-cocks, heath-fowls, pheasants, wood and water snipes." Like a good Dutchman, he made a special study of the winds of the New World—"the swift and fostering messengers of commerce."

He noted the contours of the land, the character of the soil in different regions, the native trees and fruits: "The mulberries are better and sweeter than ours, and ripen earlier." He counted "several kinds of plums, wild or small cherries, juniper, small kinds of apples, many hazelnuts, black currents, gooseberries, blue India figs, and strawberries in abundance all over the country, some of which ripen at half May, and we have them until July; blueberries, raspberries, black-caps, etc., with artichokes, ground-acorns, ground beans, wild onions, and leeks like ours . . ." He was intrigued by a local fruit he called "cicerullen, or water-lemons" (i.e., watermelon), which grew "the size of the stoutest Leyden cabbages," and that had "a light-textured pulp like a wet sponge in which the pips are embedded. When really ripe and sound, it melts away to a juice as soon as it enters the mouth, and nothing remains to spit out but the pips. . . . they are so refreshing and often served as a beverage."

He canvassed the gardeners, European and Indian, and, with a seventeenth-century intellectual's passion for the new scientific fad of analyzing and classifying, made an inventory of the wild herbs and edible plants for which European taxonomy had a name: "The plants which are known to us are the following, viz: Capilli veneris, scholopendria, angelica, polypodium, verbascum, album, calteus sacerdotis, atriplex hortensis and marina, chortium, turrites, calamus aromaticus, sassafras, rois Virginianum, ranunculus, plantago, bursa pastoris, malva, origaenum, geranicum, althea, cinoroton pseudo, daphine, viola, ireas, indigo silvestris, sigillum, salamonis, sanguis draconum, consolidae, millefolium, noli me tangere, cardo benedictus, agrimonium, serpentariae, coriander, leeks, wild leeks, Spanish figs, elatine, camperfolie, petum male and female, and many other plants."

Over the course of the next fourteen years, Van der Donck would create an impressive breadth of writing, nearly all of it on the topic of his new home, its inhabitants, both European and Indian, and its need for proper government. But what may be even more striking in his writing than his political skills or legal reasoning is the sheer exuberance that rises from the pages. The man simply fell in love with America. He saw its promise and its grandeur. He reveled in its rawness, and the opportunity it provided. Within a short time of his arrival his mind had skimmed far beyond the plodding mercantile thoughts of the West India Company officials who ran the New Netherland colony; he saw the continent not just as a source of exploitable materials but as a new home, a virgin base for the expansion of the civilization that had nurtured him. He understood that this was a land of incomprehensible vastness (even the Indians "know of no limits to the country" westward, he wrote, and "deem such enquiries to be strange and singular") into which a new society, an extension of Europe, could grow. He understood that it would need a framework of laws, a system of justice, and he was brazen enough to think he could help carve out such a system. That isn't to say he could have foreseen the New World colonies one day breaking free of their motherlands. He was a product of the seventeenth century, not the eighteenth. But he was, as his writings make plain, one of the first genuine Americans. He was so not because of where he came to live, but because of the expanse of opportunity that opened inside his breast once he arrived—opportunity he imagined not for himself alone but for others.

It's hard to say when that feeling took control of him. Probably in those first months when he wasn't reveling in the landscape he was focused on the practical execution of his work. For he had a job to do, and he threw himself into it with what his employer soon found to be inordinate zeal. From the moment he touched the soil of what he called "the New American World" Van der Donck seems to have been in constant motion. The first issue he faced was that of freelance, off-the-books trading taking place between Rensselaerswyck colonists and those of New Netherland and New England. Within days of his arrival in Rensselaerswyck, he stood in full Cavalier costume before the collected farmers and tradesmen of the colony and delivered his first ordinance, which must have stirred up the lot:

> We, Adriaen vander Donck, chief officer, with the commissioners and councilors of the colony of Rensselaerswyck, to all who shall see these or hear them read, greeting. As we see and notice daily the great strife, uproar, quarreling, yes what is more, mutual discord, all of which are causes that generally bring about the ruin of a well ordered community, springing solely from the trade which our inhabitants carry on with the foreign residents . . . have seen fit to order, enjoin, and command, as we do by these, all the inhabitants of the colony . . . that they shall not undertake to buy from or exchange with the residents any goods, or in any manner let them have any beavers, otters or other furs, directly or indirectly, upon fine and forfeiture for the first offense of three times the value of the goods first bought. . . . But, if any shallops or vessels of the Company or any one else come up the river and the inhabitants want to buy anything of which they are in great need, they shall ask permission of the Officer.

Whether or not Van der Donck realized it before leaving Amsterdam, it soon became clear that his duties were less concerned with administering justice for the welfare of a new society than with serving the profit interests of the patroon. Van Rensselaer may have been an ocean away, but through his voluminous instructions he showed himself an inexorable taskmaster unwaveringly focused on efficiency. Van der Donck was to devote himself to cracking down on a black market grain trade, hunting down those who had ventured away from the colony before doing their contracted time, and prosecuting residents who bought and sold beaver pelts on the sly. Van der Donck rode the valleys of the colony on horseback and sailed up and down the North River between Rensselaerswyck and Manhattan on Van Rensselaer's business. In November 1642, he was in New Amsterdam searching for a young woman who had skipped out on her service contract at Rensselaerswyck. When he found her, he discovered that she was pregnant and nearly ready to give birth. In court at Fort Amsterdam, he did his duty by "demanding" that she return to fulfill her obligation, but then struck a deal allowing the woman to stay put until she had delivered and her baby was old enough to travel. The old patroon didn't care to see flexibility in his lawman's personality. "It is your duty to seek my advantage and protect me against loss," he barked in a letter.

Already, even from faraway Amsterdam, Van Rensselaer could detect, through reports from various quarters, a dangerous willfulness on the part of his law officer, and he began to regret choosing Van der Donck. "What pleases me now in you is the zeal and diligence which I notice in your honor in expediting several matters," Van Rensselaer wrote early on, but these same qualities came with a downside. The young man took affairs into his own hands—settling disputes as he saw fit, deciding the colony needed a brickyard, working out improvements to the sawmill and gristmill, without consulting Van Rensselaer or Arent van Curler, the commercial officer of the colony and Van Rensselaer's grandnephew. When the patroon demanded that his law officer collect late payments from tenants, Van der Donck visited their shacks, saw that they had no money, and, rather than inform the patroon that he had not carried out his wishes, simply ignored the matter. Van Rensselaer's letters soon began to nag: "Your principal fault has been that you have wanted to prevail over Corler and that you have gone ahead too independently."

Van der Donck offended the patroon's business principles when he formally protested a direct order from Van Rensselaer that forced farmers in the colony to swear an oath of loyalty to him not only for themselves but on behalf of their servants. Van der Donck seems to have taken the position that the Middle Ages were over, that servants should be held responsible for their own behavior—a notion that Van Rensselaer considered "outrageous." From this point onward in his career, Van der Donck's personality rings out from the centuries-old pages of letters, court records, and other surviving documents of the period. It is a personality well suited to tackling a raw continent and helping to forge a viable new community: willful, righteous, insistent, arrogant, hot-tempered. It comes through in his private dealings: at one point someone takes him to court to accuse him of slander (the parties arranged an "amicable and a friendly" settlement); another time an argument with a Rensselaerswyck functionary escalated until the two men, as Van Curler later gossiped to the patroon, "pursued each other with swords," and ended with Van der Donck buffeting the man. Most of all, Van der Donck's headstrong nature is apparent in his relationship with his superior. It seems remarkable that, still in his early twenties, having traveled an ocean away from the only world he had known, he immediately set to defying his patron, a man universally feared and respected as a kind of latter-day medieval prince. "Most honorable, wise, powerful, and right discreet Lord" is how people addressed letters to Van Rensselaer. Van der Donck, by contrast, in his first act on arrival at Rensselaerswyck angered Van Rensselaer by rejecting the farm set aside for him and taking another, at the far end of the colony. He then chose one of the patroon's prized black stallions as his personal mount.

And he persisted in his defiance, as evidenced in the exasperated references to him that peppered Van Rensselaer's letters to other officials of his colony (in which he tended to underline names): "I take it very ill that Officer vanderdonck . . . ," "And as to vanderdonck . . . ," "These young people, like . . . vanderdonck, do not think at all of my interests . . . ," ". . . write me especially how vanderdonck behaves in the matter . . ." The relationship that Van der Donck developed with Van Rensselaer—at first insinuating himself as an upright, model-son figure with the older man, then proceeding, stridently, almost flamboyantly, to go against him—would replay itself, first with Willem Kieft in New Amsterdam, then again a few years later with another father-figure, this time with historic consequences. One can only wonder what his relationship with his real father was like.

At times Van Rensselaer seemed to suspect that his law officer held the interests of the colonists over his own. At other times he feared the young man would attempt something like a coup d'état. "From the beginning you have acted not as officer but as director," he complained at one point, and added sourly that if and when the time for a promotion came he wished "to have the honor of the advancement myself." Van Rensselaer's fear of the young man somehow trumping him seemed borne out by a tattletale report that Arent van Curler sent him in June 1643. Van der Donck had been spending a great deal of time in the Catskill Mountains to the west of the patroon's lands, and van Curler informed his uncle that "Your Honor may be assured he intends to look for partners to plant a colonie there."

Van der Donck had indeed been roaming the mountains. His all-consuming fascination with the New World had a focal point: the native inhabitants. The pitched battles and terrorist warfare taking place to the south was between the Europeans and the tribes of the Lower Hudson Valley, which were distinct from the Mohawks and Mahicans in the area around Rensselaerswyck. The mayhem did not reach this far north. Indians remained a constant presence at the trading post and among the homes and farms of the patroon's domain, and soon after his arrival Van der Donck took up with some of them and began venturing into their lands. In Europe a sizable literature had built up by this time about the American natives, and the Dutch in particular, who were eager to develop any arguments that showed their Spanish oppressors in a bad light, had focused on the plight of the Indians at the hands of the conquistadors. At universities such as Leiden, young men read descriptions in flowing Latin of natives who "go naked" and have no knowledge of "that source of all misfortunes, money." Thus certain educated Europeans formed an idealistic image of these New World inhabitants, an image that wouldn't seem out of place in, say, the 1970s. It was perhaps with this in his mind that Van der Donck was drawn to Indian society.

He thus cracks the stereotype of a European of the time as culturally unable to see indigenous peoples as anything other than savages. Through the finely detailed observations of Indian society he later put in writing we can see him, during this period, immersing himself in the culture of the Mohawks and Mahicans, roving the wooded slopes and valleys with them, sitting in their homes, canvassing the women on their cooking methods, observing rituals, fishing and planting techniques, sexual and marriage customs, and "the sucking of their children." These two dominant tribal groups spoke different languages and had very different cultures—the Mohawks were more settled, living in palisaded villages organized around agriculture, while the Mahicans tended to move with the hunting season—which to Van der Donck helped explain why they were so often at war with one another. He would later describe these natives, for the benefit of curious European readers, as "equal to the average and well-proportioned here in the Netherlands." He characterized their houses: built snugly so that they "repel rain and wind, and are also fairly warm, but they know nothing about fitting them out with rooms, salons, halls, closets or cabinets."

He learned some of their languages, classified the Indians of the region as falling into four different language groups, and analyzed these carefully ("Declension and conjugation resemble those in Greek, for they, like the Greeks, have duals in their nouns and even augments in their verbs"). He observed their medicine men firsthand and marveled that "fresh wounds and dangerous injuries they know how to heal wonderfully with virtually nothing," and "they can treat gonorrhoea and other venereal diseases so easily as to put many an Italian physician to shame." However, he questioned the "devil-hunting" methods used for the very ill, which "make noise enough to frighten a person in extremity to death."

He studied their religious practices, and, in answer to the question of whether they could be converted to Christianity, frankly doubted it, but, in a remarkable passage, urged his country to institute a plan of social welfare among the Indians of the colony: "Public authority ought to become involved and provide for sound teaching of our language and the elements of the Christian religion to their youth in good schools established in suitable locations in that country, so that in due course they could and would teach each other further and take pleasure in doing so. It would take a deal of effort and preparation, but without such measures not much good can be achieved among them. The neglect of it is a very bad thing, since the Indians themselves say they would be happy to have their children instructed in our language and religion."

Van der Donck's major work, *A Description of New Netherland,* from which these quotes are taken, is considered a classic of early American literature, but it has been forgotten by history thanks to the fact that it was written in the language not of the eventual masters of the American colonies but of their bitter rival. (The historian Thomas O'Donnell called the book "one of America's oldest literary treasures," and said of Van der Donck, "Had he written in English rather than Dutch, his *Description* would certainly have won from posterity the same kind, if not the same amount, of veneration that has been bestowed on Bradford's *Of Plymouth Plantation*.") The neglect of Van der Donck's book mirrors the treatment American history has given to the whole corpus of records of the Dutch colony centered on Manhattan, and, for that matter, the colony itself. There has only been one published English translation of the *Description*. This translation first appeared in 1841 (the translator, Jeremiah Johnson, was not only a former mayor of Brooklyn but counted himself a descendant of Catalina Trico and Joris Rapalje), and historians have relied on it ever since for the wealth of information the book contains about the colony, the American wilderness that the first Europeans found, and the Indians.

But those generations of historians were apparently ignorant of the fact that the translation from which they were working was badly flawed. In places the translation is accurate and indeed captures the poetry and zeal in the original, but in other places Johnson completely distorts what Van der Donck has to say. The main flaw with this translation, however, which appeared most recently in a 1968 edition of the *Description*, is that it simply omits whole portions of Van der Donck's text. A major section that did not appear in print until 1990, when Dutch scholar Ada Louise Van Gastel published it in translation in an academic journal, and of which historians thus have been ignorant, shows the young Van der Donck making a serious study of the Indians' treaties, contracts, and "government and public policy." It is fascinating reading in light of Van der Donck's recently completed legal training and the work he would soon undertake in behalf of the Manhattan-based colony.* Looking at it in that context, we see a young man, who is fresh out of law school and filled with new, practical ideas about the law and how governments might function, applying those ideas in a laboratory study of an alien society.

Like a good student of Grotius who also had a practical interest in how Europeans might better deal with the natives, Van der Donck, in this "lost" section of his book, dispassionately analyzed their ideas of right and wrong. He found in force among them none of the "rights, laws, and maxims" common in European countries, but instead a general "law of nature or of nations." He shows that at least some of the Dutch colonists were aware of the nuances in the Indians' understanding of property rights, noting that to the natives "wind, stream, bush, field, sea, beach, and riverside are open and free to everyone of every nation with which the Indians are not embroiled in open conflict. All those are free to enjoy and move about such places as though they were born there." He identified their respect for certain principles of war that Europeans also held, such as giving safe conduct to "state envoys" and honoring pacts. He noted, for the sake of future emissaries, that when making an offer such as a land treaty, the protocol was to state the re-

*I am deeply indebted to Diederik Willem Goedhuys for the new translation he made of the *Description* in 1991, a vast improvement on the Johnson translation that unfortunately remains unpublished; to Ada Louise Van Gastel, whose 1985 doctoral dissertation, "Adriaen van der Donck, New Netherland, and America," outlined for me many of the problems with the earlier translation; and to Hanny Veenendaal of the Netherlands Center in New York City, who helped me to translate afresh some passages of the *Description*.

quest orally and at the same time give a suitable gift. "The offering is hung up, the request is put, and those to whom it is addressed examine and deliberate the proposition seriously. If they take the offering, the request as made is accepted and consented to, but if it remains where it hangs for over three days the matter is held in abeyance and the petitioner has to alter the conditions or augment the offering or both."

He seemed to admire that the Indians' government was "of the popular kind," but found that it had its problems. While a whole village would gather to debate matters of importance, and a chief would work like a politician to sway the people to his preferred course of action, the democracy had an abrupt ending point. If an opponent remained obstinate, eventually "one of the younger chiefs will jump up and in one fell swoop smash the man's skull with an axe in full view of everyone." Van der Donck was forced to conclude that this species of popular government was "defective and lame."

So yes, Arent van Curler was right—Adriaen van der Donck had been spending time among the Indian villages in the Catskill Mountains in 1643. And while he was up in the highlands, he began negotiations with tribes to buy a vast tract of land. Two years into what was probably a three-year contract with Van Rensselaer, Van der Donck was chafing—and planning for the future. He saw how things stood at Rensselaerswyck, saw that the old man proposed, against common sense, to run his colony as a medieval fiefdom, with serfs and himself as the law personified, and to do it all from the other end of the ocean. By now Van der Donck had undergone a change in this new world; as with Peter Minuit, what had started as a raw adventure had matured in him into something deeper. He wanted to make something here, something that would last. As with Minuit, it was almost inevitable that he would think to found his own colony.

Immediately on receiving news of this from his nephew, Van Rensselaer dispatched a man to the colony with the mission of purchasing the tract called Catskill from the Indians. He wrote Van Curler a letter filled with invective toward Van der Donck. The man had "dishonestly designed" to deny his patron his rights, which as far as he was concerned included the right to obtain any properties adjacent to his colony. The man was to be "constrained," and if he "should prove obstinate, he shall be degraded from his office."

The old man got his way: his agent outmaneuvered Van der Donck, purchased Catskill, and extended his colony by several thousand acres. But Van Rensselaer didn't live to enjoy it. It's tempting, but probably not warranted, to infer that Van der Donck's impudence gave him a literal fit. Whatever the causes, Kiliaen Van Rensselaer, diamond merchant and patroon of Rensselaerswyck, died shortly after, leaving the estate to his sons. The odd medieval fiefdom would continue, existing in its own universe through the period of the English colony of New York and well into the history of the United States (the city of Albany, later the capital of New York State, would eventually be forced to file papers clarifying that its territory was distinct from that of the duchy that entirely surrounded it). In fact, Rensselaerswyck would prosper under the on-site stewardship of Kiliaen's son Jeremias and later managers, eventually sprawling to include upward of a million acres of land and one hundred thousand tenant-farmers.

For Van der Donck, the failure of his plans for a colony near Rensselaerswyck brought about a change of thinking. He turned his attention southward. His term in office probably had another year on it, but he had given up on the northern reaches of New Netherland and began spending more and more of his time at what was the undeniable nerve center of Dutch holdings in North America.

*

By 1644, events on Manhattan were reaching a new stage. The opposition to Kieft and his disastrous Indian war had begun to coalesce and was being led by Cornelis Melyn, the farmer who had been Van der Donck's shipmate on his voyage to New Amsterdam in 1641. Melyn was in his early forties, an upright Fleming from around Antwerp, a tanner by trade, who had also brought with him on that voyage his wife, children, some farm hands, and animals, with the intention to farm a vast tract on Staten Island. His timing was dreadful. Indians destroyed his plantation, and Melyn and his family were forced to cross the North River and seek refuge, along with most everyone else, near the fort on lower Manhattan. He bought land at the spot where the "canal," or ditch, drained into the East River, and built a two-story house on it. Soon after he had a neighbor. Jochem Kuyter was a German who had done service in the Danish navy in the East Indies, then, in search of a peaceful corner of the world to settle down, arrived in Manhattan in 1639. He took up tobacco farming on the north of the island, across the river from the plantation of his friend Jonas Bronck (who would give his name to a New York City borough). Kuyter had had success with his first crops, and was hoping to turn a profit, when a Wickquasgeck assault destroyed his plans as well, forcing him to move south. The two neighbors, Melyn and Kuyter, compared notes on their mutual suffering and decided to launch an offensive against Kieft and the West India Company.

With the huddled masses in the fort close to anarchy, Kieft, in an effort to restore order, proposed naming a new council of representatives to assist him. This mollified people somewhat, and they didn't put up a fuss when he hand-picked the eight members. Naturally, he chose men whom he believed would support him. He picked Melyn as leader, figuring that the leather-worker-turned-plantation-owner ought to be grateful to the company for giving him such an opportunity for advancement. He also chose two Englishmen, acknowledging the fact that by now twenty percent of the province's population was English; one of these, Isaac Allerton, was a wily trader who had sailed with the Pilgrims on the *Mayflower,* then, feeling constricted in their society, had moved from New England to the freer atmosphere of New Amsterdam.

Kieft assembled the board on June 18. With him, probably, were Cornelis van Tienhoven, his secretary and henchman, and, as a reminder of his authority, a contingent of soldiers. Adriaen van der Donck was not yet one of the board, but he was probably present at this meeting; he had recently arrived in New Amsterdam on one of his frequent river journeys from Rensselaerswyck. Also likely to have been on hand was the town's minister, Everardus Bogardus, a stout, hard-drinking Calvinist who had begun denouncing Kieft from his pulpit.

The colony, Kieft told the men, was out of cash. The treasury had been emptied fighting the war. He now proposed to raise money by taxing beavers and beer. A cry went up from the board members. The population he proposed to tax had lost their homes, property, and family members thanks to this war. People were living in makeshift dens and wearing rags. They couldn't pay and would refuse to even if they had the money. And anyway, the men argued, such a tax, without authorization from the company in Amsterdam, was unlawful. Kieft flushed with anger. "I have more power here than the company!" he roared at the men and announced he would do whatever he felt was necessary. Whereupon Kuyter, the ex-sailor, rose menacingly, pointed a heavy finger at the director, and vowed that some day, when Kieft no longer wore the protective mantle of office, Kuyter would "certainly have him." The meeting broke up in chaos, and several days later Kieft's soldiers were seen hammering placards around the fort informing the residents of the new taxes.

A tax on beavers might have been tolerated, but adding one stuiver to every tankard of beer sold was beyond endurance; a popular uprising ensued. The people refused to pay it, and tavern keepers refused to charge it. Kieft retaliated by sending soldiers down the road to the city tavern, where they arrested Philip Gerritsen, its proprietor.

The board then took action. The members had previously written letters to the West India Company directors in Amsterdam and to the leaders of the Dutch government at The Hague, complaining of their plight, but they were disorganized and anemic petitions. These men were farmers and traders, not lawyers; these earlier letters were probably written by the Reverend Bogardus, who was as bitter toward Kieft as anyone. "Almighty God finally, through his righteous judgment, hath in this current year kindled around us the fire of an Indian war," the first letter had lamented. The tone was churchly and groveling, with refrains of "we poor inhabitants of New Netherland" and "Your Honors can easily conceive how wretchedly it fares with us, distressed people."

At the time that letter was written, Van der Donck had been sitting around campfires far to the north, playing card games with the Mohawks and Mahicans. At this point, however, the character of the opposition changes. Up to now the colonists had been fumbling, convinced that they were subject to an injustice but without direction or understanding of the mechanisms for redress of grievances—mechanisms that were of long standing in the Dutch Republic, and in which Van der Donck—the only jurist in the colony—had recently trained.

Van der Donck may have returned north after the meeting with Kieft in June, but his term as law officer of Rensselaerswyck apparently expired in August, and he was back in New Amsterdam by early October, when the Manhattan activists met again, clandestinely. The scent of heated political activity would have been unavoidable and irresistible to the young lawyer. He had journeyed from Leiden to Rensselaerswyck in search of adventure and with a young man's dreams of great achievement—of helping to found a new society in a brave new world—only to find that his dreams didn't square with Van Rensselaer's business plan. But here, in the capital of the Dutch province, was a genuine cause in the making, a political struggle at the cutting edge of legal thought. What rights did individuals have in an overseas outpost? Were they entitled to the same representation as citizens in the home country? Never before had an outpost of a Dutch trading company demanded political status. Here, Van der Donck must have thought, was his chance to make his mark.

From the fort, where Van der Donck was appearing at this time in a court case related to his duties at Rensselaerswyck, to Cornelis Melyn's house—the center of the populist opposition to Kieft and the West India Company—it was a three-minute walk along Pearl Street (one can still take it today), with the river on his right and the church and a little row of brick homes on his left. And here they all were, the merchants and traders of the colony, grieving over their dead children, wives, and comrades, bitter at the burning of the homes and acreage in which they had invested their savings, wanting to express their outrage but not quite sure how. Van der Donck knew how. He must have offered himself at about this time as their lawyer, listened to their complaints, and begun to write.

From this point onward, the archives of the colony contain an increasingly more elaborate and strident series of legal petitions and arguments, documents sent by colonists either to the West India Company or to the States General in The Hague, which were aimed at securing the political foundations of the colony. Many of these writings have Adriaen van der Donck's name on them. There are also many others that were either written anonymously or in the name of one or another of the colonists, people who were illiterate or whose level of education doesn't match the prose.

Building on an argument put forth by Dr. Willem Frijhoff, a prominent Dutch historian at the Free University of Amsterdam and an authority on the Dutch language and history of the seventeenth century, especially as related to the New Netherland colony, I have culled what I believe to be Van der Donck's work or work in which he was involved. As Dr. Frijhoff put it to me in an e-mail, these writings, put alongside that which we know came from Van der Donck's pen, constitute "a coherent vision of a new society, sprung up from an Old World–trained academic." Dr. Charles Gehring, the translator of the official records of the colony and a man who knows both the language and the personalities of the colonists better than anyone alive, agrees that Van der Donck is the only likely author of these documents. "The only other candidate is Van Tienhoven," he told me, but while Cornelis van Tienhoven was educated, intelligent, and shrewd, as Kieft's right-hand man he would hardly have been the person to craft a series of documents defying the current administration. Dr. Frijhoff finds it remarkable that no historian before him has realized that Van der Donck must have been the force behind these writings, but the neglect of a fairly obvious point is simply another instance of the way that American history has ignored the Dutch colony. This body of writing dovetails with the actions Van der Donck would soon take on behalf of the colony. Put together, these actions and writings fill out a picture of Van der Donck as the pivotal figure in the history of the colony, the man who, more than any other, and in ways that have gone unnoticed, mortared together the foundation stones of a great city. It would probably be overly dramatic to call him the unheralded father of New York City; at the very least, he is an important figure whom history has forgotten.*

By the twenty-eighth of October 1644 the petition was complete, and the

---

*My method of determining Van der Donck's involvement in these documents that have not heretofore been associated with him is fairly straightforward. The population of the colony was small. As both Dr. Gehring and Dr. Frijhoff argue, Van der Donck was the only jurist, and thus the only person capable of framing his arguments with Latin legalisms and of constructing elaborate "interrogatories." I simply broke out of the archives all documents from this period that had such features. I then took a step that I hoped would serve as a check on my surmises. I had noted in some of the documents known to have been written by Van der Donck the repeated use of an unusual word: *American*. In the 1600s, the noun, applied to a person, was very rare. European colonists didn't use it in reference to themselves: the Dutch colonists considered themselves "New Netherlanders," the English to the north were "New Englanders," and those to the south thought of themselves as "Virginians." Only very occasionally does one see "American" used in the period, when it refers to Indians. The first recorded usage in English is in 1578, in a report about Martin Frobisher's voyage to Canada: "the Americans . . . which dwell under the equinoctiall line." The usage is even rarer in Dutch writing of the period. The word typically employed by the Dutch to refer to the Indians was *wilden*, meaning natives or, as Van der Donck himself wrote, people who "seemed to be wild and strangers to the Christian religion." Van der Donck used that word, or else *naturellen*, people of nature, but he also, in a few places, referred to the Indians as Americans. Having noticed the word also used in a few instances in the legal documents I suspected were written by Van der Donck, I then did a search of the entire corpus of political documents related to the Manhattan-based colony that were retrieved from the Netherlands in the nineteenth century. I found nine occurrences of the term "American," all referring to Indians, and all nine in documents that either have Van der Donck's name attached as the author or that Dr. Frijhoff and/or I had separately concluded were the work of Van der Donck. With uncanny appropriateness, then, *American*, turns out to be a clue to the identity of Adriaen van der Donck.

difference in tone from the earlier ones is striking. Instead of circuitous groveling before an all-powerful authority, it begins by crisply laying out a history of the colony's troubles, with the finger pointed directly: "For the sake of appearances, Twelve men were called together here, in November 1641, on the subject of the murder of Claes, the wheelwright; the Director submitted to them whether the blood of the aforesaid wheelwright should not be avenged? Whereupon divers debates arose on the one side and the other . . . [but] a hankering after war had wholly seized on the Director. . . . the aforesaid 12 men could not continue to meet any longer . . . for such was forbidden on pain of corporal punishment. Shortly after, [the director] commenced the war against those of Wesquecqueck, on his own mere motion. . . ."

The letter goes on to describe how Kieft had impaneled the new board, but only after his disastrous war was well under way, and only for the purpose of rubber-stamping his plan for new taxes to pay for it—a case, it in effect argues, of taxation without representation. Then it makes plain its complaint: "That one man . . . should dispose here of our lives and properties at his will and pleasure, in a manner so arbitrary that a King dare not legally do the like." It then takes the bold step of asking that Kieft be recalled and a new governor installed, and continues prophetically, "For it is impossible ever to settle this country until a different system be introduced here," in which villagers will "elect from among themselves a Bailiff or Schout and Schepens, who will be empowered to send their deputies and give their votes on public affairs with the Director and Council; so that the entire country may not be hereafter, at the whim of one man, again reduced to similar danger."

The colonists smuggled the petition out of Manhattan in the person of the trader Govert Loockermans, who left shortly after on one of his voyages to Amsterdam on behalf of his patrons, the Verbrugge family. In Amsterdam, the letter, building on the plaintive ones sent earlier by the colonists, made an impact—but not the one the activists were hoping for. The West India Company was at that moment in disarray; losses were mounting, the various regional chambers blaming one another. The nation—and therefore the company—was still at war with Spain, and in Brazil, company soldiers had just lost a major battle against the Spanish, with whom they were locked in a struggle for control of the sugar market. Their North American outpost had foundered for too long. Memos flew back and forth between the company offices in Amsterdam and the government offices in the courtyard complex in The Hague known as the Binnenhof. For both the merchants and the government officials this letter sharpened the focus. It was dawning on them that this North American outpost was an oddity—different from the Dutch colonies in Brazil, Batavia, Taiwan, the Spice Islands, and everywhere else. Others may have caused trouble from time to time, such as the messy massacre of Englishmen at Amboyna, but there was no question of their remaining military-trading posts, firmly under company auspices.

Following receipt of this letter, the directors came to the conclusion that they had to treat Manhattan differently, not by acknowledging it as a settlement in its own right, but by cracking down. They agreed with the upstart colonists that Kieft had to go, but not for the reasons the colonists outlined. In the thirty-five years since Henry Hudson had claimed the place for the Dutch, there had never been a strong, capable leader on the ground. The directors had been appalled, earlier, to discover that after launching a war, Kieft had been unwilling to take the field—in fact, had rarely left the safety of the fort. They ignored the letter's novel assertion of rights, its talk of representative government for the province. They felt the colonists' pain, but concluded that their plight was due not to the lack of popular representation but to a governor who didn't understand the use of force.

So they began a search for a new director, and this time they didn't want an incompetent nepotist. They needed a committed company man who was also a true leader. Someone to keep the colonists in line. An administrator, yes, and a man who was something more—a skillful diplomat—but also something less. They needed a man of nerve and grit and guile, someone unafraid of pain. They needed a boss.

Chapter 8

THE ONE-LEGGED MAN

He was a serious young man—thick-necked, with a piggish face and hard eyes offset by voluptuous lips—standing on the high poop deck of a West India Company frigate, staring out into the humid air of the Caribbean Sea. On the deck below and on the surrounding ships, three hundred soldiers awaited his command. He was an administrative agent with little military experience, but West India Company officials, if they had ambitions, expected to see action. It was March 1644; he had left Amsterdam nine years earlier, and had served doggedly through the sticky malarial seasons, first in Brazil and recently on the Dutch-controlled island of Curaçao. The company was a major means of advancement for a Dutchman. Not long before the young man had been a clerk; now he commanded a fleet, bearing down on the enemy.

The island of St. Martin appeared on the horizon of emerald water and azure sky. With the Spanish empire weakened, its Caribbean and South American holdings were in play. This little island—strategically located at what the Dutch called the *hoek*, or corner, of the Antilles chain—had gone back and forth between the two European powers. The Spanish held it currently, the West India Company wanted it back, and the official was determined to get it for them. His intelligence had told him that the Spaniards had only lightly manned the fort on the island, and indeed his men hit the beach without incident, dug in, and set up a siege cannon. Then the big guns from the fort exploded. The intelligence was wrong. The fort had recently been regarrisoned; the Spaniards were armed to the teeth. But there was an upside for the Dutch commander: this would be his first opportunity to show his mettle. He ordered his men to return fire, then, with the tang of gunpowder perfuming the air, he grabbed a Dutch flag and leaped onto the mounded earth that formed their defensive wall. Apparently, in his zeal, he had moved too close, bringing himself into range of the enemy guns. He was about to plant the flag when the Spaniards unleashed their second volley. The man collapsed, his right leg shattered by a direct hit—probably a stone ball fired as a projectile. Before losing consciousness, he ordered the siege to continue.

Thanks to the abundance of wars and the rising tide of scientific inquiry, the seventeenth century saw a large increase in the amount of space medical treatises devoted to amputation. There were many techniques, all of them hideous. Typically, the patient, fully awake, was placed in a chair with two men holding him down. The doctor would use his hands to "pluck up the skinn and muscles" of the limb in question, then, as one wrote, "we cut the flesh with a rasor or incising knife . . . to the bone, the said bone must be diligently rubbed and scraped with the back of the sayd knife, which back must be made purposely for that effect, to the end the periost which covereth the bone, may be lesse painfull in cutting of the bone. Otherwise it teareth and riveth with the same, so causeth great dolour. . . . This being done, you must saw the bone with a sharpe saw . . ." Without anaesthetic or sedative the horror was often enough that the patient died before the saw finished its work. One surgeon's handbook frankly instructed doctors how to advise a patient: "Let him prepare his soul as a ready sacrifice to the Lord by earnest prayers. . . . For it is no small presumption to dismember the image of God."

But while he suffered through weeks of delirium following the amputation of his own leg, Peter Stuyvesant, the thirty-four-year-old son of a Calvinist minister, would not die, and, after the siege of St. Martin had failed, was apologetic in his correspondence with the "Honorable, Wise, Provident, and Most Prudent Lords" of the company in Amsterdam, explaining drily that the attack on the island "did not succeed so well as I had hoped, no small impediment having been the loss of my right leg, it being removed by a rough ball." With herculean exercise of will he ignored the pain and pus flowing from the angry stump and recommenced his ferocious micromanagement of the company's affairs in the Caribbean: monitoring the salt pans that were the reason for being in this palm-scaped wilderness, strategizing to keep the Dutch possessions from the lurking English,

French, and Spanish vessels and from pirates, even fussing about how to get freshly baked bread out to ships that were on maneuvers. The pain level rose, the wound festered in the heavy air, but the sheafs of instructions and resolutions kept coming. Even in a century and an arena in which guts were a necessary part of everyday life, he must have stood out.

He came from plain country. The village of Scherpenzeel in the region of Westsellingwerf in the province of Friesland in the far northern reaches of the Netherlands was known for nothing because no one knew of it at all. It was flat farmland, incised by hedges, the horizon unencumbered by castles, fortresses, cathedrals, or other sizable manifestations of civilization. It was sparsely populated. The villagers were grim, pious, stalwart, self-reliant, and he was one of them. Frisians believed in a natural, unchanging order to things. A peasant gave birth to little peasants. If you were a minister's son, your career path was preordained. Strangely, however—and this is perhaps a key to understanding his personality, the place at which it twisted away from conformity—Peter Stuyvesant did not follow his father Balthasar, the minister of the Frisian Reformed Church of Scherpenzeel. One possible explanation: in 1627, shortly after his mother's death, his pious father remarried, and immediately and zestfully set to work siring a new family with his bride. Teenaged sons tend to react strongly to such things; one of a proud and stubborn disposition especially so, perhaps. At about the time of the remarriage, Peter seems to have left home. He studied at the Latin school in the larger town of Dokkum, whose harbor also happened to be a way station for West India Company ships bound for the New World. Growing up, his literal horizon had been as low as they come; to a youth shaped by God and flat land, these vessels, jutting a hundred feet into the air, taller than anything he had seen, natural or man-made, great cathedrals of wood with spires promising real-world deliverance, must have made an impression.

He went on to attend his father's alma mater, but he enrolled as a student of philosophy rather than theology—a signal he intended to veer from expectations. Whatever career notions Stuyvesant may have had on entering university changed when he left abruptly after two years. According to a story later told by his enemies, he was kicked out after abusing his landlord's hospitality by having sex with his daughter. Whether there was any truth to that, he was proud of his university association: ever after, he signed himself Petrus, the latinized (and thus scholarly) form of Pieter.

And so the college dropout found a position with one of the going concerns of the day, signing on at the lowest administrative level. Company officers were soon impressed with his devotion to work, and gave him a rather dubious reward: a posting to the remote island of Fernando de Noronha, two hundred miles off the Brazilian coast, renowned in company ranks for its vigorous rat population. From there he was promoted swiftly to a position in the coastal colony of Pernambuco, and then to Curaçao. Like natural leaders before and since, he gathered lieutenants as he went, men attracted to his energy who saw opportunity for themselves in serving alongside him. Unlikely as it may seem given how his career would end, he had a certain fondness for the English, which would carry through his life. There were at least two Englishmen in this posse of his. The man who appears in the Dutch records as Carel Van Brugge was born Charles Bridges in Canterbury; Brian Newton had been in the company's service for twenty years. These men would ride his coattails all the way to Manhattan, and play roles in its struggle to survive.

But the most revealing of these friendships was with a young man who did not accompany Stuyvesant to Manhattan. John Farret had been born in Amsterdam to English parents. Like Stuyvesant, he won a position with the West India Company on Curaçao; the two may have met there, or perhaps earlier in Amsterdam. They formed a fast friendship that mirrored others Stuyvesant would have—with Stuyvesant in the more powerful role, and Farret almost fawning before him. But Farret had something over Stuyvesant; he had completed university, received a degree in law, and was a poet and painter. Stuyvesant envied all of these indications of culture, and their relationship built itself around his envy and Farret's ingratiating efforts to please. In a development that suggests depths of personality beneath the wooden image of Stuyvesant that history has fashioned, he and Farret kept up a long-distance correspondence . . . in verse. A lengthy catalogue of poems detailing their changing fortunes exists in the Netherlands Maritime Museum in Amsterdam, which, as far as I have been able to determine, has never been translated or published, except for a few snippets.

The existence of this cache of poetry—which was discovered in a Dutch archive in the 1920s—in itself sheds light on their relationship. It was Farret who preserved the poems and bound them in vellum together with his own illustrations, apparently proud of his association with the man who had by then become renowned for his leadership of the Manhattan-based colony. Throughout, Farret addresses Stuyvesant as "Excellency" and "My Stuyvesant." "Never a greater honor would befall me or greater reward / than that you should order me around as a servant," he asserts, and declares that "My will is tied to your will, my heart to your heart." At times the correspondence cries out for a latent-homosexuality reading (i.e., when the men write of "such pleasure" each receives from the "skilled hand" of the other); it's probably more profitable, though, to see the poems as little portals onto the relationships between seventeenth-century Dutch merchant-soldiers, in which there was a frank deference to the one's greater power and in which friendship was expressed in language as baroque as the pink-cheeked detailing in a Frans Hals portrait. Throughout the collection, Farret's verse is sprightly; Stuyvesant's ungainly. Stuyvesant admits to an inability to express himself in "rich Latin or fancy French," but Farret, in his response, insists that Stuyvesant could write poetry in those languages if he wanted to, and shamelessly refers to Stuyvesant's verse as *goddlijck*—"divine."

Stuyvesant served three years as supplies officer on Curaçao, working hard at his job and at positioning himself for advancement, and in the process making enemies, among them the commander of Dutch political and military operations in the Caribbean, Jan Claeszoon van Campen. Things could have become difficult for Stuyvesant, but he caught a major break when Van Campen died in 1642, and Stuyvesant won the position. His friends toasted him; Farret wrote a poem for the occasion, praising "Brave Stuyvesant" who was now poised for greatness, and filled with vitriol for Stuyvesant's detractors—which suggests that Stuyvesant never had qualms about making enemies.

Stuyvesant, too, had to be pleased with his success. A proud, stiff Frisian, raised on a diet of gloomy skies and thick soup, he now ruled a tropical-paradise-cum-malarial-swamp that lay in the no-man's-land of the Spanish war, from which he lorded over Dutch operations in the entire Caribbean arena. The region was the scene of vivid, hot, bloody warfare between the decaying Spanish empire and its breakaway rival. Sugar, salt, dyewood, tobacco, horses, copper—the ways to exploit the Caribbean and coastal South America were intoxicating in their variety, and while the Dutch were eager to capitalize on the weakness of Spain's grip on the region, the Spanish were unwilling to give up such a stream of wealth easily. Besides opening a new window onto the birth of Manhattan, the massive trove of Dutch documents being translated by Dr. Charles Gehring in the New York State Library contains hundreds of pages detailing Stuyvesant's time in the Caribbean and opens other windows onto the unrelentingly grim business of wringing profits out of slaves, Indians, and the land, while simultaneously battling other European colonizers. More than anything else, the documents tie together the pieces of the Dutch empire in the Americas, showing Stuyvesant overseeing with militaristic efficiency an army of suppliers, privateers, traders, and couriers passing between Manhattan and Curaçao as the Dutch sought to solidify their New World holdings. They make clear that Manhattan began its rise as an international port not in the eighteenth century, as the Port of New York, but in the 1630s, as a cog on the circle of trade moving from the Netherlands to western Africa to Brazil and the Caribbean, then to New Amsterdam, and so back to Europe.

In his Caribbean post Stuyvesant became one of the movers of that circle. He was plugged into the communication network that ran through all its nodes, and in this way began to involve himself in the affairs of the Manhattan-based colony. He got word of Kieft's troubles there, and tried to help, in what would become an extended comedy. While returning to Curaçao from the disaster at St. Martin, his ship apparently passed in the night another heading in the opposite direction. It contained four hundred and fifty Dutch soldiers who had fled from an outpost in Brazil that the Spanish had overrun. These soldiers had turned up on Curaçao, seeking food and orders. They were told there that they could assist in the action on St. Martin, but arrived late, only to receive a second wave of shelling from the Spanish guns. Eventually, they made it back to Curaçao, where the ailing Stuyvesant must have been fairly sickened by their presence: first, because had they shown up earlier they might have turned the tide on St. Martin; second, because food rations were desperately low on Curaçao, and he couldn't afford to feed them. He decided to solve two problems at one go by ordering them to New Amsterdam, where, he hoped, they could assist Kieft with his Indian troubles. He thought he had seen the last of them.

Despite the endless attempts by Adriaen van der Donck and others to advise the directors of the West India Company of Manhattan's strategic importance, it was always an afterthought for them. Brazil, with its more manageable and profitable sugar fields, was the jewel of the company's operations, and therefore the scene of the bloodiest conflicts with Spain. Complicating the situation was the fact that in coastal Brazil the Dutch were engaged in battle not directly with Spain but with the Portuguese, who were under the vassalage of Spain and who were themselves in the process of declaring independence. Like heavyweight boxers, the two empires took turns gathering momentum, unleashing a savage blow on the opponent, then bracing for the response. In one such effort, Portugal sent eighty-six ships and twelve thousand fighting men across the Atlantic from Lisbon to pummel the Dutch ships laying siege to the province of Bahia in eastern Brazil.

As grim as Kieft's war against the Indians surrounding Manhattan was, it barely registered compared with the scope of battle in the Caribbean, and especially along the Brazilian coast, where hundreds of engagements took place over three decades, great ugly mix-ups of European tactics involving musket battalions and infantry pike charges thrown in with Indian bow-and-arrow warfare, the terrain scarred by siege cannon fire, the European soldiers on both sides stifling in their laughably heavy clothing and often fighting while riddled with yaws, dysentery, and intestinal parasites. Each encounter was punctuated by the ritual of old soldiers on both sides streaming silently out from the ranks to seek out their half-dead comrades amid the corpses and help them along with a swift slit of the throat. The savagery of the battles and grimness of the besieged settlements—"leather, dogs, cats, and rats" was the diet in one town withering under a Dutch siege—speaks to the stakes involved, and also to the pitiless environment that helped shape the man whom Manhattanites would come to call "the General."

Shortly after leaving the Brazilian sphere to take charge of Curaçao, and no doubt in part to test his own mettle, Stuyvesant had led a successful attack on a Spanish outpost on the Venezuelan coast. Then he settled into the role of administrator, determined to bring Dutch order to a world of tropical chaos and laxity. He had relished the opportunity to retake St. Martin, and his fury at the failure helped feed his commitment to his administrative duties. In the midst of his work and while struggling with the pain of his wound, he took time to pen a letter to Farret, who was now back in the Netherlands, giving him the news of his misfortune. Farret responded with a poem entitled "On the Off-Shot Leg of the Noble, Brave Heer Stuyvesant, Before the Island of St. Martin":

What mad thunder ball comes roaring towards your leg
My dear Stuyvesant, and causes your collapse?
The right pillar that used to support your body
Is that crushed and stricken off this way in one blow . . .
You presented too fair a mark—O! much too cruel chance!
My Stuyvesant, who falls and tumbles on his bulwark,
Where, like a dutiful soldier, he taunted the enemy,
To lure him into the field, on the Island of St. Marten.
The bullet hits his leg; the rebound touches my heart . . .

But ignoring the pain wouldn't do—doctors told Stuyvesant the stump where his leg had been amputated wouldn't heal in the climate; if he remained, it would fester. He resisted—he had only served eighteen months as head of Dutch operations in the Caribbean—then finally gave in to the idea of recuperating at home.

A sea crossing with such an affliction would have been a brutal affair in the best of circumstances. As it happened, the voyage was horrific. *The Milkmaid* left Curaçao in August of 1644, and didn't put into Dutch port until December. By ship, canal barge, and horse-drawn cart, then, past gabled facades and through a pleasant wintry swirl of peat smoke and stewed vegetables, he was hauled to the home of his sister Anna, who lived near Leiden. Life instantly transformed; the pestilential tropical endurance test of the past nine years vanished. He was in the civilized Dutch countryside, plied with boiled meat and smoked fish, his stump salved and ministered. It was a classic scenario: the wounded soldier returning home to be cared for. And, completing it, he fell in love with his nurse. Judith Bayard was the sister of Anna Stuyvesant's husband and was living with the couple when the invalid arrived. She was no gay young thing but a decided spinster—at thirty-seven, three years older than Stuyvesant—who had previously been living with her father (a minister, which no doubt gave the two something to talk about). When her father died she had joined the household; it was natural enough that she take charge of the patient. Judith came from Breda in the south, the same town from which Adriaen van der Donck hailed. She was a Huguenot, a Calvinist whose family had fled Catholic persecution in France.

During the long weeks of his voyage home, Stuyvesant might have spent some time mulling on a side benefit of his enforced trip: that at least he would have an opportunity to get himself a Dutch bride. It must have seemed a stroke of providence that one would all but fall into his lap, or what remained of it. But courtship didn't come easily to him. His brother-in-law, the brother of the woman in question, actually seems to have bet him a quantity of French wine that Stuyvesant wouldn't have the nerve to propose marriage, and even his staunch friend John Farret was dubious, writing in yet another poem that Stuyvesant would never consummate the relationship because "Priapus has died in him." That got Stuyvesant's dander up. He tore off a response, in verse more purple and heated than usual, accusing his friend of trying to "make sure I will lose the bet of the wine" and declaring that—manly creature that he was—he fully desired the lady to "occupy this bed." Less than a year later, they were married.*

The wound healed at last, and Stuyvesant declared himself fit for duty. And so one day he came wobbling into the courtyard of the company headquarters in Amsterdam (the building still exists and is occupied by a catering company, whose waiters flit across the same courtyard giving no notice to the bronze statue of Stuyvesant in the center), sporting a new wooden leg and a reputation for grit and efficiency. At nearly the same time, a certain letter arrived in these offices. It came from Manhattan. It presented, in unusually strident and lawyerly terms, the ruined state of affairs in the North American colony. It demanded the removal of Kieft and the installation of a new governor, one who would usher in a representative government, "so that the entire country may not be hereafter, at the whim of one man, again reduced to similar danger." The directors' heads must have swiveled back and forth from the letter to the hardened young man recently arrived from the New World and eager to get back to his Caribbean post. The directors didn't like this talk of representative government coming from Manhattan any more than they did Kieft's blundering management style. Clearly the tough young Frisian before them could give a damn for Grotius or Descartes; for him the company's law was the only "natural law." He wasn't

---

*The couple traveled south to Breda to be married. The record in the Walloon (French-speaking) church for August 13, 1645, reads: "Mons. Pierre Stuyvesant, J. H. directeur de la part de la Compagni de Oestinde en Nieu Nederland et Judith Bayard jeune fille de Mons. Bayard, en sa vie pasteur de l'Eglise Franc, a Breda."

a newfangled thinker, but a stout minister's son who understood duty and station. Altogether, an excellent young man. And soon, no doubt, he would learn to manage the peg leg.

*

MEANWHILE, IN SCOTLAND, on a summer day in 1637 a woman named Jenny Geddes set in motion another chain of events. According to the story that has ossified into myth in Scotland, she was an Edinburgh "kail wife," or cabbage monger. If you subscribe to the application of chaos theory to history, then her act that day—hurling a stool—was the flapping of the butterfly's wings that led to the hurricane.

Her target on the Sunday in question was the head of one of the most learned and respected men in Scotland, Dr. Hanna, dean of St. Giles Cathedral. The dean stood in his pulpit, stately and berobed, in his hand a slender volume, fresh off the press, the title page of which, in red and black ink and with a sober but elegant border, laid out its purpose: "The Book of Common Prayer, And Administration Of The Sacraments, And other parts of divine service for the use of the Church of Scotland, Printed by Robert Young, Printer to the Kings most Excellent Majestie, M.D.C.XXXVII." The cathedral was packed with lairds and peasants alike. Everyone, apparently, knew trouble was in the air—they had come spoiling for a fight. Obliging them, the dean opened the book and began reading from it. Whereupon a piercing voice interrupted him—Jenny Geddes, crying out lustily, "Dost thou say mass at my lug [ear]?" She then picked up the stool she had brought (pews were for men—women were required to bring their own stools if they wanted to sit), took aim, and flung it at the dean's head. The place erupted.

The thrown stool was the equivalent of the Shot Heard Round the World, the event that would trip the English Civil War. From now on, King Charles would be forced to give up the role of stately monarch and take on that of a general, commanding armies loyal to him against those marshaled by Parliament. Events surrounding the war would have a multilayered impact on American beginnings, on Manhattan as well as in the English colonies.

Perhaps more than anything else, the English Civil War was a religious war. If the seventeenth century was outlined by the struggle for global empire, the outlines were filled in by warfare brought on by the clash of religious worldviews as societies endured the aftershocks of the Reformation. From the time it had broken from the Catholic Church under Henry VIII, the Church of England had adopted a moderate form of Protestantism, maintaining a hierarchy of church officials and a Rome-influenced taste for fancy vestments and fancy liturgy. Most English people were content with this, but others chafed. Puritanism was not originally an English movement but an ideological implant from the Continent, a kind of Reformation II, a call to keep the revolution going. The English Puritans looked at events in the wider world through a theological lens. They saw the religious strife sweeping the Continent—the Thirty Years' War was essentially a series of attempts by Catholic powers to reverse the breakaway momentum in Protestant countries—and developed, along with their minimalist fashion statement, a belief that England was the New Israel, the place God had anointed as the great bulwark against the Pope and his swaggering red-robed henchmen. Puritanism rolled through English society during the years of Charles's reign, winning over peasants and aristocrats alike. It provided a how-to manual for improving your personal life and a focal point for national pride. And of course there were the fine hats you got to wear.

Puritanism also had a democratic element to it. Following first Martin Luther then John Calvin, the Puritans aimed their wrath at the Catholic idea of a man-made hierarchy that thrust itself between ordinary Christians and their God. By extension, Catholic paraphernalia—the frilly priests' garb, the gaudy paintings, the candles and incense—interfered with the profound central activity of Christian life—studying and following the Bible—and were thus to be banned. Eventually, suspicion of churchly power translated into politics—the Puritans came to oppose any authority that might interfere with what they saw as their divine mission, even if that authority was their own king. Those who crossed the ocean to settle in North America may have given up on England as the New Israel, but they brought their sense of chosenness along with them. The New World would be the "New Jerusalem." The democratic seed that planted itself in the revolt against Charles would come to flower in the colonies thirteen decades later with the American Revolution. It was this combination of plain-spoken religious zeal tied to political reform that would be the Puritans' great contribution to shaping American destiny; this is why American historians and leaders, down to Ronald Reagan and his "shining city on a hill," have sung the country's Puritan beginnings. The argument in this book doesn't deny that influence, but adds to it another that played a genuine role in shaping the American personality.

What made a civil war inevitable in England was Charles, who was willfully out of touch with his subjects. With his country houses, his lacey accessories, his Catholic wife, and his great halls draped with Van Dycks and Rubenses, he existed in his own universe, and his distance from the society he governed grew with every year. At his encouragement, the clergy introduced finery into their dress and adornments to their churches—edging closer to Roman ways. (A Puritan leader characterized Charles's project to fancify St. Paul's as "making a seat for a Priest's arse to sit in.") Charles considered the Puritans just as superstitious in their way as the relic-doting Catholics they despised. He was happy to enforce a ban on the printing of their religious tracts—which sent them to the printers of Leiden and Amsterdam.

The Puritan reform movement was strongest in Scotland, and so Charles decided, with an impressive lack of political horse sense, to bring the Scots into line by introducing in their churches a new prayer book and liturgy, one that was decisively more Catholic in ritual and language. The result was Jenny Geddes lobbing her stool and, eventually, the Scots breaking out in open rebellion. Raising money to put down the Scottish uprising required Charles to call Parliament into session for the first time in eleven years. Once it had assembled, Puritan leaders had a power base from which to carry out their campaign against the king.

Dutch authorities followed every wrinkle in the growing crisis. Beginning in July 1642, Albert Joachimi, the Dutch ambassador in London—who a decade before had pleaded with Charles to release the *Unity*, which had been carrying Peter Minuit back from Manhattan when the English impounded it—wrote a series of vivid and increasingly strident dispatches to his superiors at The Hague, which read like what they were, news reports from the front lines: "Some more cavalry have made their appearance here; and infantry are continued to be enlisted by beat of drum." "News is received here of the siege of Sherborne Castle . . . those besieged have slain between two and three hundred of the Parliamentarians . . . The French Ambassador hath taken his leave of the King, and calculates to depart this week . . . A Parliamentman of quality told me, on Saturday last, that the Earl of Essex was with the army within twelve miles of Shrewsbury; that place has been fortified by the King, who keeps his main force there." The old diplomat had a sense of what was coming, and he advised his government to take advantage of Charles's embattled state and bring to an end the growing friction between the English and Dutch colonies in North America. The States General, he wrote, "should write to the King and request his Majesty to be pleased to order the English in New England to leave the Dutch undisturbed in New Netherland."

Joachimi felt the need to act because in the Dutch colony the pressure from the north was growing. Thanks to the turmoil in England, the population of New England had swelled to ten times that of New Netherland. What had been in Minuit's time a pair of low settlements (Plymouth and Massachusetts Bay), struggling against imminent death and thankful for the odd care package the Dutch representatives on Manhattan might send their way, was now four fully functioning colonies. Connecticut and New Haven had been carved out of territory the Dutch considered their own. Each of these colonies had its own administration, and all, thanks to the fact that king and parliament were busy facing one another down, acted more or less without interference from the home country. In 1643, in order to strengthen themselves, principally against the Dutch province, they formed a league, the United Colonies of New England.

Strangely, however, even as it was feeling the weight of the growing population to its north, the Manhattan-based colony also benefited significantly from the stream of refugees moving from England to New England. The Puritan revolt in England was, for all its breadth among the populace, wondrously narrow in ideology. It wasn't enough that you were a fire-breathing Protestant—you had to be the right kind of fire-breathing Protestant, otherwise the very brightness of your flame marked you as in need of theological cleansing. "Thou shalt not suffer a witch to live," declared Exodus as translated under the direction of Charles's father, and Baptists, Anabaptists, Familists, and Mennonites were all marked thereby. It is easy enough to shake one's head at the folly, but in an age awash in incantations and potions, deciding who to make fuel for the pyre was a serious matter.

So people left England in waves. But members of despised sects who chose to follow the Pilgrims' lead and emigrate to America found, to their annoyance after enduring the horrors of the open ocean, that the Puritan majority in New England had followed the same hard-line trajectory as in the old country. In fact, there was even less theological wiggle room in the open spaces of New England. Witchcraft hysteria wouldn't reach its height for some time, but communities moved swiftly to excommunicate alternative religionists and run them out. So there was a double-rebound effect during the early 1640s, with a stream of English sectarians fleeing from Old England to New, then, recalling in their desperation the vaunted tolerance of the Dutch, moving south to seek sanctuary in the Manhattan-based colony. They came straggling through the latticeworked gatehouse of Fort Amsterdam, and Willem Kieft was pleased to have them. He was seriously embattled by this point and recognized that he had to grow his population in order to survive. And—here is the inscrutability of seventeenth-century Dutchness—in addition to giving them land to settle, he also granted them liberty to practice their religion as they saw fit, a genuine rarity in the era. Forbidding his own countrymen even marginal representation while at the same time practically insisting on covering newcomers with the blanket of religious liberty that was part of his proud cultural inheritance—this was apparently not a difficult calculation. It's worth noting, too, that the colonists themselves were fully aware of their status as a haven, and proud of it. Van der Donck, writing of one of these English refugees, summed up the situation with as much of a sense of perspective as a historian from the far future might: "[He] came to New England at the commencement of the troubles in England, in order to escape them, and found that he had got out of the frying pan into the fire. He betook himself, in consequence, under the protection of the Netherlanders, in order that he may, according to the Dutch reformation, enjoy freedom of conscience, which he unexpectedly missed in New England."

Kieft made the English arrivals swear an oath to the States General and gave them land to settle, and they went about helping to build the foundation of what would become New York City. Several of these were remarkable individuals. Lady Deborah Moody, a self-possessed London aristocrat, had converted to Anabaptism and declared herself ready to die for the outré notion that baptism must be withheld until the recipient was old enough to understand its meaning. Londoners were shocked; she was in her dignified fifties when she crammed into a stench-ridden wooden ship cheek by jowl with peasants and worse, and fled to the Massachusetts Bay Colony. There, the court of Salem threatened to banish her unless she renounced her mad ways, Puritan chieftain John Endecott famously declaring "Shee is a dangerous woeman." Kieft gave her and her followers title to the southwestern tip of Long Island. The take-charge woman herself sketched the plan of her community, to be called Gravesend (the skeleton of her original plan can still be seen in the intersection of McDonald Avenue and Gravesend Neck Road). She then set about tending to her flock of baptism-conscious followers, and thus established, in the corner of Brooklyn that now includes Bensonhurst, Coney Island, Brighton Beach, and Sheepshead Bay, the first New World settlement founded by a woman.

Anne Hutchinson also traveled from England to Massachusetts to Manhattan, in search of freedom to follow her belief that individuals could commune with the divine without any help from organized religion. New England's leaders looked on her as the seventeenth-century equivalent of an anarchist—Hutchinson wanted to do away with original sin, a moral cudgel that Puritan politicians believed indispensable to maintaining law and order. Particularly alarming was the fact that she had rapidly developed a following in Boston. Kieft didn't mind—or maybe he sensed she wouldn't be around long enough to cause trouble: when she showed up in his domain, he placed her in a no-man's-land at the height of the Indian troubles. Less than a year after she and her small band of followers had settled on the land he offered (on Pelham Bay in the Bronx, on the shore of the river that now bears her name), Hutchinson, six of her children, and nine others were massacred in an Indian attack.

The Reverend Francis Doughty, the third of the three semilegendary leaders of English refugees to the Dutch colony, had been forced from his vicarage in Gloucestershire for "nonconformity," shocked the crowd in Massachusetts for preaching "that Abraham's children should have been baptized," then headed for Manhattan. He, too, received a generous grant of land from Kieft and had begun to plant what would be the first European settlement in the future borough of Queens when a vicious Indian attack changed things. Doughty survived, gave up on the wilds of Long Island, and, seeing another opportunity, ensconced himself as minister to the growing English-speaking population of Manhattan. Kieft didn't approve; he envisioned a buffer zone of communities surrounding New Amsterdam, and he insisted that Doughty take the remains of his English flock back to his Long Island tract. Doughty turns out to have been yet another strong-willed creature, and he rebuffed the director, more or less arguing that if Kieft thought these were safe times to camp out in the wilds he could try it himself. Kieft rescinded the land grant and, for good measure, threw Doughty in the fort's jail cell for twenty-four hours.

Doughty was thus a natural addition to the colony's burgeoning anti-Kieft movement. He was also naturally litigious, and found himself in court in June of 1645, accusing another Englishman, William Gerritson, of singing a slanderous song about him and his daughter Mary. It may have been here that he caught the eye of a certain young lawyer—or, more to the point, that his eighteen-year-old daughter did. We don't know where Adriaen van der Donck and Mary Doughty first met, but it appears Van der Donck was in court at this time. If there was an initial language difficulty between the patrician Dutchman and the young Englishwoman, daughter of a strident and independent-minded father, who would herself prove to be a resourceful pioneer woman, it was soon gotten over. They were married before the year was out.

The romance was put on hold for the time being, however. Shortly before the couple met, the nineteen directors of the West India Company had gathered in Amsterdam to review their affairs in various outposts. They pronounced themselves pleased with the synergy between Angola and Brazil: what had been at first a tentative notion of moving slaves from West Africa across the ocean to do work in the company's fields in South America was now a going concern. "Every thing is, by God's blessing, in a good condition," they reported to the government ministers in The Hague, sounding freakishly cheerful about their part in what would become one of humanity's saddest and ugliest endeavors, "and in consequence of the employment of the negroes, which were from time to time introduced from Angola into Brazil, in planting grain, flour is produced in such quantity that what used to always cost 8 to 10 guilders, still continues to be sold at the low rate of six stivers . . ."

Regarding Manhattan, while they were quietly arranging for Kieft's successor, the directors decided to order him to work out a peace treaty that would end the disastrous Indian war. Kieft received these instructions in mid-summer and, perhaps sensing that his term might be coming to an end, took vigorous steps to carry them out. He knew the center of power among the tribes was to the north. The Mohawks and Mahicans kept the Munsee-speaking tribes of the lower river valley within their thrall, regularly sending representatives among them demanding tribute payments. So even though the hostilities were with the more southerly Indians, Kieft determined that the wisest course would be to secure a formal peace treaty with the stronger tribes first, to ensure that the Raritans, Tappans, and other groups closer to Manhattan would follow. This, however, meant penetrating the heart of darkness to the north, exposing himself to the savages. Kieft still had rarely stepped foot outside the radius of New Amsterdam. He needed someone who knew the Indians of the north, who spoke their languages, someone whom they knew and trusted. He turned to Adriaen van der Donck.

Kieft as yet had no knowledge of the letter written the previous autumn demanding his ouster. He certainly didn't know that Van der Donck had been meeting with the disgruntled colonists. Van der Donck seems to have been playing the role of model son again, keeping himself in the director's good graces, just as he had done with Kiliaen van Rensselaer before he began defying the old man. He agreed to help.

Kieft also brought with him on the one-hundred-and-fifty-mile journey upriver Johannes La Montagne, the second member of his two-man council, and, no doubt, a contingent of soldiers. The Indians agreed to meet within the confines of Fort Orange; the officials of Rensselaerswyck also took part. One man with an official role was a Mohawk named Agheroense, who knew all the languages of the Iroquois confederation as well as Mahican and would assist Van der Donck as interpreter. Agheroense—and, presumably, Van der Donck and Director Kieft—had spent the night at the "patroon's house," where the director of Rensselaerswyck lived. He came downstairs that morning, greeted Van der Donck, who introduced him to Kieft, and the three men sat and chatted at the breakfast table while Agheroense applied his ceremonial face paint. Kieft became visibly excited as he sat watching, for the man was painting his face with a glittering gold substance. He asked Van der Donck to inquire about it; in his mind the dormant hope—first lit in all Europeans by the Spanish discoveries of gold in South America—had reawakened. Could it be that here was the answer to the colony's financial problems? If so, wouldn't it also save his own career? Agheroense handed the pot to Van der Donck, who handed it to Kieft, who asked if he could buy it to study more closely.

There had to have been a note of irony playing in Van der Donck's mind during the peace talks. The student of law and intergovernmental relations had a unique opportunity to observe. On one side of him were Indians with whom he had lived, whose society he had studied, and whom in many ways he admired, while the representative of his own people was a man he despised for his lack of integrity. In the course of the treaty discussions, it became clear to Van der Donck that Kieft had not come prepared. In his later writings about the Indians of the region, where Van der Donck described treaty rituals, he noted that the protocol was to state one's proposition orally and at the same time offer a suitable gift. The gift was to be hung up as deliberations commenced; the other side had three days to accept the offering and thus signal that an agreement had been reached. Kieft had brought no offering to be hung up. A treaty of this magnitude, with both the Mohawks and the Mahicans, would require something significant, or the chiefs would be insulted. Kieft asked Van der Donck for a loan, and promised to repay him handsomely for his service to the colony.

Van der Donck supplied what was necessary—apparently, a large cache of sewant—and, back in New Amsterdam in late July of 1645, Kieft fulfilled his promise. He gave Van der Donck what he most wanted: his own domain, the patent to a vast tract of land. It was ideally situated, too: not in the far hinterlands to the north but adjacent to Manhattan. Van der Donck's grant began on the mainland directly to the north of the island, continued along the river for twelve miles, and carried eastward as far as the Bronx River—a total of twenty-four thousand acres. For his services, then, and for keeping his feelings about Kieft in check, he became lord of much of what is today the Bronx and southern Westchester County. He moved at once to purchase the land from the Indians, and over the next year he and Mary got to work, hiring tenant farmers to clear land and carpenters to build a house and a saw mill. (The saw mill became so vital to the community that later grew up in the area that the river on which it stood—and, later, a parkway that ran along it—would be named for it.) With such a vast tract came a kind of unofficial title. In the Netherlands, a *Jonker* (or *Yonkheer*) was a young squire or gentleman of property. From this time on, the Dutch records refer to Van der Donck as "the Jonker." Long after his death the title would re-main informally associated with the property—"the Jonker's land," people would say. In the English period, this was shortened to "Yonkers," and so it is that a city in lower Westchester County has embedded in its name the only wan tribute American history has ever paid to Adriaen van der Donck.

On his return to Manhattan, Kieft immediately plunged into arrange-ments for a peace treaty with the Indians of the region. On August 30, 1645, under "the blue canopy of heaven," the whole town assembled in front of the fort. A stately array of chiefs had assembled—Oratany of the Hackin-sack, Sesekemu of the Tappan, Willem of the Rechgawawanck, Mayauwetinnemin for the Nyack, and Aepjen of the Wickquasgeck—either on behalf of their own tribes or in some cases "in the capacity of attorneys of the neighboring chiefs." Both sides agreed to "a firm and inviolable peace," and agreed that future disputes would not be settled by violence but discus-sions. Twenty men on both sides made their marks or signatures at the bot-tom of the treaty. Adriaen van der Donck was not present, but his soon-to-be father-in-law, the Reverend Doughty, was among the signatories. The next day Kieft issued two proclamations: one ordering a day of general thanksgiving, the second ordering an investigation of the mine from which the Mohawk's intriguing gold material had come. He believed he had pulled off a triple coup: saved his job, stopped the war, and—if preliminary tests on the gold substance were correct—found something that would bring pros-perity to the colony and, maybe, an end to the residents' grievances.

He was right about the end of the Indian war, but about nothing else. Everything was collapsing about him. The civil war in England had reached a climax on a June morning in the grassy Northamptonshire uplands, when a massive conflict between the pikestaffed forces of Parliament and the king's cavaliers ended with the Puritan cavalry wing under Oliver Cromwell—crying, "God is our strength!"—cracking the royalist army in half, resulting in the surrender of four thousand of its troops. The English turmoil had the effect of further emboldening the Puritan New Englanders. They had already carved two massive chunks out of the Dutch territory (Connecticut and New Haven), and were continuing to push, shiploads of them crossing the sound from the mainland to the easternmost tip of Long Island and setting up bivouac communities on Dutch soil. To the south, Kieft's failure to pursue the Swedish incursion that Peter Minuit had started on the South River was proving disastrous. The colony of New Sweden now had three forts and maybe three hundred settlers. Its capable military commander had outflanked the Dutch trading post on the river and convinced the Indians of the region to trade exclusively with Swedish agents. As for the gold substance, it was found to be pyrite—fool's gold.

Regarding the colonists and their grievances, Melyn and Kuyter had only begun to mount their opposition to the West India Company and its feudal treatment of them. They now had an ally, a man of property who had a vested interest in the community, who had precisely the skills they needed, who recognized that the colony's problems, external and internal, could only be solved by a dramatic change of status, and who had secretly committed to carry the fight as far as it would go—to the very inner court of the halls of government at The Hague. Van der Donck was poised. He had reached the moment in life when a man moves from student and observer to actor. By 1647 he had a wife and the estate he had longed for. Ironically, he would now have little time for either. The struggle was to be all-consuming, a cause, a chance to apply the principles of justice in an unprecedented way.

The day of Kieft's replacement came at last. In a way, Kieft must have been ready for it: it had happened once before, when he was run out of the French port of La Rochelle. He was a man burdened by the deaths and dismembering tortures he had ordered. As he stood on the waterfront on May 11, 1647, watching a skiff approach from four newly arrived ships at anchor, the strain and darkness had to show in his eyes and face; his breath must have fairly stunk with it. It was a cerulean spring day, and, like characters at the end of an act of a play, all the residents of the community were gathered alongside him, headliners and minor players alike: Joris Rapalje and Catalina Trico, along with their children and grandchildren; Anthony "The Turk" van Salee and his wife Griet Reyniers—both respectable now, but still cantankerous—and their four daughters; Anna van Angola, a widowed African woman who had just received a patent for a farm on Manhattan, as well as Antony Congo, Jan Negro, and other black residents, slaves and free; assorted Danes, Bavarians, and Italians, and a handful of area Indians; Cornelis Swits, son of the murdered Claes Swits; the English refugee leaders Lady Deborah Moody and the Rev. Francis Doughty; Everardus Bogardus, the beer-swilling minister who had assisted the colonists' effort against Kieft by excoriating him from the pulpit; the activists Kuyter and Melyn; the company henchman, Cornelis van Tienhoven, who had slaughtered and tortured Indians while in Kieft's service and was hoping to be kept on in the new administration. And there, too, on the cobbled quayside stood Adriaen van der Donck and his English wife Mary—it is from Van der Donck that we have one of the extant descriptions of this scene. The mood was festive. Shouts went up; celebratory cannon blasts were fired. The day of deliverance had come.

Then, slowly, like gray rain, the silence fell upon them. From a distance they would have seen first the hardness and smallness of the eyes, like sharp pebbles set in the broad plate of the face. Then the flash of the sun on his breastplate must have caught their attention, and the sword at his waist: the efficient, meticulous, militaristic parcel of him. Finally they would have watched him unpacking himself from the boat, and noted at once, as people do such irregularities, that curious movement of his, an unnatural stiffness, and no accompanying grimace or flinch, as if in defiance of pain itself. And all eyes then naturally moving down, and seeing it, the leg that wasn't there.

Chapter 9

THE GENERAL AND THE PRINCESS

He came with a retinue: four ships of soldiers, his posse of "councilors," and a wife. He impressed the colonists gathered on the quayside with his grim decorum, his soldier-statesman demeanor. "Peacock like, with great state and pomposity" was Van der Donck's summing-up of their new leader's arrival. The people had likewise turned out in their best: we can imagine, on this spring day in 1647, lots of floppy-brimmed hats, lace collars, tight trousers or hose ribboned at the knees, and wide-topped boots—a scene out of Rembrandt on lower Manhattan.

A formal ceremony took place—the passing of the torch of leadership—beneath the sails of the windmill and the dilapidated walls of the fort and against the stupendous backdrop of the harbor. In his remarks, Stuyvesant vowed to act "like a father over his children." His signals of power were clear-cut: while the men of the community had removed their hats in his honor, he kept his on. While the colonists remained standing, he took a chair.

Kieft spoke, thanking the colonists for their loyalty and faithfulness to him. It was pure cant, the empty stuff employed by politicians everywhere, and in a normal Dutch outpost it would have been swallowed in silence. But he made the mistake of pausing to give the community the chance to thank him in return, as protocol suggested. Jochem Kuyter filled the pause, giving vent to a sailor's lungful of taunts, the effect of which was that what Kieft deserved was something other than thanks. Cornelis Melyn added a few loud comments of his own. Others began to chime in; the ceremony was about to devolve into a familiar chaos.

Then, somehow, everyone was looking at Stuyvesant. He had presence;

people felt it, followed his cues. Now, they shut up. Stuyvesant, of course, had been apprised of the entire situation; in fact, thanks to having seen the file in Amsterdam, which contained the colonists' complaints, he knew more about it than Kieft. He must have had for Kieft the withering disdain that a military officer holds for another who has failed to earn the respect of his subordinates. On the other hand, it would have gone against his every instinct to side with the rabble against authority. He knew at least some of the leaders of the activist camp, knew the names Melyn and Kuyter. He assured the community that under his administration justice would be applied equally and swiftly. Then he brought things to a quick conclusion.

He must have been shocked by this indication of the level of chaos and insubordination in the colony. Curaçao he had run as a military dictatorship, which had worked out in everyone's best interest; he had witnessed the same in Brazil. These outposts were wild lands, in which people were bound to lose all sense of civilization, to devolve into syphilitic delirium and allow themselves to be picked off by savages, disease, and lurking European foes, unless strict order was maintained. Anyone who had come to live in such a place understood that it operated under martial law—they were in no position to demand a voice or express outrage at the management of affairs. It would be necessary for him to remind them of that. And once he did, and they saw the benefits of it, the harmonious society that was possible under a Calvinist corporation, they would quickly fall into line.

There would be no honeymoon with his subjects (for that was how he referred to them). From this, the moment of his arrival, he was immersed in the unique political currents at work in the colony. With the welcome ceremony unceremoniously ended, he and his wife turned and made hastily for their sanctum, their new home, which lay just behind them. Fort Amsterdam was a four-sided structure with bastioned guard towers at its corners. Passing through the front gate and by the secretary's office, the Stuyvesants would have entered the central courtyard. The place was like a refugee camp. All along the right side of the courtyard were the barracks of the company's soldiers, the backbone of the director-general's power in the colony. But soldiers spilled out of the barracks; they were bivouacked around the courtyard and elsewhere in the town. Stuyvesant would have recognized among them some familiar faces, for it was because of him that the town was overrun. The shipload of soldiers who had fled from Brazil to Curaçao, whom Stuyvesant had sent to aid Kieft in New Netherland, were still here. They had arrived at the end of the Indian war, and Kieft hadn't known what to do with them. They were languishing now, underfed, demanding back pay, roaming drunkenly through the streets, causing fights, and destroying property—another problem for Stuyvesant to deal with.

On the left side of the courtyard was the church and, beside it, the gabled brick house reserved for the director-general. Here the newly arrived couple took a few moments to settle in. Stuyvesant rested his aching stump. Judith began the process of recovering from the ordeal of the voyage. She had to have been her husband's equal in grit considering that she had arrived four months pregnant, meaning that she had spent most of the first trimester of her pregnancy being tossed by the Atlantic.

And then the regime began. The change from the old order was immediately apparent. Gone was the leisurely schedule of Thursday council sessions. The new director would be active on every front every day. Cornelis van Tienhoven got his wish—Stuyvesant kept him on as secretary—but he may have regretted it: the volume of paperwork in the secretary's hand—proclamations, propositions, resolutions, judgments, commissions, summonses—increased dramatically and at once.

Stuyvesant had known what the place needed even before coming; his few hours here only confirmed him in his conviction that order—the kind he could bring, a mix of military structure and corporate efficiency, all shot through with a heartfelt Calvinist focus on sinners groveling before a stern God—was the cure. A drunken knife fight broke out the Sunday afternoon after his arrival; on learning that such were regular occurrences, he issued a pair of commandments: the first forbidding tavernkeepers from selling liquor on Sunday (until two in the afternoon), the second decreeing that anyone who drew a knife "in passion or anger" could face six months' imprisonment on bread and water; if he wounded someone with the knife, the sentence jumped to eighteen months.

His justice was blind when it came to distinguishing between colonists and West India Company sailors and soldiers. No one could accuse him—as they had Kieft—of favoring company employees. When two of the sailors from his voyage here were caught in violation of the ordinance forbidding sailors to go ashore without permission, he sentenced them "to be chained for three consecutive months to a wheelbarrow or a handbarrow and put to the hardest labor, strictly on bread and water."

But these were window dressing—straightforward "quality of life" directives that would play fairly well with the populace. The real issue to be dealt with was the semi-organized mutiny that was festering. As he marched around the little town those first few days, he had with him a piece of paper that fairly burned a hole in his pocket: a copy of the October 1644 letter sent by the colonists, in the names of Jochem Kuyter and Cornelis Melyn, demanding Kieft's recall. Ironically, the letter had achieved its purpose, but in so doing it had brought to the colony a man who looked on such acts as treason. The documents of the Manhattan-based colony give an idea of the complexity of Stuyvesant's mind: on the one hand, and in contrast to the standard view of him, he had a genuine appreciation of nuance, a politician's ability to play opponents off against one another, a capacity to weigh alternatives. For instance, historians have been mystified as to why Stuyvesant chose to retain Kieft's secretary; Cornelis van Tienhoven was greedy, dishonest, and famed for his lechery, all traits that the prim Stuyvesant—the man history remembers—would have abhorred. But Van Tienhoven was also one of the most intelligent men in the colony, a tenacious debater who was doggedly loyal to the West India Company, a man capable by turns of carrying out negotiations with area tribes in their own languages or leading pitiless military assaults on the very same villages. Clearly, Stuyvesant was able to weigh the man's various traits against one another and select according to his benefit. At other times, however, the more elemental Stuyvesant, who saw the world in the black and white of orthodox Calvinism, would predominate. This letter he had carried with him from Amsterdam struck him deeply. Its authors had violated the principles upon which the Dutch empire was founded, principles of order that had a theological underpinning and that had resulted in the creation of a successful and civilized society; the very clarity of the transgression in itself must have been satisfying. He would handle it with the decisiveness it deserved.

Meanwhile, a few steps away down the dusty riverfront streets of the town, clandestine meetings were taking place. The new director had promised a formal review of the case of Kieft versus the citizens of New Netherland, and Kuyter, Melyn, the jurist Adriaen van der Donck, trader Govert Loockermans,

Englishman Thomas Hall, a brilliant and multitalented Bohemian from Prague named Augustin Herman, and several other residents of New Amsterdam had taken Stuyvesant at his word and were preparing their case. Stuyvesant had no idea of their intentions, the depth of their commitment. Someone making a casual study of this portion of the records would be confused by the masses of pages, filled with impassioned invective and arguments, devoted to what ought to have been by this date—1647—a stale issue. They had complained about the director and had succeeded in getting him ousted; the war was over. Couldn't they all get on with their lives?

They were getting on with their lives. With the threat of Indian attacks removed, prosperity was returning. The ring of hammers on nailheads was constantly in the air; housing starts were up; fields were being cleared and plowed for planting; the harbor's shipping lanes were busier than they had ever been. And these men didn't want it to happen again—the sudden immersion in chaos. Once again they were building something; now they wanted a voice in the decision making. It hasn't been given much attention in the history books, but the little community on Manhattan represented one of the earliest expressions of modern political impulses: an insistence by the members of the community that they play a role in their own government. There were two major forces at work in the Dutch Republic, and this face-off pitted them squarely against one another. First was that of the empire builders, the merchant-princes and their military-trading captains, the slavers and slaughterers, the builders of outposts whose stone skeletons today form curious weed-strewn tourist attractions in places as far-flung as Ghana, Brazil, and Sri Lanka. The other force was intellectual and political; its roots lay in the Renaissance; it expressed itself in the philosophy of Erasmus, Spinoza, Grotius, and the adopted son Descartes. It had taken root in the trade-oriented, outward-looking cities of Amsterdam, Rotterdam, Antwerp, and Leiden; and through Kuyter, Melyn, and especially Van der Donck, it had exported itself to American soil. These men examined their situation from two perspectives. First, they had families to think of. But beyond the simple human impulse to protect, they had these ideas in their heads, having to do with being in charge of their own destiny—ideas still fuzzy and immature in relation to how they would develop in the next century, but also fresh and vital. They had passion.

Stuyvesant meanwhile had spent most of his years in an isolated farming province or in military outposts where life was a series of orders given and orders obeyed. He was smart, deep, honest, and narrow. He had little knowledge of intellectual currents in the wider Dutch world, let alone the wider European world. The situation had the makings of a showdown.

Through the days of early June, then, in private homes or the "clandestine groggeries" that Stuyvesant would later complain of, drinking ale from green stubbled-glass goblets, while those around them held to more innocuous games like backgammon and cribbage, the activists laid out a legal case against their former leader, which they believed would become a vehicle for winning a form of representative government for the colony. It's clear that Van der Donck held the pen, and shaped their anger into argument. He laid out, first of all, a long and highly legalistic series of "interrogatories" to be proposed to various men who had played parts in the crisis surrounding the Indian war. The slate of questions to be posted under oath to Hendrick van Dyck, a West India Company soldier who had led attacks on the Indians, cut directly to the core of the conflict and Kieft's responsibility for it:

1. Is he not well aware that the late Director General Kieft, did, on the night between the 24th and 25th February, in the year 1643, send a party of Soldiers over to Pavonia by the bouwery of Jan Evertzoon, and behind Curler's plantation on the Island of Manhatans and cause them to kill a party of Indians, with women and children, who lay there?

2. Did Mr. Kieft previously propose this expedition to the Council, and subsequently communicate it to him as Officer of the Soldiers, which he then was; and did he vote for it?

3. Were not the Indians much embittered by this act; and did not the general war between our Christians and these Americans* follow the next day, and date its commencement from that time?

4. Is it not also true, that all those Indians had fled to the above described place some days before, through dread of the Maicanders;† in the hope of being protected by our people from their enemies?

5. Did not we, the Dutch, in this country, live in peace with these Indians before and until this cruel deed had been wrought on them over at Pavonia and on the Island Manhatans?

*Note the use of *Americans* in reference to the Indians—see footnote p. 143.
†I.e., the Mahicans.

The questions for Van Tienhoven, Kieft's secretary and enforcer, began with the disastrous effort to force local tribes to pay a tax to the company for their protection, and grew, in perfect trial lawyer fashion, into a web of damning accusation:

1. Can he, the Secretary, not fluently speak the Manhatans language, which was used by the Indians hereabout?

2. Did he not, therefore, act as interpreter to the late Director General Kieft, with those Indians?

3. In what year was he sent to those Natives to collect the contribution of maize from them; if he was not employed, who then was?

4. To how many tribes was this done; and how are they named?

5. Did those Indians willingly consent to this contribution; or did they then protest against it; and what were their debates about it?

6. Can he report in writing—if not, verbally—the result of this mission, which Mr. Kieft entrusted to him?

7. In what terms did he endeavor to persuade the Indians to consent to the contribution?

8. In what year was he, deponent, sent by Mr. Kieft to the Raritanus; and did he not go there with a party of armed soldiers and sailors under the command of Heindrich, captain of the *Neptunus*?

9. What order did the Director give him, the Secretary, particularly in this case; and how did he execute it?

10. Did Mr. Kieft give any different orders to the soldiers generally, when they stood in front of the director's house, previous to setting out?

11. Were not similar expeditions sent out in the same year against the Raritans; and does he know what was the reason and object of them; and what was then accomplished?

12. Did not the Raritans revenge themselves the next year; killing four Christians, on Staten Island; and did they not afterwards destroy the houses of David Pietersen?*

In mid-June 1647, Stuyvesant gathered the parties—Kieft on one side, Melyn and Kuyter on the other—for a meeting he intended to be swift and decisive, at which the adversaries would sit quietly and listen to him lay out the situation and render his judgment. He was stunned to receive these long

*I.e., David de Vries.

lists of questions, together with demands that they be posed to the parties indicated and a call for the reorganization of the colony. He was known for his temper, and—his soldier's training winning out over his Calvinist up-bringing—salty language, and this was a perfect time to unleash some of it. He ordered a hasty end to the session, read through the documents that evening, and, the next day, reconvened his council—which consisted of sup-porters of Kieft's former government and men he had brought with him from Curaçao—to help him judge the matter. He had, however, already made up his mind—the pages of interrogatories only sharpened his convic-tion—and he gave his councilors a list of helpful questions to consider as they read over the material. These questions offer an exquisite window into his mind, and onto what might be called the Dutch Empire mind-set, when it came to the matter of popular government:

1. Was it ever heard or seen in any republic that vassals and subjects did without authority from their superiors, conceive, draft and submit to their magistrates self-devised interrogatives to have them examined thereon?

2. Whether it will not be a matter of very bad consequence and prepare the way for worse things to have two malignant private subjects arrogate to themselves the right and presume to subscribe for the entire council in-terrogatory articles on which to examine the former board, without being authorized thereto by their superiors or orders of the commonalty? I say malignant subjects, in view of the animosity between them and the late director and council, by whom they were held and proved to be dis-turbers of the public peace . . .

3. Whether, if this right be granted to these cunning fellows, they will on ac-count thereof hereafter not assume and arrogate to themselves greater au-thority against us and the appointed councilors, to usurp similar, yes, greater power in opposition to us, should our administration not suit their whims?

Stuyvesant's yes-men said yes—they agreed with him wholeheartedly that, in the words of the Englishman Brian Newton, "evil consequences" would ensue if these colonists were allowed to proceed in framing a full-blown legal argument against the lawful administration of the colony.

Stuyvesant rejected out of hand the notion that Kuyter, Melyn, and the others were acting as representatives of the colonists via the original board of eight men that Kieft had called together. These men represented of no one but themselves.

Several things now happened virtually simultaneously. Kuyter and Melyn complained that Stuyvesant and his council were prejudiced in favor of Kieft and the West India Company (they might have noted that Kieft, while awaiting passage to Holland, now sat as a member of the council), and therefore any verdict they rendered would be tainted. Stuyvesant, meanwhile, apparently showed Kieft the letter in which, three years earlier, this same handful of men, acting as they said on behalf of their constituents in the colony, had demanded his ouster. The directors in Amsterdam had never shown the document to Kieft. He studied the letter in a growing rage, the realization dawning that his career's ignoble end had come not thanks to the opinion of the directors in Amsterdam but at the hands of his own colonists.

Stuyvesant had banked on this reaction: acting more or less in concert with Stuyvesant's wishes, Kieft then wrote a formal complaint, declaring that these men had endeavored "with false and bitter poison, to calumniate their magistrates and to bring them into difficulty," complaining that they had "dispatched in an irregular manner and clandestinely sent off, that libellous letter," and demanding that they be prosecuted and his name cleared.

This was what Stuyvesant needed to move forward. He sent a messenger running down Pearl Street to Melyn and Kuyter's houses with a copy of Kieft's letter and an order that they submit a response within forty-eight hours. The leaders of what was rapidly becoming a political party then assembled to prepare their answer. It had to be done with some secrecy: Cornelis van Tienhoven's house stood right next to Kuyter's and Melyn's along the East River shore, and Stuyvesant was keen for information about other conspirators. If there was a time to back down, to respond gingerly and throw themselves on the mercy of the new director-general, it was now. They chose the opposite tack. The letter they crafted on June 22 is long, legalistic, courtly, precise, and unflinching. It is also pure Van der Donck.

The man had been steadily enmeshing himself in the affairs of New

Amsterdam for three years now, and especially since his recent marriage and move to his estate to the north of the island. As an attorney, he had appeared before Stuyvesant and his council. And as he had with Kiliaen van Rensselaer and Willem Kieft, he had begun insinuating himself with Stuyvesant from the moment of the new director's arrival. Stuyvesant evinces a fondness for him early in their relationship; it's not hard to imagine the Stuyvesants inviting Van der Donck and his English wife Mary Doughty (by Dutch custom women often kept their maiden names) into the director-general's home. Van der Donck and Stuyvesant's wife, Judith Bayard, must surely have reminisced and talked of mutual acquaintances in their common hometown of Breda. As Stuyvesant spent time with Van der Donck—who at twenty-nine was eight years younger than him—he found him capable and ambitious, a man he could develop into a West India Company official, a man who could help him in managing the colony. As he had with other father figures, Van der Donck took pains to present his model-son visage to Stuyvesant. The week before the preparation of the response to Kieft, Van der Donck magnanimously offered to put on his own account with Rensselaerswyck farmers a shipment of three hundred and fifty bushels of wheat and oats that the new director-general would need for the coming year for his family and animals. Stuyvesant accepted the offer.

At the same time, Van der Donck was involving himself in the affairs of the wider community, representing sailors, merchants, widows, and farmers in court, and associating himself with the colony's ministers, who were naturally men of influence in the community. Van der Donck comes across in the records from this period as a budding politician, a man working hard to make friends in both high and low places. While making himself useful to the director, he was also assisting his friend Melyn—whom he had known since their crossing together six years earlier—and his co-conspirators. And it is clear where his sympathies lay—indeed, it would soon become evident that his whole reason for building a political base was as a platform from which to fight the cause that by now burned inside him.

The letter crafted in response to Kieft's is channeled into the firm banks of legal protocol, but a river of emotion flows through it. It is addressed to Stuyvesant and his council, and begins with a flourish and a bracing succinctness:

Honorable Gentlemen!

The written demand of the late Director General Kieft was sent to us by the Court messenger about 9 o'clock on the 19ᵗʰ June of this year, 1647, with express orders to answer thereunto within twice 24 hours. Coming then to the point—

Item by item, then, it rebuts Kieft's charges that in the earlier letter to the directors in Amsterdam they had libeled him in representing the state of affairs. In some instances emotion shows through in biting irony:

The piles of ashes from the burnt houses, barns, barracks and other buildings, and the bones of the cattle, more than sufficiently demonstrate the ordinary care that was bestowed on the country, God help it, during the war.

At other times, such as when disputing Kieft's charge that the council had agreed with his plan to tax the Indians, it is all business:

The agreeing to the Excise is seen by 3 letters, E., F., G.; by the Acts of the 18, 21, 22 June, 1644, and therefore no further declaration is necessary.

Raw emotion is allowed to emerge once again on the subject of the slaughter of neighboring Indian villages:

It is chiefly manifest from their own act, that the Indians conducted themselves like lambs, before the melancholy spectacle of which they were the victims in the year 1643 over at Pavonia and on the Island Manhatas. Be it remarked, that they allowed themselves, their wives and children to be slaughtered at that time like sheep, and came (so to speak) like lambs to lie in our arms. We appeal in this case to the entire Commonality and to each member of it individually, who hath survived that time, to say how murderously the Indians were then treated. Would to God we may be found to be liars on this point.

Rather than sidestep the issue of whether the colonists have a right to involvement in their government, the letter takes the matter on directly. The late director-general took on "princely power," the council of eight was the closest thing to a representative body in the colony, and in the face of the outrageous decision to launch a war against the Indians the council acted properly in protesting. In the manner of the "elegant law" that Van der Donck studied at Leiden, the letter lines up ancient authorities to speak on the matter: Diogenes, Ambrose, Aristides, and Xenophon all weigh in on the rights and limitations of rulers in making the decision to go to war. Before Stuyvesant and his council, Kieft had demanded that Melyn and Kuyter be sent to Amsterdam and tried there "as pests and seditious persons." The letter now demands the right to go there, not as Kieft styled the two men but "as good patriots and proprietors of New Netherland." The case should be put to the highest governing body in the nation; the issue was not this particular war, this particular colonial administrator, but the rights of citizens in a far-flung outpost. It was a landmark issue; a test case. "Let us then once see what the law of nations thinks of it," the letter demands, calling on Grotius's recently minted principles of law.

Stuyvesant responded in kind, with an unusually long legal analysis of the situation, suggesting that he, too, saw the matter as a showdown between two competing views of the law. He called on his own ancient authorities, including biblical ones, which reveal his views of governance: "Thou shalt not revile the gods, nor Curse the ruler of thy people" (Exod. 22:28); "curse not the king, no not even in thy thought" (Eccles. 10:20); "Be subject unto the higher powers" (Rom. 13:1). Finally, military man that he was, he called on the Articles of War: "To utter words tending to mutiny and rebellion demands capital punishment." Technically, after all, the Dutch Republic was still at war with Spain, and Manhattan was an outpost of that war. As much to make an example for the colonists to note as to enforce the law as he saw it, he expressed his view that Cornelis Melyn, as avowed leader of a treasonous party, be put to death, while Jochem Kuyter should be banished and his property confiscated. Melyn expressed his intention to appeal the sentence in Holland, and Stuyvesant (as quoted by Van der Donck) shot back with black wit: "People may think of appealing during my time—should any one do so, I would have him made a foot shorter, pack the pieces off to Holland and let him appeal in that way."

Nevertheless, at the urging of his council, Stuyvesant amended the sentences of both men to banishment from the colony—effectively giving them an opportunity to appeal—and ordered them to depart by the first available ship.

A remarkable number of vectors then came to bear on a single object: the ship *Princess Amelia,* 600 tons, ringed with thirty-eight guns, riding at anchor out in the harbor, her hull neatly packed with 200,000 pounds of red dyewood she had picked up in Curaçao. It was the same ship that had brought Stuyvesant here; she was now ready for her return to Amsterdam. Her commander, a twenty-eight-year-old named Jan Claesen Bol, was, like John Farret, one of Stuyvesant's admirers: during his three-month layover on Manhattan, he had sat on Stuyvesant's council, overseeing the matter of Kieft v. Melyn and Kuyter. By mid-September, additional cargo—about 14,000 beaver pelts—had been stowed away, and she was ready for passengers.

And so they came: Kieft, eager—now that he had, in Stuyvesant, a powerful ally—to return home and defend himself, to clear his name and see his accusers punished; Kuyter and Melyn, armed with sheafs of documents, ready to appeal Stuyvesant's verdict before the States General in The Hague; the Rev. Everardus Bogardus, with whom Kieft had also tangled. And a good many of the lost contingent of soldiers who had bounced from Brazil to Curaçao to Manhattan, raggedly and repeatedly crossing Stuyvesant's path, were on board as well, the director having ordered them home in hopes of finally getting them off his back.

They set sail on August 16. The crossing was uneventful. And then, in a bizarre climax to the whole affair, Captain Bol made a classic mariner's error, mistaking the Bristol Channel (a.k.a. the False Channel) for the English Channel. The ship ran aground off the coast of Wales. Heavy surf heaved it up and down in three titanic hammerings, dashing it to pieces against the rocky bottom. For days after, Welsh farmers combed the beach for beaver pelts and other items of value: once-cherished pieces of lives transformed into flotsam.

*

THE INITIAL NEWS of the wreck of the *Princess* must have stunned the residents of New Amsterdam. The general view, once the initial shock wore off, was that God had been unusually straightforward in punishing Kieft for his many sins, and that the other passengers had had the misfortune of being too near the lightning bolt. The house of the director-general was probably not decked out in mourning either. Stuyvesant had tolerated Kieft because of his position; he had supported not the man but the office. As for Melyn and Kuyter, they had been misguided followers of an incoherent new line of thinking that was dangerous and immoral. He must have seen the wreck, in its totality, as an instance of the pure and terrible justice of the Almighty. There had been ugliness on both sides; as with Sodom and Gomorrah, and in the time of the Great Flood, the Lord had chosen to wipe the slate clean. But even in the direst of times He had kept faith with His people, by pre-serving a leader. Noah had been spared from the Flood, Moses was chosen to lead His people from waywardness. Now Stuyvesant could lead. He could turn his attention to matters of genuine importance.

And so he did, moving with ferocious competence. Had a lesser man been given the commission to strengthen the Dutch hold on their North American territory, the English would have swept in decades sooner than they did, and the Dutch imprint on Manhattan Island would have been too faint to make a difference to history. The problems that literally surrounded the colony were considerable and they had been allowed to fester. Stuyvesant had stepped into a chess game in which his predecessor had been an inferior player who had committed his resources into one ill-conceived strike while ignoring attacks from other areas. Stuyvesant as-sessed the threats, ranked them in order of priority, and went to work. He saw at once what historians later failed to recognize: that New England was not monolithic; there were four separate colonies, each with its own agenda, and they had a hard time getting along. The two southern colonies, Con-necticut and New Haven, were aggressive toward the Dutch; the other two, Stuyvesant sensed, wanted to find a way to live with their neighbor. New Plymouth, after all, had been founded by English Pilgrims who had spent long years as guests of the Dutch, and so were predisposed toward them. Massachusetts was likewise amenable; it was the largest and most powerful of the New England colonies, and John Winthrop, its elderly governor, who had devoted nearly two decades to fashioning a Puritan utopia in the New World (it was he who coined the phrase "City upon a Hill"), was, despite age and ill health, still the most influential man in New England. (It was largely because he had chosen to live there that Boston, rather than any of the other villages founded about the same time, became the capital.)

So Stuyvesant targeted Winthrop. "Honored Sr," began the letter he dictated to Winthrop (at the other end of the pen, translating into English, was one of Stuyvesant's English hangers-on, George Baxter). "I shall be boulde to propose to your wise Consideration, that your selfe, with other indifferent men of yor Countriemen . . . may be pleased to appoint the tyme & place, where & when yourselfe & they will bee pleased to give me a meeting . . ."

Stuyvesant knew that while powerful forces in England wanted to wrest control of his colony, in the chaos caused by the civil war, the New England colonies had largely been free to govern themselves as they saw fit. If he could cement a treaty with the leaders of the four respecting borders, it would be a great step toward putting his colony, as well as theirs, on a permanent footing. As it happened, Baxter, who delivered the letter in person, arrived in Boston while leaders of the four New England colonies were gathered there for a meeting, so Winthrop showed it to them. He then wrote back that while his illness had left him with a "Crazines of my head," he was still fit enough to agree with his fellow New Englanders that all wanted likewise to live in peace with the Dutch colony and all "doe readilie embrace yor friendlie motion concerning a meeting." The leaders also jointly sent a similar letter to Stuyvesant, welcoming him to America, "hoping all the English Colonies shall enjoy within your limits all the fruites of a neighbourly and friendly correspondency in a free concourse," and laying out a number of items that needed to be hashed out, including illegal trading activities and a high tariff being charged at Manhattan for shipping. Stuyvesant knew that the civil war in England had increased the New Englanders' reliance on Manhattan as a shipping hub. It must have pleased him that they raised the issue at once—he could use it as a bargaining chit in working out an agreement on borders. The New Englanders signed themselves "Your lovinge Friends the Commissioners of the vnited Colonies."

Next, Stuyvesant pivoted southward. He commissioned a detailed report on events that had taken place in the region the Dutch called the South River. It had been ten years since Peter Minuit led a Swedish expedition up this waterway that the Dutch considered a vital part of their North American territory. It would be no accident that the future cities of Philadelphia, Trenton, Camden, and Wilmington would spring up in this region. Stuyvesant could see, as Minuit had before him and William Penn would after, that water power, water transport, ocean access, and hundreds of square miles of richly exploitable wilderness could be translated directly into industry and commerce.

Kieft had ignored the foreign presence in this southern territory, and the Swedes had used that time to dig in. The leader of New Sweden now was Johan Printz, a great hog of a man whose four-hundred-pound body, as it lumbered within the palisades of his central fort, was less dressed than sided in the armor of the Swedish military. Printz had served as an officer in the Thirty Years' War, leading troops into battle in Germany and Poland before being discharged for surrendering the town of Chemnitz to a Saxon army. His New World posting was a chance to redeem himself by turning this wilderness into a functioning, profit-making colony. The Indians of the region gave him the nickname Big Belly, and he was as formidable in military guile as he was in size. The Dutch had constructed their original military-trading post on the river in what must now have seemed the distant past: 1624, when they were still considering making this region the capital of their colony. They had built Fort Nassau at the confluence of the South River and what they called the *Schuyl Kill*,* or Hidden River—convenient, they believed, to the Indians bringing furs downriver from the west.

But there was a flaw in this placement. The trading post was on the east side of the river, so that the Indians had to ford it to reach them. Peter Minuit had seen this problem from the beginning. So when he made his dramatic return to America to found New Sweden, he erected Fort Christina on the west, outflanking the Dutch and making the Swedes instantly more attractive to the Minquas (a.k.a. the Susquehannocks), the tribe that dominated the fur trade in the valley. When Johan Printz took over the Swedish colony, his first move was to further stymie the Dutch by constructing another fort farther downriver, nearer the bay, thus giving the Swedes effective control of the South River. Kieft did nothing to counter this, but the Dutch got help from an unexpected ally: the mosquito. The Swedes had built on a swamp. Soon the fair-skinned soldiers looked, one commander wrote, "as if they had been affected with some horrible disease." The soldiers called the place Fort Myggenborgh—Fort Mosquito; the bugs won, and it was soon abandoned.

*Technically, Schuylkill River is a redundancy since *kill* means river or waterway.

But Printz was far from finished. He began an elaborate rumor campaign among the Indians to the effect that the Dutch were planning to slaughter them; at the same time, he sweetened the deals Swedish traders were making with them. Then complaints started streaming into Stuyvesant's Manhattan headquarters from soldiers and company officials stationed on the South River. The Dutch had recently built another trading post on the river, but even before it was finished Printz erected a Swedish fort so close to it that the structures nearly touched. The massive Swede was as snide as he was wily, and the Dutch knew he was rubbing their noses in it. The Swedish fort, one officer whined in his report to Stuyvesant, "is the greatest insult in the world . . . for they have located the house about 12 or 13 feet from our palisades, depriving us thereby of our view of the stream." "My lord," another official wrote, "I firmly believe that he [Printz] had it built there more to mock our lords than to expect that it could realize any profit for him, since there is room enough beside our fort to build twenty such houses . . ." Sitting in his office on Manhattan, Stuyvesant was now able to summon a clear mental picture of his southern territory: the flat landscape; its placid river; warships whose masts were surmounted not with the orange, white, and blue flag of the United Provinces* but the blue and yellow cross of Sweden; the hidden inlets echoing with the cadences of the Swedish tongue as the golden-haired Nordics bartered with the Indians, struggling to comprehend their allegiances and business tactics.

Stuyvesant knew from the start that the real threat was from the English, not the Swedes. Dutch forces had already chased out English settlers who had sneaked south from the New Haven colony and tried to stake a claim on the Schuyl Kill. Stopping English activity in the region was paramount, for the Dutch, with their focus on waterways, knew what the English as yet did not: that the South or Delaware River began not in the south but far to the north of Manhattan, and wound its way three hundred miles southward (it would serve as the border between the future states of New Jersey and Pennsylvania) before emptying into Delaware Bay. Thus, if the English ever got control of it, they would have a stranglehold on Manhattan, and the Dutch colony would vanish.

*The colors of the Dutch flag of the seventeenth century were adopted in 1915 by the city of New York in recognition of its origins. There is thus a bizarrely direct connection between the colors flown by Dutch privateers cruising for booty on the Spanish Main three hundred and fifty years ago and the jerseys worn today by the New York Mets and the New York Knicks.

But Stuyvesant also understood the need to attack the Swedish problem before it sapped his colony's strength. He must have had a dossier on his rotund opposite in New Sweden, as he did on John Winthrop in Massachusetts. The three men had quite a bit in common. All were autocratic, moralistic Protestants. Printz, like Stuyvesant, was the son of a minister who had been groomed for the ministry but shifted at the last minute into military service. Stuyvesant may have known of Printz's failure on the battlefield; at any rate, he began laying out a course of action to consign New Sweden to history's dustbin. Eventually, he would have to journey to the region personally. For now, however, he issued sheafs of instructions. He ordered his representatives to buy up more land from the Delaware and Minquas. He wanted the Dutch forts on the river repaired. He wanted them stocked with goods, since the Minquas had complained about traveling far with their furs only to find the Dutch traders out of supplies. This was especially important, he wrote, because Printz had not been receiving regular shipments from Sweden.

Another issue: Minquas Indians had complained to him that New Amsterdam's dominant trader, Govert Loockermans, while on a foray on the South River, had killed their chief. Loockermans denied it, claiming he had only roughed the chief up a bit. In a clear example of Stuyvesant's political instincts winning out over his Calvinist upbringing, he instructed his official on the river to "inquire diligently into the circumstances and truth of the matter, and should you find Govert Loockermans to be at fault, conceal it so that on our part the Indians are given no occasion for new discontent." Then he added brightly, "I thank you very much for the eel which you sent."

*

MATTERS RIGHT OUTSIDE his front door were equally pressing. The fort itself was tumbling down and had to be rebuilt from the ground up. Besides that, Stuyvesant informed his council, the place needed "a school, church, sheet piling, pier and similar highly necessary public works and common buildings." It all had to get started more or less at once, as far as he was concerned. He had a duty to the place, and beyond that, it was his home; he cared about it. If it was to survive against the threats that loomed on all sides, then "this our capital" had to be made strong. He had kept Johannes

La Montagne, the Walloon medical doctor who had been the second member of Kieft's government, as a member of his own council, and La Montagne argued that the fund-raising that was necessary for these projects could only happen if he had the colonists on his side. And the only way to do this was to allow the residents to elect a board of representatives to advise him. Stuyvesant agreed. Following the custom in Dutch towns, the residents would select "à double number of nine persons" from among "the most notable, most reasonable, most honorable and most prominent" of them, and out of this group he, Stuyvesant, would then choose "a single number of nine" to serve. The first board included the Bohemian Augustin Herman, Dutch trader Govert Loockermans, English tobacco farmer Thomas Hall, and Michael Janszen, a close friend of Adriaen van der Donck, at whose home Van der Donck stayed when he remained in New Amsterdam overnight.

Van der Donck himself was not among the first "double number of nine," but the method of its selection helps explain his vigorous networking during this time. The board was to be the vehicle for political change in the colony, and becoming a member required winning the support both of the residents and of Stuyvesant himself. It's hard to avoid seeing Van der Donck as calculating, given the determined, almost fawning way he assists Stuyvesant in this period. Thanks to his marriage, Van der Donck was by now proficient in English, and he volunteered for a novel assignment when a Scotsman named Andrew Forrester made his way through the Dutch towns of Long Island— Vlissingen (later, Flushing), Heemsteede, Gravesend, and New Amersfoort—in September of 1647, waving a large square of parchment, covered in writing and seals, which he declared to the startled residents, made him governor of the entire region by virtue of a grant from the English crown. He arrived finally in New Amsterdam and, before a snickering crowd, demanded that Stuyvesant surrender to him. "Wherefore I had him taken into custody and on the next day placed under arrest at the City Tavern at the Company's expense," Stuyvesant later explained to his council.

It was a pretty bewildering turn of events. "What shall be done with said pretended governor?" Stuyvesant wondered aloud to the council. Was the man insane, or was this an organized tactic on the part of the English that needed to be treated with proper diplomatic niceties? Stuyvesant accepted the help of Van der Donck, and of two other English-speaking men, to investigate. They studied the commission, interrogated Forrester, and concluded that the man was the somewhat potty agent of the estate of an English lord who claimed title to Long Island and surrounding lands. With the assent of Van der Donck and the others, Stuyvesant decided to put the man in irons and ship him to Amsterdam, where government officials could sort through the matter.

The Forrester case was bizarre, but by no means unique. The settling of the North American continent had gone on long enough that it was now firing the imaginations of a fair number of European eccentrics. One sort particularly intrigued was the English noble of modest circumstances. Such men had seen with their own eyes the piece of paper King Charles bestowed on Lord Baltimore, by which he became master of his own private realm in the New World. The dream that took shape in some such minds was of a return to the Middle Ages; America in its virgin freshness they saw as a land of opportunity where dreams could come true, but, in a quixotic reversal of the direction that history would take, their dreams were all about the past, the halcyon days of knights and damsels, when their ancestors were still men of substance. Sir Ferdinando Gorges was one such nobleman who actually did receive title, back in the days of King James, to a huge chunk of North America, which he hoped to divide into medieval estates that he would distribute among his closest associates, who would build castles, gather squires and courts, drink mead, and clobber one another in pageants. Gorges died without ever setting foot in the New World, his dream died in the chaos of the civil war, and his tract eventually became the state of Maine. (Two hundred years later, when the U.S. government, during its own civil war, constructed a military installation on an island in Portland Harbor, somebody had the inspiration to name it after him as a nod to the odd dreamer who inadvertently founded the state, and so it remains Fort Gorges.)

Shortly after Forrester's appearance, yet another eccentric from the British Isles pitched up on the New Amsterdam waterfront with a similar claim. It was, in fact, the second visit from Sir Edmund Plowden, who had also shown up during Kieft's tenure, brandishing a document signed by the deputy general of Ireland, which, he said, gave him title to the area extending from Long Island westward beyond the Hudson River and including all of present-day New Jersey and parts of Delaware and Maryland. Plowden had it all worked out. The kingdom would be called New Albion, and he, its lord, would be styled the Earl Palatine of New Albion. Long Island would henceforth be known as the Isle of Plowden. There was apparently another arraignment at the fort in New Amsterdam, at which Van der Donck seems again to have served. Plowden declared that prior to his arrival in New Amsterdam he had been to New Sweden to inform its governor of his title, and was very much annoyed at the way he had been treated. Stuyvesant, who was perhaps getting used to the drill by now, and who must for once have sympathized with Johan Printz, simply told Plowden to leave the colony. Returning to England, Plowden published a little book called *A Description of the Province of New Albion,* in which, under the dazzling pseudonym of Beauchamp Plantagenet, he extolled the virtues of the new realm and especially of the Earl Palatine himself. He eventually wound up in an English debtors' prison.*

There was one other madcap, and ultimately tragic piece of business at the time of the Forrester episode—late 1647—with which Van der Donck may have assisted Stuyvesant. Harmen van den Bogaert, the onetime barber-surgeon who thirteen years earlier had made the first daring journey westward deep into Iroquois country, had been an active member of the colony ever since. He had married and fathered four children, had purchased an interest in a privateer called *La Garce,* which he then accompanied on a raiding voyage to the Caribbean, then served as supply master to the company, first in New Amsterdam and then at Fort Orange. He had also been involved in the affairs of the murdered wheelwright Claes Swits, to whom he had apparently been related.

In addition to all of this, Van den Bogaert had a secret, which he kept as quiet as possible since its discovery would almost certainly lead to a sentence of death. He had a fondness for men.

In the Calvinist Dutch colony, as in the Puritan English colonies, homo-

---

*The Plowden affair would not end here, but would go on and on, as a kind of Pythonesque subplot to American colonial history. In 1784, amid the confusion at the end of the Revolutionary War, an Englishman named Charles Varlo appeared in the new country brandishing Plowden's charter, which he had somehow purchased. Varlo distributed handbills to various Americans detailing his rights to a significant portion of their newly won land, and apparently delivered an address in several places "to the people of New Albion." We can only imagine his surprise when he reached St. Mary's, Maryland, which was held to be the seat of New Albion, and found there a man named Edmund Plowden—a descendant of the original, who had kept his ancestor's dream alive and traveled to the New World to claim his palatinate. This Plowden settled at an estate in Maryland called Bushwood, and Plowdens continued to live there for many generations. Charles Varlo returned to England and published his memoirs, which he called *Floating Ideas of Nature.*

sexuality was a crime on a par with murder. Van den Bogaert thought he had found a discreet outlet in the person of his young black servant, Tobias; we have no idea how Tobias felt about the relationship, but somehow the two men were caught in flagrante. Van den Bogaert fled. In 1647 New Netherland, however, there were few places to hide. You couldn't exactly lose yourself in a crowd—everyone knew everyone else. He might have tried to stow himself on a ship, if one were departing, but upon discovery he would have been shipped back for punishment. Instead, he went back to the one place he knew of where few others Europeans had been—into Mohawk country, retracing his journey of years earlier. It was autumn now, not winter, so the going would have been less difficult, but he was alone this time, traveling across dozens of miles of virgin woodland without a guide.

He made it to one of the villages that had befriended him years before, and presumably was welcomed by the inhabitants. Meanwhile, Nicolaes Coorn, who had taken over from Van der Donck as the law man of the independent fiefdom of Rensselaerswyck, did a bit of Sherlock Holmes–style reasoning, and sent a woodsman named Hans Vos off westward through the same forests on what may have been America's first bounty hunting expedition.* In a sequence foreshadowing the Wild West of two hundred years later, Vos cornered Van den Bogaert in an Iroquois longhouse used to store grain, and a shootout commenced. Van den Bogaert, once the hero of the colony, now laid low by his sexual proclivities, attempted a distraction by setting fire to the place. Vos caught his man anyway, and brought him back to Fort Orange. Coorn then wrote to Stuyvesant, informing him of the event and asking what should be done with the man.

Stuyvesant wrote back that he himself would stand in judgment at Van den Bogaert's trial, but not until spring, when the ice on the northern stretches of the river had broken and ships could get through. Before that, however, Van den Bogaert, certain of Stuyvesant's judgment and desperate beyond reckoning, escaped from the prison in the fort. As he ran across the frozen expanse of the river, he fell through a hole in the ice and drowned.

So ended the life of the barber-surgeon turned explorer, but the affair didn't end there. Shortly after, the Mohawks—in a turn of events that sug-

---

*In the small world of the Dutch colony, Vos would later require legal services, and would hire Adriaen van der Donck to represent him.

gests the depth of their understanding of European ways by this time—sent a delegation to Manhattan to sue the West India Company for damages resulting from the loss of their building and its stores of supplies. In deciding the matter, Stuyvesant might have taken counsel from Adriaen van der Donck, who knew the Mohawks and their methods of deciding grievances better than anyone in the colony. Stuyvesant concluded that the Indians were in the right, and ordered the sale of Van den Bogaert's Manhattan property, the money from which would pay what he acknowledged was the company's debt to the Indians.

Van der Donck seems to have assisted Stuyvesant with yet another matter at about this same time, this one crucial to Stuyvesant's leadership and to the colony as a whole. Besides the threats from the English, Swedes, and Indians, there remained the ongoing problem of insubordination from the semiprivate domain of Rensselaerswyck. With the death of Kiliaen van Rensselaer, the estate was now under the ownership of the diamond merchant's son, and in March of 1648 a new director arrived to run the place. Unluckily for Stuyvesant, Brant van Slichtenhorst, a bluff fifty-nine-year-old with vast experience as an administrator in the Dutch Republic, was virtually his equal in grit and resolve. He understood the language of the charter that Van Rensselaer had won from the West India company, which, in a throwback to the glory days of the Middle Ages for which men like Edmund Plowden pined, gave him almost autocratic powers. Stuyvesant read things differently; his own commission obligated him to rule the entire colony of New Netherland, which included the manor of Rensselaerswyck. It was a dispute over political jurisdiction, and Van Slichtenhorst brought it to the surface just weeks after he started work.

Stuyvesant had sent to Rensselaerswyck a seemingly innocuous proclamation declaring the first Wednesday of May a day of public fasting and thanksgiving throughout the colony. It was common of leaders in all Dutch communities, following storms, fires, invasions, or harsh winters, to set aside a formal day of thanks to the Almighty for seeing the inhabitants through the ordeal. But when the proclamation was handed round during church service in Rensselaerswyck, Van Slichtenhorst saw the symbolism in it, which he considered an infringement of his office. He stomped back to his headquarters and fired off a defiant protest.

Stuyvesant, too, understood the importance of symbols of power and the need to back them up. Almost immediately he set sail from New Amsterdam with a full military escort. When, some days later, the company sloop put in before Rensselaerswyck, Van Slichtenhorst extended him the courtesy of firing a welcoming salvo from the estate's cannons, but when they met and Stuyvesant ordered him to stand down and obey the greater authority of the Dutch colony, Van Slichtenhorst replied sharply, "Your complaints are unjust. I have more reason to complain, on behalf of my Patroon, against you."

It was only the beginning of a strident territorial battle between the two men, which would result, among other things, in the founding of the city of Albany. More to the point, we can see here another step in the dance between Stuyvesant and Van der Donck. Van der Donck seems to have accompanied Stuyvesant on this trip. It would have been natural for Stuyvesant to call on his experience: Van der Donck had spent his first three years working as the legal enforcer at Rensselaerswyck; he knew the politics and personalities of the fiefdom and of the West India Company's Fort Orange. And, indeed, the court records of Rensselaerswyck show that, after a long absence, Adriaen van der Donck appears again in the fiefdom's court in July 1648—exactly when Peter Stuyvesant made his trip northward.

So we have a nice picture coming into focus, of the correct, zealous, militaristic, thirty-eight-year-old leader of the colony, working energetically and with considerable creativity to establish control over his domain and secure its position. And as he assesses the men around him, he comes to rely on the thirty-year-old lawyer who knows so much of the law, the land, and the natives, and who goes out of his way to be of service.

December came. As the last day of the year approached and the ever-present winds off the harbor turned icy, the residents of New Amsterdam met to choose the first replacements to the board of nine representatives. Van der Donck's careful politicking in the community paid off—he was chosen as one of a pool of potential representatives. It was then a foregone conclusion that Stuyvesant, in selecting half of the men from this group, would pick the young man who had been of such service to him. And from the new board's first meeting, Van der Donck, who had already done much behind-the-scenes work with several of these men, stood out, both in the eyes of his fellow representatives and of the director. The others named him their leader and gave him a title—"President of the Commonalty." For a short time—a period of days, really—Stuyvesant was well pleased. Together, he must have thought, they could do great things.

Chapter 10

THE PEOPLE'S CHAMPION

The sun rose on September 28, 1647, to reveal, bobbing in the steel-colored waters off a gnarled limestone headland on the Welsh coast called Mumbles Point, a lone human figure, nearly lifeless, clinging to a spar of wood. All morning and well into the afternoon the man rode the waves, until at last they tossed him onto a sandbar two miles from shore. Along with the sputtering realization that he was alive came more information: there were other people here, similarly storm-tossed and stranded. Working together, they constructed a makeshift raft out of pieces of debris, and so made their way to the shore.

There, Cornelis Melyn found that his friend and fellow prisoner from the court of Peter Stuyvesant, Jochem Kuyter, was also alive. When the *Princess* broke up, Kuyter had been on the aft part of the ship, which cracked off in one large piece and floated, with him aboard, toward the scavenging Welshmen onshore. In all, 21 of the 107 passengers and crew members survived the wreck. Kieft died, the minister Bogardus died, and so, too, did most of the West India Company soldiers Stuyvesant had sent back to the Netherlands.

But surviving drowning was only the first stage of what would be an epic escape from fate's grasp. The two Dutchmen managed to cadge a few beaver pelts from the flotsam, which they sold in a nearby town, possibly Swansea, and, using these funds, made their way through the rutted, civil-war-scarred countryside to Bristol, and then to London, which they reached about three weeks later.

From our vantage, the seventeenth century seems an odd combination of the archaic and the modern. On the one hand, no infrastructure to assist shipwreck victims existed; you had to fight for survival, on land as much as against the waves. Then again, institutions that would feel instantly familiar today had a way of kicking into gear. As the various survivors of the wreck of the *Princess* staggered into London, insurance companies lined up to handle claims, lawsuits were filed, and public examiners picked up their quill pens, dipped them into pots of black iron-gall ink, and took testimony from survivors and eyewitnesses. The tangle of suits and claims took years to settle.

Melyn and Kuyter had hoped to find in London the long-serving Dutch ambassador, Albert Joachimi, who would help them to get home, but he was in Holland. Diplomatic relations were complicated by the war: King Charles was in prison, and no state in Europe yet recognized the government that Parliament had installed. The two disaffected citizens of the New World languished for months in England before finally winning passage to Holland, where they arrived around the end of the year. But the calamity had eroded none of their resolve; if anything, the shipwreck and its result—Kieft drowning and both of them surviving—reinforced their belief in the justness of their cause. They would even tell the story, in later years, that one of them had encountered Kieft on the waves just as he was about to go under, and that the former leader, in extremis, had admitted he had been wrong in his management of the colony and wrong to oppose them, and asked their forgiveness. Not the sort of confession a judge would be likely to accept, but a good indication of how thoroughly vindicated, how righteous and flush with new life and purpose, the two Manhattanites felt after the wreck of the *Princess*.

*

THE WALK FROM the City Tavern on the waterfront in New Amsterdam to the fort at the southern tip of the island was a matter of two minutes or so. It was pleasant enough: stepping out of the tavern—so common a place for transacting business it was now a semiofficial headquarters for many merchants and traders—you found yourself smack on the shore of the East River, looking out on the ships at anchor and across to the farmsteads in the village of Breuckelen. You turned right and walked south, with the river to your left and a row of gabled houses on your right, crossed the little bridge over the canal, continued down the narrow lane extending from it called, sensibly enough, Bridge Street, and there stood the fort, the ragged heart of town. Someone made this simple journey in the first days of January 1649 and delivered a letter to Director-General Stuyvesant. It was from the new assembly that represented the people of the colony and from now on would stand apart from Stuyvesant's council, which represented the company. The people in New Amsterdam and surrounding towns were calling this assembly the Board of Nine.* The letter informed the director that the Board would like leave to send one or more representatives to The Hague in order to appeal for the Dutch government to take over management of the colony.

The petition—in effect a request to be allowed to emasculate him—infuriated Stuyvesant. It must have confused him as well. He had actually lauded many of the activities the Board had undertaken in its first year in existence. The members had taken seriously their duties as representatives of the people and served a useful role. When residents brought them complaints about merchants fixing their prices on bread and wine, the Board appealed to Stuyvesant to stop it, and he did. Then, getting bolder, they laid before him a list of measures they said would improve the economy. He fulminated a bit at their effrontery, then, on second thought, decided to take "more closely into consideration and deliberation the petition and written remonstrance of the nine elected selectmen, our good and dear subjects," and made the suggested changes. But now, suddenly, the arrogance of these men had shot off the scale. It must have seemed especially strange given that his dutiful protégé, Van der Donck, was now in charge of the Board.

At the moment, there wasn't much time for him to dwell on the matter. Another issue was pending, which at first blush seems quite removed. Stuyvesant had to arrange a celebration in honor of an event that had occurred in Europe the previous year. In 1648, in the German city of Münster, negotiations involving representatives from across Europe had culminated in the signing of a peace treaty between Spain and the Dutch Republic. Eighty years of war was officially at an end. The echoes of this great event would reverberate even to the island of Manhattan. The West India Company colony had been founded, after all, as a base for carrying out the war. Manhattan, in the eyes of strategists in the Netherlands all those years ago,

*Officially, the Board represented the residents of the villages of New Amsterdam, Breuckelen (later Brooklyn), New Amersfoort (the future Flatlands section of Brooklyn), and Pavonia (Jersey City, New Jersey).

had been considered a staging area for launching raids on Spanish vessels coming to and from South America and the Caribbean, such as those carried out by Willem Blauvelt. All that was now in the past. The West India Company directors in Amsterdam would have to rethink the status and future of their North American possession.

In fact, the Münster peace treaty and the petition from the Board of Nine were related. Both were elbows from the forces of history into the gut of Peter Stuyvesant, urging him toward the future, toward a new vision for the colony. The peace treaty was something that he needed to accommodate. But he chose to ignore the petition, saying he would first have to inform the inhabitants of the several English villages that had begun under Kieft and continued as loyal components of the Dutch colony. Then he put the matter aside.

But the Board did not. From the City Tavern, Adriaen van der Donck was busy greeting and machinating with everyone from ship's captains to fur traders to bakers and distillers, all of whom had an interest in the future of the colony, and all of whom had something to say. Businessmen in the Netherlands had renewed their involvement in Manhattan since the end of Kieft's war with the Indians. Traders in New Amsterdam, with their ties to the world's greatest trading power, were among the most sophisticated on earth. Van der Donck and his fellow Board members met with them and listened as they described the conditions necessary to maintain a stable trade. He catalogued their output, and calculated that eighty thousand beaver pelts per year were passing through Manhattan on their way to the fur market in Europe. Because it was so important to the colony, he himself had become an authority on the beaver. He had raised the creatures, studied their life cycle, read everything that the ancient Roman authorities had written about them. (Later he would make it his business to disabuse Europeans of some erroneous beliefs that had originated with Pliny and others, notably about the miraculous powers of beaver testicles. "None of these," he concluded confidently about the Latin writers, "had ever seen a beaver.")

At the same time, Van der Donck was aware that the beaver trade was only, as he put it, "the means for the initial settlement of this fine country by Europeans." Tobacco was just as important a product, and one with a future. Amsterdam was already the tobacco capital of Europe; that fact, combined with artfully cost-cutting Dutch shipping and trading practices (they pioneered the concept of buying in bulk), led English tobacco farmers in

Virginia to rely on Manhattan as a shipping center. The world tobacco trade was in the first stage of its centuries-long surge, and even at this early point the Dutch had developed a marketing savvy that a Philip Morris, a Procter & Gamble, or a Frito-Lay might admire. They created a variety of blends, mixing premium Virginia leaf with lower-grade Manhattan product as well as Dutch-grown to suit a range of tastes and price points, added flavorings (lavender, nutmeg, rosemary, coriander, dill, vinegar), and paid careful attention to packaging. There was even a kind of advertising in the form of popular still life paintings involving tobacco motifs.*

The civil unrest in England only increased Virginia's dependence on Manhattan as a shipping center. The year before, when it looked as though England would block its colonies in North America from using foreign shippers, the governing body of Virginia derided its own shippers for their high prices and declared that Manhattan was vital to Virginia's economic survival. The recent excavation of the Jamestown settlement has uncovered Delft pottery, Dutch coins and pipes, and Chinese ceramics that came via Dutch shippers—all indications of the Virginians' reliance on Manhattan, and of the power of the Dutch Republic, which by now was not only the leading shipper in the world but the largest maker of manufactured goods.

All of which is to make the point that, where American history has always portrayed Manhattan succeeding as a commercial center only after the English takeover, in fact it was in the late 1640s that the city of New Amsterdam began its rise to become the hub of North American shipping. And now—starting on January 1, 1649, when he took his place on the Board of Nine—Van der Donck began in earnest to organize the businessmen who made the port function.

At the same time, he and his wife were beginning the task of developing their gargantuan estate along the river, just a stone's throw from the northern shore of the island. In keeping with the grandeur of his dream, Van der Donck had given his estate a name: Colen Donck, a compaction of "Van der Donck's Colony." He had building plans; he knew what crops he wanted to plant; he had made lists of the jobs that needed to be filled and the numbers and kinds of workers he wanted to recruit from the home country. Archaeological evidence suggests that he and Mary may have chosen a site for their

*The Netherlands is still renowned for its tobacco connoisseurship, and, not entirely coincidentally, one of the major Dutch cigarette brands is called Peter Stuyvesant.

home at the southern end of a long flat expanse that would have been ideal for large-scale farming. In 1910, New York City workers digging a sewer trench in this area of the present-day Bronx came across what proved to be the foundation of a seventeenth-century farmhouse. A 1667 map of this area shows a house labeled "Van Dunks." The only archaeological excavation of the site was done in 1990, and while the archaeologists found that the integrity of the site had been destroyed by the sewer trench, so that they could not obtain any further information from it, the sewer diggers had found Dutch bricks (slimmer than standard American or English bricks and of a yellow color), Delftware pottery fragments, combs, mirrors, lead window frames, pipestems, even wampum beads. Taken together with the early map of the area, these support the idea that this was the spot where Adriaen van der Donck decided to pursue his American dream. If this was indeed the location of the Van der Donck home, there is a pleasant appropriateness: today the area is Van Cortlandt Park in the Bronx, a vast, weedy stretch of grass informally subdivided into fields and pitches in which Bangladeshi and Guyanese cricketers, Irish hurlers, and Japanese softball players compete, none of whom, surely, has ever heard of the man who once lorded over the area and who helped make New York City a multicultural enclave.

The location had a lot going for it. The soil was rich, which Van der Donck could have discovered from the Wickquasgeck Indians from whom he had obtained title to the land—they kept a village here, which may have remained through Van der Donck's time.* A long, lazy stream ran along this stretch of farmland, skirted the house, and snaked down into the creek that separated Manhattan from the mainland, which the Dutch had named Spuyten Duyvil, or "devil's spout," after the dangerous eddies caused by the tide. By following this in a light sloop, or even in a canoe bought from the Indians,† the leader of the Board of Nine, in anticipation of the millions who would commute into Manhattan, could have made his way into the Harlem River, and then, riding with the tide, headed southward along the coast of the island, and come to dock at the small pier in front of the City Tavern.

---

*The site of the supposed Van der Donck house is just behind the gardens of the Van Cortlandt House. The Indian village, which was called *Mosholu* or *Keskeskick*, was located at what is now the Parade Ground.

†There are several references in the records to settlers using Indian-made canoes, and someone who had spent much time among them would have recognized their convenience.

The agitating residents of the town would have grouped themselves around that same shoreline one day in January 1649 to see an amazing sight: a ghost being rowed to the dock. It wasn't a total shock—Cornelis Melyn had written to his compatriots from Bristol, telling them about his and Kuyter's survival—but seeing the man in the flesh had to have reinforced what they had felt on getting word of their survival and Kieft's death: that they had a genuine cause, and that it was just.

As soon as Melyn could get into a secure space, free from eavesdroppers (his own house, perhaps—there, just a few steps up the shore to the right of the pier) with Van der Donck, Govert Loockermans, Augustin Herman, Jacob Couwenhoven, Thomas Hall, Jan Evertsen Bout, Michael Janszen, and others who considered themselves a part of this new political party, he opened his satchel and spread before them the fruits of his time in the homeland. Documents. Papers dramatically inscribed with the flourishes of government business and tied with ribbons bearing heavy official seals.

From the moment they had landed in the United Provinces, Melyn and Kuyter set about making their case, trying to undo Stuyvesant's sentence against them and in the process to make men of power in the home country appreciate the value of their North American colony. They found national politics in a swirl with the signing of the peace treaty with Spain; old alliances were shifting. Before, supporting the West India Company, which had been organized as a for-profit venture to raid Spanish shipping, had been the patriotic thing to do. Now people were free to consider other visions for the North American colony. It took months, but Melyn and Kuyter won a remarkable concession from the governing body, which now lay on the table: a mandamus, an order from the government of the Dutch Republic to the Director-General of the colony of New Netherland. The members of the Board of Nine must have gasped as they read the document—in its tone and language it was an utter vindication of their position. It decried "the war that Director Kieft illegally and contrary to all public Law, had commenced against the Indians" and the atrocities "which must startle the Christian heart that hears of them." It approved of the fact that popular representatives had been chosen to ensure that such calamities didn't happen again; it noted that Kieft, and after him Stuyvesant, had hampered these representatives. Stuyvesant's sentences against the two men were revoked, pending appeal, and Stuyvesant himself, or a representative, was to return to the home country to explain his conduct.

And there was more. Willem, the Prince of Orange—leader of the army and symbolic head of the Dutch state—had felt strongly enough about the matter that he wanted to weigh in on it as well. He wrote a personal letter, which Melyn had with him:

To Petrus Stuyvesant, Director of New Netherland, the 19th of May 1648
Honorable, prudent, and discreet, specially dear.

You will receive by the bearers hereof, Joachim Pietersen Kuyter and Cornelis Melyn, the commands which the High and Mighty Lords States General have resolved to communicate to you, to the end that you allow these people to enjoy their property free and unmolested there . . . we are disposed earnestly to admonish you hereby, in addition, expressly notifying that you shall have to allow said petitioners, peaceably and without objection to enjoy the effect of their High Mightinesses aforesaid resolution.

> *And herewith,*
> *Honorable, &c.*
> *Willem,*
> *Prince d'Orange.*

All of this was riveting to the Board of Nine and their supporters. For the first time they understood that there was a new era taking shape in the home country. And the new climate gave them an opportunity to state their case for a government that would put the colony on a secure footing.

In one of his responses to requests from the Board to be allowed to send delegates to The Hague, Stuyvesant had stalled by suggesting that, as representatives of the people, the Board should be sure that what they were proposing was indeed the will of the people. Now, emboldened by the support from Holland, the Board members decided to follow his suggestion. They would ask the people—one by one—whether they felt there was a need for a reform in government. In a remarkably direct approach to democracy, Van der Donck, Loockermans, Janszen, Herman, and the other members of the Board walked out the front door of the tavern, divided the streets of New Amsterdam among themselves, and began knocking on doors. People must have had a lot to say, because once the canvassing was finished the Board decided to compile a dossier. Van der Donck took on the task of collating the complaints and distilling the thoughts of the entire commonalty into a single document.

Stuyvesant watched the canvassers marching through the town and, as far as he was concerned, openly instigating revolt. He sat on his fury for a time, then it erupted. At some point during the months of January and February 1649, while Van der Donck was putting together his brief, there was a confrontation between the leader and his onetime disciple, in which Stuyvesant tried to comprehend how the younger man could turn on him, perhaps even gave him an opportunity to back down, and then finally severed personal ties. Unfortunately, Van der Donck doesn't record the details of the meeting, saying only that "the General" had, from the time of the door-to-door canvassing, "burned with rage."

This was the moment when Van der Donck finally showed his hand. Three times now he had gone through the same series of maneuvers with men in power—ingratiating himself as he worked into a position of some authority, then suddenly turning brash, defiant, willful. Now he let his true feelings, his patriotic fervor, show. Stuyvesant would surely have countered that it was he who was acting in the best interests of the colony, pointed out that they were beset on all sides, and made plain that any effort to undermine him in such circumstances was tantamount to treason. Both men had strong points. Stuyvesant was indeed holding the colony together. But at the same time he was blind to what Van der Donck saw: that military and diplomatic maneuvering vis-à-vis the English, Swedes, and Indians would only hold for a short while, that without a revamp of its entire structure the colony would die from within.

There was no compromise possible for either man. As a last attempt at coming to an understanding, Stuyvesant apparently offered to work together: the Board would share the information it had gathered with him, and he would take their advice under consideration. But this would defeat the whole purpose of the delegation, which was to be independent of the West India Company. Van der Donck informed him, as he later wrote, that the Board "would not communicate with him or follow his directions in anything pertaining to the matter."

That cut it. The confrontation ended with Stuyvesant exhibiting what

Van der Donck called "a bitter and unconquerable hatred" for the members of the Board, "but principally against those whom he supposed to be the chief authors" of the move to undermine him. As Van der Donck describes this encounter for the benefit of officials in the Netherlands and characterizes Stuyvesant's change of feelings toward certain once-trusted comrades, the formality of the prose actually seems to heighten the emotions involved, leading one to believe that there really had been warm feelings between the two men: "these persons had been good and dear friends with him always, and he, shortly before, had regarded them as the most honorable, able, intelligent and pious men of the country, yet as soon as they did not follow the General's wishes they were this and that, some of them rascals, liars, rebels, usurers and spendthrifts, in a word, hanging was almost too good for them."

Stuyvesant had reached his limit. Whenever he decided to move, he did it forcefully. One day at the beginning of March, probably accompanied by a contingent of West India Company soldiers, he marched around the corner from the fort to the home of Michael Janszen—the Board member with whom Van der Donck had been friends since the time both had lived at Rensselaerswyck. Van der Donck had, as usual, been staying here, but no one was home at the moment. They searched the place and found the sheaf of papers that contained the lists of residents' complaints and laments about the colony and its management, and also the draft document Van der Donck had been preparing. Stuyvesant took it, and what he found in it confirmed him in his next step. The next day, he had Van der Donck arrested and imprisoned. Then he hastily sent Philip de Truy, his "court messenger," to the members of his council and to some of the Board of Nine, demanding their presence at an emergency "supreme council."

The men—fifteen in all—assembled in an atmosphere of great tension. Stuyvesant's face, even in light moments, had a jowly grimness to it, and he cannot have seemed anything but black as they waited for him to announce the reason for the unusual gathering. Then he told them that Van der Donck had been arrested and charged with *"crimen laesae majestatis"*—high treason. The documents found in his possession "grossly slandered" the director-general and contained "great calumnies" against the government leaders in The Hague.

At this moment Stuyvesant's vice-director, Lubbert van Dinklagen, the only lawyer in the colony besides Van der Donck, stunned his superior by interrupting him with a formal protest, charging that "the honorable director . . . has heretofore done and still does many things" on his own, without informing his council, "also because he has caused Adriaen van der Donck to be placed under arrest" without consulting them. It was an electric moment. That Stuyvesant now had insubordination from his own council of hand-picked members—indeed, from his second in command—must have shaken him and given new hope to the Board members present, all of whom had to have been fearing for their own lives as well as Van der Donck's.

Stuyvesant collected himself, and, changing tactics, turned on Van Dinklagen. He read out a passage from the confiscated writings in which Van Dinklagen supposedly defamed the government in Holland. Van Dinklagen, indignant now, denied he had ever said such things and demanded to see the pages where they were written. Stuyvesant refused. Then he asked each man present to state for the record his opinion on what should be done with Van der Donck. Van Dinklagen spoke up first, insisting that, in accordance with Dutch law, Van der Donck be examined on the matter and then released on bail. But Brian Newton, who had served Stuyvesant loyally since Curaçao, who had been at his side when he lost his leg, declared that the man should remain in prison and be interrogated there. Most of the others agreed. Augustin Herman, in an act of defiance against the entire proceeding, refused to give an opinion.

Stuyvesant had summoned only six of the Board members to this special council—seemingly out of fear that the whole group of them would vote against him. With six of them and eight of his trusted advisors, plus himself, he could be more sure of a favorable outcome. Now, however, it looked as though Van Dinklagen and one or two others would swing the other way, so he adjourned the session without calling a vote. Two days later, he assembled his ordinary council, without the Board members, and "by a plurality of votes" it decided to keep Van der Donck in custody until a committee had investigated the case. Two days following that, on the eighth of March, with Van der Donck still in confinement, people from all the villages in the area around Manhattan gathered in the church at Stuyvesant's bidding to debate a matter that would have serious import for the colony. Shortly before this public meeting, Stuyvesant had gathered with his council and declared that he would read a "writing" to the populace. Presumably it contained an account of Van der Donck's treasonous behavior and Stuyvesant's decision on punishment.

But he never got to read it. After Van der Donck's arrest and the abortive special council, his compatriots had gathered with Cornelis Melyn and plotted a nervy countermove. Now, in the church, before nearly the entire population of New Amsterdam and the surrounding villages, just as Stuyvesant was getting ready to speak, Melyn rushed to the podium. The States General had given him the task of carrying their mandamus to New Amsterdam and serving it on the director-general himself, or naming some other officer or officers to do so. It was a legal technicality—the serving of a summons— but Melyn, who had a flair for theatrics, wanted to make the most of it. He now declared in a loud voice his intention to fulfill the wishes of the States General by having the Board of Nine serve the mandamus on Stuyvesant. Then he handed it to Arnold van Hardenbergh, a member of the Board, and asked him to read it.

Stuyvesant knew what the document contained, and had no wish to have its chastising language, ordering him back to Europe like a misbehaving child, aired in front of his constituency. He declared there was no need to read the document, as he was ready to receive it. "I must have the copy," he roared, and reached out to grab the thing. In the scuffle, the document was torn and the heavy wax seal that marked it as an official order of the Dutch government came off. Everyone watched in amazement then as the disc of wax fell, floated toward the ground, and then hung, dangling by a strand of parchment. The symbolism was blatant: here these men stood in the holiest building in the colony, defaming it with their raised voices, while the seal of government dangled between them. In the gasp of silence that followed, Melyn informed Stuyvesant that, if he wanted a copy of the document, there was one for him as well as one to be read to the populace.

The crowd erupted at that point. Stuyvesant must have had soldiers on hand, and things were starting to look ugly. He was a born leader; never had he endured such a breakdown of authority. His impulse was to crack down hard, but he also saw that the place was on the verge of chaos; the event, he later wrote to the States General, was "so shaped that massacre and bloodshed might have been the result, had we not converted ourselves from the highest to the lowest, and permitted the indecent service of the summons."

Recognizing that his enemies had trapped him, he brought the assembly to order, and directed the man to read the scolding document.

When it was done, with all eyes on him, Stuyvesant spoke with wrathful brevity:

"I honor the States and their Commission, and will obey their Commands, and send an Agent to maintain the judgment, as it was well and legally pronounced."

And then he left.

It was surely the most humiliating moment of Stuyvesant's life. "Mutinous and insulting" he would later call the spectacle. His soldier's pride, his simple, country-bred dignity, had been trampled. He believed steadfastly in his commission, his devotion to the colony was real, and already he was achieving results vis-à-vis the English to the north, but none of this mattered to these men who seemed bent on self-destruction.

Melyn was surely impassioned, but he tended to be too histrionic even for his fellow agitators. Stuyvesant was right to complain about how the man, even before reaching Manhattan, had gotten off the ship in Boston and bragged to the English that he had a commission to send Stuyvesant back to Holland as a prisoner. Such behavior didn't help Stuyvesant in his dealings with the New England governors. Then again, Stuyvesant had provoked the men. It's hard to imagine that the Board would have gone along with the spectacle in the church had Stuyvesant not taken Van der Donck into custody. The crime of high treason was, of course, punishable by death. Their necks were all on the block. He had raised the stakes, and forced them to do the same.

At this moment, with his popularity at a low ebb, Stuyvesant walked into a political scandal. It happened that a case of muskets arrived in port at this time. When people found out that it was Stuyvesant himself who had ordered them, and that he intended to sell them to the Indians, in order to maintain goodwill, it became the talk of the town. While the residents were barred from selling firearms to the Indians, the director himself was doing just that, apparently for his own personal gain, and at a time when firearms were in short supply even among the colonists. Stuyvesant was forced to explain his behavior before his own council, but whether or not he had committed a crime he was guilty of violating the politician's first rule: never to give the appearance of wrongdoing. He was thrown on the defensive.

So it was while he was under this cloud that Stuyvesant had to decide what to do with Van der Donck. If he had had the support of his council and the people, he may have executed the man. As it was, however, his onetime loyal lieutenant, Van Dinklagen, was now firmly against him, watching his every move to see that he acted in accordance with Dutch law. It was probably at his insistence that Stuyvesant realized he could not try and punish the man based solely on the sheets of papers confiscated from him—especially as Van der Donck had, from confinement, agreed that it was possible some of what was contained in the pages was in error, since it was raw data that he had compiled from residents. So Stuyvesant ordered Van der Donck to "prove and establish or to revoke what he has injuriously written." For the time being, Van der Donck was released from confinement. He was, however, banned from serving on the Board of Nine.

Van der Donck stepped outside into the late winter daylight a new man. By imprisoning him, Stuyvesant had anointed him as the people's champion. If Stuyvesant was now on the defensive, Van der Donck, the one under criminal charge, was flush with momentum. And by ordering him to prove the truth of what he had written, Stuyvesant in effect gave him a license to pursue the business of governmental reform.

And so he did. Walking the gabled streets of the young, rude, vibrant town, with the rough winds of early spring at his back and the inhabitants greeting him and congratulating him in their unique mix of accents and languages, he must have felt that everything he had done—from his university days at Leiden to his free-form stint as the lawman of Rensselaerswyck to his diligent politicking among the Manhattanites—had led to this moment. People knew him as an estate owner—*Jonker* ("Young Squire") is what everybody called him on the street. And that role sharpened his profile as activist: he had the stature of a landowner, and yet he was clearly not following the path of a man like Kiliaen van Rensselaer, who had tried to milk the New World of profits from the comfort of his Dutch home. Van der Donck was invested in the colony personally, in its people and its future.

Everything now went into preparations for a delegation to the Dutch Republic. Legally, all the principal players should be involved, so, beginning the day after he was released from prison, Van der Donck fired off a series of summonses—to Van Dinklagen, La Montagne, Brian Newton, and other councilors and officials—requesting each man "to appear by the first opportunity at The Hague, before their High Mightinesses." He delivered these, received their answers (mostly variations on, "Of course I won't go"), and recorded the whole thing in a flurry of paperwork. He can't have expected the entire government of the colony to up and sail to Holland to defend itself, but getting these things down on paper was, to him, a necessary step.

It annoyed Stuyvesant no end—so much so that, on May 8, he issued a new ordinance:

> Whereas it is daily observed that . . . great abuses are committed in the writing and procuring of depositions by private persons who are neither pledged thereto by oath nor qualified thereto by official authority, whereby frequently many things are written to the advantage of those who have the papers drawn up, interspersed with sinister, obscure and dubious words . . . to the great prejudice and damage of the parties; therefore, in order to prevent this result, dangerous in a republic . . . we annul and declare invalid . . . all affidavits, interrogatories, or other instruments serving as evidence, which are written by private individuals . . .

Undeterred, through May and June, writing like a man possessed, Van der Donck pulled together all the information that he and his colleagues had collected from residents and constructed what would become perhaps the most famous document to come out of the Manhattan-based colony, the *Remonstrance of New Netherland*, an eighty-three-page formal complaint, which he intended to present to the governing body in The Hague and which would in time root the Manhattan colony's structure in Dutch law and, eventually, help give New York City its unique shape and character. Its opening words carry the full measure of Van der Donck's thoughts and emotions. He managed to bundle together in a few lines his exuberant pride in Dutch exploration and discovery, his passion for his adopted homeland, even his familiarity with the local Indians. At the same time, for the benefit of government officials who had little knowledge of the colony, he put the matter of its future development in a concise and accurate historical context, going straight back to the beginning:

> Among all the enterprising people in the world, who search for foreign countries, navigable waters and trade, those who bear the name of Netherlanders will very easily be able to hold their rank among the foremost, as is

sufficiently known to all those who have in any wise saluted the threshold of history. It will, in like manner, be also confirmed by our following Relation, for in the year of Christ 1609, was the Country of which we now propose to speak, first found and discovered at the expense of the General East India Company—though directing their aim and design elsewhere—by the ship *Half Moon,* whereof Henry Hudson was master and factor. It was afterwards named New Netherland by our people, and that very justly, for it was first discovered, and taken possession of, by Netherlanders and at their expense, so that even at the present day, the natives of the country (who are so old as to remember the event) testify, that on seeing the Dutch ships on their first coming here, they knew not what to make of them . . . We have heard the Indians also frequently say, that they knew of no other world or people previous to the arrival of the Netherlanders here. For these reasons, therefore, and on account of the similarity of Climate, Situation and fertility, this place is rightly called New Netherland. It is situate along the North Coast of America, in the latitude of 38, 39, 40, 41, 42 degrees, or thereabouts. . . . The land of itself is fertile, and capable of being entirely cultivated by an abundance of people . . .

Many other supporting documents were necessary—a formal petition asking the States General to take charge of the colony, and dozens of pages of heavily annotated "additional observations" on the state of affairs, the West India Company's "tyranny," and the need for "suitable municipal government." It was a major legal undertaking, appropriate to the gravity of the situation and the potential that Van der Donck and his colleagues saw in the island of Manhattan, the river it lay in, and the continent to which it formed the gateway.

Stuyvesant meanwhile had decided he couldn't stop the Board from sending its delegation, but he would counter them. It was unthinkable that he would go himself in response to the mandamus; he was in the midst of delicate diplomacy with the New England governors and with chiefs of the Raritan, Nyack, and other area tribes. To travel personally, he explained to the States General, "we cannot do consistently with honor and oath." He would send Cornelis van Tienhoven both to represent him against Melyn's charges and to represent his government in the battle for control of the colony. But while Stuyvesant remained busy managing the affairs of the colony, an instance of how remarkably bluntly he could maintain a grudge occurred on June 14, when a trader named Jacob Loper appeared before him asking for a license to trade on the South River. "Whereas the said Loper married the daughter of Cornelis Melyn," Stuyvesant's decision was recorded, for all to see, "the honorable director general is of the opinion that the request cannot be granted."

The Board of Nine, meanwhile, chose a delegation consisting of two of its members—trader Jacob van Couwenhoven and farmer Jan Evertsen Bout—and its ex-leader, Van der Donck. If Stuyvesant protested that he had released Van der Donck from prison with the express order that he not engage in official business, there is no record of it. Van der Donck would certainly have countered that he was only following the order to "prove and establish or to revoke what he has injuriously written."

The men prepared to leave. Van der Donck spent time with his wife on their estate, making lists of supplies needed and skilled workers he should hire in Europe. He agreed to represent a woman named Annetie van Beyeren, who lived in the Long Island village of Vlissingen (i.e., Flushing), in the settling of her affairs in the home country. And he took on one other piece of legal work in the last days before departure. Willem Blauvelt, the sometime pirate, had been a swaggering presence on the island for many years, and his frigate, *La Garce,* had been a financial interest for many of the prominent men of New Amsterdam, including Augustin Herman, Jacob van Couwenhoven, who was about to accompany Van der Donck to Holland, and former director Kieft. With the full backing and support of the colonial government, the frigate had, throughout the past several years, set off for the West Indies and returned bearing Spanish prizes: ships laden with tobacco, sugar, ebony wood, and wine. All the partners in the venture received profits from these raids; this sort of activity had been the centerpiece of the West India Company's business in the New World.

With peace, however, privateering had become illegal. But Captain Blauvelt had had a hard time coming to terms with the news. Recently, as before, an eager crowd had gathered on the waterfront at the cheery sight of *La Garce,* the Dutch flag snapping at the mast, approaching with a fine prize in tow. The problem was Blauvelt had snagged the Spanish bark "in the river of Tobasco in Campeachy Bay" (on the west coast of the Yucatan Peninsula) five months after the peace treaty was signed, setting off in a series of law-suits. Van der Donck had been hired by one of the owners of Blauvelt's vessel, and took part in untangling the mess until the day before he sailed for Europe. It was a fitting last piece of business, since it signaled the end of the old order on Manhattan.

There was a final encounter between Van der Donck and Judith Bayard, Stuyvesant's wife. He met her on the street on July 29. Whether they talked and had somehow maintained cordial relations we don't know. She may have been preoccupied: the Stuyvesants' first son, Balthasar, was now twenty-one months old, and the second, Nicholas, a baby of seven months. At any rate, Van der Donck handed her a letter from Melyn to Stuyvesant—which he himself had surely helped write. Stuyvesant still had not allowed Melyn use of his land and property, as the mandamus had ordered. The letter demanded that he do so, and also that he make available to the delegates such documents as they required to present their case, and to do it soon since "time is short and the vessels are making ready."

Judith handed the letter to Stuyvesant, who slashed out a reply, which he titled, "Answer to Cornelis Melyn's disrespectful Protest handed to my Wife, as she says, by Adriaen van der Donck and A. Hardenbergh," in which, through clenched teeth, as it were, he granted the man use of his property, and declared, "Who the delinquent is, God and the law have to decide."

From this letter we have the information that Stuyvesant planned to send his representative Van Tienhoven on the readying vessel, which means that Van der Donck and Van Tienhoven—the sweaty, corpulent, wily defender of Stuyvesant and the West India Company—must have stood on the deck of the same ship as the low spread of the village, with its windmill and fort prominent, receded into mist. Ahead of Van der Donck lay the distant continent of his birth.

Chapter 11

AN AMERICAN IN EUROPE

In January 1646 a coach, drawn by six horses, labored through the frozen ruts of a road in the German countryside. With gilt woodwork and attendants tricked out in scarlet capes and hats, it made a vivid impression against the dead landscape. Two rows of retainers rode ahead, swords at their sides. Peasants by the roadside couldn't help but gawk as the entourage passed.

Inside the coach sat a sixty-one-year-old man, his sedate attire in contrast to the grandeur of the vehicle. He had a tapered beard and sharp eyes, an expression of sad, solemn decency. Sharing the cabin with him were his wife and their granddaughter. All three of them must have been weary as they neared the end of their one-hundred-twenty-mile journey. Just now, as they rounded this bend, the steepled skyline of the city of Münster came into view.

The man's name was Adriaen Pauw. He had long been one of the most important men in the Dutch Republic, and now he was about to attempt something that, should it come to pass, would transform European history. He was quite conscious of this—so much so that he would commission the above-described painting of the moment of his arrival to document his role in history. He believed that he and his like-minded colleagues had an opportunity to redraw the rules by which nations had governed themselves for centuries, to lay a new course for politics and for human affairs.

As Pauw's carriage rumbled along, nearly every state in Europe was at war and had been for the entire lifetime of most inhabitants. Going back into the Middle Ages, it had been generally accepted that war was the natural state of nations, that a country defined itself in large part by its clashes with enemies and alliances with friends. In the early 1640s, however, one of those epochal changes of thinking began to occur in the minds of men from different nations and traditions. The new mind-set had its intellectual origins, most notably, in the Dutch jurist Hugo Grotius, the man who was the guiding light to Adriaen van der Donck and other law students of the era. Twenty years before, Grotius had put forth the idiosyncratic proposition that peace was the natural state of mature, civilized nations, and war ought to be considered only as a last resort, and even then should be governed by rules to which all parties subscribed. Remarkably, monarchs paused in the midst of flinging their armies at one another to read Grotius's book. King Gustavus Adolphus of Sweden supposedly kept *De Jure Belli ac Pacis* on his person as he led his troops into battle.

Grotius's radical concept had gained momentum in the intervening years and was now decidedly in the air. The peace negotiations at Münster would be unlike anything that had come before in world history. Each envoy, in expression of his government's awareness of the magnitude of the undertaking, arrived with an entourage of knights, halberdiers, trumpeters, archers, foot soldiers, and an army of retainers; the French delegation numbered one thousand people. As it became clear that a treaty would be reached, each envoy commissioned a suite of portraits of all the dignitaries—the collection in Gripsholm Castle near Stockholm, still intact, runs to seventy-four paintings.

Negotiations actually went on in two places at once—Münster and Osnabrück—and linked together the eight decades of combat between Spain and the Dutch provinces on the one hand and the three decades of brute slaughter that had occupied much of the rest of Europe. Needless to say, Thirty Years' War and Eighty Years' War were names given after the fact; at the time it was simply endless strife.

It was all self-consciously monumental because, as the participants were well aware, it was the first time representatives of European nations had come together as separate political entities rather than as units under the umbrella of the Vatican or the Holy Roman Empire, acknowledged one another as sovereign, and tried to work things out on their own. It was the birth of secular politics, the forerunner of Versailles, Paris, Camp David, and the United Nations, the creation of a political map of Europe that would hold into the twenty-first century. It was, in a political sense, the launch of what historians would one day decide to call the modern era.

Adriaen Pauw cut an unusual figure in Münster. The term "baroque," so fitting to the age, applied as much to personal fashion as to art; ambassadors considered themselves diplomatic peacocks whose personal finery informed others of their nation's magnificence. As a representative of the anomalous Dutch republic, Pauw was one of the few non-nobles in attendance, and his drab Calvinist dress—a study in gray, black, and white—was a signal of what, as far as the Dutch were concerned, the negotiations were all about.* The purpose of the gathering was to get Spain—with the most determinedly regal court in Europe—to acknowledge the independence not only of its long-rebelling protectorate, but of a nation that proposed to exist without a monarchy. Virtually all the titled envoys to the peace negotiations—the Duke of Longueville, Count of Peñaranda, Papal Nuncio Fabio Chigi, Count Hugo Eberhard Kratz von Scharfenstein, Johan Ludwig, Count of Nassau-Hadamar, Count Palatine Charles Gustav—had trouble swallowing this; the very word *ambassador* had always had as its referent a royal court. Pauw was no spartan—he lived in a castle with a moat, surrounded by fields of red-and-white-striped tulips that were his own personal hybrid—but there was a point to be made.

In the end, peace prevailed at Münster and Osnabrück. The marathon negotiations were followed by appropriately baroque treaty preparations, then, in 1648, by the signings themselves (history has linked the two treaties by referring to them jointly as the Peace of Westphalia). And then the parties started. They went on for years, crisscrossing central Europe like brushfires. For most of Europe, the celebration was at the end of decades of slaughter. In the United Provinces of the Netherlands, the feelings were much more acute. Independence, recognition, vindication—the results of the treaty amounted to, on a societal level, a catalogue of psychological power terms. When Pauw, his fellow Dutch envoys, and the Spanish representatives put their signatures and seals to a single piece of paper, it signaled the Moment, the ignition of the Golden Age. Publishers ran off copies of the treaty, which became a bestseller. Celebrations flared through every city and village in the seven provinces. Plays, poems, salutes, parades, porcelain tiles, sermons, drinking bouts, brothel binges, painting commissions, public works projects—in

---

*There was also a linguistic irony in Pauw's drab appearance, since his last name meant "peacock."

every possible human manifestation, the Dutch proclaimed the new age. The euphoria built steadily over the months following the signing.

It was into this atmosphere—of a society conscious of a future laden with prosperity, peace, and power, and alive to the possibilities of secular politics—that Adriaen van der Donck sailed in the beginning of October 1649. He found his homeland reborn, the cause for which his grandfather had fought and become a hero vindicated. The war into which he himself had been born and raised was over. It was a new world, a new country.

But it was not Adriaen van der Donck's country—not anymore. Whatever joy he experienced and celebrations he took part in, he seems not to have wavered in his commitment to his adopted land. He was a prototype of a species that would number in the millions in the coming centuries: the European who crossed the ocean and found, in the vast continent at the other end, a new home and purpose. He was an American.

Into the harbor at Texel, the grassy, windswept North Sea island from which Henry Hudson had set out forty years earlier, the ship sailed. From there Van der Donck and his colleagues, Jacob van Couwenhoven and Jan Evertsen Bout, would have boarded a public transport boat, and so sailed southward, into the famed forest of masts that was the harborfront of Amsterdam, the most vital city on earth.

Of course, the city had not waited for the signing of a document as the signal to begin its golden era. Prosperity had been building for decades now, and so had Amsterdam. The city had more than doubled in size since Henry Hudson's time, and it was now thirty years since its merchant rulers—with impressive confidence in the city's future growth—had conceived of a staggering urban development project, now nearing completion: a series of concentric canal rings. The canals of Amsterdam are so iconic that many people assume they have always been there, but they were dug, by hand, hundreds of tons of earth moved out and sand brought in, forests' worth of pilings driven into the banks, a truly massive feat of engineering and city planning. The result was the creation of some of the first suburbs, for the idea was to encircle the core of the city—with its dens of commerce, sex, and drink—with neighborhoods of elegant housing for the army of newly rich, each home backed by ample gardens and provided with access, right out the front door, onto the state-of-the-art in urban transit systems.

Here, aside from the incessant thrum of construction, all was serenity and gentility. In a foreshadowing of modern real estate marketing, the canals themselves were named in blatant appeal to their upwardly mobile clientele: you had the option, depending on the precise altitude of your pretensions, of living on the Herengracht, or Gentleman's Canal, the Prinsengracht (Prince's Canal), or the Keizersgracht (Emperor's Canal).

Van der Donck had been away for nearly a decade. As for his comrades, Jacob van Couwenhoven, in his thirties, had followed his father to Manhattan as a teenager, and Jan Evertsen Bout had been in the New World since 1634. For all three, roaming into the heart of the city, following the waterway called the Damrak to the central plaza of the Dam, would have been a frontal assault on the senses.

It was also a premonition of the society they were in the process of helping to create an ocean away. In the Dam, the city's main square, the results of Amsterdam's years of accepting foreigners were on vigorous display. Turbans, saris, and skullcaps mingled in with musketeerish ensembles; the confused remark of a visiting Frenchman—"It appears at first not to be the city of any particular people but to be common to all as the centre of their commerce"—was one that would be echoed in coming centuries by visitors to Amsterdam's offspring across the Atlantic, New York City. The hawkers—Cantonese, Franconians, Gujaratis, Livonians, Lorrainese, Ashkenazim—contributed as much to the visual cacophony as the pyramids of goods each had laid out at the bases of columns ranged around the place. The whole parade of exotic outlanders, Dutch guardsmen, and stout, aproned housewives was set to music by itinerant lutists, fiddlers, bagpipers, and hurdy-gurdy boys; everyone was fueled by street-corner pancake sellers. René Descartes, back in Amsterdam after his years in Leiden, found comfort in the anonymity of the bustle. "I can walk out each day in the bustle of the crowds with as much freedom and ease as you have in your paths," he wrote to a country friend. (Then again, it may have gotten to him in the end: in the wake of peace, just as Van der Donck was arriving in Amsterdam, he left for the court of Queen Christina of Sweden, never to return.)

The availability of goods and services was stupefying to newcomers: sacks of pepper still giving off the perfumes of southeast Asia, bricks of sugar from the humid deltas of Brazil, hogsheads of Virginia tobacco, Turkish carpets, not to mention berths to Genoa, Smyrna, and Sumatra, and real estate offerings for homes going up at the as-yet-unfinished south end of the canal ring or in the new Jordaan area to the west. You could buy scientific measuring devices, tools for dissecting corpses, or, if you were foolish enough, a pair of spectacles, which were associated with a weak intellect ("to sell someone eyeglasses" was Dutch slang for "to deceive"). Sex, of course, was another product arrayed in plenitude—tourists could obtain a map of the city's red-light districts, which featured women whose whispered sighs came with French, Swedish, and German accents. If they weren't put off by the charming nicknames of some of the girls (e.g., Krentecut: "Currant Cunt"), the new arrivals might have found the sheer variety hard to pass up.

Art and printing were among the goods on offer. There were stalls in which art brokers sold paintings created for the home market, with an emphasis on those two iconic Dutch genres—landscape and still life—that in their very nature spoke of a society broken loose from religious dominance of its mental life and that satisfied a secular consumer urge for evocative scenes and a precise, almost Eastern fascination with ordinary objects in the here-and-now (the terms themselves came into English via the Dutch *landschap* and *stilleven).* Prints were common as well: at this moment those depicting the signing of the Treaty of Münster were everywhere, though, if you preferred, you could also find copies of the papal brief denouncing the treaties (much Vatican property had been "secularized" in the agreements). There were also engraved portraits of the signers of the treaty, pictures of various Dutch towns reacting to news of the treaty, and of companies of soldiers swozzling beer in celebration of the treaty.

In addition to the increase in intensity, there had been a big change in Amsterdam's central square since Van der Donck had left for the colony of Rensselaerswyck in 1641. One whole side of it, formerly a sprawling neighborhood, had been leveled, and in its place now stood the pilings and foundations of what would become the city's monument to itself in its ascendancy, a new Town Hall, built on classical lines, filled with art and slogans aligning the Dutch Republic with Rome and Greece. It was dedicated not only to the peace of '48 but to Peace itself, for, in the first waves of idealism following the diplomatic language about "eternal peace," people really did seem to believe that they had just lived through the war to end all wars.

As the tourist Van der Donck stood observing the first courses of stones being laid, that idea was still credible.*

But the Manhattanites didn't linger in the big city. Their business was pressing; they left soon after they had rested themselves, heading southwest.

Three centuries earlier, the corner of Holland that was their ultimate destination had been the country property of Willem, Count of Holland. Over time, it became useful as a commodious and convenient spot at which the medieval warlords of the region could meet and hash out differences. It was surrounded by a hedgerow that must have been a stunning feature of the landscape because people of the area took to calling the property itself 's Gravenhage—the Count's Hedge. Even after the meeting spot became formalized into a court and a town grew up around it, the name stayed, though it was often shortened to Den Haag, which English emissaries transliterated as "The Hague." From a provincial court, it grew into a national capital with the start of the war for independence.

The city that Van der Donck and his colleagues entered in October of 1649 was small and stately—"the largest village in Europe," people liked to call it—with meadows on one side, an oak forest on another, and the dunes of the coast a short distance away. Planned government town that it was, it had its broad tree-lined avenues where, of an evening, men of standing would promenade or ride in carriages with their families. Everything was clustered around the central government plaza called the Binnenhof, a four-sided fortress-like complex featuring government offices around the sides and, in the center, the thirteenth-century Knights' Hall, the original meeting place of the medieval nobles.

It was a clunky, byzantine style of governing the Dutch had devised, but in essence each of the seven provinces sent a delegation to the States General of whatever size they chose, though each province had only one vote. The few dozen men sat together around a single table, the title of president passing weekly from one province's lead delegate to the next. The tricky part was that all decisions required a unanimous vote, which made for intense politicking and few resolutions, something the Dutch seem not to have minded terribly, trusting in the adage that the less the government actually did the better.

*The finished building remains a tourist site, but its town hall function ended when it was converted into a palace in the nineteenth century by Louis Napoleon, so that it is now known as the Royal Palace.

On October 13, not more than a few days after their arrival, Van der Donck and his comrades won a spot on the States General's daily calendar of business and took the opportunity to present the document Van der Donck had crafted on Manhattan, the "Remonstrance of New Netherland, and the Occurrences There, Addressed to the High and Mighty Lords States General of the United Netherlands, by the People of New Netherland." Van der Donck the jurist, a bit over thirty years of age, took the lead. Years of struggle against Kieft and then Stuyvesant—winning a seat on the representative body, canvassing Manhattanites, being imprisoned and released, and finally sailing back across the ocean—had led to this. In addition to the "Remonstrance," he laid before the governing body several supporting documents, including a letter from the Board of Nine introducing him and his colleagues and, as a coup, a letter of reference he had coaxed out of Van Dinklagen, Stuyvesant's disgruntled vice-director. "These persons are thoroughly conversant with the situation of the country," he had written of Van der Donck and his colleagues. "I hope your High Mightinesses will be pleased thereby and extend them a favorable audience . . ."

It was a ripe moment for the Manhattan delegation to present its petition. The nation was still in the throes of its independence celebrations, and the speed with which the rulers took up the matter suggested that they were amenable. They knew the name Manhattan well by now, knew of the West India Company's mismanagement of the colony, and were ready to do something about it. The delegation presented itself with clarity and a distinct élan. Above all was their call for "suitable municipal government" for New Amsterdam. Van der Donck first painted for them an idyllic word picture, asking them to imagine this island, "Manhathans . . . the Capital of New Netherland," with its glorious geographic placement, "very well adapted on account of the convenience of the river," and an ideal base from which "we may pursue our country's trade . . . from Terra Nova to Cape Florida . . . to the West Indies and to Europe, wherever the Lord our God shall be pleased to permit." Then came the looming threat: the New Englanders, he added, were "fully aware that our country is better than theirs," thus the States General had to move swiftly to increase trade and settlement. Otherwise, the English would surely take over, and "It will lose even the name of New Netherland, and no Dutchman will have anything to say there."

Van der Donck's personal style is apparent not just in the individual elements of the presentation but in its exhaustiveness. He could not be content with the lengthy "Remonstrance" on its own, but had added to it a "Petition of the Commonalty of New Netherland to the States General." Then, for the benefit of the committee members who would study the matter in detail, he added a long section of "Additional Observations on the Preceding Petition." This, in turn, he footnoted to within an inch of its life, so that every aspect of the delegates' case—the limitless potential of the colony, the legality of the Dutch claim to the territory, the rights of the people who inhabited it—was covered, documented, supported, cross-referenced. The man's exuberance comes through in the utter mania of his documentation, which reads in parts like the output of a law clerk on amphetamines. A single sentence of what are already "Additional Observations" might have eight footnotes. At one point, in a sentence in which Van der Donck says that he and his colleagues presume to know the reasons for the colony's mismanagement, which he then goes on to enumerate, he footnotes the word *presume* in order to add: "Not that there is any doubt of it; for it is as clear and notorious as that the sun emits light."

Then came the props—supporting materials to give the rulers graphic reminders of the fat promise of their overseas province. Beaver pelts were laid before the high and mighty gentlemen, still reeking of the American forests, seeming almost illicit, in this civilized setting, in their bushy fecundity. And there were samples of unspecified "fruits" of the land, which, given the season and timing of the journey, might have meant tobacco, pumpkins, squash, beets, apples, nuts, corn, and certainly sacks of grain, of which the colonists were proud ("I have seen rye," Van der Donck himself would write elsewhere, "which grew so tall that a man of common size would bind the ears together above his head").

Realizing that, like as not, these rulers had no clear idea of the geography in question, Van der Donck also produced a meticulous hand-drawn map—probably created by Augustin Herman, who was a skilled cartographer—showing the province in its entirety and covering the coast from Maine to Virginia and extending as far west as central Pennsylvania.

There was perhaps one further piece of documentation, the original of which has only recently come to light. In 1992 a researcher at the Austrian National Library came across two pieces of a colored pen-and-ink townscape that had for decades been shelved separately. Fitting them together, he realized he had an early view of New Amsterdam—one that fits into the history of the Dutch colony at precisely this moment. This delicate, ephemerally colored illustration (reproduced on the cover of this book) shows a motley spread of dwellings—some of wood, some gabled brick—hugging the shoreline, and a crude fort sporting the Dutch flag. There are no people in the scene. There is reason—which will be discussed below—to believe that Van der Donck brought this almost haunting portrait of his colony's capital to cap his presentation.

All of this work—the delegates' own efforts and those of others on Manhattan who were supporting them—was done, Van der Donck declared, with a touch of feeling surely unusual in an official communication, "for the love of New Netherland." Then, having spread these layers of details and baskets of bounty before the men of government, he exited with a graceful pirouette, adding that he hoped the mighty rulers would "interpret most favorably this our presumption."

Presumption was the right word. The nerve of the Manhattan activists requires a bit of unpacking to appreciate. The Dutch system in the seventeenth century was one in which power was apportioned through well-worn channels. The States General was a fairly weak national body, rather like the original confederation that existed for the first eight years of American independence (the customary title of "High and Mighty Gentlemen" being something in the nature of a compensation); it had sway in overseas matters, such as overseeing colonial affairs, but most power was held by the provinces, and by the great overseas trading companies, which functioned almost as branches of government. The maintaining of overseas trading posts by these companies—and their right to make money from them—was deeply embedded in the system. Yet Van der Donck was quite explicit in what he asked of the leaders: "In our opinion this country will never flourish under the Honorable Company's government. . . . It would, therefore, be better and more advantageous for the country and themselves were they rid of it and the remnant of their property transported hence." Remove the niceties and the request is: "Get them out of here, and their belongings, too." It was a call to change the system, to strip West India Company shareholders of a property into which they had put enormous amounts of money and to have the central government take it over directly and give it political status within the Dutch system.

For Van der Donck, Melyn, Govert Loockermans, Augustin Herman, and their colleagues to expect the States General to undercut the entire political-economic system for the sake of a few merchants and settlers clustered on a distant island was certainly bold. So bold, in fact, that some historians have seen their mission as a freak, a pipedream—very forward-looking, perhaps, and in a way anticipating the political demands made during the American revolution, but basically out of step with the times.

But it wasn't. As an illustration of how Van der Donck's undertaking meshed with other events, shortly before the delegates had set sail from Manhattan, news of the beheading of King Charles reached the colony. As Van der Donck arrived in Holland, a debate was being waged via pamphlets—which, in the era before the coming of newspapers, were the national soapboxes—on the rights of the people and the limits of monarchs. It was sparked by the presence in the Dutch Republic—to be precise, at the Honselaardijk Palace near The Hague, where he had been living in splendor and taking as full advantage of Dutch haven as had waves of humbler refugees from across Europe—of none other than Charles's son and would-be successor, the future Charles II. One prominent intellectual took the line of traditionalists and argued that even if King Charles had been guilty of crimes that warranted execution, primogeniture—the law by which power transferred in a hereditary monarchy—demanded that his son, who had not participated in the crimes, should become the new king, and thus that it was right for the country to harbor him until the Cromwellian madness had passed. But other people felt uncomfortable about harboring a fugitive royal. In the freewheeling public forum of the Dutch Republic, a law student from the University of Utrecht, a young Dutchman very much of Van der Donck's ilk, fired off a responding pamphlet, which was printed and read everywhere, declaiming that, in the new Europe, and in a newly independent republic, such attachment to royalty was out of step with the times. Monarchs, he declared, derived their power not from God but from the people. Van der Donck's cause was not king-versus-people, of course. But this debate about the limits of a king's power shows that what it was about—the right of a people to have a voice in their government—was a subject very much in the air at the time the Manhattan delegates presented their case.

There was also outright political activism in the air. As Van der Donck was beginning his mission in The Hague on behalf of the colony, a former

Jesuit named Franciscus van den Enden was organizing a kind of Socratic academy in Amsterdam, encouraging young men to experiment freely with ideas of democracy and social equality. The most famous student to emerge from Van den Enden's coterie was Baruch Spinoza, the Amsterdam Jew who would become notorious in his lifetime, and legendary beyond, for continuing to develop the principles of modern philosophy laid down by Descartes. Some of the ideas that would emerge from this circle—democratic government, communal living, joint ownership of property, questioning the literal truth of the Bible, a public school system—sound almost freakishly modern, which makes the point that the roots of the modern world go back farther than is often thought.

Van den Enden's circle would have had a natural affinity with Van der Donck and his idealistic scheme for his colony. It's possible that Van der Donck got to know them during his time in Holland. Certainly they eventually came to know of the Dutch colony, perhaps as a result of his efforts, and would come to make it the focus for one of their schemes, a bizarre, proto-Communist experiment in utopian living. A decade after Van der Donck's mission, Van den Enden would write a draft constitution for such a community, to be based in the American colony. The group actually won a charter for the venture, and in 1663 forty-one latter-day Pilgrims, led by Pieter Plockhoy (who has become known as a father of socialism), settled on Delaware Bay, on land Stuyvesant had won back from the Swedes. But the timing was bad. Just months later, the English took over the whole Dutch colony of New Netherland, and when they did they destroyed the utopian settlement. Plockhoy himself would survive and live the last thirty years of his life in the New World, ending his days upriver, a resident of the new city of Philadelphia.

Like Van der Donck's mission, these projects were probably overly idealistic, products of the first wave of thinkers to come along in the wake of men like Descartes and Grotius, who had aspired to shift the center of human effort from the church to the human mind. But if, in the end, Van der Donck and his colleagues would not get all they wanted, they would change the system and pave the way for a new society. Why American history has overlooked their accomplishment has to do in part with Anglocentrism and also probably with something as mundane as the way colonial studies have traditionally been divided in American universities: English departments focusing on the English colonies, the Spanish colonies covered in the Spanish department, and so on. This meant both that the Dutch colony was relegated to the margins (few American universities have Dutch departments) and that colonial studies as a whole were approached narrowly. The discipline of history has broken down some of those walls in recent years, as it's become clear that educated Europeans of the seventeenth century were aware of the world and their place in it, and were affected by distant events. To understand events in one region therefore requires an appreciation for what was going on elsewhere. The fact that one volume of primary source material crucial to understanding what the Dutch did on Manhattan Island is entitled *Curaçao Papers* illustrates the point. There were global networks even then.

Give Van der Donck's mission its context, therefore, and it pops into relief. On the one hand are the records of the colony, still being translated and published, which show a churning settlement inhabited by a mix of tough individuals who see the possibilities of the place and want to explore them. It was a society—something worth fighting for. Then, too, the colonists were quite connected to the wider world. What fueled Van der Donck and his colleagues, what drove them in their idealism, was the spirit of the age. Extraordinary things were happening in Europe, and they knew it. They wrestled with the implications of the Treaty of Münster, and the broader Peace of Westphalia. Like the delegates to the treaty talks, like the members of Van den Enden's circle, they were following in the footsteps of Hugo Grotius, applying his principles of law to their New World colony.

It's also notable that, as radical as the colonists' petition may have been, it was treated seriously in the halls of government. Following the initial presentation, the high mightinesses shuffled in their chairs, flipped through pages, discussed the matter, and appointed a committee to explore it in depth. It had been a nagging issue; now was the time to deal with it.

There must have been some reveling that night in The Hague. The three Americans had to have been delighted with their first appearance before the governing body. But if they hoped for a speedy resolution of their case, they were soon disappointed. Within a matter of days, the States General found itself in the middle of a royalist crisis of its own, which had been building for some time and which now swept all lesser matters aside. The civil war in England was not an isolated event. The Dutch government wasn't based on a constitution, but was a patchwork of institutions and laws, some quite forward-thinking, others relics of the feudal past. It was a republic, but it also had its noble families, and it had a first family, the House of Orange and Nassau. By long tradition, the Prince of Orange was elected as Stadtholder—an office akin to president, but one whose duties were ambiguous. The ambiguity had been a source of irritation to the previous Prince of Orange, Frederik Hendrik, who had served as Stadtholder since 1625, had led the armies to victory in the war on Spain, and steadily and astutely increased his power during his life. His ultimate objective was to convert his family to the status of monarchy, but his big step in that direction had been fantastically ill-timed: in 1641 he had married his fifteen-year-old son, Willem, to Mary Stuart, the nine-year-old daughter of Charles I of England. At virtually the same moment, the English civil war began, and by the end of the decade Charles, to whom Frederik Hendrik had linked his fortunes, was headless.

From the beginning, the Dutch were annoyed that their noble family had hitched itself to royalty, and to doomed royalty at that. Frederik Hendrik's second major blunder was to try to waylay the peace talks at Münster. The Eighty Years' War had been very good for his family; it had made his father, William the Silent, into an icon, the "father of the nation." Beyond that, the Stadtholder was the head of the army; peace with Spain would mean a shriveling of his significance. But the merchant rulers of the province of Holland, and especially of the city of Amsterdam, had determined that peace was in their interest, and history moved in their direction. The peace treaty was signed, and just as it became clear that he had lost, Frederik Hendrik died.

The matter was far from over, however. The new Stadtholder, Willem, was, at twenty-one, volatile, arrogant, and as indifferent toward his advisors as he was toward his English child-wife. He was smart, but wild, and soon proved a more dangerous force than his father. Only days after the Manhattan delegates had presented their petition, the States of Holland—the regional assembly of the province of Holland, which also met at The Hague—voted to decommission many of the soldiers in its pay. It ought to have been an ordinary postwar measure; the world over, when wars are concluded, armies downsize. But every soldier lost was a lessening of the Stadtholder's power, and Willem reacted as if stung. He sent out orders of his own to the army officers, instructing them to maintain their troops. The officers obeyed the prince. The joyous atmosphere of The Hague instantly clouded. The States General hastily arranged to talk things over with the prince. He agreed to a reduction in troop totals, but only if those let go were Dutch. This sent a chill through the nation's chattering classes; all knew that a sizable portion of the army consisted of mercenaries, and that, in the event of a schism between the prince and the States General, these would be more inclined to stay at his side, less likely to succumb to patriotism. It was suddenly clear that Willem, feeling his power threatened, was actively considering a military move against his own newly independent nation. In fact, Willem was even more intent than his father had been to exchange the title of Stadtholder for a crown. In secret meetings with the French ambassador, he had already accepted French offers to help him achieve what the ambassador referred to in a report as "a grandeur far beyond that of his predecessors."

With the government in a state of crisis, business on all lesser matters came to a halt. Van der Donck refused to sit still, however, and used the time to strike out in another direction. The colony wasn't merely a political cause; it also needed settlers, traders, shippers. Maybe most of all, it needed publicity. So he switched from politician to public relations agent, and went off in search of a printer who would publish his "Remonstrance." It wouldn't be easy; the document was a sustained attack on one of the most powerful companies in the country. It would have to be a publisher unafraid of controversy.

He found his man. Michiel Stael was a twenty-four-year-old baker's son who, in the wake of the peace treaty, had left his hometown of Delft to come to the capital and set up as a printer of books and pamphlets. The time was right for it: Europe was churning with activity in the aftermath of Westphalia, and the Dutch Republic was the publishing capital of the Continent. Where at the turn of the century there had been four publishers in The Hague, there were now thirty-nine. Stael was eager to make a name for himself. At the time Van der Donck found him, he had just begun, publishing a few pamphlets for the French market. The work he was soon to do reveals a sharp taste for controversy. Nearly all his output for the years 1649 and 1650 would be political, and the titles suggest both the international nature of his business and the hot-off-the-press currency of their contents: "Two Letters of General Cromwell, Telling the Particulars of the Battle Between the English and Scottish Armies at Dunbar," "Propositions of the Ambassador of Spain to the Lords States General," "Letter of a Private Individual to the Parliament of Paris on the Detention of Princes Conde, de Conty and Longueville." He had a penchant for radical politics; the following year he would get in trouble with the law for producing publications critical of some of the leading men in Holland—proving that even in the most liberal of publishing climates there were limits. At one point he would be put in the stocks. His career would climax with him being chased by law officers through the streets of The Hague and into an inn (the Bend of Guinea), where he would escape through a window. He would turn up in Rotterdam a few years later and continue publishing.

Van der Donck found Stael in the cramped apartment he shared with his wife, their child, and his business partner. The print shop was also on the premises, and, appropriate for a man drawn to danger, the place looked out across the outer court of The Hague onto the Gevangenpoort, a squat brick building with an arched gateway that gave entrance into the government complex and also served as the town prison.* With his penchant for sticking it to men in power, Stael must have been delighted by Van der Donck's document and its radical proposal to divest the West India Company of one of its own provinces. As a businessman, he must also have sensed a market for the work—the West India Company was widely seen as a failure now, its share price, once as high as 206 guilders, having fallen to 14—and a ripe target for ridicule. He agreed to publish the "Remonstrance."

Stael apparently introduced Van der Donck to an engraver named Hendrik Hondius, who lived a few doors away on the Buitenhof. Van der Donck wanted his map of New Netherland to be published alongside the "Remonstrance," and it seems that Hondius put him in touch with his brother-in-law in Amsterdam, Johannes Jansson, to engrave it. If Van der Donck had done nothing else, publishing this map would have merited a place in history. The so-called Jansson-Visscher map (Claes Visscher produced a corrected edition) would be reprinted thirty-one times between 1650 and the mid-1700s, would become the definitive map not only for the Dutch but for the English as well, and is still reproduced today as the most accurate rendering of north-

---

*The Gevangenpoort still stands and is today a museum of torture and punishment.

eastern North America in the colonial period and one of the most beautiful examples of early mapmaking. It would show up in drawing rooms, shipping offices, and libraries across Europe, and thus help permanently afix Dutch names—from Cape May to Lange Eylandt to Roode Eylandt (Rhode Island)—to much of northeastern America. It also represents a fine example of the little-studied genre of cartographic propaganda: the conscious use of maps, especially by the Dutch and English, to imprint their mastery of the globe onto European minds. The Jansson-Visscher map purports to show northeastern North America dispassionately, but in fact the Dutch colony is given central position, and, more to the point, the map associates the name of New Netherland with a distinct portion of the globe, an arc of the continent from Cape Cod to Delaware. This followed Van der Donck's dogged insistence on adhering to the broad boundaries originally established by Henry Hudson and the explorer who followed him, Adriaen Block.

There was one other item of propaganda embedded in the map. The little pen-and-ink view of New Amsterdam, which Van der Donck had apparently brought with him to illustrate the mournful countenance of the colony to the States General, was to serve a second function. Just as he would use the "Remonstrance" twice—once to impress the rulers with the woeful condition of the colony, and again as a public relations tool to entice settlers—Van der Donck seems to have taken the piece of art to the engraver Johannes Blaeu and asked him to create something from it suitable for publication. The finished colored engraving, labeled "NIEUW AMSTERDAM op 't Eylant Manhattans," would appear in stand-alone editions as well as an inset view on later editions of the map; it follows the pen-and-ink illustration in every detail, except that where the original artwork shows a tumbledown village devoid of humans, the Manhattan town in Blaeu's engraved view is pert and orderly—chimneyed, gabled, weather-vaned, and bristling with life. Van der Donck's personality—unflagging boosterism for his New World colony and a willingness to flex the truth to suit his audience—is stamped on these items, which are now housed in museums and libraries around the world.

About this time, with the States General preoccupied and Stael getting the "Remonstrance" ready for publication, Van der Donck journeyed south to his native city of Breda to visit his family. Of his two sisters, three brothers, and their spouses and children, most seemed to have been living in

Breda at this time. His sister Agatha had gone off to Amboyna with her husband, an official in the East India Company, but had returned after he died there; his sister Johanna was soon to marry a local merchant. So we can imagine a boisterous homecoming, there in the (comparatively) sunny southern city, with its buildings clustered in medieval fashion around the Gothic church. A year before, however, Van der Donck's parents had done something unusual for the times, even in what was the most progressive society in Europe: obtained a legal separation. Even more remarkable, it was Van der Donck's mother, Agatha van Bergen, who agreed to pay alimony to her husband. Little is known about Van der Donck's father, Cornelis; clearly, what money and prestige the family had came from the Van Bergen side. It was Adriaen van Bergen, namesake and grandfather of Adriaen van der Donck, who had become legendary for his role in the liberation of Breda from the Spanish, and the fact that Agatha van Bergen was willing and able to pay her husband one hundred guilders per year suggests that the money was hers by inheritance.*

The family greeted the long-gone son. It was a different human being who had returned to them; the bookish boy had become a man, with a wider gait and firmer grip. He had tramped over purple mountains, slept on forest floors, shared meals in native longhouses. For nine years he had breathed a different air. It was in his eyes and voice: Van der Donck arrived in Breda irradiated with enthusiasm—whatever feelings he had over his parents' separation were not enough to quel it. To all his relations, he talked up the American colony that was his home and his cause as a land of opportunity. The only thing that was missing from this potential paradise he himself was in the process of arranging: good government. His passion, coupled with the admiration they must have felt for him—he who had gone into the wilderness and returned a leader of men, a statesman, presenting his case before the national government—swept his family members off their feet. Over the next two years, both of his parents—separately—would liquidate their holdings, pack up everything, and board ships for Manhattan. So, too, would go one of his brothers, his wife, their son, and several servants. His zeal seems to have engulfed everyone in its path.

---

*Where in England, and the English colonies, property was passed down to the eldest son, in the Dutch system it passed to all children, regardless of gender.

In The Hague, meanwhile, the colony's petition had been put back on the government calendar. Cornelis van Tienhoven—who had been working behind the scenes to undercut the Manhattan delegation—appeared several times and regaled the high and mighty leaders with information intended to show that the colony was not so bad off. Taxes levied at Manhattan, he argued, were favorable compared with what New Englanders paid. There was good farmland available to settlers. And in what is perhaps the earliest record of Manhattan's high cost of living, he produced a comparison chart of the going rates for farm animals in New Netherland and New England: a farmer on Manhattan could sell a year-old sow for twenty guilders, where in Boston it would only fetch twelve.

There is an irony in the contrasting views of the colony presented by the bitter rivals Van der Donck and Van Tienhoven. Van der Donck, in his effort to win support for an overseas province that he believed could in time out-earn the entire home country, stressed the bleak state of affairs there, at every turn skewing things toward the desperate, in many cases depicting as current the situation that had existed a few years earlier, in the aftermath of the Indian war. Van Tienhoven's more vibrant depiction may have more accurately reflected the current state of affairs. The irony is that Van der Donck's more forceful and elegant presentation, which after all was intended ultimately to bolster the colony, has over the long term swayed historians and contributed to the image of the Dutch-led settlement as congenitally defective.

Despite Van Tienhoven's presentation before the committee, as Van der Donck returned to The Hague the real excitement was taking place outside the government chamber. Michiel Stael's pamphlet version of the "Remonstrance"—dramatically retitled *Remonstrance of New Netherland, Concerning Its Location, Fruitfulness, and Sorry Condition*—had hit the streets, and it was making a stir not only in The Hague but in Amsterdam, Haarlem, and elsewhere. The *Remonstrance* gave a grim picture of recent events and the colonists' struggle, but Van der Donck's descriptions of a vast, fertile land, "capable of being entirely cultivated by an abundance of people . . . many very fine flats and maize lands" and "very good meadows" that "could with little labor be converted into good tillage land," of rich soil that bears crops "with less labor and tilling than in the Netherlands," made an impression. His trademark tangents of poetic cataloguing (the trees of the colony: "post-oak . . . butter oak . . . oil nut . . . hickory . . . water-beech . . . hedge beech, axhandle wood, two sorts of canoe wood, ash, birch, pine, lathwood, Imberen or wild cedar, linden, alder, willow, thorn, elder") added to the allure, inflaming the imaginations of people who had lived all their lives on forestless plains and polders.

The response to the publication—and to the accompanying map and illustration of New Amsterdam—was immediate. Perhaps through Stael—whose address was given on the title page—people contacted the delegates and pronounced themselves ready to go, to pull up stakes and seek their fortunes on Manhattan. The directors of the West India Company were flabbergasted. "Formerly New Netherland was never spoken of," they wrote to Stuyvesant, "and now heaven and earth seem to be stirred up by it and every one tries to be the first in selecting the best pieces [of land] there." Van der Donck and his colleagues acted quickly. They found a ship's captain in Amsterdam willing to convey settlers to Manhattan. People streamed to the harbor; in a short time, one hundred and forty settlers, all paying their own way, had been accepted, and the skipper, Willem Thomassen, pronounced the ship full to capacity. He turned away hundreds more.

Van der Donck then moved to capitalize on this outpouring of interest in the colony. He composed a breathless petition to the committee of the States General—addressing in particular its chairman, Alexander van der Cappellen, whom Van der Donck knew to be an enemy of the West India Company—in which he described the turn of events: the ship now lay ready to sail, and its skipper and owners attested that had they six more such ships they would be able to fill them. "[I]n the hope of better government," Van der Donck wanted the States General to see, "more passengers begin to set their faces toward New Netherland, according as the passage and opportunity offer." With his customary attention to details, he then got the ship's captain to attest as much before a notary.

It seems to have been a classic case of popular will exerting sudden pressure on politicans. The same day that Van der Donck presented the evidence of popular interest in the colony, the States General fired off a series of letters to the various chambers of the West India Company, asking them to send representatives to The Hague to appear two weeks hence in a joint meeting with the delegates from Manhattan, to confer "on the whole subject of New Netherland," and concluding: "Wherein fail not." A week later, Van der Donck got the Amsterdam chamber of the company to sign a contract with him and the other delegates to charter a ship capable of conveying an additional two hundred settlers to Manhattan. The company would front the costs, and the delegates would arrange the details. The ship would set sail before the first of June.

He was the consummate promoter now, working on all fronts, and getting results. By now he had a close working relationship with the members of the committee of the States General that had been assigned to deal with the colony, and they were showing distinct signs of favoring the cause, each of which elicited a protest from Van Tienhoven. On the committee's recommendation, the States General decided to send a notary from The Hague to the colony; the reason for Van Tienhoven's anger was that in doing so the leaders were taking certain political powers away from Stuyvesant and his council—away from the West India Company—and investing them in an official of the government. From Van der Donck's perspective, it was a step in the right direction.

Then, in April of 1650, came the decisive ruling. With nearly all the principals gathered in the chamber—Van der Donck and his colleagues as well as representatives from most of the regional chambers of the West India Company—the committee issued a "Provisional Order respecting the Government, Preservation and Peopling of New Netherland." No doubt all leaned forward in their chairs as a member of the committee labored through swaths of boilerplate before declaring that the committee, "having inquired into the system of government hitherto maintained in New Netherland," had concluded that the members of the States General "cannot, and ought not any longer approve of the perverse administration of the privileges and benefits granted by charter to the stockholders of the West India Company [while] neglecting or opposing the good plans and offers submitted for the security of the boundaries and the increase of the population of that country." There it was—the clear signal of the committee's verdict.

Then came specific orders to be put into effect. First and most importantly, "within the city of New Amsterdam a municipal government . . ." Until such a government came into being, the Board of Nine would continue, "and have jurisdiction over small cases arising between Man and Man . . ." The committee also referenced the sudden popular interest in emigrating to the colony: "Private vessels proceeding to the north parts of

America and the islands thereabouts, shall be obliged to convey over all passengers who will present themselves to be taken to New Netherland . . ." And there was a recommendation that a sum of fifteen thousand guilders be put into an account for the benefit of would-be settlers who could not afford the passage.

Off on its own, unadorned by editorializing commentary, was a separate order: "Petrus Stuyvesant, the present Director, shall be instructed to return home and report."

That was it. The meeting was over—the government had given its unequivocal support to the cause of the delegates. The company representatives were outraged; the Amsterdam chamber quickly prepared a rebuttal. Van der Donck, meanwhile, moved in for the kill. Not content even with this ringing endorsement of his presentation—for the orders still left the West India Company in charge of the colony—he addressed the committee. He was no longer a tentative outlander; six months of appearing at The Hague had given him confidence.

"Noble, Mighty Lords," he began, flourishes of exultation empurpling his prose. "The very laudable zeal which their High Mightinesses and you, Noble Mighty, have been pleased to evince as well for the preservation of whatever yet remains by God's especial blessing in ruined New Netherland as for the restoration of the sad and prostrate affairs there, supplies me with confidence and courage to lay before you, Noble Mighty, some means which will be highly necessary, and, according to all human calculation, advantageous and profitable to their High Mightinesses' design herein . . ."

He didn't want the States General to forget that the suffering of the settlers of the Manhattan-based colony was due to the disastrous actions of certain West India Company officials—"how much innocent blood, as well of heathens as of Christians and even of sucklings, hath been unnecessarily and barbarously shed." He asked the committee to accept into the record the list of interrogatories to be put to Van Tienhoven that he had drawn up on Manhattan. Van Tienhoven and others responsible for the Indian war should be prosecuted, he declared.

Van der Donck had determined that Van Tienhoven was disliked in The Hague, and hoped to build on that antipathy to broaden the provisional orders into an outright removal of the West India Company from the colony.

But the committee took no action on that front. It did, however, approve of a plan to send two of the delegates—Bout and Van Couwenhoven—back to Manhattan, at the head of a party of settlers, both to convey to Stuyvesant the rulings and to bring a shipment of guns for the defense of the colony. They headed off at once, exchanging exultant farewells with Van der Donck, who would stay to see that the committee's order was adopted by the States General.

Before they left, Van der Donck penned a secret letter they were to deliver. It was addressed to Dr. La Montagne, who had served under both Kieft and Stuyvesant and whom Van der Donck now pinpointed as vital to the power politics being played. This letter was only discovered in 1997—by Dr. Jaap Jacobs, one of the preeminent Dutch historians working on the New Netherland colony—in the Amsterdam Municipal Archives; like a flashlight piercing a centuries-darkened room, it shows Adriaen van der Donck, at this most critical moment of his embassy to The Hague, alive to the wider currents of the era, playing the game of politics with zest and cunning. It also shows that he considered himself leader of the activists' cause. "The old friendship and familiarity bids me to write you these few lines in haste, in order that you may remain assured of our good will towards you," Van der Donck begins, addressing the man who had sat in judgment on him when Stuyvesant had imprisoned him, but who seems to have taken pains to remain neutral in that and other debates. "I have verbally charged and pressed upon Jacob van Couwenhoven many things to tell you from me, to which I refer." Then Van der Donck begins massaging in the classic manner of politicians of every era. Certain of triumph, he assures La Montagne that "you will be included in a good position" in "the next government, which we expect shortly." Then he comes to the point: "It will be very good if you join ranks with the complainants. And it is my request that you will assist the Nine men as much as possible with advice and action . . ." Then he switches tacks to let La Montagne know that the winds of favor have changed direction, and that it wouldn't be wise to remain with the West India Company representatives: "It is well known here that the authors of the war are not punished as they should have been . . . Tienhoven is not in much esteem here and . . . his actions and those of director Kieft regarding the war are damned here by the whole world. The directors try to do their best to defend Stuyvesant, his secretary and their supporters, but they themselves, except for a few, are not in much esteem but are regarded with suspicion . . ."

Clearly, Van der Donck foresaw a time in the very near future when New Amsterdam, and the entire Dutch colony, would be taken over by the government, given normal political status, and made an integral part of the republic. In one of his petitions to the States General, he stresses the vital role he sees the colony playing in the future of the newly independent nation: "this State . . . alone is of greater extent than the Seventeen Dutch Provinces,* and . . . in the hour of need, will be found a strong arm, by the assistance it will render in people and provisions; for after the population shall have increased, your High Mightinesses will carry on a very large trade from the one to the other of your own countries—hinc inde et inde hinc— without any save your High Mightinesses' having control or authority over it." Such an arrangement would have been unprecedented—almost as if New Netherland were an eighth province in the Dutch republic, a noncontiguous state along the lines of an Alaska or Hawaii. Had it happened, of course, history—American, English, and Dutch—would have turned out much differently. In the spring of 1650, at least in Van der Donck's mind, it was a real possibility. The government was on the side of the colonists, Stuyvesant had been recalled, and Van der Donck, an ocean away from Manhattan, was laying out a new administration.

*Here he is referring to all the provinces traditionally considered by the Dutch as part of their domain, including those that did not become part of the republic but would one day form the nation of Belgium.

Chapter 12

_____

A DANGEROUS MAN

After all, Peter Stuyvesant was a country boy. Besides, a military compound was no place for toddlers to toddle, no place for a woman. So, sometime around 1650, he must have loaded his wife and their two young sons into a wagon and headed north up the Highway. Within five minutes they were in open country, meadows and pastureland punctuated by stands of forest. The road turned sharply to the right to skirt the bouwerie of his secretary, Van Tienhoven, then cut northward, elbowing through wilderness, before opening, on the left, onto an expanse of lots that were being farmed by freed slaves. Soon this area would form a village in its own right, which for a time would be called Noortwyck, or North District, before a settler from the Long Island village of Greenwyck (Pine District) would relocate here and give his property that name. (It would seem to be from this, not from English sources, that Greenwich Village would receive its name.)

Turning right off the Bouwerie Road, as this stretch of the trail was known, Stuyvesant brought his family down a lane and into the patch of the island he was in the process of taming as his own. In its marshy serenity—snipes and widgeons alighting on swampy ponds, stiff winds coming off the river bending the grasses, cows hunkering under bruised skies—it may have reminded him of home. It was two miles from the pit of troubles that was the capital city of his domain, and it must have seemed an ocean away. From the beginning, the West India Company had set aside this stretch of acreage for the use of the director of the colony, to be farmed by his workers, and so Kieft and his predecessors had used it. Stuyvesant had other ideas. He was a family man now, and he wanted to put down his roots. Within the year he would arrange to buy the farm, called Bouwerie Number One, outright from the company, and then purchase acreage on both sides of it, giving him a plantation stretching from the East River west to the center of the island and covering approximately three hundred acres. Here he built a manor and a chapel. Here he would live out his life and be buried, and here, over the parade of centuries, flappers, shtetl refugees, hippies, and punks—an aggregate of local residents running from Trotsky to Auden to Charlie Parker to Joey Ramone—would shuffle past his tomb.*

Leaving Judith with the young armfuls of Balthasar and Nicholas, he rode daily from this retreat into the maelstrom, greeting, as he passed the company orchard and cemetery and approached the cluster of streets of the town, the matrons, Indians, tapsters, smugglers, sailors, Africans, toughs and urchins, the refugees and erect citizens and slope-shouldered, eye-patched miscreants that formed his populace. And they in turn, at the unmistakable sight of him, with his cuirass and sword, a military princeling on his steed, offered lusty hellos or muttered curses depending on their political views. And then he disappeared into the fort, stiff as oak and ready to work. He was forty years old, beset by troubles on all sides, but possessed of a personality that fed on adversity.

The wounds kept coming, and many were still being inflicted by Van der Donck, even from an ocean away. Every time the Dutch flag appeared in the harbor these days, the sheaf of news that came with it was stippled with his doings. These "seditious persons, like Cornelis Melyn, Adrian van der Donck and some others . . . seem to leave nothing untried, to upset every kind of government," the company directors wrote him in February 1650. By April they had apparently learned of Stuyvesant's onetime chumminess with Van der Donck and were exasperated that he had given the man an intimacy that he had then exploited for political purposes. "We suppose that you have trusted too much in some of these ringleaders or become too familiar with them," they wrote, "now that their ingratitude and treachery have come to light, you must still act with the cunning of a fox . . ."

It was annoying to be scolded in this way and infuriating that Van der Donck seemed to have charmed the States General into siding with him and his cronies. Stuyvesant had by now heard of the provisional orders for the

---

*As a nice metaphor for the way history has muddled Manhattan's Dutch period, Stuyvesant's tombstone, embedded in the foundation of the Church of St. Mark's-in-the-Bowery, manages to get both his age and title wrong.

reorganization of the colony, but no one had yet sent him a command to enforce them. Far from doing so, he reacted to the threat of Van der Donck's mission by becoming not more conciliatory but more summary. He had finally had enough insubordination from his vice director, Van Dinklagen, and had the man thrown in prison. He placed spies among the Board of Nine and their associates. He virtually gave up on the quaint idea of allowing the people a voice in their government, and more and more took to deciding matters on his own. Augustin Herman and the other leaders of the opposition sent Van der Donck a stream of correspondence, keeping him updated on these turns of events. "We live like sheep among wolves, one friend not being able to speak to another without suspicion," one dispatch read. "He proceeds no longer by words or writings," went another, "but by arrests and stripes." Reading the pages of complaints against Stuyvesant, you feel in his harshness the uncorking of a long-bottled fury the sources of which are at least guessable. There was the dutiful son of a minister who had watched his godly and upright father remarry and lustily devote himself to his new young bride. There was the would-be wooer so embarrassingly pent up that the brother of the woman he wished to marry bet that he would be unable to ask for her hand. Finally, there was the administrator who put his trust in a young protégé only to see him turn on him and upend heaven and hell to have him ousted.

Meanwhile, he had to deal with matters on other fronts, because the incoming ships were packed with new arrivals, seasickened and unwashed but ready to stake a claim, and this also was a result of the delegation: "Many free people are coming over in this ship. . . . Many free people have taken passage on these two ships. . . . It looks as if many people will come over by every ship . . ." There was a hint of annoyance in the directors' letters— "people here encourage each other with the prospect of becoming mighty lords there, if inclined to work"—but they had to admit that "it may have a good result."

The irony was that while Van der Donck was pushing with zeal to oust Peter Stuyvesant from his post as director of the colony, Stuyvesant himself was executing some brilliant diplomacy, working hard to ensure the stability of the colony in the face of its steadily encroaching neighbors to the north. Indeed, it is due to the successes of both of these bitter rivals that New York City would develop as it did. Had either failed, the English would probably have swept in before Dutch institutions were established, New York would have become another English New World port town like Boston, and American culture would never have developed as it did.

In his three years on Manhattan, Stuyvesant had nudged and tweaked the New England governors to get them to settle boundaries. They had declared their desire to meet, but had nattered and stalled. And when the aged John Winthrop, on whom Stuyvesant had depended as his best advocate among the Puritan crowd, died in 1649, that upset things further. But brazenness was part of Stuyvesant's arsenal. He recognized the maxim that force can help bring the other side to negotiate, and he put it to work. It happened that a Dutch trading vessel owned by an Italian businessman based in Amsterdam had put into harbor at New Haven. Stuyvesant had determined that the vessel—the *St. Beninio*—was engaged in smuggling. According to Dutch claims, the entire New Haven colony lay in Dutch territory. By now there were so many English settlers there that the point was academic, but Stuyvesant saw the ship's presence as the pretext for an attention-grabbing act. He had previously sold one of the West India Company's ships to the deputy governor of New Haven, with a promise to deliver it. Now—with utter audacity considering that he was at the same time sending polite diplomatic letters to the governor—he undertook a bit of derring-do generally reserved for wartime, known as cutting a ship out of harbor. He had the vessel to be delivered to New Haven stuffed, Trojan horse–like, with soldiers. As her skipper brought her into the harbor at New Haven, he came in alongside the *St. Beninio,* his soldiers leaped aboard, cut the ship's lines, took command, and piloted her out to sea and back to New Amsterdam.

As expected, Theophilus Eaton, the rigid Puritan governor of New Haven, fired off a letter, practically tripping over his clauses in his outrage,* declaring that Stuyvesant had violated his colony's territory and absconded with a ship doing peaceable business there. Stuyvesant replied with mock innocence ("For what have I either written or done, that may seeme offensive . . .") while at the same time asserting that it was a Dutch ship, it had violated Dutch laws, and—the zinger—that the Dutch regarded the territory in question as theirs by right of first discovery. In subsequent letters he

*"And now latelie in a ship belonging to Newhauen, as bought by Mr. Goodyeare, yow haue sent armed men, & (without lycence, not soe-much as first acquainting any of the magistrates of this Jurisdiction with the cause or grownds thereof) ceised a shipp within our harbour . . ."

politely reminded the New England governors of the overwhelming might of the Dutch navy, without bothering to mention that virtually none of that might was under his control.

At the same time, he massaged John Endecott, Winthrop's replacement as governor of Massachusetts (we "Congratulate and reioyce that our neighbours there have Chosen soe worthy & prudent a successour"), in hopes that Endecott would continue Winthrop's tack of treating with the Manhattanites. It worked—the two forged a relationship. Indeed, one of the curiosities of Stuyvesant's term in office was his tendency to impress and even befriend potential enemies—English ones in particular—while treating his own colonists more or less like dirt. Eaton of New Haven and Edward Hopkins of Connecticut remained moody about the Dutch, but the combination of Stuyvesant's wooing of Endecott and his brinksmanship with the southern New Englanders—stealing a ship, resurrecting the Dutch claim to their lands, and brandishing the bogeyman of the Dutch navy—got results. Endecott and the other leaders of Massachusetts wanted peace; they forced the other New Englanders to agree to Stuyvesant's offer to meet and hash out boundaries, and instructed their delegates to "doe your utmost endeavor to make up an Agreement between [the Dutch] and Newhaven & Conecticott least if a warre or broiles arise betweene them wee be chardged and encoragged in it."

The governors wanted to meet in Boston; Stuyvesant suggested Manhattan. The compromise was Hartford, some miles up what the Dutch called the Fresh River. It was a humming little community of pious breakaways from the other New England territories, but right in its midst sat a squat and forlorn outpost manned by a handful of Dutch soldiers. Twenty-seven years earlier traders from Manhattan had been the first Europeans to establish themselves here, but the population of the Dutch colony was too thin to enable them to cover the region, and they had been forced to watch the English muscle in. Stuyvesant alighted from his ship in September of 1650, pegged up the quay, no doubt greeted Gysbert op Dyck, the commander of the Dutch fort, and greeted his four fellow statesmen. With him as secretaries and interpreters were two Englishmen, George Baxter and Thomas Willett; had things gone differently, this no doubt would have been an occasion where he would have relied on Van der Donck.

The negotiations were intense but cordial. The New Englanders pulled out their best wines and otherwise treated Stuyvesant like a visiting head of state. Eaton and Hopkins did not want to give quarter, but Stuyvesant and Endecott had stacked the deck in their favor by ensuring that all of New England's negotiators were from the less anti-Dutch colonies of Massachusetts or New Plymouth. In the final agreement, Stuyvesant gave up only what was already lost: the territory now indisputably occupied by New Haven and Connecticut. In exchange, he won acknowledgment by the English of a "permanent" boundary between them and the Dutch colony. The negotiators drew a north-south line that ran through Long Island and the mainland, and gave the eastern two-thirds of the island and territory on the mainland east of present-day Greenwich, Connecticut, to New England, and western Long Island and lands west of the same point on the mainland to the Dutch. Today, the division of Long Island into counties with distinctly Dutch and English names—Nassau and Suffolk—reflects this agreement, though the county line runs about ten miles east of the Hartford Treaty line. The Dutch were also allowed to keep their meager trading post, bravely named the "House of Hope," in Hartford.*

It was a remarkable achievement for Stuyvesant. He had used diplomacy and bluffing to leverage what little military power he had to advantage; he had given up only what had already been lost, and in exchange won from his English neighbors recognition of his colony's sovereignty. The two southern New England colonies were disgruntled, but the line held: throughout the lifetime of the Dutch colony, there would be no invasion from the north.

*

IN THE HAGUE, meanwhile, Van der Donck had been making progress as well. Then, once again, the Prince of Orange upset things. On June 5, regular business at the States General chamber was disrupted when the hotblooded Willem, still incensed over the attempt by the province of Holland to reduce the size of his army, appeared in person and announced that he intended to lead a contingent of soldiers to all the cities of Holland to explain to the military commanders of each that the only valid orders regarding disbanding would come from him. Van der Donck was no doubt in the crowd that gathered in the center of The Hague three days later to observe the

*The fort lives on—sort of—in the name of Huyshope Avenue in downtown Hartford.

grim spectacle of four hundred soldiers, Willem flamboyantly at their head, assembling and riding off in the direction of Dordrecht.

The mission failed. In the face of this major power struggle between the prince and the strongest province in the republic, the towns of Holland closed ranks behind their provincial leaders; some even refused the prince entry. He returned to The Hague in a rage, stalked into the chamber where the States of Holland met, and demanded that the members from the city of Amsterdam pull back on their call for troop reductions. The Amsterdammers, feeling flush, were in a position to respond with legalities. Technically, they informed Willem in an icy reply, it was the stadtholder who served at the pleasure of the provincial assembly, not the other way around. If anyone was in the position of giving orders, it was the States. There was no possible rationale for keeping wartime troop levels intact. In their inactivity, the soldiers would soon start getting into trouble. It was time they went to their homes.

Willem's response was unprecedented: he ordered the arrest of several members of the provincial assembly. They were taken to nearby Loevestein Castle and held prisoner.

The news of this shocking breach of authority swept through The Hague. Crowds gathered spontaneously on the streets and plazas around the Binnenhof, and even as they gossiped they were further alarmed by the spectacle of mounted mercenaries gathering on the perimeter. Van der Donck's hot-blooded printer, Michiel Stael, seems to have put out a pamphlet on the affair, for which he was slapped with a libel charge.

Then came the decisive stroke. At the end of July, Willem Frederik, cousin of the Prince of Orange, led ten thousand troops on an all-night march across Holland. Their mission was to take Amsterdam by force. All of Holland was in shock: Willem was restaging the play that had just run in England, at terrible cost to all. A coup d'état was in progress.

But Willem's power play was foiled by the weather. Traveling across the province by night and in a lashing storm, the army arrived at the gates of Amsterdam well past daybreak, by which time the city magistrates had had warning and prepared defenses. Having lost the element of surprise, Willem Frederik paused. A delegation from the States General hurried to the scene to negotiate a settlement. A messenger brought the Prince of Orange the news of the army's blunder while he was at the dinner table. Seeing the end of his dream of royalty, he stormed into his private apartment, where, in the words of one writer, he "was heard stamping his feet and throwing his hat upon the floor." Soon, the prince and the city reached a compromise on troop reductions. The crisis had passed.

Then, Willem obliged history by dying immediately on the heels of his failed power grab. In an effort to wind down from the affair, he went on a hunting trip with his cousin and fell ill from what was apparently smallpox. On the night of November 6, the States General gathered for an emergency session to hear the startling news that the twenty-four-year-old prince was dead.

Willem's coltish lunges for power kept the case of the Manhattan-based colony shelved for months. All the parties concerned stood on the sidelines and waited to see the outcome of the larger battle between the nation's leading nobleman and its most powerful city. In the course of the mad summer of 1650, it must have struck Van der Donck that his far-off colony, for all its seeming lawlessness, was hardly more chaotic or fragile than the civilized and supposedly stable home country. Far from trying to seize anything by force, he and his colleagues were following the rules—indeed, they were among the first Americans to exercise a right that would achieve near-hallowed status in the colonies and later in the nation: the right to petition the government for redress of grievances.

With the madcap interlude at an end, the government could return to something like normal, and Van der Donck's cause did not seem to have been hurt by the delay. Less than two weeks after Willem's death, Van der Donck was again before the States General, as was Van Tienhoven. All through the winter and into the spring the two men alternated in presenting their cases as Van der Donck tried to have the provisional orders for the re-organization of his colony put into force and Van Tienhoven tried to block them. Van der Donck had his foe repeatedly on the ropes, as the States General asked Van Tienhoven several times to submit answers to Van der Donck's interrogatories concerning his conduct during the Indian war. Each time, however, Van Tienhoven managed to dodge the issue.

Then, astonishingly, in the middle of this high-level politicking that was surely the most important work of his life, Van Tienhoven vanished. The States General had gotten word that the man might attempt to flee the country, and the governing body took the unusual step of issuing a decree forbidding him from leaving, to no avail. As information about his disappearance began to trickle out, the facts proved not only to be a blow to Stuyvesant and the West India Company, but an embarrassment as well. Despite being grossly overweight, "of red and bloated visage," and sporting a prominently juicy cyst—not to mention having a wife and children in New Amsterdam—Van Tienhoven fancied himself a lady's man, and his vanishing had at its root, in addition to growing doubts over the chances of his mission at The Hague, sex. The girl, Lysbeth Croon, was the daughter of an Amsterdam basketmaker, and Van Tienhoven had assured her that he was single and wanted to marry her on Manhattan. The matter blossomed into a full-fledged sex scandal, with witnesses dragged before notaries to give testimony of prurient behavior observed. (An undertaker's wife testified that Van Tienhoven had paid her three guilders to find a room for him and his young miss, which she did, "at the house of a grocer . . . at the sign of the Universal Friend." A tavernkeeper's wife reported that he "evinced great friendship and love, calling her always, Dearest, and conversing with her as man and wife are wont to do, sleeping in one bed.") Van Tienhoven was collared by the sheriff of The Hague and fined, and shortly afterward he and the girl fled the country, boarding a ship bound for Manhattan.

So it was with some exuberance that Van der Donck appeared before the entire governing body on February 10, 1652, to make the final argument on behalf of his colony. His adversary had literally fled the field, and in the room were some of the most distinguished men in the country. Adriaen Pauw, who had hoped to retire after successfully concluding the Treaty of Münster, had been called back into service in the aftermath of Prince Willem's abortive coup, and now led the Holland delegation. Pauw would have had some personal interest in the American colony; two decades earlier, his brother, one of the directors of the West India Company, had founded one of the early patroonships on the Hudson River, to which he had given the latinized form of his last name, Pavonia. (He soon abandoned the project and sold the land back to the company, but it was the first permanent settlement in what would become New Jersey, and eventually became the cities of Hoboken and Jersey City.) Also present was Jan de Witt, who would soon rise to become leader of the nation and one of the great European statesmen of the age.

To these assembled worthies Van der Donck made an elaborate presentation energized by his and his colleagues' convictions: that Manhattan and its surrounding territory represented a vital foothold on the unexplored world of the North American continent; that the West India Company had squandered this opportunity, but that it wasn't too late to reverse things. What was needed was new thinking. The leaders should abandon the old ways that allowed the company's bureaucracy to treat it as a feudal possession, and instead take this land across the ocean into the bosom of Dutch law, give its people the rights of Dutch citizens, and give its capital the status of a Dutch city with all the rights and protections that that entailed. Then they would see it flourish, and the Dutch Republic would reap the rewards.

Sensing victory, Van der Donck struck hard on the negative tack, summarizing the case against the West India Company and Stuyvesant, and, in typical fashion, methodically supporting his case with letters, journal entries, resolutions from the Board of Nine, and sworn statements that his colleagues in New Amsterdam had sent him over the previous months, all of which showed that Stuyvesant had not only failed to carry out any of the reforms their committee had voted on but had taken to ruling by fiat. His justice had become summary and brutal, especially against members of the Board (he had confiscated property and threatened them with imprisonment or banishment unless they swore that they knew "nothing of the Director and his government, but what is honest and honorable"). He had even blocked the notary sent over by the States General, forbidding him from doing his job; this man had then joined the opposition, and his letters were included in the sheaf of complaints Van der Donck exhibited.

Nevertheless, the letters revealed that there was still great hope on Manhattan that Van der Donck's mission would achieve results. "The people here are somewhat solaced on learning from the despatch that the affairs of New Netherland are beginning to be thoroughly and truly considered by their High Mightinesses, but they anxiously expect absolute Redress," one letter read. "Whatever you have done there for the public interest, I, for my part, do especially approve," Augustin Herman wrote to Van der Donck. "We are anxiously expecting the approval of the redress and a change."

These updates on the situation in the colony had an affect on the assembly. Among other things, they drove home that the community on Manhattan could no longer be considered an ad hoc collection of soldiers, fur traders, and whores, for whom martial law could suffice. These were men of standing, who had risked everything on the promise of North America, and their government had a responsibility toward them.

Van der Donck went on to discuss the Hartford Treaty, which he found particularly appalling. Not being in Stuyvesant's position on the front lines, it was easy for him to denigrate the agreement for giving up land to the English. As Van der Donck saw it, the New England governors had "pulled the wool over the Director's eyes," and Van der Donck rued the loss of "many fine bays, kills, rivers and islands . . . and the beautiful Fresh River [the Connecticut River], where full fifty Colonies or more might be planted. . . ."

The presentation was thorough, and Stuyvesant had no one to counter it. The chambers of the West India Company, asked by the government to respond, began to split into factions. The Manhattan-based colony had been "monopolized" by the chamber from Amsterdam, declared the Zeeland representatives, and its mismanagement was Amsterdam's fault. The members from Dordrecht agreed, and suggested a reorganization of the colony's government. Sitting in their pretty little canalside offices just down the road from the house where Jan Vermeer was beginning his quiet career of creating quiet masterpieces, the members from Delft concurred that something had to be done "in order that so magnificent a country may not go to ruin by bad government and management."

The States General was wholly won over, and at last took the first steps toward a massive reorganization of the colony. Under pressure from the government, the Amsterdam directors sent Stuyvesant a grudging directive: "in order to silence everyone," he was to establish a municipal government in New Amsterdam with "a bench of justice formed as much as possible on the laws of this city." The order was nearly lost in the shuffle of circumstances, but it would be enacted, and would change history.

There was some question whether Stuyvesant would have time to charter a city government, however, because in late April the States General drafted the letter Van der Donck had worked and waited for. It was telegraphically blunt:

To Petrus Stuyvesant, Director General in New Netherland

Honorable, &c. We have, in view of the public service, considered it necessary to require you, on sight hereof, to repair hither, in order to furnish us circumstantial and pertinent information, as to the true and actual condi-

tion of the country and affairs; also, of the boundary line between the English
and Dutch there. Done 27 April, 1652.

The letter demanding Stuyvesant's recall was handed to Van der Donck to deliver in person. Holding it, stepping out of the chamber into the courtyard of the Binnenhof, he must have felt light-headed, drunk on his achievement. And crossing the colonnaded plaza—the same public square in which, seven decades earlier, the leaders of seven separate Dutch states had signed a declaration of independence from Spanish rule—had to underscore the historical nature of it.

Had Van der Donck been a diarist of the likes of his younger contemporary Samuel Pepys, the page for this day would have been starred, and we might have had from it a follow-up scene of revelry at a Hague taphouse, with a throng of bureaucrats, in black hats and flowing capes, high boots perhaps topped with lace cuffs, suddenly conscious of their routine lives and routine government jobs as they gathered around the victorious representative from a far-off land, expressing keen interest, between pinches of snuff and swallows of Rhenish wine, in his holding-forth on every aspect of his country, from its mythic-sounding flora and fauna, to the island capital so enticingly positioned to exploit the continent, to the intriguing sexual forthrightness of the native women. ("They make light of their virtue," Van der Donck would write, and while they scorn "kissing, romping," and other sexual play, "at the right time they will decline no proposition and almost all of them are available and ready to carry on with abandon.") There is little doubt that the government types were taken with Van der Donck. The day before his victory, the States General voted a resolution granting him the right to pass his New Netherland estate on to his heirs—a power reserved for fiefholders such as Kiliaen van Rensselaer, and an indication both that Van der Donck was looking forward to returning home (and siring heirs) and that the officials had been won over as much by the man as by his vision for Manhattan.

It was with this vision in particular that he would have regaled listeners. This new government would definitively establish Manhattan Island as the free-trading hub of the Atlantic. It would guarantee its place as gateway to the North American continent for generations of Europeans. It would be modeled on "the laudable government" of the home country, with personal guarantees of freedom of conscience deriving directly from the Union of Utrecht (". . . each person shall remain free, especially in his religion . . ."), the de facto Dutch constitution, which dated to the beginning of the war for independence and codified the nation's adherence to ideas of tolerance. And it would be based, too, on certain inherent rights of the people—even to overthrow their rulers should they become oppressive—which stemmed from the so-called Act of Abjuration, the Dutch declaration of independence from Spain.

Van der Donck was exultant, of course, believing that his work in Europe was at an end, and went through a blizzard of errands preparatory to departing for home. He had been away two and a half years, and his property was suffering in his absence. He hired several employees who would serve six-year contracts at Colen Donck. His wife had come to join him in the Netherlands sometime in the preceding year, and together they now purchased supplies and had them loaded for passage.* He had recently helped his mother sell some of her property, and now she, his brother, sister-in-law, and their servants were preparing to emigrate to Manhattan also. It was springtime: renewal was in the freshening winds, and the victorious emissary would soon be at sea, sailing homeward.

In May, Van der Donck appeared before a government committee formally asking to be allowed to return to Manhattan and resume his previous political role—"to hold peaceably the office of President of the Commonalty in New Amsterdam." He planned not only to be in the colony for the change of administration, not only to deliver personally Stuyvesant's walking papers. He planned to lead the new government.

*

IT NEVER HAPPENED, of course. The shot that sank Van der Donck's mission—robbing him of a major historical achievement, leaving him instead a spectral presence in history, author of a still-remarkable but shadowy contribution—came from a thoroughly unexpected quarter. It wasn't Stuyvesant

---

*The ship's manifest listing Van der Donck's supplies still exists, and gives a nice snapshot of a settler's needs: whetstones, millstones, baskets of nails, "farmer's stockings," shoes, linen, "coarse woolen cloth," hats and caps, kettles, ribbons, thread, books and paper, "2 boxes and 2 barrels of steel," "8 casks of bird lime," "10 anckers of brandy," "32 cakes of soap," and a whopping "300 lbs. of pepper and 20 lb. cinnamon," suggesting Van der Donck hoped to do some trading in spices on Manhattan.

who upset things—his plans, too, would be waylaid by events. The disruption didn't come from the New England colonies or the Indians of New Netherland, or even from the Swedes camped out along the Delaware River to the south. Its origin was a grim and tempestuous creature who had burst to life, fifty-three years earlier, in the swampy fens of the east of England. As historical figures go, Oliver Cromwell, like Peter Stuyvesant, remains a deeply unlovable sort—complicated and vigorous, but somehow enduringly repellent. Cromwell has been studied endlessly, and yet he remains, in Churchill's words, that "smokey soul."

But, as with Stuyvesant, history has pasted a cardboard mask onto Cromwell. True, both men were grim, fixable types. On the other hand, Cromwell was not only the originator of the British empire, he was also a shaper of American beginnings. Where the Stuart monarchs had looked on the colonies as a source of income, Cromwell helped root America's myth of origin by viewing it through his religious lens. His spiritual conversion came in his thirties ("Oh, I have lived in and loved darkness and hated the light . . ."), and his Puritanism was virile and practical. He was all for the settling of North America, and, like John Winthrop, he considered New England a shining city on a hill, a potential promised land. At one point he even considered emigrating himself.

As a boy he was physical, tough, and exhibited "no effeminate characteristics," one chronicler felt compelled to state. He entered Parliament just before Charles dissolved it, and rose to prominence as a critic of the king. When civil war broke out he became a general who inspired devotion. His was the dominant personality in the military junta that took power; he was not yet the Lord Protector, but he was the boss in a rudderless moment in which one was needed. There was nothing of the modern psychologist about him, no notion of giving his countrymen time to heal and find themselves in the aftermath of suffering. The only path out of the ruins led directly to global dominance. With the backing of the nation's businessmen, he raised taxes and ordered the building of a new fleet of warships; under him, the modern English navy came into being. From within the rubble of civil war, he became the architect of empire.

His zeal was primordial. He planned at first to export England's Puritan revolution and set royal heads rolling along the bowling greens of Europe; it didn't catch on, but, transplanted to New England, the Puritan sense of mission, of being chosen by God, seeded the American idea of manifest destiny: of a people preordained first to conquer the continent and then to lead the world.

What did gain traction was his plan to overtake the Dutch as Europe's trading empire—with him the balance in the rivalry between the two nations begins to shift from the Dutch to the English. His "western design" had several components. In the Americas, he would aid New England and try to dislodge the Dutch from Manhattan Island, which by now English traders were beginning to see as crucial to control of the continent. In the Caribbean, Cromwell eyed another island locus: Jamaica, which he would capture from the Spanish in 1655, would become a slave-trading base. He wouldn't get Manhattan, but English "success" with the Jamaica project would of course yield centuries of profits and misery, from the cane fields of the Caribbean to the cotton fields of the American South.

During the civil war, trade between England and its North American colonies had collapsed, and Manhattan had grown in consequence. Now Cromwell hoped to break the Dutch monopoly on trade—in Europe and Asia as well as North America—by means of legislation. The problem with this tactic, so often employed throughout history, is that one can't expect a rival nation to abide by one's own laws, and the Dutch didn't. It happened that the first action in Cromwell's assault on the Dutch trading empire occurred at virtually the moment Van der Donck won his case in the States General. While Van der Donck was shifting from his victory and petitioning the States General to let him to return to Manhattan, in the straits of Dover, one hundred and fifty miles southwest of The Hague, portions of the English and Dutch fleets encountered one another. The weather was brewing and there was a strong northeastern wind. The system of communicating by means of flags and sail position had yet to be developed, and each side was confused about the other's intentions. Foremost in the minds of both commanders was the so-called Navigation Act, the piece of hard-core protectionism that Parliament had recently passed, which was aimed directly at the Dutch. With it, England had declared that only English ships would be permitted to deliver products into English ports. An impertinent clause in the bill called for foreign vessels sailing in the Channel to lower their flags in salute. When this information made its way to the Continent, Dutch commanders expressly ordered their vessels not to do any such thing.

The two men who stood with feet firmly planted on the swaying decks of their respective men-of-war, eyeing the foreign sails and assessing what to do, were both destined to become legendary figures, and together form a tableau that encapsulated the odd cross-currents of the times. Robert Blake, head of the English fleet, was a flowing-haired, Oxford-educated son of wealth who had taken to sea only recently at the age of fifty. Maarten Tromp, the leathery, pug-like Dutch commander, had gone to sea at age nine, serving under his father's command. When he was twelve, the ship was taken by English pirates, his father killed, and the youth pressed into service as a pirate's slave. He had risen through the ranks of the Dutch navy, and was now admiral of the fleet and the greatest seaman alive. The twist with these two personalities that so characterized the times was that Tromp, of humble origins, was a firm supporter of the House of Orange and of the English Stuarts (he had actually been knighted by Charles I for assisting in his struggle against Parliament), while Blake the dandy was an anti-royal Parliamentarian.

Accounts of what happened off Dover differed, but all agreed that the battle was sparked by Tromp's failure to lower his flag in recognition of English sovereignty. From four o'clock in the afternoon until nine in the evening, forty-two Dutch vessels and twelve larger, more heavily armed English ships hauled off at one another, sometimes from point-blank range, in an encounter that surprised both sides for its savagery. In fact, decades of tensions had built to this. At least some Dutch statesmen had seen it coming. Months earlier a courier pouch had arrived at The Hague with a curious document. It was printed in English, but even those who couldn't read that language could make out the word *AMBOYNA* in large red letters across the title page. A London publisher had reprinted the inflammatory pamphlet of twenty-eight years earlier, describing atrocities committed by the Dutch on Englishmen on the island in the East Indies. Of the two great statesmen in the Dutch government, the twenty-seven-year-old Jan de Witt preferred to believe that this bit of resuscitated jingoism represented only a random stirring among the English rabble, but as wise old Adriaen Pauw glanced over the pamphlet he knew it meant the English were whipping up the populace, preparing them for war.

Events now tumbled quickly toward war. Pauw left for London to take part in emergency talks with Cromwell's Council of State (where, incidentally, the man he would have dealt with as Cromwell's translator and foreign speech writer was no less a figure than the poet John Milton). In The Hague, the mood of magnanimity and optimism that had spread through the republic since the "eternal" peace of '48 had vanished. The government cycled onto a war footing. Orders went out to ships at sea and to outposts across the globe to strengthen their defenses.

The impact of all of this on Adriaen van der Donck was spectacular. The West India Company's fortunes had fallen steadily in recent years, and Van der Donck's assault had further crippled it. But with the first rumors of a war with England, the company, which after all had originally been conceived as a quasi-military entity, came roaring back to life. Its once-powerful directors flushed again with influence. Under pressure from them, and fearing that this was the wrong time to institute liberal reforms, the States General completely reversed its rulings on the Manhattan-based colony. They rescinded the recall of Stuyvesant, and ordered Van der Donck personally to hand back the letter of recall they had given him. On top of that, Van der Donck's activism, which only weeks before had been lauded as the full flowering of Dutch legal progressivism being applied, in a test case, to the nation's overseas province, suddenly looked positively dangerous. He was detained and refused permission to return to America. The ship bearing his family members and belongings left for Manhattan without him. Overnight, things had turned upside-down. He was no longer a patriot but a radical, someone to keep watch on.

*

THE DUTCH REPUBLIC'S declaration of war against England in July of 1652 was a kind of coming of age for both nations. Their recent histories had been so intertwined that they often seemed like siblings, shifting endlessly from argument to cooperation to vindictiveness. The gunboat salvos in the Channel signaled that in the struggle for control of the indescribably lucrative international trade in this first era of globalization each saw the other as the only real adversary. Their rivalry would dominate the century and give shape and substance to American beginnings.

The First Anglo-Dutch War, as history has titled it, was a true and literal trade war. A peasant in either country could have been forgiven for feeling it lacked pungency: no homes were burned, no villages sacked. The entire thing took place at sea, with England going after the Dutch herring fleet and spice- and fur-laden merchantmen, and the Dutch forced to defend their trading empire. ("The English are about to attack a mountain of gold," Pauw wryly remarked at the outset, "we are about to attack a mountain of iron.")

Which did not mean the war lacked in ferocity. The pent-up grudges on both sides came out in a series of savage exchanges that rewrote the books on naval warfare and began the buildup of tactics, rules, and technological innovations that reached a peak more than a century later in the age of Horatio Nelson. The clashes in the Channel and the North Sea that murderous summer marked the debut of "line of battle" fighting, ships of each fleet arrayed stem to stern so that their side-mounted guns could form a long deadly chain. In the culminating sea battle, the largest in world history to date, more than two hundred ships formed opposing ribbons along a sixteen-mile corridor, hulls screeching against one another and cannon unleashing inhuman mayhem (this era before the exploding shell featured such low-tech innovations as the broadside of chains, which sliced through rigging and scissored bodies to pieces). The ships caught up in the encounters were reduced to floating wrecks literally caked in gore, "their masts and tackles," one correspondent aboard an English vessel reported, "being moiled with brains, hair, pieces of skull."

Cromwell had caught the Dutch leaders off guard. While he had built a new generation of larger warships, the States General, after nearly coming to civil war with the Prince of Orange over their insistence on decommissioning the military, had laboriously downsized since the peace of '48. As a result, the States General and the regional chambers of the East and West India Companies were now forced to drop all other concerns as they focused on the task of defending trade routes and rigging more ships for battle.

Van der Donck, his cause shelved, himself an exile in his home country, thundered like a caged animal. For months he roamed restlessly back and forth between The Hague, Amsterdam, Leiden, and Breda. In Leiden, he returned to the university and received his *Supremus in jure* degree, which allowed him to appear before the Dutch supreme court. In Amsterdam, he went again to the States General asking to be released, but learned that, at the instigation of the company, word had gone out to every ship captain departing for the Americas that anyone who received him on board would face punishment. In Amsterdam he organized a group of influential friends and together they entered the stately West India Company headquarters to meet with company officials. But this only gave them a chance to loose their pent-up invective over his efforts to rob them of their colony. He was a dangerous man, a "notorious ringleader," illegitimate representative of a "lawless and mutinous rabble." He reported this to the States General, and used everything he could think of to appeal to them, pleading that his farm in America was "going fast to ruin," that he was personally being subjected to "an extraordinary civil banishment," even reminding them that he was a descendant of the great patriot responsible for liberating Breda during the war for independence. It got him nowhere. The bureaucratic wall had gone up.

Then, indefatigable still, he hit upon another idea for promoting his colony. His embassy was at a standstill, his family had gone on to Manhattan. He was alone and rudderless. In this gap in his life, images gathered. Wild raw mountains, and the river with its majestically broad belly reigning over the landscape. An autumn afternoon in which, following days of rain, a sudden burst of sun ignited the world, cows in a primordial meadow lit to glowing by it, the grass iridescent. Himself, ten or twelve years younger, sitting before the fire in a Mohawk longhouse with its hundred or so inhabitants, discussing theology of all things, agreeing with the dark-eyed chiefs in their belief that God was almighty and good, but arguing against their notion that God was too preoccupied with his eternally enticing female companion deity to pay notice to the affairs of men, thus leaving the devil to hold sway over the Indians in their smoke-filled dwellings, the Europeans on their island stronghold, and people across the waters of every hue and language, all of whom, in the Indians' cosmology, wallowed in wickedness.

His mind filled with these images, Van der Donck spent the months during the height of the war closeted away with pen and paper, and emerged with the manuscript of a book, *A Description of New Netherland,* which brought a humanistic, scientific sensibility to bear on the colony he had come to love. The *Description,* from which I have quoted throughout this book, was unabashedly a paean to the America that Van der Donck knew. He arranged it thematically, devoting sections to the waters, woodlands, wild vines, minerals, winds, seasons, and of course the Indians, each of which received the doting attention of one who had been too long absent.

At the end of the book, in order to make a direct appeal to his audience, he broke out of his anatomical dissection of the colony in favor of a much-used convention of the times, the dialogue. In this case, it was a "Dutch patriot" and a New Netherlander, the former, having read all that came before, standing in for the reader and posing questions. Van der Donck doesn't much trouble to disguise himself in the cloak of the anonymous New Netherlander, but launches into opinions that, as before, in the *Remonstrance* and elsewhere, show an almost eerie foresight. Manhattan and its surrounding region will grow exponentially, he assures his listener, and not so much because the Dutch people themselves will leave their homes for it but because the Netherlands has had a long tradition of welcoming refugees from elsewhere in Europe. It is these masses—"from eastern Europe, Germany, Westphalia, Scandinavia, Wallonia, etc."—who, having steeped themselves in the Dutch tradition of tolerance, will populate the colony, increasing its multiethnic flavor and its strength and vigor.

In this reverie of his, Van der Donck seems practically to summon the vast sweep of the coming centuries' migrations, the huddled arrivals being processed at Ellis Island, the barrios and ghettos coming into being. Aiding this future mass migration, making it happen and making it stick, he sees a unique cultural glue: "the Dutch have compassionate natures and regard foreigners virtually as native citizens," with the result that whoever is "prepared to adapt" can make a go of it in their system. This freakish burst of historic clairvoyance is tempered somewhat by his assured statement that the colony would remain Dutch, that would-be emigrants had no need to fear an English takeover anytime "in the next fifty years."

Van der Donck won a license to publish his work, but publication was withheld because, with the war raging, the government didn't want to draw attention to the colony, which it now feared the English might invade.

At last, late in 1653, four years after his arrival, Van der Donck received permission to leave for Manhattan. But it came at a price. The forces that had branded him a danger had not let go. The heads of the Amsterdam chamber took particular delight in assuring him that his cause was shattered. Finally he understood what he had been up against all these years—that the power he had been attempting to thwart was rooted in the vastness of the Dutch empire. He had been too far ahead of his time, and now he understood it. For the first time in his life, he described himself as "wholly disheartened and cast down." He penned yet another petition, different in tone from anything he had ever written:

> The undersigned, van der Donck, humbly requests consent and passport of the Board to go to New Netherland, offering to resign the commission previously given him as President of the community, or otherwise as its deputy, and promising upon arrival in New Netherland and taking up residence there, to accept no office whatever it may be, but rather to live in private peacefully and quietly as a common inhabitant, submitting to the orders and commands of the Company or those enacted by its director.

His request was granted. He was forbidden from engaging in public life and forbidden to practice law in the colony, on the remarkable grounds that there was no other lawyer in the colony, and thus no one with the knowledge to stand up to him in court. (Actually, Lubbert van Dinklagen, Stuyvesant's former vice-director who was also a trained lawyer, was still in the colony, but he had likewise been silenced by Stuyvesant following his backing of Van der Donck's mission, and had gone into retirement on Staten Island.)

Over a period of several weeks prior to his voyage, Van der Donck turned up repeatedly at the office of an Amsterdam notary public named Jacob de Winter, each time with one or more men and women. Together they sat while the notary carefully inscribed the terms and conditions of a contract, and then each signed or made his or her mark on the paper:

> June 4, 1653. Adriaen van der Donck, patroon of his colony in New Netherland, takes Hendrik Cornelisz Broeck into his service as carpenter for a period of three years. He will sail to New Netherland with his own tools. The passage will be paid by Van der Donck . . .
>
> June 13, 1653. Adriaen van der Donck, patroon of his colony in New Netherland, takes Jan Mewesz. and Evert Jansz., both from Steenwijk, into his service as carpenters . . .
>
> June 16, 1653. Adriaen van der Donck . . . engages Helena Wand for a period of six years . . . Helena Wand is obliged to do the household and such as a maid-servant and to assist his family. She will receive as annual wages f36 besides board and lodging.

July 26, 1653. Adriaen van der Donck, living in New Netherland, engages for his colony Henrik Claasz., pottery-maker from Rotterdam . . .

July 28, 1653. Adriaen van der Donck, free man in New Netherland, engages as gardener for a period of three years: Gommaart Paulusz., from Antwerp. . . . Paulusz. shall be obliged to keep the garden of Van der Donck, to set, to plant, to clip and do similar jobs . . .

Van der Donck had apparently succumbed: he would give up his political pretentions. But he hadn't abandoned his home, or the idea of America. And even in defeat he left evidence for the persistence of his vision: records that foreshadow the course of the coming centuries, momentarily shining the light of history onto a handful of individuals who became caught up in the idea of a land of opportunity across the ocean, and followed him there.

The Dam Square in Amsterdam, at about the time of Van der Donck's arrival in the Dutch Republic to present the case of the Manhattan colonists. *(Amsterdams Historisch Museum)*

The so-called Jansson-Visscher map, which Van der Donck had printed in the Dutch Republic about 1650, became the definitive map of the American northeast for more than a century and helped imprint Dutch names on many American places. *(Collection of Joep de Koning)*

Above: The somber view of New Amsterdam that Van der Donck presented to the Dutch government in his effort to convince it to take over the colony. *(Photographic Archive of the Austrian National Library, Vienna)* Below: The print based on the earlier image, which presents the town in a considerably more promising light and which Van der Donck published to encourage settlers to emigrate to the colony. *(Collection of Joep de Koning)*

The title page of Adriaen van der Donck's *Description of New Netherland*, written in exile, into which he poured his passion for his adopted home. *(New York State Library)*

BESCHRYVINGE
Van
NIEUVV-NEDERLANT,
(Ghelijck het tegenwoordigh in Staet is)
Begrijpende de Nature, Aert, gelegentheyt en vrucht-
baerheyt van het selve Lant; mitsgaders de proffijtelijcke en-
de gewenste toevallen, die aldaer tot onderhout der Menschen, (soo
uyt haer selven als van buyten ingebracht) gevonden worden,
ALS MEDE
De maniere en ongheneynte eygenschappen
vande Wilden ofte Naturellen vanden Lande.
Ende
Een bysonder verhael vanden wonderlijcken Aert
ende het Wesen der BEVERS,
DAER NOCH BY GEVOEGHT Is
Een Discours over de gelegentheyt van Nieuw Nederlandt,
tusschen een Nederlandts Patriot, ende een
Nieuw Nederlander.
Beschreven door
ADRIAEN vander DONCK,
Beyder Rechten Doctoor, die teghenwoor-
digh noch in Nieuw Nederlant is.

T'AEMSTELDAM,
By Evert Nieuwenhof, Boeck-verkooper/ woonende op 't
Russtlandt in 't Schrijf-boeck/ Anno 1655.

A Representation of the Battell fought betweene the English Fleet, commanded by his H. Prince Rupert, and George Duke of Alb.

English and Dutch ships arrayed in "line of battle" formation during the Second Anglo-Dutch War. *(National Maritime Museum, London)*

Opposite: This redraft of the 1660 plan of New Amsterdam is visual evidence for the immediate impact of Van der Donck's mission to the Dutch government. Seven years after his efforts brought municipal government to Manhattan, the plan shows a well-organized town with regular streets and lots, fortifications, and a canal. Thanks to a census conducted at the same time, we know the occupants of each of the 342 structures. The wall along the northern (right) edge eventually gave Wall Street its name, and the broad street heading northward from the fort became Broadway. Improbably enough, the original of this plan was discovered in the early twentieth century in a Medici palace in Florence. *(Collection of the New-York Historical Society)*

John Winthrop Jr., the wildly ambitious governor of the Connecticut colony, duped Stuyvesant into believing he was a friend.

James, Duke of York, for whom New York was named.
(National Maritime Museum, London)

Nieuw Amsterdam *volugs* Nieuw Jorck *geued*
ende bewoven by de Nederlanders op den 24 Aug 1673
geulegd aen de Engelse onder uitgesien

This image shows New York in 1673, during the moment when Dutch forces retook it from the English, as indicated by the soldiers on the street and the cannon firing from the fort. At far right is the palisade "wall" for which Wall Street is named. *(Library of Congress)*

Jan Luyken's seventeenth-century engraving of a Dutch *baas*, or master (in this case a pewterer), with his young apprentice. It was in Dutch Manhattan that the Americanism "boss" was coined: just one of the influences, large and small, the colony would have on the country.

One of the 12,000 pages of the manuscript records of the Dutch colony based on Manhattan, which survived centuries of neglect and are now being translated and made available. This document, which has yet to appear in published translation, was written on August 30, 1664, by New Amsterdam's leaders as English frigates sit in the harbor and they debate whether to surrender or fight. *(New York State Archives)*

Charles Gehring, who for three decades has translated the records of the Dutch colony centered on Manhattan. *(Dietrich Gehring)*

PART III

THE INHERITANCE

Chapter 13

BOOMING

On a Thursday morning in the thick of winter, 1653, seven men left their narrow, low-ceilinged homes and the warmth of their Delft-tiled hearths, stamped through the streets of lower Manhattan, and entered the gates of the fort. Assembled in the council room there, they swore an oath of service to the States General, then bowed their heads as a minister intoned a prayer—". . . Thou hast received us in Christ . . . make us fit through Thy grace, that we may do the duties imposed upon us . . ."—that signals, among other things, that we are well before the era of the separation of church and state.

Adriaen van der Donck was still in the Netherlands, struggling against the political fatwa that was preventing him from returning to America, when their honors, the magistrates of the newly incorporated city of New Amsterdam, transacted their first, brief piece of business, putting their signatures to a statement "herewith [to] inform everybody that they shall hold their regular meetings in the house hitherto called the City Tavern, henceforth the City Hall, on Monday mornings from 9 o'clock, to hear there all questions of difference between litigants and decide them as best they can." Two and a half weeks later, in a physical break from the government of Peter Stuyvesant and the West India Company that was visible to all, they convened at the three-story building on the waterfront that had long been the center of the town's activities. In case anyone missed the significance, the bell in the courtyard out front sounded the change of government.

It was very modest. But it meant something to those involved. For years the settlers of Manhattan Island had insisted that their community was more than a military or trading outpost, that they were not serfs forced to toil for a distant master, but citizens of a modern republic entitled to protection under its laws. As of February 2, 1653, with the signing of a municipal charter, New Amsterdam was a city. The magistrates were quite aware of the heritage of the political offices and legal traditions they took on. The government they formed had a structure—there were two co-mayors and a panel of judges, which, when combined, formed the legislative body—copied from Amsterdam and based on Roman-Dutch law, the Roman part of which had come to Holland by way of the Holy Roman Empire, which in turn traced itself all the way back to the caesars and the Code of Justinian. When, in February of 2003, the speaker of New York's city council cut into a birthday cake and gave a champagne toast in honor of the three hundred fiftieth anniversary of the city's charter, it was to these gatherings in the former tavern that he paid homage.* The city dates its political foundation not to the English takeover, when it was named New York, but to this moment.

Then again, so what? Aside from the bit of arcana that New York is perhaps unique in the United States in that its legal roots go back to ancient Rome, does it mean anything? The political founding of a city may be interesting to a narrow clique of historians but of justifiable indifference to the rest of the world. For that matter, it's also worth noting that Stuyvesant blunted the power of the city government by initially refusing to allow popular election: he himself appointed its first officers.

What matters is what the founding of city government on Manhattan led to. The idea posed at the beginning of this book was that New York City is different in its origins from Boston, Hartford, and other early East Coast cities. It was different because a sulky but dogged English explorer named Hudson happened to chart the area for the Dutch. But it would only matter in the long term—its difference would only stick—once it had a real structure. Municipal incorporation provided that structure, one born of long experience containing and maintaining peace among a dozen cultures. The proclamation that Stuyvesant's superiors forced on him as a result of Van der Donck's efforts granted "to this growing town of New Amsterdam" a government "to be framed, as far as possible and as the situation of the country permits, after the laudable customs of the city of Amsterdam, which

---

*The festivities were held in the Museum of the American Indian, on the site of the fort. A sort of flattened tribute to the original city hall exists in the form of a brick outline of its location on the sidewalk at the corner of Pearl Street and Coenties Slip.

gave her name to this first commenced town . . ." Thus the achievement of Adriaen van der Donck. This was the foundation that New York City was built on, and, spreading in every direction, it would color and mold the American continent and the American character.

The two matters that occupied the new government in its first weeks form a diptych of the settlement's concerns, which always seemed to veer between the historic and the ridiculous. Into the newly outfitted council chamber, on its first full day in business, burst a raucous knot of locals who were near to blows. Joost Goderis was a harried man; he was married to a woman with a wayward eye; the fact was well known in the town, and he was fed up. He'd recently been out oystering on Oyster (i.e., Ellis) Island, and as he canoed back to Manhattan he encountered his supposed friend Gulyam d'Wys loitering on shore with a gang of young toughs. D'Wys wanted to give the boys something to laugh at, and so he told Goderis (as the court recorded it) "that Joost should give him, deft., a better opportunity to have sexual connection with his, pltf's., wife." When Goderis tried to maintain his dignity by feigning confusion, d'Wys helpfully explained that "Allard Anthony has had your wife down on her back." The boys with him laughed and called the man a cuckold who "ought to wear horns, like the cattle in the woods." Goderis hoped the new municipal board was the sort of body to help a man in emotional distress, and gravely brought the matter before the magistrates.

At the same time, and on a darker front, the magistrates were grappling with daily reports of fallout from the war between England and the Dutch Republic. Stuyvesant—who had fought against the forming of a town government, but who for now seemed to welcome the opportunity to share the burden—regularly stumped over from the fort with three-month-old news from Holland. As in all wars, the reports contained a mix of paranoia, rumor, and inscrutable behavior. "The government in England is at present very odd," one letter informed Stuyvesant; according to informed sources, the English were demanding "that all apprentices shall again wear blue caps." While the Dutch leaders pondered that one, it had also become apparent that the American colonies of both countries were in play in the conflict. The West India Company was to begin gearing up once again for privateering work, as it had against Spain. The company proposed that "5 or 6 ordinary, but well manned, frigates" should use Manhattan as a base for attacking English colonies. At the same time, the States General was afraid of a surprise attack, and reported that it was "certainly informed that New Netherland is in great danger and imminently exposed to invasion," and ordered Stuyvesant and the city magistrates to reinforce defenses.

The magistrates, with Stuyvesant sitting in on their session, took action. The first decision was "to surround the greater part of the City with a high stockade and a small breastwork." To fund it, the magistrates raised money from the town's wealthiest residents, Stuyvesant matching the top figure of one hundred and fifty guilders. Then they plunged into the details: the palisade along the northern perimeter of the town would be comprised of twelve-foot oak logs, each eighteen inches in circumference and "sharpened at the upper end." These would be sunk three feet into the earth and be fortified by a four-foot-high breastwork. Payment to the builder, the government declared, "will be made weekly in good wampum." A crier was sent out, declaring that the town council was asking for bids to carry out the work. Englishman Thomas Baxter signed on to provide the wood, and the thing was built by early July. In the long term, what's notable about this first public works project orchestrated by the town government is not the wall itself but the street that ran along it. It's a safe bet that no matter how wildly they tended to dream, the magistrates could not have imagined that this rough pathway would replace the gleaming, colonnaded bourse of Amsterdam as the epicenter of global finance. It's also worth noting that the wall along Wall Street was built not to keep Indians out, as folklore has it, but to keep the English out.

While the Manhattanites were fearing an attack from New England, the residents of Connecticut, New Haven, Massachusetts, and Plymouth were likewise feeding on a steady diet of rumors that the Dutch were about to move northward against them. One of these rumors—that the Dutch had hired Indians to massacre New England families while they were at church—made it to London, and was packaged by an enterprising printer in the most explosive way. The memory of the killing of ten English traders by Dutch soldiers on the far-off Southeast Asian island of Ambon or Amboyna three decades earlier hadn't died in England, and had been rekindled the year before by republication of the inflammatory pamphlet reporting the event. Now, someone in the English colonies, possibly associated with the government of either Connecticut or New Haven, had the genius to use Amboyna specifically to stir the New Englanders against the multiethnic Dutch-run colony to their south. The new pamphlet that swept through England and was shipped to America was titled "The Second Part of the Tragedy of Amboyna: or a True Relation of a Most Bloody, Treacherous, and Cruel Design of the Dutch in the New Netherlands in America. For the total Ruining and Murthering of the English Colonies in New-England." It was a double-barreled shot of ethnic hatred, decrying the Indians as "bloody people, fit instruments for so horrid a design," and lauding an English colonist who had "in one night cut off fourteen hundred of them," while also seeing the plot as an instance of the genetic wickedness of the Dutch, "Amboyna's treacherous Cruelty extending its self from the East to the West Indies, running in its proper channel of Dutch blood . . ."

The pamphlet was a model of wartime disinformation, forcing the Dutch government to carry out an investigation and deny the accusation while keeping the flame of English public opinion stoked. Months earlier, several New England leaders had disembarked at New Amsterdam to meet with Stuyvesant on the matter. He had assured them that his people had no designs on the English colonies. While on Manhattan, however, the Puritans got an eyeful of the rude, boisterous, growing port city, through which, they well knew, much of their own region's trade passed. If England were to make a play for the Dutch colony and so gain a lock on the interior of the continent and the shipping center of the entire coast, it had better be soon. The trade war was as good a pretext as any, and anyway the story was too good not to use. In addition to supplying the material for the "second Amboyna" pamphlet, the New England governors wrote to Cromwell personally and put the case that his so-called Western Design, by which England would weave the lands of the Atlantic Rim into the beginnings of an empire, would be perfectly served by conquering the island at the mouth of the Hudson River. Cromwell, who had just assumed the title Lord Protector and with it many of the trappings of the king he had helped behead, liked the grandiosity in the plan, agreed it was time to carry it out, and wrote back to say he was sending a four-frigate flotilla and a company of soldiers to Boston, whose "utmost assistance may be given for gaining the Manhattoes."

At this juncture, Adriaen van der Donck finally sailed back to Manhattan. It's frustrating, but not surprising, that we have no record of his homecoming. People viewed him as a hero; residents had followed every action he undertook in The Hague on their behalf. The new magistrates had him to thank for their jobs, and must still have considered him the leader of the re-form party. But there was no public display—no one wanted to incur the wrath of Stuyvesant. It's especially frustrating that we are forced to imagine the encounter between Van der Donck and Stuyvesant, which had to have been freighted with emotion. When last they had been together, Stuyvesant had imprisoned Van der Donck for treason. Since that time, the onetime protégé had spent four years in the Dutch Republic hectoring the govern-ment for Stuyvesant's removal, and had actually succeeded, only to have the decision reversed. Now, having gambled everything and lost, he was return-ing and putting himself at Stuyvesant's mercy. The only item we have shows Van der Donck, shortly after his arrival, asking Stuyvesant for access to the records of the colony, so that he can add to the book he had written, which was still awaiting publication in Amsterdam. Stuyvesant turned him down, citing the advice of the company directors, who warned of "new troubles" from "Meester Adriaen van der Donck," and feared he would turn "the Company's own weapons . . . upon itself." Stuyvesant could be a dangerous enemy. Van der Donck had to proceed with extreme caution, and the fact that he drops from the official records at this point suggests that he did.

But that doesn't mean he stayed out of politics. Certainly on his arrival he was busy with domestic matters, reacquainting himself with his property and helping his newly arrived relatives adjust to America. His mother moved into a house on Pearl Street looking out across the East River to the Breuckelen meadows, and his sister-in-law needed help dealing with her teenaged son, who was a bit of a handful (Gysbert van der Donck, along with his friend, the son of Cornelis Melyn, was a member of the gang who had taunted Joost Goderis as a cuckold). But it doesn't fit Adriaen van der Donck's character that he would be content with domesticity.

In fact, he seems to have picked up right where he left off in The Hague, only now working behind the scenes. Within weeks of his return, there was a new political uprising against Stuyvesant. With the colony on the upswing, towns in the vicinity of Manhattan (which would later be incorporated into the boroughs of Brooklyn and Queens) were growing, and the leaders of sev-eral of these—Gravesende (later Gravesend), Vlissingen (Flushing), Middel-burgh (Newtown), Heemsteede (Hempstead), New Amersfoort (Flatlands), Breuckelen (Brooklyn), and Midwout a.k.a. Vlackebos (Flatbush)—began clamoring for their rights. Piracy had sparked the controversy. It was still commonplace in the colony; a recurring problem stemmed from locals who, having failed to make a go of things through legitimate business, turned pirate. The most recent villain was well known to all: Thomas Baxter, who had supplied the oak posts for the "wall," was marauding along Long Island Sound, stealing horses. The residents of outlying towns assembled to declare that if the company couldn't protect them they would stop paying taxes.

Some historians have explained this breach between Stuyvesant and the Long Island towns as a Dutch-English encounter. There were many English residents in these towns and there was a war on between the Dutch and the English, therefore, according to the reasoning, the agitation amounted to an internal revolt, a way of assisting England in the war. The episode has also been used to support the standard notion that any yearning for political rights that existed in the Dutch colony could only have come from its English residents. This is a misreading of events. The confusion seems to stem from the fact that the petition presented to Stuyvesant in December was written in English and then translated into Dutch. But the "Remonstrance and Petition of the Colonies and Villages in this New Netherland Province," in which colonists complained of the "arbitrary government" Stuyvesant exercised, follows Dutch legal forms. John Brodhead, the nineteenth-century historian who gathered the records of Van der Donck's doings in The Hague and who was intimately familiar with Van der Donck's writing, noticed a similarity in tone between Van der Donck's *Remonstrance of New Netherland* and this current remonstrance, with its spirited rejection of Stuyvesant's continued rule by fiat. Another early historian of the period noted the similarity in style of this complaint to the earlier complaints written during Kieft's time—for which, as detailed in Chapters 7 and 9, there is ample evidence of Van der Donck's involvement.

In demanding a voice in their affairs, the residents of the Long Island towns—Dutch and English both—were reacting not to the war but to the founding of the municipality of New Amsterdam. In fact, the magistrates of the New Amsterdam government not only supported their petition to the West India Company; they called on these leaders to travel out of their wooded plains and valleys, cross over on the Breuckelen Ferry, and join with them in the capital to craft a formal complaint. In other words, this minirevolt that Stuyvesant found himself faced with at the end of 1653 was a direct result of Van der Donck's achievement in The Hague, and it was also a direct continuation of that work, an attempt to push Stuyvesant and the company further toward political reform. It took place within weeks of Van der Donck's return. Van der Donck was uniquely suited to act as intermediary between the Dutch and English leaders: his wife was English, and his father-in-law, the firebrand English preacher Francis Doughty, was now minister of Flushing, one of the towns that was party to the complaint. Van der Donck also knew well the Englishman who penned the remonstrance. George Baxter had been around since Kieft's time, like Van der Donck had assisted Stuyvesant as an English translator, and had even served on Stuyvesant's council during Van der Donck's trial—and therefore, like Van der Donck, had split with Stuyvesant after once being close to him.

As a final piece of evidence, Stuyvesant seems to have complained to his superiors about the possibility of Van der Donck being behind this latest insurgency. In response to a letter of his that is now lost, the directors write: "We do not know, whether you have sufficient reason to be so suspicious of Adriaen van der Donck, as all the charges against him are based upon nothing but suspicion and presumptions, however, we shall not take his part, and only say that as we have heretofore recommended him to you on condition of his good behavior, we intend also that he be reprimanded and punished, if contrary to his promise he should misdemean himself."

The picture that emerges, then, is not one in which English interlopers come into the colony, lay in wait for several years, and then, Trojan horse–like, emerge at time of war to add to the Dutch troubles. Indeed, there is no indication in this encounter of the English residents expressing a longing for English government. As they point out in their complaint, they had fled to these parts to escape it, and hoped to put down roots in the area surrounding Manhattan to take advantage of the more liberal justice of the Dutch Republic, the government of which, they noted, was "made up of various nations from divers quarters of the globe." What they wanted was exactly what Van der Donck had strived for all these years: an end to the West India Company's rule, and a spread of rights through the rapidly growing towns of the colony. Such rights, the remonstrance declared, in a phrase out of Grotius that Van der Donck liked, were based on "natural law."

So the movement Van der Donck had launched was still animating the people of the colony, and in fact had spread. It was the continuation of a long, sustained, well-reasoned appeal for political reform that came not from England but from the early-modern heart of the European continent.

It did little good, however. Stuyvesant reacted to the remonstrance in trademark fashion. The directors of the West India Company, he declared, were "absolute and general lords and masters of this province." The petition was denied. Stuyvesant was nothing if not consistent.

Then again, Stuyvesant himself was in danger of being trumped: violent change was bearing down on the colony while this debate still echoed. Unknown to everyone, Cromwell's squadron left England in February of 1654. New Amsterdam would have been quickly subdued—the West India Company's soldiers were spread thinly around the colony, and hundreds of New Englanders, alarmed by the threats of a Dutch invasion, had declared themselves ready to follow an English military leader in a preemptive strike.

But fate—i.e., the weather—intervened. The storm-tossed squadron didn't arrive in Boston Harbor until June. As Major Robert Sedgwicke, commander of the fleet, wrote to Cromwell, the very day he was about to embark from Boston with "nyne hundred foote" and "one troope of horse" for the assault on Manhattan, "there arrived a shipp from London, bringing with her diverse printed proclemations of peace between the English and the Dutch." Jan de Witt had hammered out a treaty with Cromwell, yielding England control of the Channel while retaining trading supremacy in the Mediterranean and in Asia. The First Anglo-Dutch War ended with the North American sphere unchanged. The invasion squadron was called back home.

*

ONE MIGHT SAY that this is the point in history when Manhattan became Manhattan. With a rudimentary representative government in place, the island rapidly came into its own. Stuyvesant and the West India Company still officially ran the place, but, whether they were Dutch, English, or any of the other nationalities represented in the colony, the businessmen—the fur traders, the tobacco farmers, the shippers of French wines, Delft tiles, salt, horses, dyewood, and a hundred other products—increasingly got their way. As the business leaders won positions in the city government and became political leaders, others—bakers, tavernkeepers, school teachers, ministers—came to them for support. These alliances strengthened New Amsterdam's municipal government, which, in its turn, set a flurry of development in motion. Roads were paved with cobbles. Brick houses replaced wooden ones; tile roofs came in (mostly red and black, giving the town a crisp finish), and the old thatch ones were banned as a fire hazard. A proper wharf was built off Pearl Street. A street survey of New Amsterdam was commissioned. As the town picked itself up, it took on that defining Dutch characteristic: tidiness. Its streets and stoops were swept clean. Trees were aesthetically pruned; gardens took neat diamond, oval, and square shapes. An order went out forcing farmers to tear down pigsties and chicken coops that occupied prominent roadside positions. Owners of vacant lots on the main streets were slapped with an extra tax to encourage them to develop their property. The ditch that had been chopped through the center of the town was widened into a proper canal, its banks reinforced with pilings and crossed by pretty stone bridges, which, together with the gabled buildings, gave the town a strong echo of its namesake. Taverns were even more numerous than before, but staggering, puking drunkenness had abated somewhat. The taverns now functioned as clubs for traders and businessmen to meet, places where news was exchanged, and maybe dens for sampling that wanton new elixir, coffee.

It was still a port town, with tentacles that stretched across the globe, so piracy and whoring, syphilic scabs and cutlass scars, remained fixtures. But you get glimpses, too, of the well of ordinary life that any society draws from and that, in its quiet, pious normalcy, falls outside the margins of official records. A family gathers in the evening around the hearth, the father reading the Bible and carefully recording special events inside its front cover. A minister, writing home to Europe, recounts his weekly circuit on the Breuckelen Ferry between the churches of Long Island, New Amsterdam, and "Stuyvesant's Bouwerie." An "orphanmaster" describes the progress of his charges.

The place was maturing, thanks largely to the municipal leadership on Manhattan. It gave people a sense that this island on the edge of the wilderness, which had always veered sharply between lawlessness and tyranny, had become a place where families could let their dreams take root.

In what might have been seen as a good omen, one of the colony's dodgiest residents, Kieft's and Stuyvesant's longtime henchman, Cornelis van

Tienhoven, disappeared at this time, with appropriate flamboyance. Fleeing from The Hague, where he was opposing Van der Donck, and later turning up on Manhattan with a young mistress, had made him a laughingstock; we can only guess how his wife greeted him. Stuyvesant had kept him on for a time, but he soon became too much of a liability. He had bullied colonists for years, and there was a growing sense that he was involved in cooking the company's books. As troubles reached a climax, he vanished one day in 1656, with his hat and cane found floating near the shore. Stuyvesant wanted badly to cover the matter up, have his association with the man forgotten, and quickly declare a death by drowning. But people felt they knew better—for one thing, Van Tienhoven's brother, who had also become entangled in financial irregularities, vanished at about the same time, and later turned up on Barbados. Whatever happened to Cornelis van Tienhoven is one of the unsolved mysteries of New Netherland.

But Manhattan wasn't the only eventful part of the colony; it wasn't just the island capital that took off after 1653. Only a year before the municipal government came into being, in an effort to resolve his dispute with the up-river duchy of Rensselaerswyck, Stuyvesant had created by decree the town of Beverwyck on territory staked out around Fort Orange. The beaver trade for which it was named was still flourishing, and the community came into being seemingly overnight. Mills, brickyards, and tile yards were laid out and produced the materials for creating a town whose citizens were self-consciously urban enough to construct a poorhouse as one of their first community projects. By 1660 it was the colony's second city, with a thousand residents. Compared with New Amsterdam, it kept its remote, Wild West feel. Through the records we get fleeting views of Indians as ordinary participants in town life. They are boarders in residents' homes, sitting by the fireside of an evening with pewter mugs of beer. One shows up, purse in hand, at the baker's house to buy cakes. Once, in 1659, two Mohawk chiefs ask for—and receive—an extraordinary session of court in which to present grievances against Dutchmen who have been abusing their people. For the twelve years in which it existed, before morphing into the town of Albany, Beverwyck was a hardscrabble place, poised between the looming mountains and the vast river, the thunk of beaver skins on countertops the sound of commerce. But it was also a well-ordered community, with a court of justice that functioned identically to the one in New Amsterdam and those in

Holland. In makeup it was more Dutch than New Amsterdam, but still a quarter of its residents came from outside the United Provinces, and with Germans, Swedes, French, English, Irish, Norwegians, and Africans, it had a far more mixed population than New England towns.

In Amsterdam, meanwhile, men like Seth Verbrugge and Dirck de Wolff—the coiffed and groomed merchant princes who ran Europe's trade from their red leather chairs and ornately carved desks, their walls hung with framed maps showing their global sway, their wives collared in lace and studded with diamonds—took advantage of the newfound stability on Manhattan. They gave their agents there greater sway and purchasing power, and the agents used their contacts with English and Dutch merchants from Canada to Virginia to Jamaica and Brazil to make their island port the hub of Atlantic trade. The new products appearing in New Amsterdam's shops speak of a more refined life for its inhabitants—medicine, measuring equipment, damask, fine writing paper, oranges and lemons, parakeets and parrots, saffron, sassafras, and sarsaparilla.

With municipal government on Manhattan came an innovation whose effect would long outlive the colony itself, and help to impress the island's legacy into the American character. Going back into the Middle Ages, cities throughout Europe had offered a form of local citizenship to inhabitants: English cities had their freemen, Dutch towns their burghers. Amsterdam had recently installed a new, two-tiered system, and the local government on Manhattan promptly copied it. The so-called great burgher was a powerful trader who contributed sizable sums for civic improvements and, in exchange, got the right to trade and had a voice in setting policy. What was different was the offering of small burgher status. Nearly every resident of New Amsterdam applied for it, and it gave even the humblest—shoemakers, chimney sweeps, tailors, blacksmiths, hatters, coopers, millers, masons—a stake in the community, a kind of minority shareholder status. The system encouraged inhabitants to support one another and largely did away with the itinerant traders who used to sweep in, make a quick profit, and then leave. It also made for a more egalitarian place than New England, where the number of freemen, or town citizens, never exceeded twenty percent of the population. In New Amsterdam, nearly everyone—rich and poor, the coiffed and the scabby—was part of the same club. When shipping increased in the port, all benefited.

Added to this, workers in the colony never organized themselves into the guilds that had held sway in Europe since the Middle Ages. This was probably because the West India Company did its best to bar the guilds, fearing their power. But this form of union-busting turned out to have an advantage. Artisans branched out: a baker might own land, invest in a shipment of tobacco, and earn extra income as a soldier. Young men who entered the colony's rolls as humble artisans rose to heights, and a muscular strain of American upward mobility was born. Frederick Flipsen (a.k.a. Philipse) traveled to Manhattan from Friesland and signed himself a lowly carpenter when he became a small burgher in 1657; at the time of his death in 1702, after a long career of multifaceted wheeling and dealing, he was one of the wealthiest men in America, his upriver estate, the famous Philipsburg Manor, encompassing ninety-two thousand acres of what would become Westchester County (including, incidentally, all of Adriaen van der Donck's former holdings).

There is a linguistic inheritance that would come along with this new relationship to work. Frederick Flipsen's workers, and the assistants to the colony's smiths, wheelwrights, bakers, and gunstock makers, had a looser relationship to their superiors than did workers in traditional guilds; a wheelwright's apprentice might also serve beer in the tavern or help bake bread. In time the typical Dutch word for master—*baas*—would take on a different connotation in the New World, and an Americanism came into being. And no Americanism is more American, and at the same time more New York, than boss. From Tweed to Corleone to Springsteen, the ur-bosses are all-American and utterly New York.* As New Amsterdam gave way to New York, the word would have a natural attraction for English colonists, too, because in its adapted usage it frankly distinguished itself from the power system that held sway in Old England; it spelled out a different kind of power relationship. "No," it says, "we have no class system in place here, but there is someone in charge. I'm not your master, lord, or sovereign, but I am your boss. Now get to work."

In this period of growth and activity, we see the emergence of other customs and usages that would influence American culture—little things,

---

*Yes, Springsteen is a New Jersey icon, but New Jersey was after all part of the Dutch colony, and from that time to now at the center of Manhattan's sphere of influence. And, while we're at it, Springsteens were among the original Dutch settlers of New Netherland.

meaningless in themselves, but indications that the Dutch colony never really died out, but became part of something larger. In October of 1661, there was a grain shortage in the city, and the municipal government issued an order to the bakers of the town to restrict themselves to baking bread and not "to bake any more *koeckjes*, jumbles or sweet cake." It's the tiniest of things, but note the Dutch word. It is pronounced "cook-yehs." Literally, little cakes. More than a century later, with the publication of *American Cookery*, the first American cookbook, in 1796, Amelia Simmons would lock in print what had by then become a standard usage. It's because the first Manhattanites called them that that Americans would never eat biscuits, but cookies.

While they were waiting (or not) for the bakers to produce their sweets, the women of New Amsterdam were inclined to pick up a head of cabbage, chop it finely, slather it with vinegar and melted butter, and serve it alongside, maybe, a platter of pike with smoked bacon, or veal meatballs. *Koolsla*—"cabbage salad"—was their straightforward name for the dish. Again, jump forward a century. In 1751 a Swedish traveler in the Hudson Valley, in describing a meal his Dutch landlady had served him, fused into the written language a term that was still given the original Dutch pronunciation but now had a phonetic American spelling: cole slaw.

As the town expanded and developed its seasonal routines and rituals, those of the dominant culture tended to prevail. We can imagine how the colony's most iconic legacy got established: every year in early December children of non-Dutch families in New Amsterdam had to have pouted at being left out of something good. As in the home country, the Dutch children would break out in song:

> Saint Nicholas, good holy man,
> Put on your best coat,
> Then gallop to Amsterdam . . .

And on the sixth of the month, the saint's feast day, they would wake to find that he had left treats for them. This, surely, was unbearable; among the English, the French, the German, the Swedish families of Manhattan, pressure was brought to bear on parents, and the Dutch tradition was adopted, and, later, pushed forward a couple of weeks to align with the more generally observed festival of Christmas. So *Sinterklaas* began his American odyssey.

All of this activity—children clamoring, bakers baking, tradesmen muscling their way to the top—intensified as Manhattan matured in its last decade under the Dutch. How New Amsterdam flourished in the years following the establishment of the municipal government is an area that has only recently been studied in depth, thanks largely to Charles Gehring's translation work. Ironically, however, the very intensity of activity in this period of the colony's life has slowed the translating of its records. "In the late 1650s I'm dealing with much more complicated legalese," Dr. Gehring told me one day in 2002 as I sat observing him at work in his office in the New York State Library. His desk was stacked with volumes of an eighteenth-century guide to Dutch, Latin, and French legal terms; the shelves behind him were lined with the forty massive volumes of *Het Woordenboek der Nederlandsche Taal,* the definitive historical dictionary of the Dutch language from the year 1500, and the ten-volume *Middelnederlandsch Woordenboek,* which focuses on the sixteenth century. "There's more legal activity now because there are more people," he said. "And there are more arguments. In the early days the land grants were vague because there was plenty of land. By now people are more packed in, and they are fighting about where property lines are. So you find Stuyvesant having to employ surveyors. And then you see the municipal government order a street plan with all the building lots indicated."

All of this paints a picture of Manhattan in its Dutch phase very different from the haggard, inept settlement we get in traditional tellings. But while trade and shipping details suggest that the region was thriving, they aren't what most mattered about the place. Who was there, how they got along, how they mixed—that is the colony's unheralded legacy. From the French Atlantic coast, the pine forests of Denmark, the streets of London, they made their way to this island, and, thanks to a farsighted program started by the city leaders, found someone waiting to offer them "burgher" status as they came off the ship. If they couldn't afford citizenship dues ("twenty guilders in beavers"), they could pay it on installment. Eventually, maybe, they found a way to make enough guilders, beavers, or hands of wampum to convince them that it was worth staying.

The village of Harlem (Nieuw Haarlem, after the city in Holland), founded at this time at the northern end of Manhattan, was a kind of microcosm of this microcosm of the future American society. The initial bloc of thirty-two families who staked out lots along its two lanes came from six different parts of Europe—Denmark, Sweden, Germany, France, the Netherlands, and what is now southern Belgium—and spoke five different languages. Perched alongside one another on the edge of a wilderness continent, families that would have broken up into ghettos in Europe instead had to come together, and learned a common language.

Nothing better shows the kind of mixing that took place in this setting than a phenomenon that was unprecedented elsewhere in the colonies: intermarriage. Scan the marriage records of the Dutch Reformed Church of New Amsterdam and you find a degree of culture-mixing in such a small place that is remarkable for the time. A German man marries a Danish woman. A man from Venice marries a woman from Amsterdam. Isaac Bethloo from "Calis in Vranckryck" (i.e., Calais in France) weds Lysbeth Potters from "Batavia in the East Indies." Samuel Edsall, reared in the English countryside around Reading, finds himself on Manhattan, where he somehow manages to woo a girl named Jannetje Wessels who spent her early years in the wild heath country of Gelderland near the German border. A Norwegian marries a German. Swedish-English. Danish-Swedish. Prussian-German. German-Danish. French-Dutch. In all, a quarter of the marriages performed in the New Amsterdam church were mixed. Intermarriage also appears among the Africans of the population, as when a man from the island of St. Thomas marries a woman from West Africa, and there are instances of marriage between whites and blacks.

It's easy to imagine Van der Donck, newly returned from Europe and strolling through New Amsterdam, comparing the rush of cultures in its streets to the mix he found on the Dam square in Amsterdam. He had come back to witness something that he himself had helped bring about: the forging of America's first melting pot. It so happened that in this melting pot the common language to which everyone defaulted was Dutch. And it was a seventeenth-century Dutch sensibility—a mix of frankness, piety, a keen business sense, an eye on the wider world, and a willingness to put up with people's differences—that formed the social glue. Already, a type was forming, which visitors were beginning to remark on: worldly, brash, confident, hustling.

Of course, equality was not part of the fabric of this pluralistic society. It wasn't even an ideal. Tolerance—call it grudging acceptance—was the major leap forward in human civilization that had recently occurred, which helped form the societies both of the Dutch Republic and the Manhattan colony. But in the seventeenth century no one believed that blacks and whites, men and women, Catholics and Protestants, were equals, or should be treated as such. Last among the unequals were the Africans. The slaves in the colony were the human workhorses. In trying to get a sense of what life was for the African Manhattanites, however, it's necessary to erase from your mind the idea of the fully formed institution of slavery as it existed in, say, the American South in the early 1800s. The institution was in its early days, and there was a strong belief in the Netherlands that it was morally wrong to buy and sell human beings, so that in the records of the colony you see a queer range of perspectives on Africans and their condition. There is the pious Reverend Jonas Michaelius referring to the black women who have worked in his house as "thievish, lazy, and useless trash," and there is Stuyvesant, sounding the classic slaver, accusing a woman slave of theft, denouncing a man for his "laziness and unwillingness," and decreeing that both be sold "for the maximum profit of the Company." But there are also more than a few cases of owners freeing slaves after a number of years, on the belief that they had done their time, and there are even a few occasions when Europeans are recorded as working for freed Africans. A number of Africans owned property, and Stuyvesant himself declared, in an as-yet unpublished document, that their ownership was to be looked on as "true and free ownership with such privileges as all tracts of land are bestowed on the inhabitants [of this] province." Slaves also had some legal rights: repeatedly, slaves appear in court, filing lawsuits against Europeans.

It's also necessary to keep in mind the scale of slavery in the colony. Manhattan was far removed from the sugar fields of Brazil and the Caribbean, where slave labor mattered. In its first decades there were no more than a few dozen slaves scattered across the colony at any one time; by the time of the English takeover there were about three hundred. What's notable in the records is less the presence of slaves on Manhattan than the development of the West India Company's slave trade. At first the company had refused to sully itself with the slave trade, but after failing in its other business ventures and seeing the money to be made from the transshipping of humans, it reversed course and became a significant player in one of history's ugliest episodes.

The island of Curaçao was transformed into a processing station for tens of thousands of chained, disease-riddled, and seasickened West Africans, and the records show Stuyvesant—whose title was after all Director-General of New Netherland, Curaçao, Bonaire, and Aruba—in the midst of running the North American colony, managing from afar his vice-director on Curaçao, Matthais Beck. What jangles in reading their correspondence are the humdrum, helter-skelter inventories of goods being moved around the Atlantic, as in a ship that arrived in Curaçao in August 1660 carrying "724 pine planks . . . 1245 pounds of English hardbread . . . 2 barrels of bacon . . . 75 skipples of peas . . ." and "10 Negroes" valued at "130 pieces of eight."

Africans weren't the only group to receive less-than-equal status. Cultural diversity management was about the last item on Peter Stuyvesant's list of job skills, and it's safe to say he was less than thrilled to see Manhattan's streets becoming an ethnic kaleidoscope. Religion was at the root of it: Stuyvesant despised Jews, loathed Catholics, recoiled at Quakers, and reserved a special hatred for Lutherans. Which is to say, he was the very model of a well-bred mid-seventeenth-century European. Religious bigotry was a mainstay of society. The four New England colonies to the north were founded on it. Across Europe it was universally held that diversity weakened a nation. Of course, the United Provinces of the Netherlands were supposed to be the exception to this rule, but the blanket of tolerance got a bit tattered on the transatlantic voyage. It's strange that the one nod that history has given to the Manhattan-based colony—as a cradle of religious liberty in the early America—is off base. Not that it is wrong exactly, but it needs to be combed out.

Dutch tolerance was indeed renowned throughout Europe, but it continued to be debated in the country, and every decade or so brought a shift in the prevailing cultural winds. One such shift had occurred in 1651. When the stadtholder, Willem II, died following his attempted coup d'état, leaders of all the Dutch provinces bent toward The Hague for a Great Assembly, the first such gathering since 1579, when the separate provinces met to hash out a common nation. The main topic was supposed to be what to do about the lack of a stadtholder, but the assembly turned into a debate on tolerance. The orthodox Calvinist faction chose the assembly as the occasion to push the line that the whole tolerance business had gotten out of hand—that, in effect, before you knew it the streets of Amsterdam would be filled with drug dens and legalized prostitution. A wave of hardline sentiment rippled outward, and it became fashionable for a time to crack down, in particular, on Catholics, Lutherans, and Jews.

It was in this atmosphere that Stuyvesant, whose feelings were strongly antidiversity anyway, moved against the religious groups that had proliferated as the colony had grown. When the Dutch Reformed ministers asked him to block Lutherans from worshipping on the grounds that it "would pave the way for other sects," so that eventually the place "would become a receptacle for all sorts of heretics and fanatics," he did so with gusto. In 1654 twenty-three Jews, some of whom had fled the fall of Dutch Brazil, showed up seeking asylum. You can almost see Stuyvesant shaking his head at being told that, on top of the usual heap of issues he had to deal with, he now had a Jewish population. His reaction was matter-of-fact, and perfectly in character: the Jews were "a deceitful race" that would "infect" the colony if he didn't stop them. He barred one from buying land, "for important reasons." He even refused to allow them to take turns standing guard with the citizens' militia, citing "the aversion and disaffection of this militia to be fellow soldiers of the aforesaid [Jewish] nation." If they didn't like it, he told Jacob Barsimon and Asser Levy in a terse decree, "consent is hereby given to them to depart whenever and wherever it may please them." But Abraham de Lucena and Salvador Dandrada, leaders of the Jews, knew their rights in the Dutch system, and appealed to the Dutch Republic. The Jewish community of Amsterdam applied pressure in the time-honored tradition of politics, and won. Stuyvesant's superiors reminded him loftily of the "each person shall remain free in his religion" law (and added that certain influential Jews had invested a "large amount of capital" in the West India Company), and ordered him to back off.

But it was English Quakers who pushed tolerance to the limit. They had followed other sects that had fled from Old England to New, and then southward into Dutch territory. There they began proselytizing in the largely English towns of Long Island. With their sermonizing and taunting and the jiggling fits of spiritual frenzy for which they were named, they all but invited Stuyvesant's disdain. They were, in his estimation, a threat to the peace and stability of the colony, and probably out of their minds as well. He thought he was being magnanimous when, instead of banishing them, he sent them an English preacher—none other than Adriaen van der Donck's father-in-law, Francis Doughty—but they rejected him, and continued holding their own avant-garde services. When Stuyvesant forbade the town of Vlissingen from abetting them, thirty-one of the villagers, all English, followed the Dutch form of complaint by signing a remonstrance to Stuyvesant. The law of "love peace and libertie . . . which is the glory of the Outward State of Holland," they reminded him, extends even "to Jewes Turkes and Egiptians." Therefore, they respectfully refused to obey. The so-called Flushing Remonstrance is considered one of the foundational documents of American liberty, ancestor to the first amendment in the Bill of Rights, which guarantees that the government "shall make no laws respecting an establishment of religion, or prohibiting the free exercise thereof." But here, too, history has spun it as a Dutch-English story, with the English in the role of lovers of liberty and Stuyvesant, standing in for his non-English colony, as the reactionary boob. In fact, the currents running through the colony were more complex, the Netherlands being the source both of a legal code of tolerance and, at times, of the failure to adhere to it. If the first amendment hearkens back to the Flushing Remonstrance, the Flushing Remonstrance clearly bases itself on the religious freedom guarantee in the Dutch constitutional document.

True to form, Stuyvesant responded to the English remonstrance with a series of arrests and imprisonments. His orthodox roots were showing in all of this: he was pushing hard, and against the inexorable forces of history, for his colony and the island he considered home to become, somehow, eventually, pure. If he had had his way, he would probably have picked off foreign religious elements one by one, scaring each away, until, like the New Englanders he seemed to admire, he had a religious monoculture, a Calvinist oasis in the New World.

But the place had its own character, and it was evolving rapidly. Thirty years later, one of Stuyvesant's successors, Governor Thomas Dongan, casually referenced the varieties of religious experience that had proliferated by then in the New York colony. Besides a Church of England presence, a Dutch Calvinist population, French Calvinists, Dutch Lutherans, and Roman Catholics, there were "Singing Quakers; Ranting Quakers; Sabbatarians; Antisabbatarians; Some Anabaptists some Independants; some Jews."

"In short," he added to sharpen the point, "of all sorts of opinions there are some, and the most part, of none at all." Stuyvesant must have lurched in his grave.

*

IF THE GROWTH of the colony brought Stuyvesant headaches, it also brought opportunity—bursts of happiness, even—into his otherwise stormy life. One day in late summer 1655, he found himself with a good sun overhead, the feel of a swaying deck beneath him, and enough wind to fatten the sails and flutter the long thin strands of his hair. Once again, as in his salad days in the Caribbean, he was at sea, heading a flotilla of seven gunboats and three hundred soldiers, bearing down on the enemy. Then, he had been thirty-four, and his assault on the Spanish at St. Martin was squelched by the "rough ball" that had shot off his leg. Now forty-five and in command of a thriving province, he was determined to win the day.

Off the starboard stretched a long ribbon of forest-backed beach that looked every bit as wild as when Henry Hudson had sailed along it in the other direction five decades earlier. Rounding Cape May and advancing into the shoaly bay and then up the river that formed the most neglected area of his domain, he anchored between the two Swedish forts on the western shore. Here he deployed with precision, dividing his men into five companies, sending a contingent of fifty marching off to occupy the only road in the region, thus cutting off communication between the two forts of his enemy, and setting the rest to building a six-foot-high breastworks a stone's throw from the nearer fort. He sent into the fort an ensign named Dirck Smith, accompanied by a drummer escort. The message he carried was a straight-up demand: unconditional surrender.

The Anglo-Dutch War was over. A wave of prosperity was washing through the colony. And with the recent fall of Brazil to the Portuguese, the West India Company had finally—belatedly—committed itself to the Manhattan-based colony, sending troops and ships. So Stuyvesant was at last able to devote his formidable attention to his southern region. The Swedes had maintained their presence here for seventeen years now, settling the region sparsely, in part by bringing in "forest Finns." Decades before, Sweden had encouraged this particular group of Finns who lived near the Russian border to settle in a remote area of central Sweden, which the Swedish government had wanted cleared. The Finns had a way of life that revolved around "burn-beating" to clear forest and then cultivate the land, making them the perfect subgroup to tame dense, virgin woodland. But they turned out to be too good at their task; when they refused to curtail their way of life and stop decimating forests, the Swedes began shipping them to America. Together with the forest Finns, the Swedes had developed settlements on the South River and cultivated a steady fur trade with the Indians of the region, which had rankled both Kieft and Stuyvesant. They had also taken control of one of the Dutch forts on the river. Now Stuyvesant had come to demand, as he put it, "restitution of our property."

After a brief wait, the Swedish commander stepped out to survey the force arrayed against him, then asked to be allowed to communicate with his superior in the other fort. "His request was firmly denied," Stuyvesant later wrote with satisfaction, "and he left discontented." Finally the Swedish factor, a man named Von Elswick, arrived on the scene to parlay. He and Stuyvesant met on the edge of a marsh just below the fort. The insects of high summer roared around them, the sun glinted off Stuyvesant's armor; his self-assured body language reflected the presence of the hundreds of soldiers behind him. The men apparently spoke in a mixture of languages, falling to diplomats' Latin for precision. Both knew that Stuyvesant had gathered an overwhelming force. The matter was simple: would the Swedes fight and die needlessly, or surrender the Delaware River region to the Dutch?

Von Elswick had no choice but to give in, but as he surrendered he aimed a verbal kick at Stuyvesant. *"Hodie mihi, cras tibi,"* he said in prophetic Latin. *Today it's me, tomorrow it will be you.* He meant it as a vow—that the Swedes would one day return. In fact, it was prophetic in a different way, as in nine years' time another power, in the role of the bigger fish, would give Stuyvesant the same ultimatum he was now offering the Swede.

Stuyvesant parried the jibe and took possession of the forts. New Sweden vanished into history. He took immediate steps to settle the region, which he knew was the only hope for keeping control of it. He started with the Finns whom the Swedes had brought in as laborers. He decided to invite them to stay, and in fact he gave them incentives to continue settling the wilderness. Like so many other aspects of the Manhattan-based colony, this decision would rattle down the centuries, affecting American history in oddly resonant ways. The Finns did indeed put down roots, and over the final decade of Dutch rule more would join them, as word spread in the old country. From the early 1700s into the early 1800s their descendants would migrate down the Appalachian Valley, through the South, and out into the heartland of the new country. They brought with them their forest-clearing skills, which literally opened the American frontier, and something more as well. Throughout northern Europe, this group was renowned for its way with wood, and as the Finns spread they brought their technology with them, and it caught on. There is a long trail of evidence—V-notching, roof construction, and a kind of modular floor plan—to support the idea that the American log cabin, which rooted Appalachia and shaped Abraham Lincoln's Indiana boyhood, thus originated with the Finns of central Sweden and spread following the Latin-Dutch-Swedish parlay between Stuyvesant and Von Elswick in a bee-loud glade along the Delaware River.*

Stuyvesant felt full of himself as he prepared to head back to Manhattan. His colony was thriving. (That it was due in large part to the semirepresentative government that he had bitterly fought was another matter.) The border agreement he had hashed out with the New Englanders was holding. And at long last he had regained control of the southern region, and without firing a shot. As he prepared to board his flagship, the ache in his stump must have dulled somewhat.

*

IF HE WAS experiencing a rare problem-free moment, however, it was about to end. One hundred and fifty miles to the north, canoes were in the river, moving fast through the predawn, paddles knifing the water. On September 15, 1655, six hundred Indians made landfall at the southernmost point of Manhattan Island, below the fort, then flowed through the streets of the town, firing arrows, swinging axes, setting off screams, shrieks, alarms. Similar raids took place to the north on the mainland and on Staten Island, where Indians burned down homes, killed several dozen Europeans, and took more hostages.

Historians have thought it an odd coincidence that this brief "war"

---

*A bit of anecdotal support: when I told my Swedish-Norwegian father-in-law—who owns a log cabin in the traditionally Scandinavian country of northern Minnesota—about the Finns as the originators of the American log cabin, his response was: "Around here everyone knows that if you want a log cabin built, you call a Finn."

should take place while Stuyvesant happened to be away to the south sub-
duing the Swedes. Trying to make sense of it, some grabbed at an incident
in which a Dutchman killed an Indian woman for stealing peaches, decided
that this had launched the mayhem, and named it the Peach War. But the evidence for what actually sparked the raids is there, lying in the records. The
European residents of New Amsterdam could distinguish between the various tribes of the region, and in reporting the events of September 1655 they
noted that the attackers seemed to be from everywhere: "Maquas, Mahikanders, the Indians of the North River from above to below," they wrote to
Stuyvesant. And, strangely, they noted the presence of a chief of the Minquas or Susquehannocks—the tribe from the South River region, precisely
where Stuyvesant had sailed. Such a multicultural Indian gathering makes
no sense—unless you flip your view of events around, as some recent historians have done, and see it from the Indians' point of view.

We are so used to looking at encounters between whites and Indians
through the prism of later centuries that it's hard to fathom that in the 1600s
the Indians saw themselves as the dominant players. As far as the Minquas
of the South River were concerned, they had devoted seventeen years to
cultivating a trading relationship with the Swedes, only to see Stuyvesant
and his soldiers destroy it. So the Indians retaliated. In doing so, they were
in effect protecting the Swedes, who brought them valuable supplies and
who, being weaker than the Indians, deserved their protection. It has also
become clear in recent years that East Coast Indians regularly formed alliances with distant tribes. If we grant them that much sophistication, then
the reports of the Manhattanites make sense: a Minquas chief orchestrated
the attack, and it was a direct result of Stuyvesant's dismantling of New
Sweden.

The misnamed Peach War was a blip in the life of the Manhattan-based
colony: it was over in a matter of weeks. But it plays a bigger part in this
story. Here again, as in so many other places, we have to fill in gaps with
guesses. We have to imagine a party of Indians who had come from afar to
attack Europeans. Just north of Manhattan, in a long valley, they come
across a patch of civilization: a farmhouse, a saw mill, fields under cultivation. They raid the house; a man inside rises up to defend his family. He has
always maintained good relations with the Indians of the area, but these are
from elsewhere and make no distinctions between whites who are friends or

enemies. The man is murdered. His wife escapes, or perhaps is taken prisoner for a time. It is over quickly, the roaring, defiant cries that signal the
end of a life swallowed by the wooded hillsides.

The man was Adriaen van der Donck. For some periods of his life his
presence and personality are so vivid that he seems to step three-
dimensionally out of the pages of historical records. But the image of him in
his last years, since his return from Europe, is flat and dim, and the circumstances of his death are sketchy. The death itself isn't even recorded. We
know only that Van der Donck was alive in the summer of 1655, that he was
dead before January of 1656, and that his house was ransacked by Indians
during the multitribal attack in September. So we have to stitch the rem-
nants together with surmise. Interestingly, it's from Stuyvesant that we first
hear of Van der Donck being dead, in an indirect reference. As the Manhattanites try to make sense of the Indian attacks, Stuyvesant tells the members
of his council of a Wickquasgeck Indian, from the area around Van der
Donck's home, coming to discuss what he knows. This Indian, Stuyvesant
mentions, "had been a good friend of Van der Donck, and had taken care of
his cows for some time." Thus the verb tense serves as the man's death notice, and the mention of him in conjunction with the attack adds another
piece of evidence as to how he died. Since Stuyvesant himself never understood the likely connection between his military actions in the South River
and the attacks around Manhattan, it probably never occurred to him that
he had been indirectly responsible for the death of his onetime nemesis.

Van der Donck's wife, Mary, survived him. Her father, the Reverend
Francis Doughty, had recently accepted a position at a church in Virginia
and, following her husband's death, she joined him there. She found regular
work as a medical practitioner, purging, sweating, setting bones, and delivering babies. Eventually she married an Englishman named Hugh O'Neale,
but, oddly, continued to appear in the records as "Mrs. Van der Donck (alias)
O'Neale." Having given up on the vast estate for which her husband had had
such plans, Mary signed it over to her brother, who sold it. And so very
quickly after his death at the age of thirty-seven, Adriaen van der Donck—
with no progeny or property to recall him to the living—was a forgotten man.

But no—that's not quite true. In a strange twist, his book, *A Description
of New Netherland*—into which he had poured his knowledge of the colony,
its people, its natives, its plants, winds, insects, mountains, snows, dangers,

and promises—his book, which had been admitted for publication and then withheld due to the war, came out in the Netherlands right around the time of his death. It became a best-seller, and went into a second edition the following year. Once again, this time posthumously, Van der Donck sparked a wave of interest in a faraway place called Manhattan, an island where ordinary Europeans could throw off the ancient shackles of their castes and guilds and sects. A place to which, now, yet more mixes of peoples—Croats and Prussians, Flemings and Limburgers, Copenhageners and Dieppois—would pin their dreams.

To the front of the second edition of the book, the publisher attached a poem that sung both the author and his subject:

> So, reader, if you desire, travel there freely and full of joy.
> Although named for the Netherlands, it exceeds it far.
> Does such a journey not appeal? Then lend your eyes
> To the book by Van der Donck, which like a bright star
> Shows the land and people, and will teach you further
> That the Netherlands, through her care, can govern New Netherland.

It wasn't very good verse. But it was as close as anyone would come to memorializing the man who first saw the promise of Manhattan Island, dreamed its future, and devoted his life to making the dream real.

The passion for the New World colony that had fueled Van der Donck outlived him. Less than a year after his death and on the heels of the publication of his book, the municipal government of Amsterdam put together an elaborate plan for a colony of its own. Three hundred settlers signed on to emigrate, and the city drew up long lists of start-up supplies—400 pairs of shoes, "50 pairs Prussian blue stockings," "100 red Rouen caps," "8 firkins vinegar," 250 pounds of cheese, 15 hams, 30 smoked tongues—with which it furnished them. Impressed by Stuyvesant's vanquishing of the Swedes, they decided to plant the new settlement on the South River, around one of Stuyvesant's forts. And so it began all over again: a new crop of arrivals, new hopes. "I have been full 5 or 6 hours in the interior in the woods," wrote one of the settlers, a schoolmaster, shortly after landfall, "and found fine oak and hickory trees, also excellent land for tillage. . . . I already begin to keep school, and have 25 children." They called the settlement New Amstel.

Today it is the city of New Castle, Delaware, and on its central square a tiny, late-seventeenth-century Dutch house of sturdy brick and red-shuttered windows bears testimony to the belated effort to heed Van der Donck. The desires, now, were to exploit the colony's potential and to catch up with English expansion in North America. One would be realized, the other would not.

Chapter 14

NEW YORK

Unless you are a member of the Dead Sea Scrolls sect or a follower of the philosopher Hegel, it would probably be a mistake to think that the English takeover of Manhattan was inevitable. The fall of Rome, the defeat of the Spanish Armada, the American colonists winning their war for independence, the Allies defeating Hitler—we have a tendency to imagine that past events, especially the big ones, had to happen the way they did. But really to believe that is to subscribe to a doctrine that holds that our acts aren't our own, that we are only cogs in a machine carrying out preprogrammed instructions.

In hindsight, however, the takeover does have a certain obviousness. Partly that's because history books have portrayed the event that way, giving us the image of the English population of New England as an inexorable force of nature swelling until, like a glass overflowing, it poured southward almost unconsciously, flooding the Dutch colony. But looked at another way, you might say that the colony cast off its Dutch parent. The seed that Henry Hudson transported to a distant island rooted and grew, and, really, outgrew the mother plant. It was the luckiest thing in the world for Manhattan—for America—that the English wanted it so badly, because, though no one could see it at the time, the Dutch empire was already on the wane, and the English one was only beginning its rise. Van der Donck's mission had been all about the forces of history; his appeal was for the leaders of the Dutch government to take note of them. But the system that fueled the Dutch Golden Age wasn't built to last. The English, meanwhile, especially those in America, would begin experimenting ornately and obsessively with ideas of liberty, unfettered reason, the rights of man. Put elements of the two together—seventeenth-century Dutch tolerance and free-trade principles and eighteenth-century English ideas about self-government—and you have a recipe for a new kind of society. You can almost see the baton passing from the one seventeenth-century power to the other, and at the very center of that changeover is Manhattan.

But no one in the Dutch colony—or for that matter in New England—saw the end that finally came. It wasn't a result of hordes of New Englanders sweeping south. What happened was more calculated, and involved a global set of players, and, like any good final act, some sudden reversals.

The figure at the center of it all, of course, was Peter Stuyvesant. Stuyvesant's main adversary was a man he would never meet—a man whose first, brief, appearance in the history books came years earlier. In 1642, Stuyvesant was still barking orders under the tropical sun of Curaçao, Kieft was in charge on Manhattan, and Van der Donck was the lawman up north, roaming the vast estate of the Amsterdam diamond merchant Kiliaen Van Rensselaer. Meanwhile, outside the village of Boston, nine young men stepped from a simple clapboard building onto a long sward of grass. It was endless wilderness just beyond the surrounding cow pastures and apple trees, but they and the cluster of people gathered around them saw the event through the lens of civilization, embued it with centuries of English tradition. The nine young men were the first class of graduates of the college founded with money granted by a Puritan minister named John Harvard.

Overseeing the ceremony was John Winthrop, governor of the Massachusetts colony, with whom Peter Stuyvesant would forge a close relationship. But the man who, more than any other individual, would engineer the takeover of Manhattan was one of those nine young scholars stepping into a New England morning in early fall. His name was George Downing. He was a grim, athletic nineteen-year-old possessed of an ambition bordering on aggression, and he happened to be Governor Winthrop's nephew.

As with most of those first generations of Harvard graduates, Downing yearned for London. Shortly after the ceremony, he sailed there, saw the civil war taking shape, pronounced himself a Puritan revolutionary, and fought with the Parliamentarians. As the new government came into being, Oliver Cromwell saw the intellect and bulldog ferocity in the young man and made him his ambassador to The Hague. There, Downing proved himself English to the core, which meant, among other things, fostering a loyal hatred of the Dutch. Really, he was an ungainly choice for a diplomat, unless you are more interested in sticking it to the country in question than in smoothing things. In place of the suave manners usually considered necessary in diplomacy, Downing was brusque and obstinate. Jan de Witt and the other leaders of the Dutch government found him repellent, and his colleagues in the English government didn't much care for him either. The diarist Samuel Pepys worked under him and frankly pronounced him (to his diary, anyway) a "perfidious rogue."

But Downing had the diplomat's knack of getting what he wanted, and nothing shows it better than his management of his own fate following Cromwell's death in 1658 and the restoration of the Stuarts, in the person of Charles II, to the throne. Downing had been among the most vicious of the anti-Royals, hunting down friends of the Stuart family, and now the same royal family had returned to power. Turning on a dime, he boldly asked the new monarch to excuse his waywardness in supporting Cromwell, and blamed his faulty judgment on his having come of age in the unstable climate of the New World. He then demonstrated his loyalty to the king by trapping and arresting three of his own friends, men who had sentenced Charles's father to death. Downing's shamelessness was rewarded not only by Charles reappointing him to his position as Dutch ambassador, and later knighting him, but, eventually, by the naming of Downing Street in London after him. (Downing College at the University of Cambridge has his name on it, too, as a result of a bequest he made.)

So Downing resettled himself at The Hague, and recommenced loathing the Dutch and their trade hegemony and searching, as duty compelled him to do, for cracks in it. Back in New England, meanwhile, the leaders—men who were theologically even more strident than the home country Puritans— were at least as disoriented by the restoration of the Stuarts as Downing, and most were not nearly as adept at switching gears. One result of their quandary, notable for American history in a number of ways, was the struggle for power and territory among the leaders of the English colonies in the early '60s. Massachusetts, with its long-standing royal charter, was on firmest ground. But the two southern colonies, Connecticut and New Haven, had formed in an ad hoc way, settlers spilling southward into territory the Dutch had claimed; as yet they had no official sanction in England. It was now necessary to petition the royals they had long despised. For New Haven, where Puritanism was purest, this was galling, and the leaders balked.

One man in Connecticut, however, had more flexibility. John Winthrop, the governor of that colony, was the son of the other John Winthrop, governor of Massachusetts and the patriarch of all the New England Puritans, and thus the cousin of George Downing. The elder Winthrop had long since died, much to the chagrin of Peter Stuyvesant, who had relied on his pro-Dutch leanings in his dealings with the New England leaders. Stuyvesant now—with disastrous misjudgment—looked to the son for level-headed leadership among the Puritan firebrands. The younger Winthrop has been portrayed by history as a quiet, modest achiever, forever in the shadow of his father. This small, dark knife of a man has not been given credit either for his accomplishments or his political cunning.

In 1661, having overcome his anti-Royalist impulses, Winthrop proposed to travel to London to petition Charles for a charter for his colony. His guile shows itself first in his eagerness to go, second in the manner of his leave-taking. After promising William Leete, his counterpart in New Haven, that he would also deliver the petition for a charter that the colony had belatedly cobbled together, he sailed off, literally leaving the man standing on shore still holding his document. Next, he chose not to leave from Boston but instead made arrangements with his friend Peter Stuyvesant to sail from Manhattan. Of course, the island was a major travel hub, but sailing on a Dutch ship meant arriving in Holland first and then having to cross to England. Stuyvesant doesn't seem to have found it odd.

Sailing into the Dutch harbor on July 8, Winthrop was shocked by the sound of cannon fire coming from the fort. But the shock turned to delight: his friend Stuyvesant was giving him the honored greeting of a head of state. (The Dutch records inform us that no less than twenty-seven pounds of gun powder were consumed "to salute Governor Winthorp [sic]".) Stuyvesant liked Winthrop. He seemed to like all Englishmen. Hartford was fast-growing but unkempt, and Stuyvesant proudly showed the visitor around his trim little capital: here the fort, here the new brick home of the director himself (Stuyvesant having decided he ought to have a house outside the fort as well as his distant farm), here the newly reinforced wall along the northern perimeter, complete now with guard towers and a central gate at the Highway. Winthrop apparently kept up his stream of convivial chatter, asking lots of questions, complimenting the director on how far he had come with his town. He spent thirteen days in New Amsterdam, and by the end of it he had detailed notes on the place, its fortifications, and troop numbers.

Trying to imagine Stuyvesant's plight at this time gives some sympathy for him. He knew there were English machinations over his colony, and must have been livid over the company's failure to send soldiers for its defense. And yet, when his own people expressed similar anger at being left without protection, he had to defend the directors' decisions.

And while he was wary of the English, Stuyvesant couldn't resist comparing notes with Winthrop on their respective colonies, and expressing frank envy of the monocultures of New England while complaining how his own population was comprised of the "scrapings" of all countries. As pressures grew, he seems to have become more and more a solitary figure, and an oddly evocative image of him at this time comes into view. One of his apparent sources of pleasure was tropical birds, with which he had presumably become fascinated in his years in the Caribbean. Over the years he had instructed company officials on Curaçao to send him birds (one packing slip indicates "To the honorable lord director-general P. Stuyvesant," "Four parrots in two cages" and "Twenty-four parakeets"), so that he must have built up quite an aviary by this time. On his farm, alone with the bright squawking of his pets, he must have tried endlessly to parse the problem of how to deal with the English, weighing trust versus suspicion.

Stuyvesant's bonhomie toward Winthrop extended right up to the latter's departure: fifty-five soldiers lined the harbor as Winthrop's ship headed for open water, and unleashed a full military salute. At the other end of his journey, Winthrop arranged a meeting with the directors of the West India Company. Here he played up the fellow-Protestant connection, and the normally reserved men of business were convinced. "He has always shown himself a friend of our nation," they wrote to Stuyvesant, encouraging him in his trust.

If anyone found it suspicious that Winthrop proposed next to travel from Amsterdam to The Hague, it could have been explained away as a family matter. George Downing, English diplomat in residence there, was after all his cousin. They had last seen each other in New England, and were on familiar enough terms that later Winthrop wrote several times to Downing, who was famously stingy with money, to chide him for keeping his mother living near poverty. Secret consultations being what they are, we don't know the details of the meeting between the two cousins in September of 1661, but a map that Winthrop had drawn up of New Amsterdam's fortifications was soon circulating in government channels; this, logically, was the moment in which information about the current military status of the Dutch colony was transferred to English authorities.

Then—this historically momentous journey proceeding to the next phase—it was on to London for Winthrop. Charles II's coronation had taken place just five months earlier, and the city, having thrown off the heavy drape of Puritan rule, was in the midst of its libertine Restoration hoedown, with thundering alehouses, saucy maids, and theaters packing in crowds to see productions of *Hamlet*, '*Tis a Pity She's a Whore*, and puppet shows satirizing Puritanism. From all of these Winthrop carefully averted his eyes as he applied himself to the task of winning royal favor.

In drab contrast to the satiny surroundings of the king's council chamber, Winthrop—a gray little man with a hooked nose and arched, sardonic-looking eyebrows—bowed low and bowed often that autumn and winter, he smiled through the small indignities (being routinely confused with Josiah Winslow of the Plymouth colony, realizing midway through the discussions that the king thought "Massachusetts" and "New England" were one and the same) and emerged with a document that embodied all of his desires, desires he had kept secret from everyone, most of all his New England colleagues. When the charter was finally presented to them, they were staggered. Charles had given Connecticut a grant that extended from the Massachusetts border south, including the Dutch territories, and west as far as "the Pacific." Winthrop's quiet, modest, understated ambition was now revealed. He wanted all the territory between Massachusetts and Virginia. He wanted his land to stretch to the Pacific Ocean—never mind that no one had any notion how far it was. He wanted everything. And he got it.

New Haven officials were apoplectic at the idea that Winthrop proposed to engulf their colony, but it was a fait accompli—he had the royal signature—and, truly, he was so nice about it, so patient in explaining why it was for the good of all, that his opposite, Governor Leete, gave in quickly, thus ensuring that the future United States would contain no state of New

Haven. The bitterest Puritans of the colony talked about picking up stakes and heading for the Dutch territory, where they knew they would be welcomed, but their leaders also knew that Winthrop had that next in his sights.

Stuyvesant, meanwhile, had gotten wind of Winthrop's charter. He wrote to his friend, asking him to confirm that he would respect the Hartford Treaty boundary lines they had drawn up more than a decade earlier. Winthrop's reply was a deft little evasion. The West India Company suggested to Stuyvesant that because of "your anxiety over the patent lately obtained by Governor Winthrop," he should shore up his defenses. But they didn't give him the troops or ships to do so, despite his appeals.

Stuyvesant had troubles quite aside from Winthrop. The boom that had come to New Amsterdam in the eight years since the granting of its city charter was accompanied by a draining away of confidence in Stuyvesant and the West India Company. There had been that chance, in the months following Van der Donck's return, for Stuyvesant to support the reform that people had demanded, and give the entire colony a semblance of popular representation. Then again, the company would probably not have allowed it. At any rate, that was his last hope to win the hearts of the people. Soon after, English colonists on Long Island and on the mainland, who had sworn allegiance to New Netherland, began flipping that allegiance, declaring themselves residents of Connecticut. Winthrop encouraged this and in part engineered it. Stuyvesant complained to the directors that Long Island and "West Chester" were turning English; there had been encroachments on Jonas Bronck's and Adriaen van der Donck's former estates. While the city was thriving, the colony, he wrote, was in "a sad and perilous condition."

Now Winthrop prepared to make his big move, to bring the entire Dutch colony within his jurisdiction. One by one, towns on the mainland were ordered to "yield obedience" to Connecticut, and begin paying taxes to Hartford. Winthrop was no longer Stuyvesant's friend; now he and his colleagues in Connecticut were "unrighteous, stubborn, impudent and pertinacious." New Netherland was disintegrating, and Stuyvesant didn't have the means to stop it.

But no—the end didn't come that way, with an invasion from the north. Winthrop was just about the wiliest creature of all those involved in this end game—the wiliest, that is, but one. His cousin, George Downing, had the better of him there. Downing took the information about Manhattan that Winthrop had given him and put it to other uses. From his diplomat's offices in The Hague, Downing had the wider view of things. He saw the globe scored with the crisscrossing lines of Dutch trade routes. Dutch outposts stippled the coast of India like a beard; they were scattered across the Indonesian archipelago; the Dutch were the only nation on earth with whom the closed islands of Japan would trade. They had control of the spice trade, of cotton, indigo, silk, sugar, cotton, copper, coffee, and dozens of other products. And now, as they moved into West Africa, Downing saw them about to secure an advantage in the one commodity that would tip the balance in the decades ahead: human beings.

In June of 1661, Downing appeared before the States General, and made an expansive appeal on behalf of his nation. England and the Dutch Republic, he intoned, must "be instruments of good and not of hurt to each other." The matter of trade was thorny, but, he advised sagely, "the world is large, there is trade enough for both." This was hogwash. After negotiating a trade treaty with Jan de Witt, he went to London, where he promptly directed his indominable energy to convincing the king that now was the time to hit the Dutch hard, with soldiers, ships, and cannon fire. Living as he did in the bosom of Holland's Golden Age, he had seen the changes brought by the waves of wealth—dour Calvinist clothes swapped for satins and swaggering French fashions, country estates tricked out with faux-Roman pillars, the children of rich merchants (as evidenced by many portraits) growing fat and pink as young sows—and he believed the Dutch had gone soft. Their Atlantic Rim possessions were ripe for picking, starting with the slaving posts in West Africa. "Go on in Guinea," he thundered to the king's council. "If you bang them there, they will be very tame."

Downing was playing to the choir; overwhelmingly, according to Samuel Pepys, the court was "mad for a Dutch war." The only man who really mattered, however, wasn't so sure. The second Charles Stuart to sit on the English throne was a man of wide interests. He was obsessed with clocks, enjoyed redesigning the royal gardens, and spent late nights at "the Royal Tube" (his telescope). He loved dogs, horses, singing Italian songs, tennis (he played daily), and sex (possibly daily—the notorious Nell Gwynn was among his many mistresses and "royal bastards" was a category of palace expenditure). His court was the epitome of licentiousness, a mirror image of the years that had preceded it. He had been a teenager when anti-royal forces put a price on his head, and after years hiding in barns, forests, and foreign palaces, he was now where he was meant to be, and ready to live it to the full. He cared about foreign policy, but didn't seem to have an overriding philosophy of where to steer the country. He wasn't especially fond of the Dutch, but admired them, and had some gratitude toward them for putting him up in The Hague. He wasn't sure about launching military raids.

His brother, however, was. James Stuart, at twenty-eight, was bigger and bluffer than the king, a full-out athlete and lifelong soldier, aggressive and full of tally-ho, altogether more of a man's man. He wasn't well liked by the people and some historians have branded him a stooge, but he had something his brother lacked: constancy. When he later converted to Catholicism it was after long deliberation, and he stayed with it despite the fact that it got him deposed only three years into his reign. It was James who saw the magic in Cromwell's idea of an English empire. His brother had made him head of the Admiralty, and from that position he was determined to make good on Cromwell's dream.

The plan began to take shape in 1661. As a first step, the men at the center of power in London—politicians, royals, merchants—agreed that the American colonies, which had been left to themselves while the nation's attention was diverted by civil war, needed reorganizing. Charles and James didn't trust the Puritan leaders there, and soon after the king had sent Winthrop away with his charter it was agreed that it had been a mistake to give the New Englanders leave to take control of Manhattan and the Hudson River corridor, which meant access to the interior of the continent.

Downing then took the lead in arguing for a master plan involving the whole Atlantic Rim. Reading the letters, minutes, and military instructions surrounding this evolving plan, it's remarkable to comprehend that so much history—the changeover of Manhattan Island, the consolidation of the American colonies, the ramping up of the slave trade into an epoch-changing institution, the transformation of West Africa, the Caribbean, South America, and North America—was quite calculated and stemmed from a series of meetings among a rather small group of men in London in the years 1661 and 1662.

James backed the plan, and pushed for the king's endorsement. Warfare was a language that the prince knew and felt comfortable with. In his years of exile he had volunteered and fought valiantly under the French in their war against Spain, leading men in musket-and-horse charges on the snowy plains of northern France and achieving the rank of general, then, when the vicissitudes of the age dictated that the English royals-in-exile should back the Spanish, promptly switching sides and fighting with equal bravery for Spain. Having risked his life a dozen times for lesser ends, he was more than ready to commit himself now to something as big and vital as this. The first objective was to wrest control of the slave ports of West Africa from the Dutch. The prince organized a company to fund the operation, which got the flourishing title of The Company of Royal Adventurers Trading into Africa. (The Royal Mint commemorated James's desire to exploit the "Guinea Coast" by striking a new coin, which, popularly known as the guinea, would long outlast the trade.) Reorganized as the Royal African Company, this enterprise would become the single greatest shipper of slaves from Africa to America. (The prosaic-sounding 1667 announcement of its public offering of stock stands in stark relief to the impact the words would have down the centuries: "the Royal Company being very sensible how necessary it is that the *English* Plantations in *America* should have a competent and a constant supply of *Negro-servants* for their own use of Planting, and that at a moderate Rate, have already sent abroad, and shall within eight days dispatch so many Ships for the Coast of *Africa* as shall by God's permission furnish the said Plantations with at least 3000 Negroes, and will proceed from time to time to provide them a constant and sufficient succession of them . . .")

In the company's first mission, James picked a roguish Irishman named Robert Holmes and sent him in command of two ships to go raiding in the Cape Verde islands and down the Guinea Coast. Holmes did all that was asked of him: the initial result of James's first corporate adventure was a rout of the Dutch slaving posts. The Dutch ambassador expressed his government's outrage to King Charles (the two countries were after all at peace), and the king tried to brush the matter aside: "And pray, what is Cape Verde? a stinking place; is this of such importance to make so much ado about?" Meanwhile, the ringing success encouraged both the prince and the diplomat to move to the next stage. Downing was sure he could talk his way out of anything. "What ever injuries the Dutch doe them," he wrote of James's warships, "let them be sure to doe the Dutch still greater and lett me alone to mediate between them . . ."

Charles now had some confidence in the geopolitical gambit, and he gave Downing and his brother their next card to play. Settlement of North America had become a primary long-term objective; the slave business was intertwined with it. In March of 1664 the king signed his name to an extraordinary document. In making a gift "unto our Dearest Brother James Duke of York, his Heirs and Assigns" of a vast stretch of the North American continent (". . . Together with all the Lands, Islands, Soils, Rivers, Harbors, Mines, Minerals, Quarries, Woods, Marshes, Waters, Lakes, Fishings, Hawking, Hunting and Fowling and all other Royalties, Profits, Commodities and Hereditaments to the said several Islands, Lands and Premises . . ."), he was being more than generous. Much of the land indicated—from Maine to Delaware—he had only recently granted to Winthrop for his Connecticut colony. The gift to his brother was meant to erase that mistake. The "Duke's Charter" took care to single out the "River called Hudsons River," and it was in this that men in Whitehall who were attuned to global economic events were particularly interested.

Like an elephant in the dawn, the full girth of the continent to the edge of which the European colonies had clung for four decades was gradually becoming apparent. It was also apparent by now that the New England colonies were on a kind of shelf, landlocked, unable to access future potential. The beavers of the northeast were on their way to extinction; the future lay to the west, which meant, first, up the Hudson River. And the key to it was Manhattan. This was borne out by the fact that much of their own trade went through Manhattan, which, English leaders now calculated, cost them ten thousand pounds per year in tobacco shipments alone. Having identified the island as the linchpin of the American colonies, a committee at Whitehall determined in January 1664 that it was necessary to take it, and soon. Further, they wanted it in the hands of one of their own men rather than the New Englanders.

Having made their decision, the committee moved quickly. The charter was signed in March; the next month, James summoned a man named Richard Nicolls. Nicolls was forty years old, a lifelong royalist who had stayed at the prince's side all during his Commonwealth exile and fought with him in France. He was smart and capable, which was just as well. James told him he was being entrusted with North America. He would command four gunships and four hundred and fifty men; they would leave within the month. Shortly after, James himself took to sea, cruising the Channel in a naval exercise, smelling the future on the sea air, fully aware that his attack on Manhattan would have to be followed up by further assaults on the Dutch.

Nicolls, meanwhile, sailed west. The squadron had good conditions to start. Then on day sixteen they were hit by crosswinds and foul weather, and in "very great Fogge," Nicolls, on his flagship, the thirty-six gun *Guinea,* lost sight of two of his ships. Ten weeks after leaving Portsmouth, the vessels made landfall, two on Cape Cod, the other two away to the south at Piscataway.

When he came ashore at Boston, Nicolls dispatched riders with letters from King Charles to the New England governors, informing them that steps were about to be taken for "the welfare and advancement of those our plantations in America." Arguably the man in the colonies most shocked by Nicolls's arrival was not Stuyvesant but John Winthrop. Nicolls had been ordered by James to "putt Mr Winthropp . . . in mind of the differences which were on foot here"—i.e., that the king had reneged on his promise. Winthrop's dream of a continent-wide colony of Connecticut vanished in a stroke. Smart politician that he was, however, he swiftly adjusted his expectations. While the Massachusetts leaders stalled and grumbled, unhappy with the idea of relinquishing power to the crown, Winthrop offered his services in negotiations with Stuyvesant, which Nicolls accepted.

Stuyvesant, meanwhile, was, of all places, one hundred and fifty miles north of Manhattan, at Fort Orange, where there were problems with the Mohawks. He hadn't been caught off guard, but he had been misled. Through one of his English friends he had learned of the English squadron even before it landed, and had his capital dig in—setting watches, preparing defenses, sending men out along Long Island Sound for news of the ships' arrival. Then a remarkable letter arrived from Amsterdam. Before the squadron had left, Downing had taken the unusual step of informing the Dutch government of its existence—in order, he said, to assure the Dutch that their colony had nothing to fear; England was merely sending a commander to overhaul the administration of the New England colonies.

The Dutch leaders were completely duped; the directors insisted Stuyvesant needn't be alarmed. Nicolls's mission would not affect him, and as to the English residents of the Dutch colony, they would "not give us henceforth so much trouble" because they "prefer to live free under us at peace with their consciences" than risk being persecuted by "a government from which they had formerly fled." So Stuyvesant relaxed his guard, went up the Hudson as planned, and as soon as he arrived at his northern outpost news of impending disaster reached him. He sailed back to Manhattan to find the island in turmoil. The English gunboats were perched at the entrance to the lower harbor, cutting off the river and Manhattan Island. People stepping off the ferry from Breuckelen talked of inhabitants of the English towns forming themselves into companies of foot soldiers. Sailors from a Dutch boat anchored in Gravesend Bay reported the English ships had fired on them.

Stumping into the fort, Stuyvesant dictated a letter to the colony's secretary, which was delivered to Nicolls's ship, asking his business and declaring hopefully that Stuyvesant was not "apt to entertaine any thing of prejudice intended against us." Nicolls's reply came the next morning, a messenger delivering a letter informing Stuyvesant that "in his Majesties Name, I do demand the Towne, Scituate upon the Island commonly knowne by the Name of Manhatoes with all the Forts there unto belonging, to be rendered unto his Majesties obedience, and Protection into my hands." The king did not relish "the effusion of Christian blood," but if the Dutch did not surrender they would invite "the miseryes of a War."

Stuyvesant's reaction to this thunderbolt was stylishly in period: he returned the letter because it was unsigned. Whereupon Nicolls fired off another:

These to the Honorable the Governor of the Manhatoes.

Honoured Sir.

The neglect of Signing this inclosed Letter, when it was first brought to your hands, by Colonell Geo: Cartwright, was an omission which is now amended, and I must attribute the neglect of it at first, to the over hasty zeale I had dispatching my Answer to the Letter I received from you dated 19/26th instant, I have nothing more to add, either in matter of Forme, then is therein expressed, only that your speedy Answer is necessary to prevent future inconveniences, and will very much obliege.

Your affectionat humble Servant
RI: NICOLLS.

Townspeople were rushing through the streets with news and gossip. Stuyvesant tended to be calm in such situations. By now he had the pertinent details. There were maybe five hundred men in New Amsterdam able to bear arms. Nicolls had nearly twice that, plus forces totaling a thousand or more amassing on Long Island, plus the firepower of his ships. The fort had its cannons, but it was so low on gunpowder they were inconsequential. It was probably hopeless, but Stuyvesant doesn't seem to have had second thoughts: they would fight to the death. Anything else, he informed the leaders of the city government, "would be disapproved of" at home.

At this juncture, a rowboat, with a white flag aloft, approached the shore. In it, of all people, was Winthrop, along with several other New Englanders. They asked for a meeting, and Stuyvesant led them to a tavern. Winthrop urged his "friend" to surrender, and handed him a letter containing Nicolls's terms. They were generous terms—extravagant almost—and yet Stuyvesant was unmoved. Later, at the City Hall, the city officials demanded to see the letter and show it to the citizens. Stuyvesant knew his people: resistance would cave once they heard of the favorable terms. So he tore the letter to pieces.

At this, the room went wild. Long-stoppered feelings came flooding out. The company, Stuyvesant himself, the colony's government—it was all a sham; it had never been anything else. For years they had lodged requests and petitions, asking for a voice in government, and he had sneeringly rejected them, declared them childish fools who didn't understand the complexities of government, and all along he had been nothing but a good soldier blindly carrying out the orders of a bankrupt bureaucracy. Now he expected them to fight and die on his orders. Why should they? Why spill their blood, and try to hold the attackers off, when they all knew the West India Company had sent no reinforcements, despite his appeals. It would have been one thing had the company denied their petitions for reform on the grounds that its way was better, but it never had a way.

Finally, the town leaders demanded once again to see the letter. In an odd bit of comedy, Stuyvesant offered them the pieces, which Nicasius de Sille took and carefully pasted back together.

Meanwhile, with no answer from Stuyvesant, Nicolls had moved his ships forward, within shot of the city. The English Long Islanders, with muskets and pikes, were gathered along the Breuckelen shore. Some French privateers who were in the area had gotten news of the events, and rushed to the scene as well.

There is then an almost Shakespearean scene, in which Stuyvesant climbs heavily onto the battlements of his fort and stands there, gazing at the guns trained on his town, his long wisps of hair flailed by the wind. He seems, in this moment in which he will be forever frozen in history, almost to have achieved the status of a tragic hero, his leadership, his particular stew of character strengths and flaws, having built this impressive place but also having caused his own people to turn against him. (To add a family dimension to the betrayal, his seventeen-year-old son, Balthasar, had come out on the side of the city leaders.) There was a lone gunner at his side, awaiting his command to touch light to powder. It must have been tempting. A single cannon blast at the ships riding at anchor just beyond the walls would be enough. It would unleash a rain of violence, a storm that would swallow the place, ending the torment, ending things the way they ought to end, in good, quenching blood and fire.

Then, in his direst moment, the church came to give comfort. Two ministers of the town, father and son, both with the ponderous, sonorous name of Megapolensis, appeared at his side. It's hard not to think of Stuyvesant's father here, to imagine the lifelong battle inside him between stalwart devotion to the church, personified in his father's ministry, and that streak of stiff rebelliousness. Maybe it was the church that swayed him. Then, too, the warships, the guns, the French privateers, and the glinting line of weaponry on the opposite shore had to have added up to something in his military calculations. He knew what the pikes and the expectant leers of the foreigners meant. It was a long-standing rule of war that if a besieged fort so much as fired a shot, the forces against it were at liberty to sack and loot; the place would be laid waste. Was he really willing to subject the people he had lived among these seventeen years to such a thing?

The ministers talked lowly to him for a while, and then the three men went down.

But he still wouldn't yield. He crafted another letter to Nicolls, referencing the history of the Dutch claim to the territory, asserting that "we are oblieged to defend Our place," informing him that he had had news from Holland about a treaty between the two countries, and suggesting that Nicolls check with the home office before taking this fateful step. It may have been a bluff, but Stuyvesant was right in thinking this move by England was rash. Contrary to Ambassador Downing's assurances to King Charles, the Dutch would fight to defend their interests. At this moment, the great Dutch admiral Michiel de Ruyter was preparing to launch an expedition for West Africa. When his sweep was over, all but one of the Dutch outposts taken in James's raids would be back in Dutch hands. Outright war would then begin, and, all told, the Dutch would win the Second Anglo-Dutch War, creating a pothole in England's road to empire.

But, pulling back to the broad view, the English were riding to the top of the historical wave. With these events of late summer 1664, the island of Manhattan would be a pivot around which the age would turn, and when it was done the floppy hats, Vermeer interiors, "merry company" portraits, and blue-and-white Delft tiles would be thrust into the past, and ahead would be the Raj and the redcoats, Britannia ruling the waves.

In the end, Stuyvesant truly did stand alone. All of his people deserted him. The leading citizens of New Amsterdam—ninety-three of them, including his son—signed a petition asking him to avert "misery, sorrow, conflagration, the dishonor of women, murder of children in their cradles, and, in a word, the absolute ruin and destruction of about fifteen hundred innocent souls." Perhaps it struck him, on reading it, that it showed he had been right all along: this rapid willingness to give up, this spinelessness, this absence of patriotism, was what came of a mongrel society. Mixing religions and races weakened a populace, and here was proof. It would be wrong to think that the citizens of the town had no sense of loyalty, but they were practical people, and at any rate they had little choice. They made clear in their final petition to Stuyvesant that they were willing to support their neighbors and their colony, but they had no qualms about abandoning the company that had left them defenseless.

And so they did. The fifteen hundred residents of New Amsterdam, the ten thousand inhabitants of the colony of New Netherland, turned their backs on the company that had long ignored them. Griet Reyniers, onetime Amsterdam barmaid who became Manhattan's first prostitute, abandoned it. So did her husband, Anthony "the Turk" van Salee, the half-Morroccan former pirate. They were now wealthy landowners on Long Island, and their four daughters were married to some of New Amsterdam's up-and-coming businessmen. Joris Rapalje, who with his bride Catalina Trico comprised the Adam and Eve of the colony, had recently died, but Catalina was still very much alive, as were her grown children and their families, and they, too, preferred to acquiesce rather than die. The same went for Asser Levy, the Polish Jew who had battled Stuyvesant over the rights of Jews, and now owned Manhattan's first kosher butcher shop, and for Manuel "the Giant" Gerrit, the African who had escaped hanging in 1641 and who for the past five years had been living as a free landowner on a small farm near Stuyvesant's bouwerie. For all of these people, living peaceably under an English prince who promised to continue the way of life they had fashioned was patently better than fighting and dying.

And so he relented. "I would much rather be carried out dead," he said, and surely everyone believed him, but instead he named six men to meet with their English counterparts and negotiate terms. They met at Stuyvesant's farm. And the next Monday, at eight in the morning, Stuyvesant, fifty-four-years-old, thick of build, with his cuirass and his limp and his small, bold eyes, led a military procession out of the fort, with drummers drumming and flags waving.

Then, as all attention shifted to the waterfront, where Nicolls and his main body of troops was coming ashore, a small party of English soldiers entered the deserted fort. Outside, the harbor winds were swirling around the interested throng of mixed nationalities who watched as an English flag went up the flagpole and listened as Nicolls declared the place renamed for his patron, the Duke of York and Albany. Inside the fort, meanwhile, a few soldiers climbed to the office of the colonial secretary, above the gate. In any change of government, gaining possession of the records is among the first steps, for to control a society's vital documents is to control its past and future. The soldiers found what they were looking for: rows of bulky leather-bound volumes, forty-eight in all, numbered consecutively on their spines, A to Z and then AA through PP. Wills, deeds, minutes, correspondence, complaints, petitions, confrontations, agreements—it was all here, meticulously maintained, year by year, day by day, the story of America's first mixed society.

Chapter 15

INHERITED FEATURES

As Stuyvesant surrendered the Manhattan colony, America's myth of origin was already coming into being. Starting in the 1660s, a handful of New England clergymen began singing the praises of their parents' and grandparents' generations, which had braved an ocean and a wilderness to start a new life. The story they wove was biblical from first to last. In their modest telling, their forebears were none other than the chosen people of God, and America (i.e., New England) was the promised land. By the time of the revolutionary generation a century later, the story had become myth. John Adams, himself a descendant of the first Puritans, revered the Pilgrims as the launchers of the American saga.

Certainly the Puritans passed down many features to the nation. They were practical, plain-spoken, businesslike, pious—all traits that Americans from Adams on have admired and tried to emulate. But, as many people have noted in recent decades, in which the Puritans have fallen out of favor, they were also self-important zealots. Their form of government was a theocracy. It was rooted in intolerance: freedom of worship, in the words of one prominent New England minister (who became president of Harvard College), was the "first born of all abominations." " 'Tis Satan's policy to plead for an indefinite and boundless toleration," declared another. The Puritans' systematic crackdown on alternative views was cruel, unusual, and lethal. People whose crime was being members of the Baptist denomination, or Quakers, or belonging to some other Protestant sect, were beaten with a knotted whip ("to cut their flesh and to put them to suffering"), put in a "horse lock" of irons, had ears lopped off. They were whipped and then tied to a cart and driven through deep snow, "the white snow and crimson blood" making a vivid tapestry. They were hanged in public spectacles. Some were hanged and then had their naked bodies dragged through the streets. These were not mass "lynchings" but sentences pronounced by judicial authorities, in regimes based on an official policy of intolerance. Later, in the 1680s, came the witchcraft mania, which has gone down in history as a particularly vivid example of the dangers of fusing government and religion.

Out of the Puritans' exceptionalism—their belief that the Old World had succumbed to wickedness and they had been charged by God to save humanity by founding a new society in a new world—grew the American belief that American society was similarly divinely anointed. In 1845, journalist John O'Sullivan coined the phrase that would carry this doctrine forward across the continent when he declared "the right of our manifest destiny to overspread and to possess the whole continent which providence has given us for the development of the great experiment of liberty and federated self government." In the early twentieth century, President Woodrow Wilson extended the manifest destiny concept to cover the globe. In the aftermath of the Great War, Wilson determined that the United States, because of "the sheer genius of this people and the growth of our power" and because it had "seen visions that other nations have not seen," had become not only "a determining factor in the history of mankind" but "the light of the world."

This conviction lives on today, and is directly traceable to the first Puritans. When the sons of those first leaders—Cotton Mather, Thomas Hutchinson, Jeremy Belknap, Thomas Prince—put their beliefs into print, their story found ready listeners. Of course, in this version of American beginnings, the tellers were English and the hearers were English. Subsequent generations were raised on the belief that America's origins were English, and that other traditions wove themselves into the fabric later. And history shows this, does it not? The thirteen original colonies were English colonies. The supporting evidence is overwhelming: the language we speak, our political traditions, many of our customs. This is all so obvious that we don't question it.

But it ought to be questioned. The original colonies were *not* all English, and the multiethnic makeup of the Manhattan colony is precisely the point. The fact that the Dutch once established a foothold in North America has been known all along, of course, but after noting it, the national myth of origin promptly dismisses it as irrelevant. It was small, it was short-lived, it was inconsequential. That wasn't *us*, the subtext runs, but someone else, an alien mix of peoples—with strange customs and a different language—who appeared briefly and then vanished, leaving only traces.

This is false. In the first place, while in population the colony was quickly outpaced by New England, it was hardly small. It covered the whole middle stretch of the East Coast and encompassed parts of five of what would be the original thirteen states. In terms of historical evidence—of written records—we have a steadily growing mountain of it, thanks to the translation and publication work now going on. But surely the most obvious reason to see the Dutch colony as significant is that we are not talking about a settlement planted in some obscure corner, in a hidden valley or on an inaccessible slope. We are talking about Manhattan. The strange thing would be if the settlers of the most geographically vital island on the continent, which would serve as the gateway between it and Europe, had *not* made an imprint on the nation that was to come.

Moving the story beyond the English takeover requires, first, realizing that "the Dutch" didn't go anywhere. The people from all over Europe who had built homes and raised families on Manhattan, on Long Island, away to the south along the Delaware River, and across the river from Manhattan in what the English first named "Albania" (*sic!*) but on second thought called New Jersey, had no reason to leave after Stuyvesant surrendered his colony. In fact, ships from the Dutch Republic, with their mixed loads of European settlers, kept arriving in New York Harbor. (Notaries in Amsterdam, blithely ignoring the political changeover, continued writing "New Netherland"— and sometimes "New York in New Netherland"—on immigration papers well into the 1680s.) And Richard Nicolls—who became the first governor of New York after accepting Stuyvesant's surrender—and his successors actually encouraged the traffic with their longtime foe. They even made a point of naming prominent Dutch merchants to their economic councils to keep the ties strong. That was because these first English governors quickly discovered they were in the awkward but titillating position of being even more keyed into world trade than London itself. With the English takeover, New York instantly became a unique spot on the globe: the only port city plugged directly into both of the world's two major trading empires. To sever connections to the great trading firms of Amsterdam would have been to strangle their long-sought possession just as it was burgeoning. The traders, bakers, brewers, barkeeps, smugglers, and scam-artists of the town soon realized the same thing the governors did, and felt the power of it: their island was no longer a Dutch settlement, and it wasn't really English either. It had its own trajectory.

The notion of an English takeover brings with it an image of starting afresh, of a house emptied of the possessions of the previous tenant and then filled with the completely different belongings of a new occupant. What happened instead was more in the nature of a cohabitation. Continuity between the Dutch and English eras was established at eight o'clock on Saturday morning, the sixth of September 1664. We can imagine a percussion of hooves on dry earth as twelve riders, having traveled north up the Highway and then east along the Bouwerie Road, came to a halt and dismounted before the façade of Peter Stuyvesant's farmhouse. Maybe they paused for a moment to breathe the country air: here were fields under cultivation and, just beyond, stands of forest alternating with salt marshes. (Today the same view takes in an Arab newsstand, a Yemenite Israeli restaurant, a pizza shop, a Japanese restaurant, and a Jewish deli.) Following precedent for such occasions, neither Stuyvesant nor Nicolls was present for the meeting that then took place, but each had chosen a slate of commissioners to negotiate the transfer of the colony. Stuyvesant's included four Dutchmen, one Englishman, and one Frenchman; Nicolls's representatives were two of his aides and four New Englanders, including John Winthrop.

We don't know details of the negotiations, which is a pity because there is the suggestion of a move on the part of Peter Stuyvesant that, if true, would amount to a kind of reversal in his long struggle with the colonists, and in particular with Adriaen van der Donck. Nicolls's private instructions from the king authorized him to inform the Dutch colonists only that "they shall continue to enjoy all their possessions (Forts only excepted) and the same freedome in trade with our other good subjects in those parts." But Stuyvesant seems to have instructed his men to push for specific guarantees, and that is what they got. The end result of the negotiations, the so-called Articles of Capitulation, is a remarkable document. Packaged into it—and extended later by the New York City Charter—was a guarantee of rights unparalleled in any English colony. "The Dutch here shall enjoy the liberty of their Consciences," it read. People would be free to come and go as they liked. Trade would be unrestricted: by all means, "Dutch vessels may freely come hither." Most remarkable, the political leaders of the colony would "continue as now they are," provided they swore an oath of allegiance to the king, and in future "the Towne of Manhatans, shall choose Deputyes, and those Deputyes, shall have free Voyces in all Publique affaires." Prefiguring the Bill of Rights, it even stipulated that "the Townesmen of the Manhatons shall not have any Souldier quartered upon them."

It's possible that this unusual slate of freedoms was authorized by the Duke of York himself, who had declared he wanted the Manhattanites to have "immunities and privileges beyond what other parts of my territory doe enjoy." If James was indeed the force behind these articles then he deserves to have his title attached to the name of the place. The thinking was that the inhabitants of the island should be allowed to maintain their way of life for the very good reason that the place worked. One has to keep in mind what an oddity the new city of New York was to people of the seventeenth century, with its variety of skin tones and languages and prayer styles coexisting side by side. The English leaders in Whitehall Palace were surely aware of this unusual characteristic of the island across the water, and they may have been confused by it, but at the same time they understood that it was part of what made the place function.

Then again, there is no record that the English offered the particular catalogue of guarantees that made their way into the Articles of Capitulation. It's logical to assume that the Dutch representatives, on Stuyvesant's orders, pushed for some of these. If so, there is an ironic twist here. Such a slate of individual rights and liberties, preserving the unique society that had come into being in the colony, was just what Van der Donck had fought for, and precisely what Stuyvesant had opposed during his seventeen years in office. Now, faced with the end of the West India Company's rule, which he had stoutly, mulishly, upheld, he seems to have made a turnaround. If his own brand of leadership couldn't save the place, then Van der Donck's vision—government commitments to support free trade, religious liberty, and a form of local political representation—afforded the best protection for its inhabitants in the uncertain future. If this is what Stuyvesant came to think in those final hours, the question is: why? Part of the answer may be that, despite the unending turmoil of his years as director of the colony, he cared about it and its people. Some of his colonists may have argued the proposition, but he apparently had a heart. The second part of the answer is that Stuyvesant understood power. If he had to give up the colony, better to divide it into channels and see that some of it flowed to the people of the colony than to have the English decide what courses it would follow. The result surely wasn't a reversal of character, not a complete break, but a bending that makes for an ironic end to Stuyvesant's long tussle with his colonists.

Maybe then Stuyvesant came away from the negotiations with some degree of satisfaction. But if so it was slim. He had lost his colony, and the directors of the West India Company rubbed salt in the wound by demanding that he return to Amsterdam to face charges of "criminal neglect" in surrendering. After a grim voyage on a ship the ironic appropriateness of whose name—*The Crossed Heart*—must have raised in him a low chuckle, Stuyvesant found himself in more or less the same position that Van der Donck had been in more than a decade earlier: making his case before the States General while the West India Company threw argument and invective at him ("neglect or treachery . . . scandalous surrender"), blocked his effort to return to America, and kept him exiled in Holland and separated from his family. As further indication that Stuyvesant had undergone something of a transformation with the loss of the colony, he included in his defense testimonials from some of the very Manhattanites who had once denounced his autocratic rule, who now declared that he had done everything in his power to keep the colony together.

The fact that Stuyvesant petitioned to be allowed to return can't be overlooked. Like Van der Donck, and yet by a very different route, he, too, had become an American. He may have packed his son off to seek his fortune in the Caribbean in the weeks after the English takeover (upon arrival in Curaçao, Balthasar Stuyvesant wrote home, inquiring about events and asking his cousin to "take care of the girls on the Manhatans" and "greet them all for me with a kiss"). But America was Stuyvesant's home, and eventually the States General granted him permission to return. He finished out his days as a resident of the rapidly growing settlement, a gentleman farmer, a grandfather, a man of renown always greeted by locals as "the General," a historical curiosity to the incoming population. The capping irony of his life was that in surrendering the colony he had finally won himself the welcome of his fellow colonists. He had joined them at long last, but not as an inhabitant of New Netherland. He died—in 1672, at the age of sixty-two—a New Yorker.

Nicolls, meanwhile, was delighted with the deal he had struck. Without firing a shot, he had gotten a thing that he knew full well was of great immediate value and of inestimable future value. All of the English leaders seemed aware of the scope of the achievement. "I saw ye towne upon the Manatos Iland reduced to the obedience of our Soveraigne Lord the Kinge," John Winthrop intoned after the articles were signed, "Wherby there is way made for the inlargment of his Maties Dominions, by filling yt vacant wildernesse, in tyme, with plantatios of his Maties subiects . . ." Nicolls fired off a letter to the Duke, practically crowing at his accomplishment, declaring New York "the best of all His Majties Townes in America," and predicting that within five years it would be the main portal for the flow of trade between England and North America.

When the news of the takeover reached King Charles, he whisked a letter to France. His sister Henrietta—the Duchess of Orleans, sister-in-law (and sometime lover) of Louis XIV—was his closest confidante. "You will have heard of our taking of New Amsterdam, which lies just by New England," he wrote to her chirpily. " 'Tis a place of great importance to trade, and a very good town." The Dutch had done marvels with the wilderness island, the king noted, "but we have got the better of it, and 'tis now called New York."

*

BUT THE 1664 surrender would not be the end of the struggle between the two empires over the colony. The takeover of Manhattan helped ignite the Second Anglo-Dutch War, which would see Dutch warships retaliate by taking the English outpost of Surinam to the north of Brazil, valuable for its sugar plantations, and the spice island of Run in the East Indies, while others sailed up the Thames tributary known as the Medway, surprising the English fleet, torching some of its finest ships, and forcing Whitehall to treat for peace. With a shortsightedness that would have made Van der Donck shake his head in sad recognition, the Dutch government allowed England, in the treaty negotiations, to have its way regarding captured territories: rather than swap them back, each nation would keep its war spoils.

Some Dutch leaders, however, apparently thought that was a bad deal. Only five years after the peace treaty was signed, the Third Anglo-Dutch War broke out, and a Dutch fleet crossed the Atlantic and set about strafing

English possessions. It attacked Caribbean ports under English control, swept into the Chesapeake and burned the tobacco fleet about to embark for England, then, in a little-known episode, sailed into New York Harbor in August 1673, precisely nine years after Stuyvesant's surrender, and retook Manhattan. Everything then happened in reverse: a Dutch commander at the head of a flotilla of gunships threatened to reduce the town; inside the fort, an Englishman was in charge, anguishing over what to do. He was outgunned and outmanned. The English surrendered; a new, Dutch-led administration was installed. The English troops paraded out of the fort just as the Dutch under Stuyvesant had done, and the town that had been New Amsterdam and then New York was given a third name: New Orange. The whole colony changed hands: the upriver trading town that the Dutch had named Beverwyck, and which Nicolls had renamed Albany after his patron, was now called Willemstad. The paperwork was barely complete, however, before it all reverted again. Fifteen months after retaking the colony, with the signing of yet another peace treaty, the Dutch gave it back.

But even this was not the end of the tug of war over the island and its trading city. Its namesake, the Duke of York, having labored for a quarter century in his brother's shadow, got the chance truly to impose his vision of empire in 1685, when Charles died and he ascended to the throne. But the rule of James II began to fall apart almost at once. Thanks to his conversion to Roman Catholicism years before, English leaders and much of the population suspected him of being a Popish puppet; real resistance mounted when he installed Catholics in important offices. When it got out that the queen was pregnant—meaning that a Catholic line was in the making—James's rule teetered.

English history has characterized the Glorious Revolution—in which James was ousted and replaced by Willem of Orange, Stadtholder of the Netherlands, and his wife, Mary—as an "invitation." There is an element of spin doctoring in this. In fact, the Dutch leader—the son of the previous Willem, who had attempted a coup d'état while Van der Donck was in The Hague—capped the century of Dutch-English rivalry by launching a full-scale invasion of the British Isles. More than twenty thousand troops hit the beach at Torbay on the Devon coast, and a month later Willem rode triumphantly into London. The Dutch army took control of Whitehall Palace and all the other power centers, and the Dutch stadtholder was crowned king of England. The so-called invitation was considered by many Englishmen of the time a thorough disgrace, but for others the facts that Mary (who was James's daughter) was the presumptive heir to the English throne and that in Willem they once again had a Protestant monarch made things all right.

This cross-pollinization of the royal leadership of two longtime rival nations would have an echo in Manhattan when a German-born New Yorker named Jacob Leisler (who, thirty years before, had served as a West India Company soldier under Stuyvesant), apparently under the impression that the Dutch-born king of England would approve, led a handful of radicals in a Calvinist-fueled takeover of the city. But Willem wasn't interested, and Leisler's Rebellion, as history has known it, ended quietly, with Leisler and an associate being hanged for treason and, for good measure, beheaded.

Maybe the main result of this remarkable span—in which the island and surrounding colony changed hands five times in three decades—was that it forced the inhabitants to solidify their identity. Which European power held ultimate control became less important to the Manhattanites than the relationships between their own ethnic communities and their ties to traders, shippers, and family in other parts of the world. What mattered was that cache of rights, which they noisily insisted be honored by whoever had just won control of the place, and which enabled the separate minority communities to flourish.

So Adriaen van der Donck's dream became real in a way he never imagined. The structure he helped win for the place grounded it in Dutch tolerance and diversity, just as he hoped it would, which in turn touched off the island's rapid growth and increased the influx of settlers from around Europe, just as he predicted. What he didn't predict was that the English would appreciate this fact, and maintain the structure, and that it would support a future culture of unprecedented energy and vitality and creativity.

*

AND SO OFF it went, spiraling upward along its path through history—the colony and city of New York, the jewel in the crown of England's North American possessions. More English settlers came, naturally enough, and also—word having continued to spread about its mixed population and the opportunities for getting ahead—French, German, Scottish, and Irish immigrants, so that by 1692 a newly arrived British military officer would complain to his uncle in England, "Our chiefest unhappyness here is too great a mixture of nations, and English ye least part."

Newcomers were fully aware of the island's Dutch roots, and noted the continued influence in everything from the gabled houses with their front stoops to the predominance of the language. But a funny thing happened. Over time the outward trappings of Dutchness became synonymous with the region's roots. And as those features faded with time, so, in this thinking, did the colony's significance.

There is an error in this, which would be perpetuated over the centuries. Some in the past have identified the continuance of the colony by examining the Dutch subculture in the Hudson Valley. They noted that Dutch was still being spoken well into the nineteenth century, and the Reformed Dutch Church continued strong. To this day the area around Albany is crammed with towns whose names—Rotterdam, Amsterdam, Watervliet, Rensselaer (after the colony of Rensselaerswyck where Van der Donck first worked), Colonie (also named for Rensselaerswyck, and retaining the Dutch spelling)—reinforce the connection. As late as the 1750s, English officials in that area needed to find Dutch speakers to help them treat with Indians because Dutch was still the only European language the tribes spoke. And of course there are the great families of colonial America—the Van Burens, Roosevelts, Vanderbilts—who are traceable by their Dutch ancestry to New Netherland.

But all of that is missing the point. What matters about the Dutch colony is that it set Manhattan on course as a place of openness and free trade. A new kind of spirit hovered over the island, something utterly alien to New England and Virginia, which is directly traceable to the tolerance debates in Holland in the sixteenth and seventeenth centuries, and to the intellectual world of Descartes, Grotius, and Spinoza. Yes, there were people in Hudson Valley towns who preserved Dutch traditions, but that was mostly a reaction to the English takeover: in the way of minorities everywhere, they entrenched, became self-conscious, and guarded and burnished their traditions, to the point where the "Low Dutch" spoken in the nineteenth century was incomprehensible to visitors from the Netherlands, a relic of the tongue spoken in the Golden Age of two centuries earlier. In fact, the irony in the case of the descendants of the original Dutch settlers is that it would be in finally blending into American culture—which they eventually did—that they paid the truest homage to their heritage.

*

THE IDEA THAT the Dutch colony made important contributions to America is not new. Two nineteenth-century historians of New York who were intimately familiar with the Dutch sources—E. B. O'Callaghan and John Brodhead—saw its overlooked significance, but they were ignored, in part because America was then in the throes of a nostalgia for its Puritan beginnings. After spending four years in Europe on behalf of the state of New York, in which he gathered thousands of documents in archives in Holland and England that pertained to New York's origins (it was from these that the story of Adriaen van der Donck's mission to The Hague would emerge), Brodhead delivered a series of talks to fashionable New York society in the 1840s and 1850s, in which he laid out a case for the unheralded legacy of the Dutch colony. He was excoriated in the press—ridiculed for suggesting that the nation could have had progenitors other than the Puritans of New England. In reacting to Brodhead's claim, one newspaper correspondent showed that the anti-Dutch bias America had inherited from England in the seventeenth century was still alive in the nineteenth; he found it particularly ludicrous that so great and powerful a country as the United States could have gotten where it had by "following the example of the policy of the petty cheese-paring of the Batavian provinces, with their windmills, and barren soil, fit only for fuel . . ." Brodhead wrote a valiant response, which does not seem to have been published, which began:

> Yielding to no one in a sincere respect for Puritanism, "wherein it was worthy," and in a due estimate of its influence upon the destinies of the United States, I must still venture candidly to express my dissent from the opinions of those who self complacently insist, on all occasions, and "usque ad nauseam," upon tracing back all the admirable features in our Social and political Organization to the "Pilgrim Fathers" and their descendants. Unmeasured eulogy of the excellent pioneers of New England colonization has become so much the fashion, that it is almost a relief to turn to the history of other American settlements and find that there are other men whose actions and influence deserve notice in the annals of our Country. To say

nothing of the "Old Dominion" of Virginia, which was permanently settled twelve years before New Plymouth, it seems to me that it is due to historical truth that the influence and the character of the Dutch who first explored and settled the coasts of New York and New Jersey should be fairly set forth.

Brodhead's voice went unheard. Part of the difficulty of making such a case came from the fact that the mass of documents that constituted the records of the colony still lay untranslated. In the 1970s two things changed. One was that the discipline of history came down off its pedestal. People were suddenly interested in social history and "multiculturalism." The other was that the translation of the records of the Dutch colony got under way. Historians began to call for a reappraisal of this piece of American beginnings. The titles of some of the scholarly papers that emerged—"Writing/Righting Dutch Colonial History," "Early American History with the Dutch Put In"—suggest the change. The names of many of the historians involved in this reappraisal, on whose work I have relied, are found in the endnotes, bibliography, and acknowledgments of this book. When Scribner's published its important three-volume *Encyclopedia of the North American Colonies* in 1993 and gave prominent attention not only to New Netherland but to New Sweden as well, it signaled that the academic view of the colony and of American beginnings had changed. In August of 2001, in the midst of my work on this book, the *New York Times* ran an editorial on the project to translate the Dutch archives, declaring that after a long time in which scholars of the Dutch colony had been "clamoring for scholarly affirmative action," the tide had turned and now "a vanquished New Netherland's influence looms larger than ever."

The idea of the colony as a birthplace of the American melting pot has been simmering for some time. In the last few decades, historians have focused on the vast chunk between New England and Virginia and dubbed the region the Middle Colonies. With the focus has come an appreciation of what this region gave the country. The Middle Colonies, as Patricia Bonomi, one of the premier American historians of recent decades, has written, were both "the birthplace of American religious pluralism" and "a stage for the western world's most complex experience with religious pluralism." Religious pluralism was the seventeenth century conduit for cultural pluralism, and the coming-together of people from different back-grounds resulted in something new, which began to be remarked on a century after New Netherland's demise. In 1782, when the French-born J. Hector St. John de Crèvecoeur wrote *Letters from an American Farmer*, one of the earliest descriptions of American society and culture, it was this region he had in mind as he asked:

> What then is the American, this new man? He is either an European, or the descendant of an European, hence that strange mixture of blood, which you will find in no other country. I could point out to you a family whose grandfather was an Englishman, whose wife was Dutch, whose son married a French woman, and whose present four sons have now four wives of different nations. *He* is an American, who, leaving behind him all his ancient prejudices and manners, receives new ones from the new mode of life he has embraced, the new government he obeys, and the new rank he holds. He becomes an American by being received in the broad lap of our great *Alma Mater*. Here individuals of all nations are melted into a new race of men, whose labours and posterity will one day cause great changes in the world.

What we find beneath the "Middle Colonies" label, the force that gave rise to Crèvecoeur's observation, is the Dutch colony. There were other forces at work, too: the Pennsylvania and Rhode Island colonies both became known for religious toleration. But the influence of the Dutch colony would be wide ranging. Such influence can't be proved deductively, but evidence to support it comes in many forms. There is, first, the simple fact that the very part of America in which multiethnic society first formed was also the region where the Dutch colony had been.

We can support the connection by looking at other legacies from the colony that also took root first in this region. An example: after Richard Nicolls took charge of New York and had become familiar with the Dutch customs he had allowed the inhabitants to maintain, he found one political office particularly useful. The colony had a law officer whose job was to prosecute cases on behalf of the government. The English system had no such officer; at the time, the victim of a crime, or his or her relative, was responsible for seeking justice. The Dutch official—called a *schout*—allowed the justice system to move more efficiently. Nicolls adopted it—the English records at first took to calling this law man the "scout"—and it spread through the other colonies. The job eventually became known as district attorney, and remains a fixture of local government in America. (It happens that one of the first "district attorneys" in America was Adriaen van der Donck, whose original posting was as *schout* of the colony of Rensselaerswyck.) In 1975, Yale law professor A. J. Reiss noted, in an article on the history of the office, "The first appearance of public prosecutors in the United States occurred when the Dutch founded the colony of New Netherland," that "[h]istorical evidence makes it abundantly clear that when this area was taken by the Duke of York in surrender in 1664 . . . the Dutch system of public prosecution was maintained where it had been firmly established by then," and that "[h]istorical records demonstrate that the 'Schout' was established within five of the 13 original colonies that became the states of the United States of America."

There are many other telltale legacies—customs and traditions and usages that spread, along with the phenomenon of American pluralism, from what was once Dutch territory. It was in the Dutch colony that an American worker first complained about "the boss." It was here that American children first longed for the arrival of "St. a Claus" (as *Rivington's New York Gazetteer* spelled it in the early 1770s, noting that the saint's feast day would be celebrated "by the descendants of the ancient Dutch families, with their usual festivities"). It was here that Americans first ate "cookies" and "cole slaw." Of course, nothing is more meaningless than cookies; the reason for mentioning such items is their ubiquity. The blob of slaw on every blue plate special served from the Depression to the Eisenhower era, riding alongside the baked beans at numberless barbecues, packed into a little plastic tub to offset the grease in a fast-food burgers-and-fries meal, ignored or absently consumed, is a modest clue to the pervasive presence of the Manhattan colony. It is a tip-off that in considering its contribution we should be looking not in obscure corners but at what is right in front of us. We won't find it in the form of Dutch pipestems buried in backyards, but in any town's telephone book, where Singh, Singer, Singleton, and Sinkiewicz fall on the same page.

Many inheritances are hard to spot because in the mix and rumble of the centuries they have become layered, altered, embedded in other, larger systems. This stands to reason: we couldn't expect much to last three centuries in pristine form. Rather, we would expect that, if a thing was useful or desirable, it would become part of the blend. Santa Claus may be the perfect example of this. It was a slim fellow in a bishop's hat whose arrival the children of Dutch Manhattan looked forward to on Saint Nicholas Eve; typically, he left treats in their shoes, but occasionally (as in a late-century drawing, "The St. Nicholas Celebration," by Cornelis Dusart), in stockings hung from the mantel. As the non-Dutch families adopted him and he gained momentum, bits of other cultural traditions stuck to the ritual; the media (Thomas Nast's cartoons in *Harper's Weekly* plumped the saint and whitened his beard) and corporate advertising (the white-trimmed red suit came compliments of Coca-Cola's iconic ad campaign in the 1930s) refined the image, and the result is a complicated collage, thoroughly American, and rooted in the Manhattan of Stuyvesant and Van der Donck.

The influence of the colony can also be spotted rippling through the layers of political history. After Van der Donck's political crusade helped cement the unique features of the Dutch colony's society, Nicolls's Articles of Capitulation guaranteed that the English would preserve the rights and privileges the residents had come to expect. When in 1686 the New York City Charter, considered by some to be the launch point of the modern city, was signed, it not only made plain those rights and privileges but was clear about their origins, acknowledging that the citizens of the "ancient City . . . Enjoyed . . . sundry Rights Libertyes priviledges [and] ffranchises" that derived not only from its English rulers but from the "Governours Directors Generalls, and Commanders in Chiefe of the Nether Dutch Nation."

You can move forward from this charter, and from the rowdy, argumentative, still mostly Dutch-speaking society that stood behind it, straight into the revolutionary period and beyond. In Philadelphia in 1787, New York's delegation to the Constitutional Convention was among those least enamored of a document that would give so much power to the federal government. Meeting later in Albany, the state's leaders decided that they could only ratify the Constitution if, among other things, a bill of specific individual rights were attached to it. The names of the twenty-six men who insisted

on this were about half English and half Dutch; the new state was already famously contentious, and its pluralistic delegation had a long history of
struggling for individual rights to account for its stubbornness.

Of course, when the Bill of Rights was adopted in 1791, no one looked to
the Dutch-led colony that had held sway a century before as having a hand
in it. There had been no written history of the Dutch period—it would be
decades before the documents detailing Van der Donck's mission on behalf
of the rights of Manhattanites would be unearthed.

The pathways along which the colony's influence spread are also part of
the evidence for its lasting importance. Starting from their settlements on
the Delaware River, the "forest Finns" literally cleared a path down the Appalachian valleys, along which Finnish, Swedish, Dutch, and other pioneers
traveled, and by the way added the log cabin to America's cultural legacy.
But the main route of expansion was to the north. The island of Manhattan
became the gateway to America for generations of immigrants, and it was
because of this that the legacy of the Dutch colony got amplified. Stepping
off the boat, the individuals in those huddled masses, arriving from Naples
or Hamburg or Le Havre or Liverpool, breathed in an atmosphere utterly
different from what they had left. The smell in the air was one they had
hoped to find, a complicated, heady perfume. It had in it the big, muscular,
fresh odors that came sweeping off the continent, full of green promise. It
was sharpened by the oily tang of industry and good sweat, accented with
kielbasa and pasta sauce, horse dung and sawdust and slaughterhouse. The
newcomers soaked it in, this odor of promise and of a reblending of peoples
into something new, and they called it American. Then they fanned out, and
brought it with them. Up the Hudson they went, which was to the seventeenth and eighteenth centuries what the Mississippi would be to later eras:
the lifeline, the broad highway of commerce and travel.

At Albany, once the site of the fur-trading post of Fort Orange, they cut
westward, into the Mohawk River valley. There, in the early nineteenth
century, industrial-age politicians discovered what Dutch pioneers had
known two centuries earlier: that promise and expansion lay westward
along this valley. In 1825, after eight years of stupendous manual labor, a
three-hundred-and-sixty-mile trench was carved through the wilderness
that Harmen Myndersz van den Bogaert had explored on his perilous foray
into Iroquois country during the harsh winter of 1634. How the Erie Canal

changed the nation is a basic piece of American history. It opened the interior of the continent, swelled the population, shifted the balance from rural to urban, helped make America an industrial power. America was transformed, and the promise that the first Manhattanites saw in their island came roaring into reality. The stream of people and goods into Manhattan became a flood. From across Europe and around the world they funneled into the island, then up the river, and so westward along the canal. And with the pipeline of commerce extending into the very heart of the continent, crossroads settlements transformed into cities, lights winking on in the dusk of the endless landscape, each with its cluster of founding ethnic groups: Toledo, Cleveland, Detroit, Buffalo, Milwaukee, Chicago, Green Bay.

That's why the story of the original Manhattan colony matters. Its impact is so diffuse that it would be perilous to declare and define it too concretely, so here is a modest attempt: it helped set the whole thing in motion. Certainly this isn't evident on the surface: the little village that Stuyvesant lorded over bore no resemblance to the metropolis, let alone the vast nation that exploded into existence to its left, any more than an acorn does to an oak. But the original settlement contributed, and is still there, mixed into the being of the island and the nation.

The legacy of the people who settled Manhattan Island rides below the level of myth and politics. They reshuffled the categories by which people had long lived, created a society with more open spaces, in which the rungs of the ladder were reachable by nearly everyone. They didn't exactly mean to do these things. There was a state policy of tolerance, which helped shape the colony, but there was also ignorance of it and refusal to adhere to it. It was a society that was both haphazard and planned. It didn't have a neat outline of the sort that spawned the Puritan myth. Then again, myths have a downside: the shining "city on a hill" became Manifest Destiny, and morphs easily into a cheap battle cry. The first Manhattanites didn't arrive with lofty ideals. They came—whether as farmer, tanner, prostitute, wheelwright, barmaid, brewer, or trader—because there was a hope for a better life. There was a distinct messiness to the place they created. But it was very real, and in a way, very modern.

It wasn't until 1908 that a Jewish immigrant, intoxicated by the possibilities, the strength, the progressiveness, the hope for breaking down old hatreds that he found in 'America's mixed society, wrote a play, which ran for

136 weeks (on Broadway, naturally) that he called *The Melting Pot*. The phrase entered the lexicon as recently as that, but Israel Zangwill was describing something that had been stewing for a long time. Of course, terms like "melting pot" and "pluralism" have long since become weighted and contentious. Should immigrants leave their old ethnicities behind or preserve them and remain in some way apart from the main culture? Instantly, the question becomes "What is an American?" Or, for that matter, "Who is English?" "Who is a German?" Or an Italian, an Israeli, or a Turk. In a world of pluralistic societies, the debate is universal.

But the strength in the mixing-of-cultures idea was undeniable for a long time. And the essence of it, the idea of tolerance, may matter more now than ever. The terrorist attack that destroyed the World Trade Center and shook the world in September of 2001 struck not only the center of American financial might but also the few square acres of lower Manhattan that was once called New Amsterdam. The fact that the one grew out of the other ought to be proof that the idea of tolerance remains a thing of power. With any luck, it will also remain the mortar of progressive society. Developing it, showing that it could work, was the messy genius of the first Manhattanites.

Epilogue

THE PAPER TRAIL

Through all the events of this story, in a council room in Fort Amsterdam and in an administrative office above the gate, the successive secretaries of the Manhattan-based colony of New Netherland did what all secretaries do: took notes and filed records. Lots were sold, houses were built, pigs were stolen, knives were drawn, liquor was taxed, property was damaged. The quill scratched its way softly across the sheets of imported rag paper. The directors issued their decrees and the leaders of the colonists their complaints. Letters streamed out—to Curaçao, Virginia, Boston, Amsterdam. The quill dipped into the ink pot, then addressed the paper again, filling row after row with the oddly curling Dutch script of the period.

What happened to these records after Richard Nicolls's troops took possession of them can be summed up in a truism: history is written by the winners. There was probably an element of spite involved in the failure of the English to incorporate the records of the Dutch colony into the first American histories. The bad blood between the two rival nations only intensified with the three wars they fought during the course of the century. The title of one of the many screeds published in England is enough to remind one of the ludicrous level of animosity: *The Dutch-mens Pedigree, Or, A Relation Shewing How They Were First Bred and Descended from a Horse-Turd Which Was Enclosed in a Butter-Box*. Another indication of English antipathy toward the Dutch, which America took in with its mother's milk, so to speak, is the tally of "Dutch" phrases in the language—"Dutch treat," "Dutch courage," "double Dutch," "a Dutch bargain," "going Dutch," "Dutch comfort"—all of them derogatory and all coming right out of the seventeenth century.

While the records of other early settlements were being preserved and accessed to create the story of American beginnings, those of the non-English colony were kicked around, fought over, forgotten. Their fitful passage through the next three centuries is an ironically dramatic reflection of how the colony itself has been ignored—Zelig-like, this archive would be connected to some of the major events and figures in American history. In 1685, after King James ordered a reorganization of the colonies, the volumes were tossed onto a stagecoach bound for Boston; three years later they made the same rough trip back to New York when the new monarchs, William and Mary, reversed the ruling. It was probably on one or both of these journeys that some volumes were lost (none of the records prior to 1638 remain, and the crucial period of 1649 to 1652, when Van der Donck was presenting the colonists' case before the States General, has vanished as well). In 1741 the fort, in which the records were once again housed (now called Fort George), was torched in what was widely considered to be a slave conspiracy. The gatehouse burned, but the records were saved by a diligent secretary tossing them out the window. It was a blustery day, and many pages blew away, but the bulk of the records remained intact.

In the buildup to revolution, New York City became a place of chaos and confusion. Bands of radicals did their best to disrupt the British administration. Threats were made on the life of William Tryon, the royal governor of the colony, so that on the morning of December 1, 1775, he found himself trying to conduct business from the lurching deck of a ship, the *Duchess of Gordon,* in New York Harbor, several hundred yards away from the populace he was supposed to be governing. A new matter of concern came to the governor's attention that morning, involving the same radical who had threatened his life. He wrote a hurried letter to the deputy secretary of the province:

Sir—As I am credibly informed that Isaac Sears, at the head of a large body of Connecticut people, intends very shortly to march into the city of New-York, to seize and carry off by violence the public records in the secretary's office, I do hereby require you, without loss of time, to put on board the ship Dutchess of Gordon, all such public acts and records under your care, as immediately concern the interests of the crown, until I can advise with his Majesty's council how they may be better secured. The records for patents for land and public commissions are of the first importance to be put on board the above ship. I am, Sir, your obedient servant, WILLIAM TRYON.

The records that Tryon was anxious to protect included not only those of the English colony of New York but those of the earlier Dutch colony as well. They remained for much of the war in the damp hold of Tryon's ship, where mold set in, the traces of which are still evident on the sheets. Then, according to a letter from the French writer J. Hector St. John de Crèvecoeur to none other than Benjamin Franklin, as the fight over the fate of the city and the colonies reached a climax, the records were moved to the Tower of London. Eventually, the victorious colonists demanded their return. Miraculously, the papers survived the turmoil of the war, although at its end the secretary of the new state of New York reported that many pages were "much mill-dewed and greatly injured"; he added, however, that he had exercised "my best endeavours to preserve them, having frequently exposed them to the sun and air, and several times had them brushed through every leaf."

With the turn of the next century, it looked as though the information in the documents would enter the historical record. In 1801 a committee of the New York State Assembly declared that "immediate measures ought to be taken to procure a translation of the records of this State, now in the Secretary's office, which are written in the Dutch language." One might expect that this directive would be taken seriously since it was authored by Aaron Burr, the most powerful man in the legislature, who was about to leave in order to serve as Thomas Jefferson's vice-president (and would three years later become infamous for killing Alexander Hamilton in a duel). But it wasn't until 1818 that a full-scale translation effort was under way. The man selected for this work—Francis Adrian van der Kemp, an elderly Dutch minister and former soldier who had emigrated to New York—did as he was asked. In four years, he produced a translation of the entire twelve thousand pages.

In fact, this episode in the history of the colony's records comes across as a kind of comedy. Such a rate of production is not humanly possible for one man. What's more, Van der Kemp had a faulty grasp of English, he was going blind at the time, and, in an effort to save his eyes as he rushed through the documents, he stopped intermittently to apply belladonna (a deadly poison). The result of Van der Kemp's tour de force effort was twenty-four volumes of handwritten translations—a fiasco of small errors, howlers, and massive, unexplained gaps—that were worse than worthless—worse because they were assumed to be adequate, were housed in the state library in Albany, and used by historians. Eventually, fate occasionally being kind, this entire corpus—which was never published and of which only the original existed—burned in a fire before it could further corrupt history.

The next attempt to bring this chapter of American history to light came in the early twentieth century. A search went out for a translator with a fluid understanding of the Dutch language of the seventeenth century, and one was found: a shy, heavy-set, Dutch-born engineer with a gift for language and a stubbornness for accuracy. But only two years after A. J. F. van Laer began work on a translation of the records, the infamous fire of 1911 struck the New York capitol, which housed the state library. Millions of volumes were destroyed. Once again, the Dutch records dodged catastrophe, thanks to the ironic fact that, being considered of lesser importance, they were housed on a bottom shelf, so that when the shelves collapsed, English colonial records that had been stored above protected them from destruction. Nevertheless, some documents were destroyed, others were badly damaged, both by fire and water, and two years of Van Laer's work was lost. Like a character in a novel, the man, seemingly shell-shocked, continued for a long time after the fire to go to work as usual. His work site was now a smoldering ruin, open to the sky, and he would poke among the debris in search of potential fragments. He continued to be employed in the state archives and eventually produced a translation of four volumes of the Dutch records (which would remain unpublished for half a century), but suffered a nervous collapse as a result of the catastrophe, and turned away from the massive, seemingly jinxed project.

And so to the 1970s, to the era of Watergate, when, as I have outlined at the beginning of this book, another effort was launched to crack the code of the Dutch manuscripts. Gerald Ford succeeded Richard Nixon as president, and selected Nelson Rockefeller, who had just completed his fourth term as New York governor, as his vice-president. Before leaving for Washington, Rockefeller arranged for a modest portion of funds to be dedicated to the project, and the hunt was on again for a translator.

The difficulty was greater than one might imagine. The Dutch language has changed enormously in three hundred years, and in the eighteenth century there was a shift in handwriting style, so that documents written prior to that are often incomprehensible to modern Dutch speakers. Then there is the vast amount of technical knowledge required: weights and measures, how many *mengelen* in an *aam*, the fact that a *daelder* is worth the same as a Carolus guilder but less than a *rijksdaelder*. The job was a niche within a niche.

It was a shock to both men, then, when Peter Christoph, a senior librarian charged with the task of finding a translator, met Charles Gehring at a conference. Gehring had finished a dissertation in Germanic linguistics with a concentration in Netherlandic studies. "Before I had a chance to say anything," Christoph said, recalling their meeting for me, "he asked me, 'In your field, do you know of any openings for someone to work with seventeenth-century Dutch documents?' I said, 'Boy, do I.' "

That was in 1974. Gehring has had only one job since, as translator of the archives of the colony. In the way of all nonprofit enterprises, there is a yearly crisis over funding to support the work. Not surprisingly, much of it comes in the way of donations from Americans of Dutch ancestry. There is also a matching grant from the National Endowment for the Humanities. As Gehring's output has been published—there are eighteen volumes in print so far—he has become a center of American colonial studies. He is succeeding not only in making the records of America's non-English colony available to researchers, but in broadening the field of colonial studies beyond its historic Anglocentric focus. As a kind of cap to his effort, in 1999 the twelve thousand pages of manuscript records of the Dutch colony were declared a national treasure by the U.S. Department of the Interior. Besides giving the charred pages a belated dignity, the designation also came with funds to help preserve them.

The historians who in recent years have written dissertations and academic papers on the Dutch colony—further broadening awareness of its significance—owe a lot to Gehring and to Janny Venema, a Dutch historian who has worked as assistant to the translator for the past eighteen years. I owe them a great deal as well. Not only have they made the records accessible through their translations, they have allowed me to work alongside them, have answered endless questions, have suggested avenues to explore,

and have given me free rein over the shelves and file cabinets of relevant arcana they have collected over the years. Just as valuable, spending time with
them has given me a greater feel for the people of the colony than I ever
could have gotten from mere books. The New York State Library occupies a
soulless 1970s building in downtown Albany, but in the corner where their
offices are located it's the age of Rembrandt and Vermeer; for the hours I'm
there, life seems richer and wilder. When Charly Gehring holds forth on the
hazards of sailing in the seventeenth century, his conversation is sprinkled
with Dutch nautical terms not heard in the Netherlands in centuries. He has
an appealing habit of talking about people in the present tense: "Van Tienhoven has a lot of skeletons in his closet, but he's also just about the
shrewdest guy on the island," he will say of a man last seen on Manhattan in
1656.

   From them, too, I've gotten a sense of the documents as artifacts, which
hold stories that don't transfer into type. Sitting with Janny Venema, looking
through browned, mold-speckled pages written in the days leading up to
the English takeover, I noticed one sheet with a distinctly different writing.
The typical scribe's hand is rounded, with intricate little flourishes; this
page was filled with thick, jagged, up-and-down strokes. "Oh, that's
Stuyvesant," she said offhandedly. "He must have been in a hurry and there
was no secretary around." It was remarkable to see how well the man's
handwriting seemed to match his personality, and indeed, the letter—which
has yet to be published—brims with immediacy. He is writing to the directors of the West India Company: English frigates are in the harbor, their
guns are trained on the city. At the bottom, Stuyvesant adds that he will give
the letter to a skipper who hopes to slip undetected through the Hell Gate
and out to sea. The fact that I was holding it was proof that the skipper
never sailed. Long Island is lost, Stuyvesant informs his bosses, and New
Englanders are massing across the river, ready to invade. The town is low on
food and gunpowder; the people tell him they aren't willing to fight for a
company that has shown no willingness to support them. The anger in the
letter is palpable: the corporate bosses had ignored his endless appeals for
reinforcements, and left him in an impossible situation. It isn't Stuyvesant
the pig-headed administrator who comes through in the harsh strokes, but a
man caught in an inept bureaucracy.

   One more, smaller example of how these weathered pages reveal fragments of human life. The outpost of Fort Orange (Albany) had its own administration, and for many years a man named Johannes Dijckman acted as secretary, taking minutes of meetings. We know little about him—just an ordinary man, of no account to history—but elsewhere there is a mention of him having a drinking problem. "Over time, you notice that his handwriting gets harder to read," Gehring said. "Then, one day in 1655, right in the middle of a meeting, the handwriting changes. A new hand picks up, and you never see the old one again." Shortly after, Dijckman appears in the deacon's account books; he's on poor relief and will stay on the dole until he dies. "Those last pages of minutes Dijckman takes are covered with stains and blotches," Venema said. "Who knows what they are: maybe just water. But maybe it's wine. Maybe tears."

TAKE A TRIP TO NEW NETHERLAND

This book relies in part on the translation work of the New Netherland Project, based at the New York State Library. Readers interested in the subject can learn more by visiting the organization's website, www.nnp.org, which has information on the colony as well as a virtual tour of New Netherland (written by the author of this book). And those who would like to support this vital nonprofit enterprise can do so online by becoming a Friend of New Netherland.

NOTES

For further details about the sources listed in these notes, please refer to the bibliography, which begins on page 352.

PROLOGUE

Page

4 "Original sources of information": Bayard Tuckerman, *Peter Stuyvesant, Director-General for the West India Company in New Netherland*, preface.

5 "measures ought to be taken": A. J. F. van Laer, "The Translation and Publication of the Manuscript Dutch Records of New Netherland, with an Account of Previous Attempts at Translation," 9.

5 destroyed the state library: See Epilogue notes for sources on previous translation attempts.

6 "It is impossible": Bertrand Russell, *A History of Western Philosophy*, 581.

8 "like a great natural pier": Mariana G. van Rensselaer, *History of the City of New York in the Seventeenth Century*, 1:49.

8 "best of all His Majties": E. B. O'Callaghan and Berthold Fernow, trans. *Documents Relative to the Colonial History of the State of New York*, 3:106. Hereafter cited as Docs. Rel.

CHAPTER 1

13 His complicated personality: I have used all of the standard sources in constructing my portrait of Hudson: Richard Hakluyt, *The Principal Navigations Voyages Traffiques and Discoveries of the English Nation*, vol. 3; Samuel Purchas, *Hakluytus Posthumus or Purchas his Pilgrimes*, vol. 13; G. M. Asher, ed., *Henry Hudson the Navigator: The Original Documents in Which His Career Is Recorded;* Henry Cruse Murphy, *Henry Hudson in Holland;* John Meredith Read, Jr., *A Historical Inquiry Concerning Henry Hudson, His Friends, Relatives, and Early Life, His Connection with the Muscovy Company, and Discovery of Delaware Bay;* Llewelyn Powys, *Henry Hudson;* and Edgar Mayhew Bacon, *Henry Hudson: His Times and His Voyages*. I've also consulted Philip Edwards, ed., *Last Voyages: Cavendish, Hudson, Ralegh, The Original Narratives;* Donald S. Johnson, *Charting the Sea of Darkness: The Four Voyages of Henry Hudson;* and Douglas McNaughton, "The Ghost of Henry Hudson."

13 Since we know his destination: The journal of Abacuk Pricket, printed in Purchas, *Hak-*

luytus Posthumus or Purchas his Pilgrimes, vol. 13, confirms that Hudson had a house in London; Powys, *Henry Hudson,* 1, says that it was "somewhere near the Tower of London." Muscovy House was originally located in Seething Lane, but, according to Armand J. Gerson et al., *Studies in History of English Commerce During the Tudor Period,* 33 (quoting Husting Roll 341, 29), the company moved prior to 1570 to a location "in the parish of St. Antholin London in or neare a certayne streete since the . . . late dreadfull fire in London called and knowne by the name of Dukes Street." St. Antholin's was on Budge Row, in Cordwainer Street Ward. In reconstructing Hudson's walk, I have used the "Agas map," reprinted in Adrian Prockter and Robert Taylor, *The A to Z of Elizabethan London;* Claes Jansz Visscher's view of London circa 1616, reprinted in John Wellsman, ed., *London Before the Fire;* and John Stow's *A Survey of London Written in the Year 1598.*

14 Among its charter members: The main argument for a line of interrelated Hudsons in the Muscovy Company is made by Read, *A Historical Inquiry Concerning Henry Hudson.*

14 "Here lyeth": Ibid., 41.

15 "sturdye Beggers": Jessica A. Browner, "Wrong Side of the River: London's disreputable South Bank in the sixteenth and seventeenth century"; and A. L. Beier, "Vagrants and the Social Order in Elizabethan England," 10–11.

15 From the bravado of its formal name: My sources on the Muscovy Company and the mid-Tudor period are David Loades, *The Mid-Tudor Crisis, 1545–1565;* Richard Hakluyt, *The Discovery of Muscovy;* Purchas, *Hakluytus Posthumus;* Charlotte Fell-Smith, *John Dee;* Raymond H. Fisher, *The Russian Fur Trade, 1550–1700;* Peter J. French, *John Dee: The World of an Elizabethan Magus;* Armand Gerson, Earnest Vaughn, and Neva Ruth Deardorff, *Studies in the History of English Commerce During the Tudor Period;* Henry Harrisse, *John Cabot, the Discoverer of North-America, and Sebastian His Son;* Garrett Mattingly, *The Armada;* Samuel Eliot Morison, *The European Discovery of America,* vol. 1, *The Northern Voyages;* Geraldine M. Phipps, *Sir John Merrick: English Merchant-Diplomat in Seventeenth Century Russia;* David B. Quinn and A. N. Ryan, *England's Sea Empire, 1550–1642;* E. G. R. Taylor, *Tudor Geography;* T. S. Willan, *The Muscovy Merchants of 1555;* and James A. Williamson, *The Age of Drake.*

15 English traders had been blocked: Loades, *The Mid-Tudor Crisis, 1545–1565,* 73.

16 Giovanni Cabotto: Samuel Eliot Morison *(The Great Explorers,* 40–41) says it was probably either Cabotto or Gabote.

16 some mariners were confused: E. G. R. Taylor, *Tudor Geography,* 86.

17 the Englishmen's Strait: Ibid., 34.

17 *fretum arcticum* . . . As with most people: Ibid., 81–85.

17 twenty-five pounds . . . six thousand pounds: Conyers Read, *Mr. Secretary Walsingham,* 3:371.

18 "near the pole the sun shines": Powys, *Henry Hudson,* 26.

20 "an age wherein": Albert Gray, "An Address on the Occasion of the Tercentenary of the Death of Richard Hakluyt."

20 the "perpetual clearness": Donald Johnson, *Charting the Sea of Darkness,* 20.

21 six-million-square-mile Arctic ice shelf: "In the arctic late winter, sea ice covers about 10 million square miles on top of the globe, while in summer the ice pack shrinks to about 6 million square miles, according to Martin Jeffries, an associate research professor of geophysics at the Geophysical Institute." Ned Rozell, "Sea Ice Reduction May Be Another Climate Change Clue." *Alaska Science Forum* Article 1255 (October 5, 1995).

21 Church of St. Ethelburga: Hakluyt, *Principal Navigations Voyages,* 3:567.

21 "This morning we saw": Purchas, *Hakluytus Posthumus,* 13:306–07.

22 "We set sayle": Ibid., 313.

22 "it is so full of ice": Ibid., 329.

22 "out of hope": Ibid., 328.

23 "sunk into the lowest depths": Ibid., 300.

CHAPTER 2

27 "magnificent fountain": Harry Sieber, "The Magnificent Fountain: Literary Patronage in the Court of Philip III."

27 "strenuous spirit": Simon Schama, *The Embarrassment of Riches*, 53.

28 sometimes even buying: H. F. K. van Nierop, *The Nobility of Holland*, 212.

28 "The Originals of the two": John Adams, *A collection of state papers . . .* , 399.

29 he may even have spent: Adriaen van der Donck, in his telling of Hudson's story, says that Hudson had lived in Holland. Although historians have dismissed this account as self-serving to the Dutch claim to New Netherland, a familiarity with the country would help to explain Hudson's quick decision to sail for the Dutch, as well as his friendships with Plancius and De Hondt.

30 "present negotiations": G. M. Asher, ed., *Henry Hudson the Navigator: The Original Documents in Which His Career Is Recorded*, 245.

30 "has found that the more northwards": Ibid., 246.

30 "there are also many rich": Ibid., 253.

31 "to think of discovering": Llewelyn Powys, *Henry Hudson*, 81.

31 "This is the entrance": Purchas, *Hakluytus Posthumus or Purchas his Pilgrimes*, 13:356.

32 "an abundance of blue plums": J. F. Jameson, *Narratives of New Netherland, 1609–1664*, 37.

32 the Moravian missionary: John Heckewelder, *History, Manners, and Customs of the Indian Nations*, 71–75

32 "a very good harbor": Quotes in this and the following paragraph are from Juet's journal as reprinted in Purchas, *Hakluytus Posthumus*, vol. 13.

33 "Juan Hudson": I. N. P. Stokes, ed., *Iconography of Manhattan Island, 1498–1909*, 2:44.

34 "as fine a river": Van Meteren, in Asher, *Henry Hudson*, 150.

34 "*Vellen . . . Pelterijen . . .*": The English and Dutch versions are in ibid.

35 Even as he was being lowered: All details in this scene come from Abacuk Prickett's account of the mutiny, as printed in vol. 13 of Purchas, *Hakluytus Posthumus*. Prickett's account is skewed and untrustworthy—he makes himself and his fellow survivors blameless bystanders in the mutiny, conveniently fingering those who had died on the return voyage as the ringleaders—but there is no reason to mistrust the details regarding weather, dress, and so on.

36 "to the great kingdoms": Asher, *Henry Hudson*, 255. The charter of the new company was made in 1612. The actual trial didn't take place until 1618, after several unsuccessful attempts to navigate the passage the mutineers claimed to have discovered.

36 Arnout Vogels: Information about Vogels comes from Van Cleaf Bachman, *Peltries or Plantations: The Economic Policies of the Dutch West India Company in New Netherland, 1623–1639*, 3–6.

CHAPTER 3

37 From Amsterdam the ships made their way: Van Cleaf Bachman, *Peltries or Plantations: The Economic Policies of the Dutch West India Company in New Netherland, 1623–1639*, 16.

38 "de rivière Hudson": I. N. P. Stokes, ed., *Iconography of Manhattan Island, 1498–1909*, 4:41.

38 "It is obvious": Bachman, *Peltries or Plantations,* 31.

38 "sinews of war": E. B. O'Callaghan, *The History of New Netherland,* 1:31.

39 "12 ships and yachts": Docs. Rel., 1:35–36.

40 "more like princes' palaces": K. H. D. Haley, *The Dutch in the Seventeenth Century,* 158.

40 The councillor who administered: A. J. F. van Laer, trans., *Documents Relating to New Netherland, 1624–1626, in the Henry E. Huntington Library,* "Provisional Regulations for the Colonists," and also Van Laer's note, p. 256: "Dr. Claes Petersz was the well-known physician Dr. Nicolaes Pietersen Tulp, the central figure in Rembrandt's famous painting called *The Lesson in Anatomy,* which hangs in the Mauritshuis at the Hague. Dr. Tulp was from 1622 to his death, in 1674, a member of the council and at different times schepen and burgomaster of the city of Amsterdam. Hans Bontemantel says that he never called himself otherwise than 'Claes Pieterss,' and that 'Tulp' was a nickname, derived from *tulp,* or tulip, which was placed over his front door."

40 Catalina Trico and Joris Rapalje: George Olin Zabriskie and Alice P. Kennedy, "The Founding Families of New Netherland, No. 4—The Rapalje-Rapelje Family."

41 Catalina Trico, now in her eighties: Joel Munsell, *A Documentary History of the State of New York,* 3:32.

41 The records of New Netherland show: References to Rapalje and Trico are scattered throughout the colonial records; the passage of their lives can be traced through the index to E. B. O'Callaghan, *Calendar of Historical Manuscripts in the Office of the Secretary of State.*

41 In the 1770s: Patricia Bonomi, *A Factious People,* 277.

41 Their descendants: Interview with Harry Macy, editor of *The New York Genealogical and Biographical Record* and a Rapalje descendant, April 2, 2003.

42 In contemporary scientific terms: United States Fish and Wildlife Service, Southern New England–New York Bight Coastal Ecosystems Program. "Significant Habitats and Habitat Complexes of the New York Bight Watershed."

42 "reeds": Robert Grumet, *Native American Place Names in New York City,* 24.

42 oysters: Adriaen van der Donck, *A Description of New Netherland,* trans. Diederik Goedhuys, 74.

42 "hilly island": Grumet, *Native American Place Names,* 23–24.

42 "Here we found beautiful rivers": Stokes *Iconography,* 4:60.

43 "It is very pleasant": J. F. Jameson, *Narratives of New Netherland, 1609–1664,* 77.

44 "hovels and holes": Van Laer, "Annals of New Netherland: The Essays of A. J. F. van Laer," ed. and annot. Charles Gehring, 12.

44 "as high as a man": Jameson, *Narratives,* 76.

46 after more than a decade: Shirley Dunn, *The Mohicans and Their Land 1609–1730,* 76.

46 "in figure, build . . . jet-black, quite sleek": Van der Donck, *Description,* 90–91.

46 "he shall be very careful": Van Laer, *Documents Relating,* 55.

47 "He shall also see": Ibid., 39.

48 He had grown up speaking: Information about Minuit's family and early life comes from C. A. Weslager, *A Man and His Ship: Peter Minuit and the Kalmar Nyckel,* 14–20.

48 "He shall have": Van Laer, *Documents Relating,* 44.

49 So he bought it: The order of events is far from clear, and historians debate whether Verhulst or Minuit was the one who purchased Manhattan Island. My account is based on my own reading of all relevant primary source material, as well as the arguments made by various historians. I side against those who in recent decades removed Minuit from his legendary position as purchaser of the island, and with those who reassign him to that position. Reasons: the substance of the "further instructions" to Verhulst and the

dates of Minuit's trip to the Netherlands and of his return suggest the directors were fed up with Verhulst and also realized, perhaps thanks to Minuit's information, that a new central base for the province was needed. Some historians have noted evidence of settlers on Manhattan prior to May 1626, but that doesn't mean the company had already bought the island. More to the point, the whole weight of the events gives a picture of Minuit taking charge and reorganizing the province, something Verhulst, given his weak leadership and position, couldn't have done.

50 humorist Dave Barry: Dave Barry, "A Certified Wacko Rewrites History's Greatest Hits," *Milwaukee Journal-Sentinel*, 26 December 1999.

50 their genetic makeup: Bryan Sykes, *The Seven Daughters of Eve: The Science That Reveals Our Genetic Ancestry*, 279–280.

50 it has been estimated: J. C. H. King, *First People, First Contacts: Native Peoples of North America*, 8.

52 such as one in South Carolina: Stuart Banner, "Manhattan for $24: American Indian Land Sales, 1607–1763."

52 sold for scrap paper: Docs. Rel., 1:xxv.

52 "surprise, mortification": John Romeyn Brodhead, *An Address Delivered Before the New York Historical Society*.

53 quotations from Van Rappard documents: Van Laer, *Documents Relating*, 45–59.

54 tabard . . . fur coat: Ibid., 180.

55 Schaghen letter: Translation from Van Laer, "Annals of New Netherland," 14.

56 "Received a letter": Docs. Rel., 1:38.

56 "Duffels, Kittles": Cornelis Melyn, "The Melyn Papers, 1640–1699," 124.

57 "deliver yearly": Charles Gehring, trans. and ed., *Land Papers 1630–1664*, 8.

57 Andries Hudde sold: A. J. F. van Laer, *New York Historical Manuscripts* 1:45. Hereafter cited as *NYHM*.

57 West India Company soldier earned: The Bontemantel Papers include a record of the salaries of New Netherland officials, from the director-general on down. These documents show that a soldier was paid eight to nine guilders per month.

57 In 1648: Janny Venema, "The Court Case of Brant Aertsz van Slichtenhorst Against Jan van Rensselaer," paper read during the 2000 Rensselaerswijck Seminar in Albany, New York.

59 "because he is well acquainted": Van Laer, *Documents Relating*, 176.

62 "All seafaring persons": *NYHM* 4:8.

62 "[E]ach and every one": Ibid., 4.

62 "notwithstanding her husband's presence": Ibid., 1:55. In vol. 4:5, of the same series, Thomas Beeche (here called Tomas Bescher) is referred to as an Englishman.

63 De Rasière added: Van Laer, *Documents Relating*, 188, 198–99.

63 *Tekel or Balance* . . . : G. M. Asher, *Dutch Books and Pamphlets Relating to New-Netherland*, 122–123.

64 "a rundlet of sugar": *Governour Bradford's Letter Book*, 3:53–54, reprinted in Stokes, *Iconography*, 4:70.

64 "a noise of trumpets": Ibid., 3:54–55, reprinted in Stokes, *Iconography*, 4:71.

66 "True . . . this island": Jameson, *Narratives*, 122.

CHAPTER 4

67 Charles I: The main sources I have used in constructing my portrait of Charles are Charles Carlton, *Charles I: The Personal Monarch*; Pauline Gregg, *King Charles I*; Lucy

Aikin, *Memoirs of the Court of King Charles the First;* and J. P. Kenyon, *The Stuarts: A Study in English Kingship.*

67 "Essex miles": J. P. Hore, *The History of Newmarket and the Annals of the Turf,* 1:155.

67 William Harvey: Ibid., 2:18.

67 in a single racing season: R. C. Lyle, *Royal Newmarket,* 11.

67 couldn't stand French people: C. V. Wedgwood, *The Political Career of Peter Paul Rubens,* 45.

67 emigrate to Canada: Carlton, *Charles I,* 184.

68 "but I must tell you": Kenyon, *The Stuarts,* 98–99. Emphasis added.

69 "the enemy": Docs. Rel., 1:55.

70 Rubens also introduced: Carlton, *Charles I,* 125, 144–145.

70 "We cannot perceive": Docs. Rel., 1:49.

71 "this intrigue was set": Docs. Rel., 1:45.

72 "brought againe to the torture": East India Company, *A True Relation Of The Uniust, Cru-ell, And Barbarous Proceedings against the English at Amboyna In the East-Indies . . . , E3.*

73 "the most assured and civill": East India Company, *A Remonstrance Of The Directors Of The Netherlands East India Company, presented to the Lords States Generall of the united Provinces, in defence of the said Companie, touching the bloudy proceedings against the English Merchants, executed at Amboyna, C2.*

73 "Bring more candles": John Dryden, *Amboyna: A Tragedy. As it is Acted By Their Majesties Servants.*

75 "barber-surgeon": Paul Zumthor, *Daily Life in Rembrandt's Holland,* 155–57.

76 By sheer luck, the journal: My account of Van den Bogaert's journey comes from his journal and the commentary on it published in Harmen Meyndertsz van den Bogaert, *A Journey into Mohawk and Oneida Country, 1634–1635,* translated and edited by Charles T. Gehring, William A. Starna, and Gunther Michelson, and on interviews with Charles Gehring and Iroquois scholar Gunther Michelson.

78 "shoot!": This is how Van den Bogaert gives it; Michelson says it actually means "shoot again."

78 "As soon as they arrived": Van den Bogaert, *A Journey into Mohawk,* 10.

80 "This white man": The chant, as recorded by Van den Bogaert: *"ha assironi atsi-machkoo kent oyakaying wee onneyatte onaondage koyockwe hoo senoto wanyagweganne hoo schenehalaton kasten kanosoni yndicko."* The words *kaying wee, onneyatte, onaondage, koyockwe, hoo senotowany* refer, respectively, to the Mohawk, Oneida, Onondaga, Cayuga, and Seneca nations. In an interview (February 7, 2002), Gunther Michelson, who translated the Mohawk for the 1988 publication of Van den Bogaert's journal, gave me his rendering of the chant.

80 man, woman, prostitute: Van den Bogaert, *Journey into Mohawk Country,* 52–63.

81 an English trader sailed: This incident comes from David de Vries's journal, published in J. F. Jameson, *Narratives of New Netherland, 1609–1664,* 186–234.

82 A letter written: Jaap Jacobs, "A Troubled Man: Director Wouter van Twiller and the Affairs of New Netherland in 1635."

83 Ramparts . . . boathouse: *NYHM,* 1:108–109.

83 Willem Blauvelt: Ibid., 2:162, 267, 323, 373.

83 "commit adultery": Ibid., 4:89.

83 "what he was doing": Charles Gehring, trans. and ed. *Council Minutes, 1655–1656,* 68–69.

84 Simon Root: *NYHM,* 4:360–61.

84 Jan Premero: Ibid., 97–100.

84 The Giant went free: My thanks to Firth Haring Fabend for sharing with me her notion
    that this case was a form of "leniency."

84 "Piere Malenfant": *NYHM,* 4:269.

85 "dishonorably manipulated": Ibid., 49.

85 "her petticoat upon her knees": Ibid., 1:107.

85 Griet was on board, too: Some details on Reyniers and Van Salee come from Leo Hersh-
    kowitz, "The Troublesome Turk."

85 hazardous crossing: Mariana G. Van Rensselaer, *History of the City of New York in the
    Seventeenth Century,* 1:119.

86 "the shirts of some": *NYHM,* 4:46.

86 "I have long enough": Ibid., 1:70.

86 measure the penises: Ibid., 4:46.

86 "a Turk, a rascal": Ibid., 1:11.

86 "If you do not know": Ibid., 67.

87 "as good neighbors": Docs. Rel., 3:18.

87 Van Rensselaer exaggerated somewhat: A. J. F. van Laer, trans., *Van Rensselaer Bowier
    Manuscripts,* 307.

87 "two days' journey": Ibid., 166, 181.

CHAPTER 5

93 its population: A. T. van Deursen, *Plain Lives in a Golden Age,* 11.

94 *Treasure of Health:* Simon Schama, *Embarrassment of Riches: An Interpretation of
    Dutch Culture in the Golden Age,* 557.

95 one-half of all books: Keith L. Sprunger, *Trumpets from the Tower: English Puritan
    Printing in the Netherlands, 1600–1640,* 29.

95 "refuse no honest": K. H. D. Haley, *The Dutch in the Seventeenth Century,* 167.

96 "each person shall": Translated from E. H. Kossman and A. F. Mellink, eds., *Texts Con-
    cerning the Revolt of the Netherlands,* 165.

96 In the 1620s: On the Dutch tolerance debates, I have relied on Jonathan Israel, "The
    Intellectual Debate About Toleration in the Dutch Republic"; Jonathan Israel, "Tolera-
    tion in Seventeenth-Century Dutch and English Thought"; and James Homer
    Williams, "'Abominable Religion' and Dutch (In)tolerance: The Jews and Peter
    Stuyvesant."

96 "Many will be": M. E. H. N. Mout, "Limits and Debates: A Comparative View of Dutch
    Toleration in the Sixteenth and Early Seventeenth Centuries," 41.

97 the tolerance advocates: Ibid., 46.

97 His *Discourses:* Dava Sobel, *Galileo's Daughter: A Historical Memoir of Science, Faith,
    and Love,* 302.

97 forty gallons of wine: Haley, *Dutch in the Seventeenth Century,* 118.

98 "in the academic Garden": T. H. Lunsingh Scheurleer and G. H. M. Posthumus
    Meyjes, *Leiden University in the Seventeenth Century,* 280.

98 Reinier de Graaf: Ibid., 283.

99 "elegant law": R. Feenstra and C. J. D. Waal, *Seventeenth-Century Leyden Law Professors
    and Their Influence on the Development of the Civil Law,* 9–11.

100 "from its conformity": Edward Dumbauld, *The Life and Legal Writings of Hugo
    Grotius,* 62.

100 Cunaeus: Richard Tuck, *Philosophy and Government, 1572–1651,* 166–69.

101 pipe tobacco: Schama, *Embarrassment of Riches,* 195.

101 "it is not permissible": The quote and analysis of the Dutch home come from Witold Rybczynski, *Home: A Short History of an Idea,* Chapter 3.

101 Descartes: On Descartes' time in and around Leiden, including his associations and battles with professors there, I am relying on Stephen Gaukroger, *Descartes: An Intellectual Biography,* 321–86.

102 "as soon as my age": René Descartes, *Discourse on Method,* 44.

102 "In general, the affairs": A. J. F. van Laer, *Van Rensselaer Bowier Manuscripts,* 520.

103 Getting experienced workers: Janny Venema, "Beverwijck: A Dutch Village on the American Frontier, 1652–1664," 366–67; Oliver Rink, *Holland on the Hudson,* 152.

103 "When convenient": Van Laer, *Van Rensselaer Bowier Manuscripts,* 524.

104 "it is named": Adriaen van der Donck, *A Description of the New Netherlands,* trans. Jeremias Johnson, ed. Thomas F. O'Donnell, 7.

105 Gillis Verbrugge: Oliver Rink, "Unraveling a Secret Colonialism, Part I," 14.

105 Dirck de Wolff: Ibid., 15.

105 baker as ship's captain: *NYHM* 3, 81.

106 looseness of society: On the "multitasking" of New Amsterdam residents, I am relying on Dennis Maika, "Commerce and Community: Manhattan Merchants in the Seventeenth Century," 38–59.

106 Govert Loockermans: David M. Riker, "Govert Loockermans: Free Merchant of New Amsterdam."

106 "tortured the chief's brother": J. F. Jameson, *Narratives of New Netherland, 1609–1664,* 208.

106 home of the pirate: Information on the location of Loockerman's home comes from Diane Dallal, archaeologist with New York Unearthed.

106 inventory of his property: *NYHM* 1, 320–22.

107 four hundred inhabitants: French priest Isaac Jogues, visiting five years later, estimated the population at between four and five hundred; it is from him that the figure of eighteen languages comes. Jameson, *Narratives,* 259.

107 "a mean barn": Ibid., 212.

107 minister's house and stable: I. N. P. Stokes, ed., *Iconography of Manhattan Island, 1498–1909,* 4:78, 79.

107 Juriaen and Philip Geraerdy: *NYHM* 1, 336–37.

107 "a dwelling house": Ibid., 338–39.

108 "30 tuns of fine salt": Ibid., 347–49.

108 No sooner had the ship: Commentators have referred to the ship arriving on August 20, 1641. I believe they are relying on De Vries's journal, in which he gives this date (Jameson, *Narratives,* 211). But the fact that the skipper of the ship was in New Amsterdam entering into contract with a merchant for the next delivery on July 30, 1641, doesn't fit with this. My guess is that De Vries got the month wrong, and that perhaps the ship arrived on July 20.

108 "sail with the first": *NYHM* 1:341–42.

109 "a silver-plated rapier": Van Laer, *Van Rensselaer Bowier Manuscripts,* 204. The description pertains to the previous, shortlived *schout;* I am assuming that Van der Donck would have received the same badges of office.

CHAPTER 6

110 inn of Peter de Winter: James Riker, *Revised History of Harlem,* 132.

111 "the just half": *NYHM* 1:19.

111 took on a partner: Ibid., 93–94.

111 "fumbled at the front": Ibid., 55.

111 "black wench": Ibid., 57–58.

112 Willem van Ruytenburch, in *The Night Watch:* This family tie was pointed out to me by
     Willem Frijhoff, who detailed it in his paper "Neglected Networks: New Netherlanders
     and Their Old Fatherland—The Kieft Case."

113 pamphlet published: "Broad Advice," in H. C. Murphy, trans., *Vertoogh van Nieu Ned-
     erland, [by A. van der Donck] and, Braeden raedt aende Vereenichde Nederlandsche prov-
     intien, [by I. A. G. W. C., pseud. Of C. Melyn], Two rare tracts, printed in 1649–50,
     Relating to the administration of affairs in New Netherland,* 139.

113 It was unique: I am obliged to Jaap Jacobs for this insight, which is developed in his
     book *Een zegenrijk gewest: Nieuw-Nederland in de zeventiende eeuw.*

113 By some estimates: Ernst van den Boogaart, "The Servant Migration to New Nether-
     land, 1624–1664," 55.

116 "I, Willem Kieft": Docs. Rel., 12:19.

116 a new society: The insight into Minuit's desire to found a new society comes from Wes-
     lager, *A Man and His Ship,* chapters 4–6.

118 "Whereas at present": *NYHM* 4:107.

119 "Whereas the Company": Ibid., 60.

119 "their womenfolk": Adriaen van der Donck, *A Description of New Netherland,* trans.
     Goedhuys, 92.

119 "These savages resemble": J. F. Jameson, *Narratives of New Netherland, 1609–1664,*
     213.

120 "Whereas the Indians": *NYHM* 4:115–16.

120 an Indian named Pacham: Jameson, *Narratives,* 211.

121 "Whether it is not": *NYHM* 4:124.

122 "being himself protected": Jameson, *Narratives,* 214.

122 "whereas we acknowledge": *NYHM* 4:125.

122 "it will be best": Ibid., 126.

122 the council of twelve: Docs. Rel., 1:202–203.

122 "And whereas the Commonality": Ibid., 203.

123 The ugliest assault: Jameson, *Narratives,* 226–29.

125 "Did the Duke of Alva": Ibid., 228; "Broad Advice," in Murphy, trans., *Vertoogh van
     Nieu Nederland,* 149.

125 It also reinforced: For specifics on the development of tolerance in the Dutch psyche, I
     am relying on Jaap Jacobs, "Between Repression and Approval."

125 In its very seeding: For this insight I am indebted to Willem Frijhoff, "New Views on
     the Dutch Period of New York."

126 the settlers tried to maintain: Events in this paragraph come from *NYHM* 2:32, 33,
     34–35, 39–40, 70, 87, 88, 96; 4:119, 197.

CHAPTER 7

129 "so much so": Adriaen van der Donck, *A Description of New Netherland,* trans. Hanny
     Veenendaal and the author, 15.

129 "The trees are then": Ibid., 48.

129 "Above the highlands": Van der Donck, *Description,* trans. Johnson, 63–64.

130 bears: Van der Donck, *Description,* trans. Goedhuys, 59.

130 eagles: Van der Donck, *Description,* trans. Johnson, 49.

130 birds: Ibid., 51.

130 winds: Ibid., 58.

130 "several kinds of plums": Ibid., 23.

130 watermelon: Van der Donck, *Description,* trans. Goedhuys, 37–38.

130 "The plants which are": Van der Donck, *Description,* trans. Johnson, 28.

131 "know of no limits": Ibid., 5.

132 "We, Adriaen van der Donck": A. J. F. van Laer, *Van Rensselaer Bowier Manuscripts,* 573–74.

132 searching for a young woman: *NYHM* 4:173.

132 "It is your duty": Van Laer, *Van Rensselaer Bowier Manuscripts,* 636.

132 "What pleases me": Ibid., 631.

132 "Your principal fault": Ibid., 636.

132 "outrageous": Ibid., 640.

132 "pursued each other": E. B. O'Callaghan, *The History of New Netherland,* 1:460.

133 one of the patroon's prized black stallions: A. J. F. van Laer, trans. and ed., *Minutes of the Court of Rensselaerswyck,* 1:61, 67–68, 79.

133 "I take it very ill": Van Laer, *Van Rensselaer Bowier Manuscripts,* 616, 649, 650, 666.

133 "From the beginning": Ibid., 631.

133 "Your Honor may": O'Callaghan, *History of New Netherland,* 1:462.

134 "go naked": Benjamin Schmidt, "Innocence Abroad: The Dutch Imagination and the Representation of the New World, c. 1570–1670," 18.

134 "equal to the average": Van der Donck, *Description,* trans. Goedhuys, 90.

134 "repel rain": Ibid., 101.

134 "Declensions and conjugations": Ibid., 115.

135 "fresh wounds and": Ibid., 119.

135 "devil-hunting": Van der Donck, *Description,* trans. Johnson, 95.

135 "Public authority": Van der Donck, *Description,* trans. Goedhuys, 133.

135 "Had he written": Thomas O'Donnell, Introduction, in Van der Donck, *Description,* trans. Johnson, x.

137 did not appear in print: Ada Van Gastel, "Van der Donck's Description of the Indians: Additions and Corrections," *William and Mary Quarterly,* July 1990.

137 "wind, stream, bush": Van der Donck, *Description,* trans. Goedhuys, 127.

138 "The offering is hung up": Ibid., 129.

138 "one of the younger": Ibid., 130.

138 "dishonestly designed": O'Callaghan, *History of New Netherland,* 1:338–39.

139 a million acres: Shirley Dunn, "Enlarging Rensselaerswijck." Dunn says at its height Rensselaerswyck extended "700,000 or more acres." I am also figuring in the Van Rensselaer tract called Claverack.

140 June 18 meeting described: Docs. Rel., 1:212–14.

140 he had recently arrived in New Amsterdam: The New Netherland council minutes for 1644 (*NYHM* 4:190) show that on June 6 Van der Donck was in court at Fort Amsterdam.

141 "Almighty God": Docs. Rel., 1:190–191. I am grateful to Dr. Willem Frijhoff of the Vrije Universiteit Amsterdam for elaborating for me his argument that Van der Donck was the author of much of the correspondence generated by the colonists, and that Bogardus was likely responsible for some of what was written in 1643 and 1644. My theory expands on his. His argument is spelled out in his book *Wegen van Evert Willemsz.: Een Hollands weeskind op zoek naar zichzelf, 1607–1647,* 735–38.

141 expired in August: A. F. A. van Laer, *Minutes of the Court of Rensselaerswyck, 1648–1652,* 1:10; Docs. Rel. 1:431, 532–33.

144 "For the sake of appearances": Docs. Rel., 1:211. The original incorrectly gives the date as November 1642.

CHAPTER 8

146 The island of St. Martin: Details of the attack on St. Martin are spelled out in Charles T. Gehring and J. A. Schiltkamp, trans. and eds., *Curaçao Papers, 1640–1665,* 32–35, and in the pamphlet "Broad Advice."

147 "pluck up the skinn": From Peter Lowe's *Discourse on the Whole Art of Chyrurgerie* (1596), as quoted in Richard A. Leonardo, *History of Surgery,* 153.

147 "Let him prepare": John Woodall, *The Surgeon's Mate* (1617), as quoted in Henry H. Kessler and Eugene Rachlis, *Peter Stuyvesant and His New York,* 48.

147 Stuyvesant letter: Martha Eerdmans, *Pieter Stuyvesant: An Historical Documentation,* 52–55.

147 ferocious micromanagement: Gehring and Schiltkamp, *Curaçao Papers,* 37–48.

148 abusing his landlord's: "Broad Advice," trans. H. C. Murphy, 160, refers to Stuyvesant as having "formerly stolen the daughter of his own landlord at Franiker, and was caught at it, and let off for the sake of his father, otherwise he would have been disgraced."

149 Van Brugge: Charles T. Gehring, *Council Minutes, 1652–1654,* 223.

149 Farret: Biographical information comes from J. D. Uhlenbeck, "Genaelogie van het geslacht Farret." He appears in most sources as Johan, but the genealogy gives his name at birth as John.

149 correspondence in verse: The poetry exchange between Farret and Stuyvesant is in the collection of the Nederlands Scheepvaart Museum, Amsterdam. I worked from a transcription done by J. P. Puype, librarian of the museum, in the collection of Charles Gehring at the New Netherland Project. Hanny Veenendaal of the Netherlands Center gave me a colloquial translation.

149 which was discovered: I. N. P. Stokes, ed., *Iconography of Manhattan Island, 1498–1909,* 4:Supplementary Addenda for 1645.

151 four hundred and fifty Dutch soldiers: Gehring and Schiltkamp, *Curaçao Papers,* 36–39.

151 He thought he had seen: My thanks to Charles Gehring for suggesting I follow these 450 soldiers who would repeatedly cross paths with Stuyvesant.

152 In one such effort: Joao Capistrano de Abreu, *Chapters of Brazil's Colonial History, 1500–1800,* 83.

152 yaws, dysentery: Medical and battle conditions in Brazil come from F. Guerra, "Medicine in Dutch Brazil."

152 "leather, dogs, cats, and rats": Duarte de Albuquerque Coelho, *Memorias diarias de la guerra del Brasil,* quoted in Abreu, *Chapters of Brazil's Colonial History,* 82.

153 "What mad thunder ball": My thanks to Elisabeth Paling Funk for translating this poem for me.

153 fell in love with: For some of the information on Stuyvesant's return to the Netherlands I am relying on Alma R. VanHoevenberg, "The Stuyvesants in the Netherlands and New Netherland."

154 "so that the entire": Docs. Rel., 1:213.

155 Meanwhile, in Scotland: There are many accounts of this scene. I am relying in part on the roundup of the earliest descriptions that appears in chapter 21 of J. Cameron Lees, *St. Giles', Edinburgh: Church, College, and Cathedral, From the Earliest Times to the Present Day.*

156 "making a seat": Charles Carlton, *Charles I: The Personal Monarch,* 166.

157 "Some more cavalry": Docs. Rel., 1:127.

157 "News is received," etc.: Docs. Rel., 1:127, 133, 134.

158 "Thou shalt not": Exodus 22:18, King James Version.

158 It is easy: I am relying on Barbara Mowat, "Prospero's Book," for an understanding of the mix of theology and sorcery in sixteenth- and seventeenth-century England.

159 "came to New England": Docs. Rel., 1:305.

159 Lady Deborah Moody: John Winthrop, *Journal of John Winthrop,* Richard Dunn, James Savage, and Laetitia Yaendle, eds., 462–63.

160 Anne Hutchinson: For Hutchinson's story, I am relying on Ibid., 473–46, and on Selma R. Williams, *Divine Rebel: The Life of Anne Marbury Hutchinson,* chapters 1, 9, and 14.

160 "that Abraham's children": E. B. O'Callaghan, *The History of New Netherland,* 1:257.

161 Doughty turns out: Information on the Doughty-Kieft conflict comes from Adriaen van der Donck's *Remonstrance of New Netherland,* Docs. Rel., 1:305, and from the pamphlet "Broad Advice," 159.

161 it appears Van der Donck: The dates Doughty and Van der Donck were both at court in New Amsterdam are in *NYHM* 4, 266–274. It's possible that only Van der Donck's opponent, Simon Pos, appeared in person on the dates mentioned in the records, in which case Van der Donck and Mary Doughty could have met later in July, when Van der Donck returned from the north.

161 "Every thing is, by God's": Docs. Rel., 1:157.

162 He came downstairs that morning: The scene between Agheroense, Van der Donck, and Kieft comes from Adriaen van der Donck, *A Description of New Netherland,* trans. Diederik Willem Goedhuys, 48–49.

163 The gift was to be: Ibid., 129.

163 twenty-four thousand acres: Van der Donck, *Description,* trans. Jeremias Johnson, ed. Thomas F. O'Donnell, xxvii.

164 On August 30, 1645: Details on the Fort Amsterdam peace treaty come from *NYHM* 4, 232–34.

164 The civil war in England: For my lightning account of the Battle of Naseby, I consulted Joshua Sprigge, *Anglia rediviva;* Mark Kishlansky, *A Monarchy Transformed,* 165–66; *After the Battle of Naseby* (painting by Sir John Gilbert); and the village of Naseby Website (www.hillyer.demon.co.uk).

166 The day of deliverance: Information on Stuyvesant's arrival comes from the pamphlet "Broad Advice," 162–64, and Van der Donck, *Remonstrance,* Docs. Rel., 1:309–10.

CHAPTER 9

167 "Peacock like": Docs. Rel., 1:310.

167 "like a father": Docs. Rel., 1:446.

169 A drunken knife fight: *NYHM* 4, 365–67.

170 "to be chained": Ibid., 369.

172 green stubbled-glass goblets: Pieces of such glasses, which were common in the Dutch Republic at the time, were excavated from New Amsterdam homes dating to precisely this period. Backgammon and cribbage pieces have also been unearthed. Sources: Joyce Goodfriend, "The Sabbath Keeper"; Anne-Marie Cantwell and Diana diZerega Wall, *Unearthing Gotham: The Archaeology of New York City,* Introduction; Nan Rothschild et al., "The Archaeological Investigation of the Stadt Huys Block."

172 "Is he not well aware": Docs. Rel., 1:195–96.

173 "Can he, the Secretary": Docs. Rel., 1:198–99.

174 "Was it ever heard": *NYHM* 4, 370–71.

175 "with false and bitter": Docs. Rel., 1:203–204.

176 magnanimously offered: *NYHM* 2, 407. The contract is for 450 *schepels;* a *schepel* equals 0.764 bushels.

176 Van der Donck was involving: For this insight into Van der Donck as budding politician, I am grateful to Dr. Ada Louise Van Gastel, who sketches it in chapter 4 of her dissertation, "Adriaen van der Donck, New Netherland, and America."

177 "Honorable Gentlemen!": The letter is in Docs. Rel., 1:205–209. I am grateful to Dr. Willem Frijhoff for sharing with me his arguments in support of Van der Donck as the letter's author.

178 "Thou shalt not revile": *NYHM* 4, 406–407.

178 "People may think": "Remonstrance," Docs. Rel., 1:310.

178 Stuyvesant amended the sentences: *NYHM* 4, 417–22.

179 the ship *Princess:* Details regarding the cargo of the *Princess* come from Charles Gehring, "Wringing Information from a Drowned Princess," and Simon Groenveld, "New Light on a Drowned Princess—Information from London."

180 It was largely: Edmund S. Morgan, *The Puritan Dilemma,* 59–61, 103–104.

181 Stuyvesant-to-Winthrop letter: Charles Gehring, trans. and ed., *Correspondence, 1647–1653,* 6–7; Baxter: Ibid., 8.

181 "Crazines of my head": Ibid., 8.

181 "hoping all the English": Ibid., 9.

181 He commissioned a detailed: Charles Gehring, trans. and ed., *Delaware Papers: Dutch Period, 1648–1664,* 1–12, and endnote 1.

183 "is the greatest insult": Ibid., 18.

183 "My lord": Ibid., 12.

184 "inquire diligently": Ibid., 22.

185 "the most notable": *NYHM* 4, 338–41.

185 a Scotsman named: The Forrester affair is detailed in Ibid., 442–45.

186 Sir Edmund Plowden: The Plowden affair is told in Van der Donck's "Remonstrance," Docs. Rel. 1:289, and the broader story is given in Murphy, "Representation of New Netherland," in Coll. New-York Historical Society, 2nd series, vol. 11, 1849, 322–26. Plowden's original 1632 petition to King Charles—stating that he and his compatriots are "willing at their own cost" to plant a colony "at a remote place, called Manati or Long Isle"—is logged in Public Records Office, Calendar of State Papers, Colonial Series, 1574–1660, 6:154. I'm also relying here on John Pennington, "An Examination of Beauchamp Plantagenet's Description of the Province of New Albion."

187 There was one other: Details of Van den Bogaert's end are found in *NYHM* 4, 480–81, and A. F. A. van Laer, *Minutes of the Court of Rensselaerswyck, 1648–1652,* 105. I have also relied on Charles Gehring et al., trans. and eds. of Harmen Meyndertz van den Bogaert's *A Journey into Mohawk Country and Oneida Country, 1634–1635,* xxi.

188 Meanwhile, Nicolaes Coorn: *NYHM* 4, 255 and Van Laer, *Minutes of the Court,* 11.

188 As he ran across: Charles Gehring, "Totidem Verbis," in *De Nieu Nederlanse Marcurius,* 4, 1988.

190 "Your complaints are": E. B. O'Callaghan, *The History of New Netherland,* 2:71–78.

190 Van der Donck in Rensselaerswyck: Van Laer, *Minutes of the Court* (July 23, 1648 entry).

CHAPTER 10

191 When the *Princess:* Information on the wreck of the *Princess* and survival of Melyn and Kuyter comes from Charles Gehring, "Wringing Information from a Drowned Princess"; Simon Groenveld, "New Light on a Drowned Princess—Information from London"; and the contemporaneous pamphlet "Broad Advice."

193 delivered a letter: The petition is not extant, but Stuyvesant refers to it in *NYHM* 4:580.

193 "more closely into": Ibid., 489.

194 He . . . calculated: Adriaen van der Donck, *A Description of New Netherland,* trans. Diederik Willem Goedhuys, 142.

194 "None of these": Ibid., 141.

194 "the means for": Ibid., 140.

195 led English tobacco: Jan Kupp, "Dutch Notarial Acts Relating to the Tobacco Trade of Virginia, 1608–1653."

195 They created a variety: Simon Schama, *The Embarrassment of Riches: An Interpretation of Dutch Culture in the Golden Age,* 196–97.

195 The year before: Maika, "Commerce and Community: Manhattan Merchants in the Seventeenth Century," 31–36; Kupp, "Dutch Notarial Acts."

195 in fact it was: Oliver Rink's *Holland on the Hudson* first made this case in 1986, and since then historians have begun to revise the Anglocentric view of Manhattan as a muddle. For example, Wayne Bodle, in "Themes and Directions in Middle Colonies Historiography, 1980–1994" (July 1994), notes the new view that the Dutch colony "rather than languishing in the decade before 1664, had a long-term developmental trajectory broadly parallel to those of many contemporary English colonies" and that this was "characterized by private enterprise."

196 Taken together with: Archaeological evidence for the location of the Van der Donck house comes from Nan A. Rothschild and Christopher N. Matthews, "Phase 1A–1B Archaeological Investigation of the Proposed Area for the Construction of Six Tennis Courts on the Parade Grounds of Van Cortlandt Park," 13–14; William Tieck, *Riverdale, Kingsbridge, Spuyten Duyvil: New York City; a Historical Epitome of the Northwest Bronx,* 4, 9; Christopher Ricciardi, "From Private to Public: The Changing Landscape of Van Cortlandt Park; Bronx, New York, in the Nineteenth Century," 16; and Anne-Marie Cantwell and Diana diZerega Wall, *Unearthing Gotham,* 264.

197 a mandamus: Docs. Rel., 1:250–52.

198 "To Petrus Stuyvesant": Ibid., 351–52.

198 They would ask: "Remonstrance" in J. F. Jameson, *Narratives of New Netherland, 1609–1664,* 349–51.

199 "burned with rage": Ibid., 350.

200 "these persons had": Ibid.

200 "grossly slandered": The arrest of Van der Donck and subsequent council session are detailed in Van der Donck's "Remonstrance" in ibid., 350–52, and Van Laer, *NYHM* 4:580–84.

201 gathered in the church: Docs. Rel., 1:321–22, 352–53.

201 Shortly before this: 4:584.

202 "so shaped that": Docs. Rel., *NYHM* 1:322.

203 had gotten off the ship: Ibid., 3:85–86; Docs. Rel., 1:321–22.

203 At this moment: "Remonstrance" in Jameson, *Narratives;* Docs. Rel., 1:311; *NYHM* 4:595–97.

204 banned from serving: *NYHM* 4:587.

205 He delivered these: Docs. Rel., 1:355–58.

205 "Whereas it is": *NYHM* 4:600–01.

205 "Among all the enterprising": Docs. Rel., 1:275.

206 he was in the midst: Charles Gehring, *Correspondence, 1647–1653*, 44–53.

206 and with chiefs: *NYHM* 4:607–609.

207 "Whereas the said": Ibid., 601.

207 But Captain Blauvelt: Ibid., 219, 603, 605; Ibid. 3:114, 121, 151.

208 Van der Donck handed her: Docs. Rel., 1:354–55.

CHAPTER 11

209 the above-described painting: My account of Adriaen Pauw riding into Münster is based on the Gerard ter Borch painting *Entry of Adriaen Pauw and Anna van Ruytenburgh into Münster*, as well as on Alison McNeil Kettering's analysis of the painting in *Gerard ter Borch and the Treaty of Münster*, and on Jonathan Israel's "Art and Diplomacy: Gerard Ter Borch and the Münster Peace Negotiations, 1646–8." Pauw arrived in January, but the painting depicts his ceremonial arrival in verdant spring, a liberty Ter Borch took, according to Kettering, because it made for a better painting.

210 In the early 1640s: My account of the Peace of Westphalia and its significance relies on Heinz Schilling, "War and Peace at the Emergence of Modernity"; John Elliott, "War and Peace in Europe: 1618–1648"; Anja Stiglic, "Ceremonial and Status Hierarchy on the European Diplomatic Stage: The Diplomats' Solemn Entries into the Congressional City of Münster"; and Volker Gerhardt, "On the Historical Significance of the Peace of Westphalia: Twelve Theses"—all in Klaus Bussman and Heinz Schilling, *1648: War and Peace in Europe*.

210 King Gustavus Adolphus: Volker Gerhardt, "On the Historical Significance of the Peace of Westphalia: Twelve Theses," footnote 6.

210 the French delegation: Israel, "Art and Diplomacy," 94.

211 he lived in a castle: J. G. N. Renaud, *Het Huis en de Heren van Heemstede Tijdens de Middeleeuwen*; tulips: Simon Schama, *Embarrassment of Riches: An Interpretation of Dutch Culture in the Golden Age*, 354.

213 "It appears at first": The quote is from French priest François Fénelon, in Christopher White, *Rembrandt*, 27.

213 "I can walk": Stephen Gaukroger, *Descartes: An Intellectual Biography*, 188.

213 he left for the court: Ibid., 412–13.

214 "to sell someone eyeglasses": Peter van der Coelen, *Everyday Life in Holland's Golden Age: The Complete Etchings of Adriaen van Ostade*, 130.

214 red-light districts: Schama, *Embarrassment of Riches*, 472–78.

215 "largest village": K. H. D. Haley, *The Dutch in the Seventeenth Century*, 64.

216 "Remonstrance": Docs. Rel., 1:259.

216 a letter from the Board: Ibid., 1:258.

216 "These persons are": Ibid., 319.

216 "Manhathans . . . the Capital": Ibid., 265.

216 "we may pursue": Ibid., 260–61.

216 "It will lose": Ibid., 264.

217 "Not that there is": Ibid., 262.

217 Beaver pelts . . . "fruits": Ibid., 346: ". . . as well as some samples of the fruits and peltries produced there . . ."

217 "I have seen rye": Adriaen van der Donck, *Description of New Netherland*, trans. Jeremias Johnson, ed. Thomas F. O'Donnell, 31–32.

217 hand-drawn map: Docs. Rel., 1:346: ". . . a perfect map of the country . . ."

218 This delicate: Joep de Koning, "From Van der Donck to Visscher"; Robert R. Macdonald, "The City of New Amsterdam Located on the Island of Manhattan in New Netherland."

218 "for the love of": Docs. Rel., 1:261.

218 "In our opinion": Ibid., 317.

219 fired off a responding pamphlet: The pamphlets debating monarchy are in the Koninglijke Bibliotheek in The Hague (Knuttel catalogue numbers 6377–6383); my source on their importance is Pieter Geyl, *Orange and Stuart*, 47–48.

220 Van den Enden: Jonathan Israel, *Radical Enlightenment: Philosophy and the Making of Modernity, 1650–1750*, 168–80; Plockhoy and Van den Enden: ibid., 176–79; Wim Klever, "Conflicting 'Considerations of State'. Van den Enden's Opposition Against de la Court's Aristocratic Republicanism and Its Follow-Up in Spinoza's Work"; Plockhoy: Bart Plantenga, "The Mystery of the Plockhoy Settlement in the Valley of Swans."

220 Why American history has: Many historians helped me appreciate this change in the way history is done. For conversations on the topic, my thanks in particular to Joyce Goodfriend of the University of Denver and Cynthia van Zandt of the University of New Hampshire; also to Karen Ordahl Kupperman of New York University and James Homer Williams of Middle Tennessee State University for talks they gave on the subject at the 2001 Gotham History Festival at the Gotham Center in New York.

221 appointed a committee: Docs. Rel., 1:319–20.

223 "a grandeur far beyond": Herbert H. Rowen, *Princes of Orange: The Stadtholders in the Dutch Republic*, 82.

223 Michiel Stael: E. F. Kossmann, *De boekhandel te 's-Gravenhage tot het eind van de 18de eeuw*, 365–66; Marika Keblusek, *Boeken in de hofstad: Haagse boekcultuur in de Gouden Eeuw;* Craig E. Harline, *Pamphlets, Printing, and Political Culture in the Early Dutch Republic*, 126.

223 Where at the turn: Craig E. Harline, *Pamphlets, Printing, and Political Culture in the Early Dutch Republic*, 73.

223 pamphlet titles: Kossmann, *De boekhandel te 's-Gravenhage;* online catalogue of the Koninklijke Bibliotheek, The Hague.

224 West India Company share prices: Jonathan Israel, *Dutch Primacy in World Trade 1585–1740*, 163.

224 Stael apparently introduced: Joan Vinckeboons, Gunter Schilder, and Jan van Bracht, *The Origins of New York*, 18.

224 map of New Netherland: Benjamin Schmidt, "Mapping an Empire: Cartographic and Colonial Rivalry in Seventeenth-Century Dutch and English North America"; Joep de Koning, "From Van der Donck to Visscher"; Vinkeboons, Schilder, and Van Bracht, *Origins of New York*.

224 The so-called Jansson-Visscher map: Robert T. Augustyn and Paul E. Cohen. *Manhattan in Maps*, 32–33.

225 Van der Donck's family: William Hoffman, "Van der Donck-Van Bergen"; Ada Van Gastel, "Adriaen van der Donck als woordvoerder van de Nieuw-Nederlandse bevolking."

227 And in what is perhaps: Docs. Rel., 1:369.

228 "Formerly New Netherland": Charles Gehring, *Correspondence, 1647–1653*, 83–84. Vinckeboons, et al., *The Origins of New York*, 17–18, while acknowledging that the rush

of interest in the colony in February and March 1650 suggests that the *Remonstrance* was published then, conclude that it must have been published later in the year, because Stael, who gives his address on the title page as "on the Buitenhof," didn't move there until March 10. But the sudden popular interest in the colony can only be explained by the publication of the *Remonstrance,* and there are several possible explanations for the information on the title page. For one, we know that Stael would later move to another address on the Buitenhof, so it's possible that, favoring the neighborhood, his earlier address was there as well. Another possibility is that Stael knew he would be moving to the prestigious address, and so set the type for it before he was actually living there, knowing that he would be in at about the time of publication. There is also no reason Stael would have delayed publication for several months. The letter of the West India Company directors to Stuyvesant, in which they say that "now heaven and earth" are interested in the colony, is dated February 16. Craig E. Harline, *Pamphlets, Printing, and Political Culture in the Early Dutch Republic,* 92, gives one month as a typical time it took to produce a published pamphlet, which would gibe with the February date, and suggests that the *Remonstrance* hit the streets at the beginning of 1650.

228 He composed: Docs. Rel., 1:376–77.

228 addressing in particular: Jaap Jacobs, "A Hitherto Unknown Letter of Adriaen van der Donck," 4–5.

228 "on the whole subject": Docs. Rel., 1:377–81.

229 "Provisional Order": Ibid., 387–91. That the order was read aloud I infer from the paragraph that seems directed to people in the room at the time, which begins: "We would, therefore, be of opinion that your High Mightinesses do, with the advice and communication of the Directors now summoned from all the Chambers of the West India Company, the major part of whom are in attendance . . ."

230 "Noble, Mighty Lords": Ibid., 395.

231 discovered Van der Donck letter: Jacobs, "A Hitherto Unknown Letter." I would like to thank Dr. Jacobs for discussing the letter and its significance with me, and for allowing me to reprint his translation of it.

232 "this State . . . alone": Docs. Rel., 1:347.

CHAPTER 12

234 three hundred acres: I. N. P. Stokes, ed., *Iconography of Manhattan Island, 1498–1909,* 6:142.

234 "seditious persons": Charles Gehring, *Correspondence, 1647–1653,* 82.

234 "We suppose that you": Ibid., 88.

235 "We live like sheep": Docs. Rel., 1:452.

235 "He proceeds": Ibid., 453.

235 "Many free people": Gehring, *Correspondence, 1647–1653,* 90, 92.

236 fired off a letter: Ibid., 13–14.

236 "For what have I": Ibid., 18–19.

236 the Dutch regarded: See Eaton's letter to Stuyvesant, Ibid., 21.

237 "Congratulate and reioyce": Ibid., 49–50.

237 "doe your utmost": Ronald Cohen, "The Hartford Treaty of 1650," 328.

237 The negotiations: On the Hartford Treaty, I have relied on Jaap Jacobs, "The Hartford Treaty"; Ronald Cohen, "The Hartford Treaty of 1650: Anglo-Dutch Cooperation in the Seventeenth Century"; and Charles Gehring, *Correspondence, 1647–1653.*

238 On June 5: Herbert H. Rowen, *John de Witt, Grand Pensionary of Holland*, 28–29.

239 put out a pamphlet: E. F. Kossmann, *De boekhandel te 's-Gravenhage tot het eind van de 18de eeuw*, 366.

240 "was heard stamping": Rowen, *John de Witt, Grand Pensionary*, 36.

240 Van Tienhoven vanished: The Van Tienhoven sex scandal is found in Docs. Rel., 1:514–17.

241 Pauw and Jan de Witt: Rowen, *John de Witt, Grand Pensionary*, 57–60.

242 methodically supporting his case: Van der Donck's "memorial" to the States General and supporting documents appear in Docs. Rel., 1:438–57.

242 "nothing of the Director": Ibid., 453.

242 "The people here": Ibid., 446.

242 "Whatever you have done": Ibid., 444.

243 "pulled the wool": Ibid., 458.

243 "in order that so": Ibid., 464–65.

243 "in order to silence": Gehring, *Correspondence, 1647–1653*, 149.

243 To Petrus Stuyvesant: Docs. Rel., 1:472.

244 "They make light": Adriaen van der Donck, *Description of New Netherland*, trans. Diederik Willem Goedhuys, 108.

244 resolution granting him: Docs. Rel., 1:470.

244 It would be modeled: M. E. H. N. Mout, "Limits and Debates: A Comparative View of Dutch Toleration in the Sixteenth and Early Seventeenth Centuries," 40–41.

245 Act of Abjuration: Stephen E. Lucas, "The *Plakkaat van Verlatinge:* A Neglected Model for the American Declaration of Independence," 192.

245 He hired several: Rockefeller Archives, Amsterdam Notarial Records Related to New Netherland, No. 2279 V, page 24. Notary Jacob de Winter. 1652 May 15.

245 "to hold peaceably": Docs. Rel., 1:473.

246 Oliver Cromwell: My main sources on Cromwell are Christopher Hill, *God's Englishman;* Maurice Ashley, *The Greatness of Oliver Cromwell;* and Antonia Fraser, *Cromwell, the Lord Protector.*

246 "Oh, I have": Fraser, *Cromwell, the Lord Protector*, 38.

246 "no effeminate": Christopher Hill, *God's Englishman: Oliver Cromwell and the English Revolution*, 39.

247 seeded the American idea: Anders Stephanson, *Manifest Destiny: American Expansion and the Empire of Right*, chapter 1.

248 Accounts of what happened: My account of the action off Dover is based on the pamphlets "A Declaration of the Parliament of the Commonwealth of England, Relating to the Affairs and Proceedings . . ." and "Nootwendige Observatien op het Antwoort van de Republiicke van Engelant op drie schriften overgelevert by d'Ambassadeurs vande H. Staten Generael . . . ," 41–43; Roger Hainsworth and Christine Churches, *The Anglo-Dutch Naval Wars*, chapter 1; and David Howarth, *The Men-of-War*, 48–67.

248 suspicions of Pauw and de Witt: Rowen, *John de Witt, Grand Pensionary*, 65, and the pamphlet "De Rechte Beschryvingh van alle het gene den Heer Adriaen Paau Ambassadeur Extraordinary." Pauw's state of mind is also apparent in his speech before Parliament, June 11, 1652, bound with "A Declaration of the Parliament of the Commonwealth of England . . ."

249 Milton in the Anglo-Dutch War: Leo Miller, *John Milton's Writings in the Anglo-Dutch Negotiations, 1651–1654*, 3–13.

250 "The English are about": Hainsworth and Churches, *Anglo-Dutch Naval Wars*, 17.

250 "their masts and tackles": Howarth, *The Men-of-War*, 60.

250 word had gone out: Docs. Rel., 1:476.

251 "going fast to ruin": Ibid., 477.

251 At the end of the book: Van der Donck, *Description*, trans. Goedhuys, 156–62.

253 "The undersigned": Gehring, *Correspondence, 1647–1653*, 203.

253 Notarial records: Rockefeller Archives, Amsterdam Notarial Records Related to New
     Netherland, No. 2280, pages 18–65. Notary Jacob de Winter.

CHAPTER 13

257 "Thou hast received": Berthold Fernow, trans. and ed., *The Records of New Amsterdam
     1653–1674*. Hereafter cited as *RNA*.

257 "herewith [to] inform": Ibid., 49.

258 Roman-Dutch law: J. W. Wessels, *History of the Roman-Dutch Law*, 22–25, 124–29.

258 "to this growing": Jerrold Seymann, *Colonial Charters, Patents and Grants to the Com-
     munities Comprising the City of New York*, 14–19.

259 cuckold case: *RNA*, 1:51, 53, 58, 59–61.

259 "blue caps": Charles Gehring, *Correspondence, 1647–1653*, 232.

259 to begin gearing up: Ibid., 226.

259 "5 or 6 ordinary": Docs. Rel., 1:484.

260 "certainly informed that": Ibid., 487.

260 the wall and Wall Street: *RNA*, 1:65–67, 69, 72–74, 90.

260 bourse: Simon Schama, *The Embarrassment of Riches: An Interpretation of Dutch Cul-
     ture in the Golden Age*, 348.

261 second Amboyna: "The Second Part of the Tragedy of Amboyna, or a True Rela-
     tion . . ."

261 who had just assumed: Antonia Fraser, *Cromwell: The Lord Protector*, 450–58.

261 "utmost assistance": John Thurloe, *A Collection of the State Papers . . .* , 1:721–22.

262 "Meester Adriaen": Gehring, *Correspondence, 1647–1653*, 220–21.

262 His mother moved: William Hoffman, "Van der Donck-Van Bergen," 233.

262 a member of the gang: *RNA*, 1:51, 61, 65.

263 The most recent: Charles Gehring, *Council Minutes, 1652–1654*, 91–93.

263 The episode has: As an example of this standard dismissing of the Dutch colony, the
     distinguished historian Dixon Ryan Fox, writing in 1940, recycled the accepted wis-
     dom that "In New Netherland we do not see Dutch groups insisting on communal
     privileges, as in New England . . ." and that ". . . local self-government came and de-
     veloped in New Netherland by reason of New England Puritan invasion." That histori-
     ans could ignore the long series of petitions crafted by the Dutch colonists, climaxing
     with Van der Donck's elaborate and impassioned mission to the Hague on behalf of
     self-government, can only be explained as Anglocentric blindness. (Dixon Ryan Fox,
     Yankees and Yorkers, 71–75.)

263 John Brodhead: John Romeyn Brodhead, *The History of the State of New York,
     1609–1691*, 2:571.

263 Another early: Mariana van Rensselaer, *History of the City of New York in the Seven-
     teenth Century*, 1:349.

264 was a direct result: My thanks to Dr. Willem Frijhoff for helping me to formulate my ar-
     gument that Van der Donck played a role in the December 1653 remonstrance.

264 Doughty in Flushing: Brodhead, *History of the State of New York*, 1:411, 555, 615.

264 "We do not know": Gehring, *Correspondence, 1654–1658*, 11.

264 "made up of various": Ibid., 92.

264 "natural law": The way it is stated in the supporting petition of the New Amsterdam magistrates is: ". . . because the laws of nature give to all men the right to assemble for the welfare and protection of their freedom and property . . ." (Ibid., 100); Stuyvesant, in his reply, rejects " 'that natural law gives to all men' such rights." (Ibid., 102.)

265 The invasion squadron: Thurloe, *State Papers,* 2:418-19.

265 Manhattan became Manhattan: I am particularly indebted to Dennis Maika, whose 1995 doctoral dissertation, "Commerce and Community: Manhattan Merchants in the Seventeenth Century," helped change the way historians look at Manhattan under the Dutch. By shifting attention from the West India Company to the new breed of merchant-entrepreneurs that came into being on Manhattan, Maika showed that the crucial date for its rise was not 1664, the year of the takeover, but 1653, the year of the municipal charter.

266 These alliances: I owe this insight to Simon Middleton of the University of East Anglia, who outlined it in his talk, "Artisans and Trade Privileges in New Amsterdam," at the 2001 Rensselaerswijck Seminar in New York City.

266 red and black: Van Rensselaer, *History of the City of New York,* 2:138; I. N. P. Stokes, ed., *Iconography of Manhattan Island, 1498-1909,* 4:129.

266 old thatch ones: Gehring, *Council Minutes, 1655-56,* 186.

266 An order went out: Stokes, *Iconography,* 4:129, quoting Van Rensselaer.

267 Mills, brickyards: Janny Venema, "Beverwijck: A Dutch Village on the American Frontier, 1652-1664," 75-81.

267 a thousand: Martha Shattuck, "A Civil Society: Court and Community in Beverwijck, New Netherland, 1652-1664," 9-11.

267 They are boarders: Charles Gehring, ed. and trans., *Fort Orange Court Minutes, 1652-1660,* 354.

267 One shows up: Ibid., 355.

267 Once, in 1659: Ibid., 463-64.

268 their walls hung: Schama, *The Embarrassment of Riches,* 313, 320-21.

268 The new products: Maika, "Commerce and Community," 128-29; Gehring, *Council Minutes, 1652-1654,* 162.

268 a new, two-tiered: *RNA,* 7:150.

268 Nearly every resident: Ibid., 150-53.

268 burgher system: Ibid., 149-54. Also, my brief overview of the "burgherright" system of New Amsterdam relies on Maika, "Commerce and Community," especially chapter 3.

269 a looser relationship: Venema, "Beverwijck," 304.

270 "to bake any": *RNA,* 3:391.

270 *koeckjes:* Peter Rose, *The Sensible Cook: Dutch Foodways in the Old and New World,* 34-35.

270 *Koolsla:* Ibid., Pehr Kalm, *The America of 1750: Peter Kalm's Travels in North America; the English Version of 1770,* 28. The sample New Amsterdam dishes (pike, meatballs) come from *The Sensible Cook.*

270 "Saint Nicholas": Paul Zumthor, *Daily Life in Rembrandt's Holland,* 185.

271 "There's more legal": Personal interview, Albany, New York, June 18, 2002.

271 If they couldn't: *RNA,* 7:200; Maika, "Commerce and Community," 224.

272 The initial bloc: James Riker, *Revised History of Harlem: Its Origin and Early Annals,* 183.

272 In all, a quarter: Joyce Goodfriend, *Before the Melting Pot: Society and Culture in Colonial New York City, 1664-1730,* 17.

272 intermarriage in New Amsterdam: Samuel Purple, ed., *Collections of the New-York*

Genealogical and Biographical Society, vol. 1, *Marriages from 1639–1801 in the Reformed Dutch Church, New York.*

273 "thievish, lazy": Stokes, *Iconography,* 4:74.

273 "laziness and unwillingness": Gehring, *Council Minutes, 1655–1656,* 267–68.

273 But there are also: Peter Christoph, "The Freedmen of New Amsterdam," *de Halve Maen,* 161.

273 "true and free": Charles Gehring, unpublished translation of New Netherland document no. 10(3).332.

273 In its first decades: Robert Swan, "The Black Presence in Seventeenth-Century Brooklyn," *de Halve Maen,* 1. Some historians have claimed that Stuyvesant himself owned forty slaves, but I think this figure is too high. It is based on a 1660 account from a minister who reports that "there are forty negroes" at the "the Bouwery." But by that time "the Bouwery" had become a village, and we know that several families of freed blacks owned property there, along what is now Fourth Avenue. So the figure of "forty negroes" surely included both slaves and free blacks.

273 by the time: Goodfriend, *Before the Melting Pot,* 13.

274 "724 pine planks": Charles Gehring and J. A. Schiltkamp, eds., *Curaçao Papers, 1640–1665,* 175.

274 One such: On these events of 1651 I am relying on Jonathan Israel, "The Intellectual Debate"; Jonathan Israel, *The Dutch Republic,* 706–709; and James Williams, " 'Abominable Religion' and Dutch (In)tolerance: The Jews and Petrus Stuyvesant."

275 "would pave the way": Stokes, *Iconography,* 142.

275 twenty-three Jews: Leo Hershkowitz, "New Amsterdam's Twenty-Three Jews—Myth or Reality?"

275 "for important reasons": Gehring, *Council Minutes, 1655–1656,* 166.

275 "the aversion and": Ibid., 81.

275 "consent is hereby": Ibid., 128.

275 The Jewish community: Ibid., 261–62; Gehring, *Correspondence, 1654–1658,* 83.

276 "love peace and libertie": Docs. Rel., 14:402–403.

276 But here, too: On the historical importance of the Flushing Remonstrance, I am relying on Haynes Trebor, "The Flushing Remonstrance" and David Voorhees, "The 1657 Flushing Remonstrance . . ."

276 "Singing Quakers": Docs. Rel., 3:415.

277 Here he deployed: Details from this scene come from Charles Gehring, *Delaware Papers,* 1: 37–47, and from Charles Gehring, *"Hodie Mihi, Cras Tibi:* Swedish-Dutch Relations in the Delaware Valley."

277 "forest Finns": My sources on the forest Finns are Terry Jordan and Matti Kaups, *The American Backwoods Frontier: An Ethnic and Ecological Interpretation;* Terry Jordan, "The Material Cultural Legacy of New Sweden on the American Frontier"; Per Martin Tvengsberg, "Finns in Seventeenth-Century Sweden and Their Contributions to the New Sweden Colony"; and Juha Pentikainen, "The Forest Finns as Transmitters of Finnish Culture from Savo Via Central Scandinavia to Delaware."

278 "restitution of our": Charles Gehring, *Delaware Papers, 1648–1664,* 39.

278 *"Hodi mihi":* Ibid., 39.

278 He decided to invite them: Ibid., 46, 54.

279 "Maquas, Mahikanders": Ibid., 35.

279 Such a multicultural: I am indebted to Cynthia J. van Zandt of the University of New Hampshire for this insight, which she outlined in a paper presented at the Annual Meeting of the American Historical Association in 1998 entitled " '. . . our river savages . . .

betook themselves (unknown to us) and went to Manhattan City, in New Holland, to exact revenge on our behalf": Cross-Cultural and Multi-Ethnic Alliances in the 17th-Century Mid-Atlantic."

281 "had been a good friend": Gehring, *Council Minutes, 1655–1656*, 204.

281 Van der Donck's wife: William Hoffman, "Van der Donck-Van Bergen," 340–41.

282 Croats and Prussians: These nationalities come from marriage records of the colony post 1656.

282 "So, reader": My thanks to Elisabeth Paling Funk for translating this poem.

282 Three hundred settlers: Docs. Rel., 2: 4; list of supplies Docs. Rel., 1: 643–44.

282 "I have been full": Docs. Rel., 2: 17.

CHAPTER 14

285 Meanwhile, outside: Samuel Eliot Morison, *The Founding of Harvard College*, 257–58; F. O. Vaille and H. A. Clarke, eds., *The Harvard Book . . .* , 25–32.

286 a "perfidious rogue": John Beresford, *Godfather of Downing Street*, 150.

286 and blamed his faulty: Ibid., 29.

287 literally leaving the man: John Romeyn Brodhead, *The History of the State of New York*, 1: 695; Robert Black, *Younger John Winthrop*, 209–10.

287 twenty-seven pounds: Docs. Rel., 2: 460.

288 He spent thirteen days: Black, *Younger John Winthrop*, 210; Brodhead, *History of the State of New York*, 1: 695. Detailed notes: Doris Quinn, "Theft of the Manhattans."

288 comparing notes: E. B. O'Callaghan, *Calendar of Historical Manuscripts in the Office of the Secretary of State*, 296.

288 parrots and parakeets: Charles Gehring and J. A. Schiltkamp, *Curaçao Papers, 1640–1665*, 115.

288 "He has always": Docs. Rel., 14: 525.

289 later Winthrop wrote: John Beresford, *Godfather of Downing Street: Sir George Downing*, 128.

289 a map that Winthrop: Doris C. Quinn, "Theft of the Manhattans," 29.

289 *Hamlet, 'Tis a Pity:* Samuel Pepys's diary for July through October 1661; Robert C. Black III, *The Younger John Winthrop*, 212.

289 confused with Josiah Winslow: Black, *Younger John Winthrop*, 244.

289 Charles had given: Ibid., 225.

290 Winthrop's reply: Ibid., 264.

290 "your anxiety over": Docs. Rel., 14: 551.

290 Stuyvesant complained: Ibid., 2: 230, 484–88; O'Callaghan, *Calendar of Historical Manuscripts*, 307.

290 "a sad and perilous": Docs. Rel., 2: 484.

290 "yield obedience": Black, *Younger John Winthrop*, 268.

290 "unrighteous, stubborn": Docs. Rel., 2: 484.

291 Japan would trade: Jonathan I. Israel, *Dutch Primacy in World Trade, 1585–1740*, 172; other products: Israel, chapters 5 and 6.

291 "be instruments of good": Beresford, *Godfather of Downing Street*, 155; Downing's attitude and convictions: Pieter Geyl, *Orange and Stuart*, 191.

291 "Go on in Guinea": Keith Feiling, *British Foreign Policy 1660–1672*, 130–31.

291 The second Charles Stuart: My characterization of Charles is based on Antonia Fraser, *Royal Charles: Charles II and the Restoration;* John Macleod, *Dynasty: The Stuarts,*

1560–1807, chapters 8 and 9; and Arthur Bryant, ed., *The Letters, Speeches, and Declarations of King Charles II.*

292 James Stuart: My characterization of James is based in part on Maurice Ashley, *James II*; Jock Haswell, *James II, Soldier and Sailor*; and J. S. Clarke, *The Life of James the Second . . . .*

292 Reading the letters, minutes: Feiling, *British Foreign Policy*, 97–131; Docs. Rel., 3:51–66; Royal African Company, "The several declarations of the Company of Royal Adventurers of England Trading into Africa . . ."

293 In his years of exile: Haswell, *James II*, 104–20.

293 Royal Mint commemorated: K. G. Davies, *The Royal African Company*, 181.

293 Reorganized as: Ibid., 346.

293 "the Royal Company being": Royal African Company, "The several declarations of the Company of Royal Adventurers of England Trading into Africa . . ."

293 "And pray": Feiling, *British Foreign Policy*, 125.

293 "What ever injuries": Beresford, *Godfather of Downing Street*, 170.

294 "Together with all": Peter Christoph and Florence Christoph, eds., *Books of General Entries of the Colony of New York, 1664–1673*, 1–4.

294 a committee at Whitehall: Feiling, *British Foreign Policy*, 124.

294 the next month: Brodhead, *History of the State of New York*, 1: 736.

295 within the month: Black, *Younger John Winthrop*, 272.

295 James himself took to sea: Ashley, *James II*, 80.

295 "the welfare and": Docs. Rel., 3: 61.

295 "putt Mr. Winthropp": Ibid., 55.

296 "apt to entertaine": Christoph, *General Entries*, 25.

296 "the effusion of": Ibid., 26.

297 "These to the": Ibid., 27.

297 "would be disapproved": Brodhead, *History of the State of New York*, I, 739.

297 pasted back together: Docs. Rel., 2: 445–47.

298 There is then: E. B. O'Callaghan, *History of New Netherland*, 2: 525–26.

298 The ministers talked: Docs. Rel., 2: 509; O'Callaghan, *History of New Netherland*, 2: 525–26; Brodhead, *History of the State of New York*, 1: 740.

298 "we are oblieged": Christoph, *General Entries*, 29.

299 "misery, sorrow": Docs. Rel., 2: 248.

299 They were now wealthy: Leo Hershkowitz, "The Troublesome Turk: An Illustration of Judicial Process in New Amsterdam."

300 Asser Levy, Polish Jew: Leo Hershkowitz, "New Amsterdam's Twenty-Three Jews— Myth or Reality?"

300 for the past five years: Charles Gehring, unpublished translation of New Netherland documents no. 10(3):329 and 10(3):330.

300 "I would much rather": Brodhead, *History of the State of New York*, 1: 741–42.

CHAPTER 15

301 Starting in the 1660s: Harry M. Ward, "The Search for American Identity: Early Histories of New England."

301 John Adams: David McCullough, *John Adams*, 245, 254.

301 "first born of all": The quote is from Urian Oakes, in Thomas Jefferson Wertenbaker, *The Puritan Oligarchy: The Founding of American Civilization,* 33.

301 " 'Tis Satan's policy": Ibid., 32.

301 The Puritans' systematic: The examples in this paragraph are from ibid., 224–40.

301 "the right of our manifest": Stephanson, *Manifest Destiny: American Expansion and the Empire of Right,* 42.

302 In the early twentieth: On Wilson's expansion of the term, and for the Wilson quotes, I am relying on ibid., chapter 4.

303 In fact, ships: Christian Koot, "In Pursuit of Profit: The Netherlands' Trade in Colonial New York, 1664–1688," talk given at Conference on New York City History, CUNY Graduate Center, October 2001.

303 Notaries in Amsterdam: Rockefeller notarial archives, Jacob de Winter, notary, nos. 2309, 2313, 2326.

304 "they shall continue": Docs. Rel., 3: 57.

304 "The Dutch here": Peter Christoph and Florence Christoph, eds., *Books of General Entries of the Colony of New York, 1664–1673,* 36–37.

305 "continue as now they are": Ibid., 35–37.

305 "immunities and privileges": Leo Hershkowitz, "The New York City Charter, 1686."

306 "neglect or treachery": Docs. Rel., 2: 420, 491.

306 Balthasar Stuyvesant: Charles Gehring and J. A. Schiltkamp, trans. and eds., *Curaçao Papers, 1640–1665,* 220.

306 He died: Docs. Rel., 3: 363–379, 419–510; John Romeyn Brodhead, *The History of the State of New York, 1609–1691,* 2: 131–32.

307 "Wherby there is": John Winthrop to the Earl of Clarendon, "The Clarendon Papers," *Collections,* New-York Historical Society (1869), 58.

307 "the best of all": Docs. Rel., 3: 106.

307 "You will have heard": Arthur Bryant, ed., *The Letters, Speeches, and Declarations of King Charles II,* 168.

307 the Dutch government allowed: Docs. Rel., 2: 516–17.

308 as an "invitation": Jonathan Israel, *The Anglo-Dutch Moment,* Chapter 3, "The Dutch Role in the Glorious Revolution," especially 124–29.

309 Jacob Leisler: David Voorhees, "The 'fervent Zeale' of Jacob Leisler"; Firth Haring Fabend, "The Pro-Leislerian Dutch Farmers in New York: A 'Mad Rabble,' or 'Gentlemen Standing Up for Their Rights'?"

309 the relationships between: Joyce D. Goodfriend, *Before the Melting Pot: Society and Culture in Colonial New York City,* chapters 4 and 5.

309 What mattered was: Milton Klein, "Origins of the Bill of Rights in Colonial New York," 391.

309 French, German, Scottish, and Irish: Goodfriend, *Before the Melting Pot,* 16, 56–60.

310 "Our chiefest unhappyness": Charles Lodwick, "New York in 1692 . . . ," 244. 371.

310 As late as the 1750s: James Tanis, "The Dutch-American Connection . . . ," 24.

310 In fact, the irony: Firth Haring Fabend, *Zion on the Hudson: Dutch New York and New Jersey in the Age of Revivals,* especially chapter 10.

311 "following the example": Newark *Daily Advertiser,* December 6, 1850.

311 "Yielding to no one": John Romeyn Brodhead, unpublished manuscript, the Brodhead Collection, Rutgers University.

312 "clamoring for scholarly": Editorial, *New York Times,* 7 August 2001.

313 "What then is": J. Hector St. John de Crèvecoeur, *Letters from an American Farmer*, 46–47.

314 district attorney derived from *schout:* W. Scott van Alstyne, Jr., "The District Attorney—An Historical Puzzle"; A. J. Reiss, "Public Prosecutors and Criminal Prosecution in the United States of America." As with nearly everything in history, the origins of the office of district attorney are open to debate, but the arguments that Reiss and van Alstyne make show a straightforward chain of influence. The most forceful argument against the district attorney office originating in the office of *schout* is interesting in that it has the classic features of American Anglocentrism. Jack Kress ("Progress and Prosecution"), notes that England had no such office, that the Dutch did, that the first district attorneys in English America appeared in precisely the area where the Dutch colony had been, and that those first district attorneys were called "scout" by the English, seemingly a clear indicator of their Dutch origin. But he then dismisses the argument on the grounds that the Dutch couldn't have made a lasting impact because the Dutch colony was small and the period of Dutch control was "quite brief, lasting only from 1653 until 1664 and that it is questionable if this was sufficient time for the institution of the *schout* to take root . . ." Besides getting the date of the colony's founding wrong by thirty years, Kress adopts the classic pattern of reasoning that American history has applied to the Dutch colony: assume the colony had no real presence, then, on the basis of your assumption, dismiss evidence to the contrary.

315 Santa Claus: Elisabeth Paling Funk, "Washington Irving and the Dutch Heritage," manuscript in progress, chapter 3: "The Popular Culture of New Netherland." My thanks to the author for sending me this portion of her work.

315 "ancient City": The charter is printed in Stephen Schechter, *Roots of the Republic: American Founding Documents Interpreted,* 91. My reading of the colony's political legacy comes in part from Leo Hershkowitz, "The New York City Charter, 1686"; Robert C. Ritchie, *The Duke's Province: A Study of New York Politics and Society, 1664–1691,* chapter 1; Paul Finkelman, "The Soul and the State: Religious Freedom in New York and the Origin of the First Amendment"; Milton M. Klein, "Origins of the Bill of Rights in Colonial New York"; Betsy Rosenblatt, "New York State's Role in the Creation and Adoption of the Bill of Rights."

315 The names of the twenty-six: Rosenblatt, "New York State's Role in the Creation and Adoption of the Bill of Rights"; "Albany Committee," *New York Journal and Weekly Register,* April 26, 1788.

EPILOGUE

320 While the records: My sources on the history, condition, and preservation of the colony's records are: The A. J. F. van Laer Papers, New York State Library; the John Romeyn Brodhead Papers, Rutgers University; the Andrew Elliot Papers, New York State Library; A. J. F. van Laer, "The Translation and Publication of the Manuscript Dutch Records of New Netherland, with an Account of Previous Attempts at Translation," New York State Library Education Department Bulletin, January 1, 1910; Vivian C. Hopkins, "The Dutch Records of New York: Francis Adrian van der Kemp and De Witt Clinton," *New York History,* October 1962; New York Secretary of State, "Inventory of Dutch and English Colonial Papers"; Hugh Hastings, ed., *Public Papers of George Clinton,* 1: 7–10; Charles Gehring, "New Netherland Manuscripts in United States Repositories," *de Halve Maen* 57 (August 1983); Charles Gehring, "New Netherland Translating New York's Dutch Past," *Humanities* (November/December 1993);

Ronald Howard, "John Romeyn Brodhead," *de Halve Maen* 59 (July 1985); Peter Christoph, "Story of the New Netherland Project," *de Halve Maen* 61 (September 1988); Charles K. Winne, Jr., "Arnold J. F. van Laer (1869–1955), An Appreciation," in A. J. F. van Laer, trans., *New York Historical Manuscripts: Dutch*, vol. 1; Application Form, U. S. Department of the Interior, "Save America's Treasures" Program, Project: Dutch Colonial Manuscripts, 1638–1670; and interviews with Charles Gehring, Peter Christoph, Christina Holden, Janny Venema.

320 Threats were made: Information about Tryon comes from Paul David Nelson, *William Tryon and the Course of Empire*, and from original documents in the Andrew Elliot Papers at the New York State Library.

320 "Sir—As I am": J. V. N. Yates, "Report of the Secretary of State, relative to the records &c. in his office," 44.

321 mold set in: Interview (August 27, 2002) with Maria Holden, conservator, New York State Archives.

321 according to a letter: It has been assumed the records spent the entire war aboard the *Duchess of Gordon* and another ship, the *Warwick*, but a letter from Crèvecoeur to Franklin, written in 1783, provides evidence that they were moved to the Tower late in the conflict. J. Hector St. John de Crèvecoeur, *Letters from an American Farmer*, 341.

321 "much mill-dewed": Yates, "Report of the Secretary of State" 46.

321 "immediate measures ought": Van Laer, "Translation and Publication of the Manuscript Dutch Records of New Netherland."

322 a fiasco of small errors: Historians had long suspected Van der Kemp's translations were flawed. Charles Gehring was able to assess just how bad they were after he discovered two volumes that had escaped destruction in the fire.

325 having a drinking problem: In fact, it is Stuyvesant, writing to the company directors, who refers to the man as the "drunkard Johannes Dijckmans."

325 "Then, one day in 1655": The change in handwriting—the moment at which Dijckman's career ends—occurs on Tuesday, May 9, 1655, and appears on page 193 of Charles Gehring, *Fort Orange Court Minutes, 1652–1660*.

BIBLIOGRAPHY

LETTERS, JOURNALS, PAMPHLETS, MAPS, PAPERS, COUNCIL MINUTES, AND OTHER PRIMARY SOURCES

Adams, John. *A collection of state-papers, relative to the first acknowledgment of the sovereignty of the United States of America, and the reception of their minister plenipotentiary, by their high mightinesses the States-General of the United Netherlands.* The Hague, 1782.

Aglionby, William. *The Present State of the United Provinces of the Low Countries as to the Government, Laws, Forces, Riches, Manners, Customes, Revenue, and Territory of the Dutch.* London: John Starkey, 1671.

Albany Committee, *The New York Journal and Weekly Register,* April 26, 1788.

Asher, G. M. *Dutch Books and Pamphlets Relating to New-Netherland.* Amsterdam: Frederik Muller, 1854.

———, ed. *Henry Hudson the Navigator: The Original Documents in Which His Career Is Recorded.* New York: The Hakluyt Society, 1860.

Augustyn, Robert T., and Paul E. Cohen. *Manhattan in Maps, 1527–1995.* New York: Rizzoli, 1997.

Bontemantel, Hans. The Bontemantel Papers. New York: New York Public Library.

Bradford, William. *Of Plymouth Plantation.* New York: Knopf, 1966.

Brodhead, John Romeyn. *An Address Delivered Before the New-York Historical Society.* New York: New-York Historical Society, 1844.

———. The John Romeyn Brodhead Papers. New Brunswick, N.J.: Alexander Library, Rutgers University.

Bryant, Arthur, ed. *The Letters, Speeches, and Declarations of King Charles II.* London: Cassell, 1935.

Church of Scotland. *The Booke of Common Prayer, And Administration Of The Sacraments, And other parts of divine Service for the use of the Church of Scotland.* Edinburgh: Robert Young, 1637.

Christoph, Peter R., ed. *New York Historical Manuscripts: English.* Vol. 22, *Administrative Papers of Governors Richard Nicolls and Francis Lovelace, 1664–1673.* Baltimore: Genealogical Publishing, 1980.

Christoph, Peter R., and Florence A. Christoph, eds. *The Andros Papers.* 3 vols. Vol. 1, *1674–1676;* Vol. 2, *1677–1678;* Vol. 3, *1679–1680.* Syracuse, N.Y.: Syracuse University Press, 1989–1991.

———. *Books of General Entries of the Colony of New York, 1664–1673*. Baltimore: Genealogical Publishing, 1982.

Clarendon, Edward, Earl of. *The Clarendon Papers*. Collections of the New-York Historical Society, 1869.

Clinton, George. *The Public Papers of George Clinton*, vols. 1 and 8. Albany, N.Y.: State Legislative Printer, 1904.

Connecticut Colony. *The Public Records of the Colony of Connecticut, Prior to the Union with the New Haven Colony*. Hartford: Brown & Parsons, 1850.

Crèvecoeur, J. Hector St. John de. *Letters from an American Farmer, describing certain provincial situations, manners, and customs . . . of the people of North America*. Philadelphia: Mathew Carey, 1793.

Descartes, René. *Discourse on Method*. Garden City, N.Y.: Anchor Books, 1974.

Downing, George, Sir. *A discourse written by Sir George Downing, the king of Great Britain's envoyee extraordinary to the states of the United-Provinces. Vindicating his royal master from the insolencies of a scandalous libel, printed under the title of "An Extract out of the register of the States General of the United Provinces, upon the memorial of Sir George Downing, envoyee, &c." and delivered by the agent de Heyde for such, to several publick ministers: whereas no such resolution was ever communicated to the said envoyee, nor any answer at all returned by their Lordships to the said memorial*. London, 1664.

Dryden, John. *Amboyna: A Tragedy. As it is Acted By Their Majesties Servants*. London, 1691.

Du Moulin, Pierre. *The Monk's Hood Pull'd Off, or, The Capucin Fryar Described*. London: James Collins, 1671.

East India Company. *A Remonstrance Of The Directors Of The Netherlands East India Company, presented to the Lords States Generall of the united Provinces, in defence of the said Companie, touching the bloudy proceedings against the English Merchants, executed at Amboyna*. London, 1632.

———. *A True Relation Of The Uniust, Cruell, And Barbarous Proceedings against the English at Amboyna In the East-Indies, by the Neatherlandish governour and Councel there. Also the copie of a Pamphlet, set forth first in Dutch and then in English, by some Neatherlander; falsly entituled, A True Declaration Of The Newes that came out of the East-Indies, with the Pinace called the Hare, which arrived at Texel in June, 1624*. London, 1624.

Edwards, Philip, ed. *Last Voyages: Cavendish, Hudson, Ralegh, The Original Narratives*. Oxford: Clarendon Press, 1988.

Eerdmans, Martha. *Pieter Stuyvesant: An Historical Documentation; compiled upon request of the Provincial Government of Friesland in Commemoration of the Pieter Stuyvesant Festival, Wolvega, Friesland, July 12–16, 1955*. Grand Rapids: Eerdmans, 1957.

Elliot, Andrew. Andrew Elliot Papers, 1767–1785. Albany: New York State Library.

England and Wales. *Articles of peace & alliance, between the most serene and mighty prince Charles II. by the grace of God king of England, Scotland, France and Ireland, Defender of the Faith, &c. and the High and Mighty Lords the States General of the United Netherlands, concluded the 21/31 day of July, 1667*. London, 1667.

Farret, Johan, and Peter Stuyvesant. Poetry exchange between Johan Farret and Peter Stuyvesant. In the collection of the Nederlands Scheepvaart Museum, Amsterdam. Photocopy, New Netherland Project, New York State Library, Albany.

Fernow, Berthold, trans. and ed. *The Records of New Amsterdam, 1653–1674*. 7 vols. New York: The Knickerbocker Press, 1897. Reprint, Baltimore: Genealogical Publishing Co., Inc., 1976.

A friend to this commonwealth. *The case stated between England and the United Provinces, in this present juncture. Together with a short view of those Netherlanders in their late practises as to religion, liberty, leagues, treaties, amities. Publish'd for the information and a warning to England.* London, 1652.

Gehring, Charles, trans. and ed. *Correspondence, 1647–1653.* New Netherland Document Series. Syracuse, N.Y.: Syracuse University Press, 2000.

———. *Correspondence, 1654–1658.* New Netherland Document Series. Syracuse, N.Y.: Syracuse University Press, 2003.

———. *Council Minutes, 1652–1654.* New York Historical Manuscripts Series. Baltimore: Genealogical Publishing Co., Inc., 1983.

———. *Council Minutes, 1655–1656.* New Netherland Document Series. Syracuse, N.Y.: Syracuse University Press, 1995.

———. *Delaware Papers: Dutch Period, 1648–1664.* New York Historical Manuscripts Series. Baltimore: Genealogical Publishing Co., Inc., 1981.

———. *Delaware Papers: English Period, 1664–1682.* New York Historical Manuscripts Series. Baltimore: Genealogical Publishing Co., Inc., 1977.

———. *Fort Orange Court Minutes, 1652–1660.* New Netherland Documents Series. Syracuse, N.Y.: Syracuse University Press, 1990.

———. *Fort Orange Records, 1656–1678.* New Netherland Documents Series. Syracuse, N.Y.: Syracuse University Press, 2000.

———. *Land Papers, 1630–1664.* New York Historical Manuscript Series. Baltimore: Genealogical Publishing Co., Inc., 1980.

———. *Laws and Writs of Appeal, 1647–1663.* New Netherland Documents Series. Syracuse, N.Y.: Syracuse University Press, 1991.

———. New Netherland Colonial Manuscripts. Unpublished translations, nos. 10(3):329, 10(3):330, 10(3):332.

Gehring, Charles T., and J. A. Schiltkamp, trans. and eds. *Curaçao Papers, 1640–1665.* New Netherland Documents. Interlaken, N.Y.: Heart of the Lakes Publishing, 1987.

Gemeente Archief, Amsterdam. *English Translations of Notarial Documents in the Gemeente Archief in Amsterdam Pertaining to North America.* Historic Hudson Valley Collections, Rockefeller Archives, Pocantico Hills, New York.

Great Britain, Parliament. *A declaration of the Parliament of the commonwealth of England, relating to the affairs and proceedings between this commonwealth and the States General of the United Provinces of the Low-Countreys, and the present differences occasioned on the States part. And The answer of the Parliament to three papers from the ambassadors extraordinary of the States General, upon occasion of the late fight between the fleets.* London, 1652.

Grotius, Hugo. *The Jurisprudence of Holland.* R. W. Lee, trans. 2 vols. Oxford: Clarendon, 1926.

Hakluyt, Richard. *The Discovery of Muscovy.* London: Cassell and Co., 1904.

———. *The Original Writings & Correspondence of the Two Richard Hakluyts.* London: Hakluyt Society, 1935.

———. *The Principal Navigations Voyages Traffiques and Discoveries of the English Nation.* 12 vols. Glasgow: 1903–05.

Hartgers, Joost. *Beschrijvinghe van Virginia, Nieuw Nederlandt, Nieuw Engelandt en d'Eylanden Bermudes, Berbados, en S. Christoffel.* Amsterdam: Joost Hartgers, 1651.

Hastings, Hugh, ed. *Ecclesiastical Records of the State of New York,* vol. 1. Albany: Lyon, 1901.

Jameson, J. F. *Narratives of New Netherland, 1609–1664.* New York: Charles Scribner's Sons, 1909; New York: Barnes and Noble, 1937.

———, ed. *Privateering and Piracy in the Colonial Period: Illustrative Documents.* New York: Macmillan, 1923.

Kalm, Pehr. *The America of 1750: Peter Kalm's Travels in North America; the English version of 1770.* Revised and edited by Adolph B. Benson. New York: Wilson-Erickson, 1937.

Knuttel, W. P. C. *Catalogus van de pamfletten-verzameling berustende in de Koninklijke bibliotheek.* 's Gravenhage: Algemeene landsdrukkerij, 1889–1920.

Kossman, E. H., and A. F. Mellink, eds. *Texts Concerning the Revolt of the Netherlands.* London: Cambridge University Press, 1974.

Lodwick, Charles. "New York in 1692: Letter from Charles Lodwick, to Mr. Francis Lodwick and Mr. Hooker, Dated May 20, 1692, Read Before the Royal Society of London." *Collections of the New-York Historical Society,* 2nd ser., vol. 2. New York, 1849.

Melyn, Cornelis. "The Melyn Papers, 1640–1699." *The New-York Historical Society Collections, 1913.* New York: New-York Historical Society, 1914.

Munsell, Joel, ed. *A Documentary History of the State of New York.* 4 vols. Albany: Weed, Parsons, 1865.

Murphy, Henry Cruse, "The Representation of New Netherland." *Collections of New-York Historical Society,* 11, 1849.

New-York Historical Society. *Collections.* New York: New-York Historical Society, 1869.

New York (State) Secretary of State. *Inventory of Records and Files in the Office of the Secretary of State, 1818.* Albany: New York State Library.

Nootwendige Observatien op het Antwoort van de Republiicke van Engelant Op drie schriften overgelevert by d' Ambassadeurs vande H. Staten Generael vande Vereenichde Provintien aen den Raedt van Staet, ter occasie van het laetste Zeegevecht tussen de Vlooten van beyde Republiicken. 1652. Knuttel no. 7148.

O'Callaghan, E. B. *Calendar of Historical Manuscripts in the Office of the Secretary of State.* Albany, N.Y.: Weed, Parsons, 1865.

———, trans. *Voyages of the Slavers St. John and Arms of Amsterdam, 1659, 1663, Together with Additional Papers Illustrative of the Slave Trade Under the Dutch.* Albany, N.Y.: J. Munsell, 1867.

O'Callaghan, E. B., and Berthold Fernow, trans. *Documents Relative to the Colonial History of the State of New York.* 15 vols. Albany, N.Y.: Weed, Parsons and Company, 1856–1887.

Olin, John C., ed. *A Reformation Debate: John Calvin and Jacopo Sadoleto, Sadoleto's Letter to the Genevans and Calvin's Reply.* Grand Rapids, Mich.: Baker Book House, 1979.

Pepys, Samuel. *The Diary of Samuel Pepys.* New York: Cassell, 1886.

Present State of Holland, or a Description of the United Provinces, The. London, 1745.

Prockter, Adrian, and Robert Taylor, eds. *The A to Z of Elizabethan London.* London: London Topographical Society, 1979.

Public Records Office. *Calendar of State Papers, Colonial Series, 1574–1660, Preserved in the State Paper Department of Her Majesty's Public Record Office.* London, 1860.

Purchas, Samuel. *Hakluytus Posthumus or Purchas his Pilgrimes.* 20 vols. Glasgow: MacLehose, 1905–07.

Purple, Samuel, ed. *Collections of the New-York Genealogical and Biographical Society,* Vol. 1, *Marriages from 1639–1801 in the Reformed Dutch Church, New York.* New York: New York Genealogical and Biographical Society, 1890.

De Rechte Beschryvingh van alle het gene den Heer Adriaen Paau Ambassadeur Extraordinary van wegen de Hoog: Moog: Heeren Staten Generael, der Vrye Vereenichde Nederlan-

den, met het Parlement van Engelant getracteert, heeft nopende een goede Vreede tusschen beyde Repulijcquen. Amsterdam, 1652. Knuttel no. 7136.

Rijksmuseum te Leiden. *Album studiosorum Academiae lugduno batavae MDLXXV–MDC-CCLXXV.* The Hague: Nijhoff, 1875.

Rivington's New York Gazetteer. December 23, 1773, December 8, 1774.

Royal African Company. *The several declarations of the Company of Royal Adventurers of England Trading into Africa, inviting all His Majesties native subjects in general to subscribe, and become sharers in their joynt-stock. Together with His Royal Highness James duke of York and Albany, &c. and the rest of the said royal companies letter to the Right Honourable Francis lord Willoughby of Parham, &c. Intimating the said companies resolutions to furnish His Majesties American plantations with negroes at certain and moderate rates.* London, 1667.

Schechter, Stephen L., ed. *Roots of the Republic: American Founding Documents Interpreted.* Madison, Wis.: Madison House, 1990.

The Second Part of the Tragedy of Amboyna: Or, a True Relation of a Most Bloody, Treacherous, and Cruel Design of the Dutch in the New Netherlands in America. For the total Ruining and Murthering of the English Colonies in New-England. Being extracted out of several Letters very lately written from New-England to several Gentlemen and Merchants in London. London, 1653.

Seymann, Jerrold. *Colonial Charters, Patents and Grants to the Communities Comprising the City of New York.* New York: The Board of Statute Consolidation of the City of New York, 1939.

Snow, Dean R., Charles T. Gehring, and William A. Starna, eds. *In Mohawk Country.* Syracuse, N.Y.: Syracuse University Press, 1996.

Sprigge, Joshua. *Anglia rediviva; England's recovery (1647).* Facsimile reproduction. Gainesville, Fla.: Scholars' Facsimiles & Reprints, 1960.

Stokes, I. N. P., ed. *Iconography of Manhattan Island, 1498–1909.* 6 vols. New York: Robert H. Dodd, 1915–1928.

Stow, John. *A Survey of London Written in the Year 1598.* Stroud, Gloustershire: Alan Sutton Publishing Ltd., 1994.

Temple, William. *Observations Upon the United Provinces of the Netherlands.* Edited by Sir George Clark. Oxford: Clarendon, 1972.

Thurloe, John. *A Collection of the State Papers of John Thurloe, Esq.; Secretary, First, to the Council of State, And afterwards to The Two Protectors, Oliver and Richard Cromwell.* 7 vols. London, 1742.

Van den Bogaert, Harmen Meyndertsz. *A Journey into Mohawk and Oneida Country, 1634–1635.* Trans. and ed. by Charles T. Gehring, William A. Starna, and Gunther Michelson. Syracuse, N.Y.: Syracuse University Press, 1988.

Van der Coelen, Peter, ed. *Everyday Life in Holland's Golden Age: The Complete Etchings of Adriaen van Ostade.* Amsterdam: Museum het Rembrandthuis, 1998.

Van der Donck, Adriaen. *Beschryvinge van Nieuw-Nederlant.* Amsterdam: Evert Nieuwenhof, 1655. Second edition, 1656.

———. *A Description of New Netherland.* Trans. Diederik Willem Goedhuys. Unpublished, 1991.

———. *A Description of the New Netherlands.* Trans. Jeremias Johnson, ed. Thomas F. O'Donnell. Syracuse, N.Y.: Syracuse University Press, 1968.

———. *The Representation of New Netherland: concerning its location, productiveness and poor condition, presented to the States General of the United Netherlands and printed at The Hague in 1650.* Trans. H. C. Murphy. New York: Bartlett & Welford, 1849.

————. *Remonstrance of New Netherland, and the Occurrences there, addressed to the high and mighty Lords States General of the United Netherlands, on the 28ᵗʰ July 1649; with Secretary van Tienhoven's Answer.* Ed. Edmund O'Callaghan. Albany: Weed, Parsons, 1856.

————. *Vertoogh van Nieu Nederland, [by A. van der Donck] and, Braeden raedt aende Vereenichde Nederlandsche provintien, [by I. A. G. W. C., pseud. Of C. Melyn], Two rare tracts, printed in 1649–50, Relating to the administration of affairs in New Netherland.* Trans. H. C. Murphy. New York: Baker, Godwin, 1854.

————. *Vertoogh van Nieu-Neder-Land, Weghens de Gheleghentheydt, Vruchtbaerheydt, en Soberen Staet desselfs.* 's Gravenhage: Michiel Stael, 1650.

Van Laer, A. J. F. A. J. F. Van Laer Papers, 1909–1952. Albany: New York State Library.

————, trans. *Documents Relating to New Netherland, 1624–1626, in the Henry E. Huntington Library.* San Marino, Calif.: Henry E. Huntington Library and Art Gallery Press, 1924.

————. *New York Historical Manuscripts: Dutch.* Vol. 1, *Register of the Provincial Secretary, 1638–1642.* Baltimore: Genealogical Publishing Co., 1974.

————. *New York Historical Manuscripts: Dutch.* Vol. 2, *Register of the Provincial Secretary, 1642–1647.* Baltimore: Genealogical Publishing Co., 1974.

————. *New York Historical Manuscripts: Dutch.* Vol. 3, *Register of the Provincial Secretary, 1648–1660.* Baltimore: Genealogical Publishing Co., 1974.

————. *New York Historical Manuscripts: Dutch.* Vol. 4, *Council Minutes, 1638–1649.* Baltimore: Genealogical Publishing Co., 1974.

————. *Van Rensselaer Bowier Manuscripts, being the letters of Kiliaen Van Rensselaer, 1630–1643, and other documents relating to the colony of Rensselaerswyck.* Albany: University of the State of New York, 1908.

————, trans. and ed. *Minutes of the Court of Rensselaerswyck, 1648–1652.* Albany: University of the State of New York, 1922.

Van Strien, Kees. *Touring the Low Countries: Accounts of British Travellers, 1660–1720.* Amsterdam: Amsterdam University Press, 1998.

Van Tienhoven, Cornelis. "Answer to the Representation of New Netherland." In E. B. O'Callaghan and Berthold Fernow, trans. *Documents Relative to the Colonial History of the State of New York.* Vol. 1. Albany, N.Y.: Weed, Parsons and Company, 1856–1887.

Wellsman, John, ed. *London Before the Fire: A Grand Panorama, from Original Seventeenth Century Engravings by Visscher, Hollar and de Witt.* London: Sidgwick & Jackson, 1973.

Winthrop, John. *Journal of John Winthrop, 1630–1649.* Richard Dunn, James Savage, and Laetitia Yaendle, eds. Cambridge: Harvard University Press, 1996.

Yates, J. V. N. "Report of the Secretary of State, relative to the records &c. in his office." Albany: New York State Senate, January 5, 1820.

SECONDARY SOURCES

Abreu, Joao Capistrano de. *Chapters of Brazil's Colonial History, 1500–1800.* Trans., Arthur Brakel. New York: Oxford University Press, 1997.

Aikin, Lucy. *Memoirs of the Court of King Charles the First.* Philadelphia: Carey, Lea and Blanchard, 1833.

Akrigg, G. P. V. *Jacobean Pageant, or The Court of King James I.* Cambridge: Harvard University Press, 1963.

Archdeacon, Thomas J. *New York City, 1664–1710: Conquest and Change.* Ithaca: Cornell University Press, 1979.

Ashley, Maurice. *The Greatness of Oliver Cromwell.* New York: Macmillan, 1958.

———. *James II.* London: Dent, 1977.

Bachman, Van Cleaf. *Peltries or Plantations: The Economic Policies of the Dutch West India Company in New Netherland, 1623–1639.* Baltimore: Johns Hopkins Press, 1969.

Bacon, Edgar Mayhew. *Henry Hudson: His Times and His Voyages.* New York: G. P. Putnam's Sons, 1907.

Bailey, Rosalie Fellows. *Pre-Revolutionary Dutch Houses.* New York: William Morrow, 1936.

Baltzell, E. Digby. *Puritan Boston and Quaker Philadelphia.* New York: Free Press, 1979.

Barnes, Donna R., and Peter G. Rose. *Matters of Taste: Food and Drink in Seventeenth Century Dutch Art and Life.* Syracuse, N.Y.: Syracuse University Press, 2002.

Barnet, Sylvan, ed. *The Complete Signet Classic Shakespeare.* New York: Harcourt Brace Jovanovich, 1972.

Beresford, John. *The Godfather of Downing Street: Sir George Downing, 1623–1684.* London: Cobden-Sanderson, 1925.

Bergeron, David M. *King James and Letters of Homoerotic Desire.* Iowa City: Iowa University, 1999.

Black, Robert C., III. *The Younger John Winthrop.* New York: Columbia University Press, 1966.

Blackburn, Roderic H., and Ruth Piwonka. *Remembrance of Patria: Dutch Arts and Culture in Colonial America, 1609–1776.* Albany, N.Y.: Albany Institute of History and Art, 1988.

Blakely, Allison. *Blacks in the Dutch World: The Evolution of Racial Imagery in a Modern Society.* Bloomington: Indiana University Press, 1993.

Bliss, Robert. *Revolution and Empire: English Politics and the American Colonies in the Seventeenth Century.* Manchester, U.K.: Manchester University Press, 1990.

Blom, J. C. H., and E. Lamberts, eds., James C. Kennedy, trans. *History of the Low Countries.* New York: Berghahn Books, 1999.

Bogert, Frederick W. *Bergen County, New Jersey, History and Heritage.* Vol. 2, *The Colonial Days, 1630–1775.* Bergen County, N.J.: The Bergen County Board of Chosen Freeholders, 1983.

Bonomi, Patricia U. *A Factious People: Politics and Society in Colonial New York.* New York: Columbia University Press, 1971.

———. *Under the Cope of Heaven: Religion, Society, and Politics in Colonial America.* New York: Oxford University Press, 1986.

Boxer, C. R. *The Dutch Seaborne Empire: 1600–1800.* New York: Alfred A. Knopf, 1965.

Brodhead, John Romeyn. *The History of the State of New York, 1609–1691.* 2 vols. New York: Harper & Brothers, 1871.

Burrows, Edwin G., and Mike Wallace. *Gotham: A History of New York City to 1898.* New York: Oxford University Press, 1999.

Bussman, Klaus, and Heinz Schilling. *1648: War and Peace in Europe.* 3 vols. Münster: Westfälisches Landesmuseum, 1998.

Calder, Isabel. *The New Haven Colony.* New Haven: Yale University Press, 1934.

Cantwell, Anne-Marie, and Diana diZerega Wall. *Unearthing Gotham: The Archaeology of New York City.* New Haven: Yale University Press, 2001.

Carlton, Charles. *Charles I: The Personal Monarch.* 2nd ed. London: Routledge, 1995.

Ceci, Lynn. "The Effect of European Contact and Trade on the Settlement Pattern of Indians in Coastal New York, 1524–1665: The Archaeological and Documentary Evidence." Doctoral dissertation, CUNY Graduate Center, 1977.

Chiodo, John J. "The Foreign Policy of Peter Stuyvesant: Dutch Diplomacy in North America, 1647 to 1664." Doctoral dissertation, University of Iowa, 1974.

Clarke, Desmond, ed. *The Unfortunate Husbandman: an account of the life and travels of a*

Real Farmer in Ireland, Scotland, England and America, by Charles Varley or Varlo. London: Oldbourne, 1964.

Clarke, J. S. *The Life of James the Second, King of England, &c. Collected Out of Memoirs Writ of His Own Hand.* 2 vols. London, 1816.

Cohen, David Steven. *The Dutch-American Farm.* New York: New York University Press, 1992.

Commager, Henry Steele. *Jefferson, Nationalism, and the Enlightenment.* New York: George Braziller, 1975.

Cooke, Jacob Ernest, editor in chief. *Encyclopedia of the North American Colonies.* 3 vols. New York: Charles Scribner's Sons, 1993.

Cooper, Victor. *A Dangerous Woman: New York's First Lady Liberty, The Life and Times of Lady Deborah Moody.* Bowie, Md.: Heritage, 1995.

Davids, Karel, and Jan Lucassen, eds. *A Miracle Mirrored: The Dutch Republic in European Perspective.* Cambridge: Cambridge University Press, 1995.

Davies, K. G. *The Royal African Company.* London: Routledge, 1999.

Denevan, William, ed. *The Native Population of the Americas in 1492.* Madison: University of Wisconsin Press, 1978.

Dietz, Johann. *Master Johann Dietz, Surgeon in the Army of the Great Elector and Barber to the Royal Court.* New York: Dutton, 1923.

Dodge, Ernest S. *Northwest by Sea.* New York: Oxford University Press, 1961.

Dumbauld, Edward. *The Life and Legal Writings of Hugo Grotius.* Norman: University of Oklahoma, 1969.

Dunn, Shirley. *The Mohicans and Their Land 1609–1730.* Fleischmans, N.Y.: Purple Mountain Press, 1994.

Dyer, Louisa A. *The House of Peace.* New York: Longmans, Green, 1956.

Fabend, Firth Haring. *A Dutch Family in the Middle Colonies, 1660–1800.* New Brunswick, N.J.: Rutgers University Press, 1991.

———. *Zion on the Hudson: Dutch New York and New Jersey in the Age of Revivals.* New Brunswick, N.J.: Rutgers University Press, 2000.

Feenstra, R., and C. J. D. Waal. *Seventeenth-Century Leyden Law Professors and Their Influence on the Development of the Civil Law.* Amsterdam/Oxford: North-Holland Publishing Co., 1975.

Feiling, Keith. *British Foreign Policy 1660–1672.* London: MacMillan, 1930.

Fell-Smith, Charlotte. *John Dee.* London: Constable & Co., 1909.

Fisher, Raymond H. *The Russian Fur Trade, 1550–1700.* Berkeley: University of California Press, 1943.

Foster, Stephen. *Their Solitary Way: The Puritan Social Ethic in the First Century of Settlement in New England.* New Haven: Yale University Press, 1971.

Fouquet, P. *Oud Amsterdam: Afbeeldingen der Voornaamste Gebouwen en Gezichten uit den Jare 1600–1790.* Amsterdam: Allert de Lange, 1923.

Fox, Dixon Ryan. *Yankees and Yorkers.* New York: University Press, 1940.

Fraser, Antonia. *Cromwell: The Lord Protector.* New York: Knopf, 1973.

———. *Royal Charles: Charles II and the Restoration.* New York: Dell, 1979.

Fremantle, Katherine. *The Baroque Town Hall of Amsterdam.* Utrecht: Haentjens Dekker & Gumbert, 1959.

French, Peter J. *John Dee: The World of an Elizabethan Magus.* London: Routledge & Kegan Paul, 1972.

Friedman, Lawrence. *Crime and Punishment in American History.* New York: Basic Books, 1993.

Frijhoff, Willem. *Wegen van Evert Willemsz.: Een Hollands weeskind op zoek naar zichzelf, 1607–1647.* Nijmegen: Sun, 1995.

Funk, Elisabeth Paling. "Washington Irving and the Dutch Heritage." Manuscript in progress.

Gaukroger, Stephen. *Descartes: An Intellectual Biography.* London: Clarendon Press, 1995.

Gehring, Charles T. *A Guide to Dutch Manuscripts Relating to New Netherland.* Albany: University of the State of New York, 1978.

Gerson, Armand, Earnest Vaughn, and Neva Ruth Deardorff. *Studies in the History of English Commerce During the Tudor Period.* New York: University of Pennsylvania, 1912.

Geyl, Pieter. *Orange and Stuart.* New York: Scribner's, 1969.

Goebel, Julius. *Law Enforcement in Colonial New York: A Study in Criminal Procedure.* New York: Commonwealth Fund, 1944.

Goodfriend, Joyce D. *Before the Melting Pot: Society and Culture in Colonial New York City, 1664–1730.* Princeton, N.J.: Princeton University Press, 1992.

Greenberg, Mark. *The Hague.* New York: Newsweek Books, 1982.

Gregg, Pauline. *King Charles I.* London: J.M. Dent & Sons, 1981.

Grumet, Robert Steven. *Historic Contact: Indian People and Colonists in Today's Northeastern United States in the Sixteenth Through Eighteenth Centuries.* Norman: University of Oklahoma, 1995.

———. *Native American Place Names in New York City.* New York: Museum of the City of New York, 1981.

Hainsworth, Roger, and Christine Churches. *The Anglo-Dutch Naval Wars, 1652–1674.* Gloucestershire: Sutton, 1998.

Haley, K. H. D. *The Dutch in the Seventeenth Century.* London: Thames and Hudson, 1972.

Hall, Michael, Lawrence Leder, and Michael Kammen, eds. *The Glorious Revolution in America.* Chapel Hill: University of North Carolina Press, 1964.

Harline, Craig E. *Pamphlets, Printing, and Political Culture in the Early Dutch Republic.* Dordrecht: Martinus Nijhoff, 1987.

Harrisse, Henry. *John Cabot, the Discoverer of North-America, and Sebastian His Son.* New York: Argosy-Antiquarian, 1968.

Hart, Simon. *The Prehistory of the New Netherland Company: Amsterdam Notarial Records of the First Dutch Voyages to the Hudson.* Amsterdam: City of Amsterdam Press, 1959.

Haswell, Jock. *James II, Soldier and Sailor.* New York: St. Martin's, 1972.

Heckewelder, John. *History, Manners, and Customs of the Indian Nations.* 1819. Reprint, Philadelphia: Historical Society of Pennsylvania, 1876.

Hill, Christopher. *God's Englishman: Oliver Cromwell and the English Revolution.* New York: Dial Press, 1970.

Holmes, Martin. *Elizabethan London.* New York: Frederick A. Praeger, 1969.

Hoppin, Charles Arthur. *The Washington Ancestry and Records of the McClain, Johnson, and Forty Other Colonial American Families.* 3 vols. Greenfield, Ohio: Privately Printed, 1932.

Hore, J. P. *The History of Newmarket and the Annals of the Turf.* 3 vols. London: Baily & Co., 1886.

Howarth, David. *The Men-of-War.* Alexandria, Va: Time-Life Books, 1978.

Hughes, Robert. *Culture of Complaint: The Fraying of America.* Oxford: Oxford University Press, 1993.

Huizinga, Johan. *Dutch Civilisation in the Seventeenth Century.* New York: Frederick Ungar, 1968.

Innes, J. H. *New Amsterdam and Its People: Studies, Social and Topographical, of the Town under Dutch and Early English Rule.* Princeton, N.J.: Princeton University Press, 1902.

Israel, Jonathan I. *Dutch Primacy in World Trade, 1585–1740.* Oxford: Clarendon Press, 1989.

———. *The Dutch Republic.* Oxford: Oxford University Press, 1995.

———. *Radical Enlightenment: Philosophy and the Making of Modernity, 1650–1750.* Oxford: Oxford University Press, 2001.

Jacobs, Jaap. *Een zegenrijk gewest: Nieuw-Nederland in de zeventiende eeuw.* Amsterdam: Prometheus, 1999.

Jameson, J. Franklin. *Willem Usselinx.* New York: G. P. Putnam's Sons, 1887.

Jennings, Francis. *The Ambiguous Iroquois Empire.* New York: Norton, 1984.

Johnson, Amandus. *The Swedish Settlements on the Delaware.* 2 vols. New York: University of Pennsylvania, 1911.

Johnson, Donald S. *Charting the Sea of Darkness: The Four Voyages of Henry Hudson.* New York: Kodansha America, 1995.

Jones, Charles W. *Saint Nichlas of Myra, Bari, and Manhattan: Biography of a Legend.* Chicago: University of Chicago, 1978.

Jordan, Terry, and Matti Kaups. *The American Backwoods Frontier: An Ethnic and Ecological Interpretation.* Baltimore and London: The Johns Hopkins University Press, 1989.

Kammen, Michael. *Colonial New York.* New York: Scribner's, 1975.

Keblusek, Marika. *Boeken in de hofstad: Haagse boekcultuur in de Gouden Eeuw.* Hilversum, Netherlands: Verloren, 1997.

Kenney, Alice P. *Stubborn for Liberty: The Dutch in New York.* Syracuse, N.Y.: Syracuse University Press, 1975.

Kenyon, J. P. *The Stuarts: A Study in English Kingship.* London: Severn House, 1977.

Kessler, Henry H., and Eugene Rachlis. *Peter Stuyvesant and His New York.* New York: Random House, 1959.

Kettering, Alison McNeil. *Gerard ter Borch and the Treaty of Münster.* The Hague: Mauritshuis, 1998.

King, J. C. H. *First People, First Contacts: Native Peoples of North America.* London: British Museum, 1999.

Kishlansky, Mark. *A Monarchy Transformed: Britain 1603–1714.* New York: Penguin, 1997.

Klooster, Wim. *The Dutch in the Americas, 1600–1800.* Providence, R.I.: The John Carter Brown Library, 1997.

Koolhaas, Rem. *Delirious New York: A Retroactive Manifesto for Manhattan.* Rotterdam: 010 Publishers, 1994.

Kossmann, E. F. *De boekhandel te 's-Gravenhage tot het eind van de 18de eeuw.* 'S-Gravenhage: M. Nijhoff, 1937.

Kupperman, Karen Ordahl, ed. *America in European Consciousness, 1493–1750.* Chapel Hill: University of North Carolina, 1995.

———. *Indians and English: Facing Off in Early America.* Ithaca: Cornell University Press, 2000.

Kurlansky, Mark. *Cod: A Biography of the Fish that Changed the World.* New York: Walker & Co., 1997.

Lane, Kris E. *Pillaging the Empire: Piracy in the Americas 1500–1750.* Armonk, N.Y.: Sharpe, 1998.

Lees, J. Cameron. *St. Giles', Edinburgh: Church, College, and Cathedral, From the Earliest Times to the Present Day.* Edinburgh: Chambers, 1889.

Leonardo, Richard A. *History of Surgery.* New York: Froben Press, 1943.

Loades, David. *The Mid-Tudor Crisis, 1545–1565.* London: Macmillan, 1992.

Lyle, R. C. *Royal Newmarket.* London: Putnam & Co., 1945.

Macleod, John. *Dynasty: The Stuarts, 1560–1807*. New York: St. Martin's, 1999.

McCullough, David. *John Adams*. New York: Simon & Schuster, 2001.

Maika, Dennis J. "Commerce and Community: Manhattan Merchants in the Seventeenth Century." Doctoral dissertation, New York University, 1995.

Mak, Geert. *Amsterdam*. Cambridge: Harvard University Press, 2000.

Mattingly, Garrett. *The Armada*. Boston: Houghton Mifflin, 1959.

Meinig, D. W. *The Shaping of America, A Geographical Perspective on 500 Years of History*. Vol. I: *Atlantic America, 1492–1800*. New Haven: Yale University Press, 1986.

Merwick, Donna. *Death of a Notary: Conquest and Change in Colonial New York*. Ithaca: Cornell University Press, 1999.

Miller, Leo. *John Milton's Writings in the Anglo-Dutch Negotiations, 1651–1654*. Pittsburgh: Duquesne University Press, 1992.

Milton, Giles. *Nathaniel's Nutmeg*. London: Hodder & Stoughton, 1999.

Morgan, Edmund S. *The Puritan Dilemma: The Story of John Winthrop*. Boston: Little, Brown, 1958.

Morison, Samuel Eliot. *The European Discovery of America*. 2 vols. New York: Oxford University Press, 1971–1974.

———. *The Founding of Harvard College*. Cambridge: Harvard University Press, 1935.

———. *The Great Explorers*. New York: Oxford University Press, 1978.

Morison, Samuel Eliot, Henry Steele Commager, and William E. Leuchtenburg. *The Growth of the American Republic*, 7th ed. Vol. 1. New York: Oxford University Press, 1980.

Murphy, Henry Cruse. *Henry Hudson in Holland*. The Hague: M. Nijhoff, 1909.

Murray, David. *Indian Giving: Economics of Power in Indian-White Exchanges*. Amherst: University of Massachusetts, 2000.

Nelson, Paul David. *William Tryon and the Course of Empire*. Chapel Hill: University of North Carolina, 1990.

Nissenson, S. G. *The Patroon's Domain*. New York: Columbia University Press, 1937.

Nute, Grace Lee. *Caesars of the Wilderness: Medard Chouart, Sieur des Grosselliers and Pierre Esprit Radisson, 1618–1710*. St. Paul: Minnesota Historical Society Press, 1978.

O'Callaghan, E. B. *The History of New Netherland*. 2 vols. New York: D. Appleton, 1848.

———. *The Register of New Netherland, 1626 to 1674*. Albany, N.Y.: J. Munsell, 1865.

Otterspeer, Willem. *Groepsportret met Dame*. Amsterdam: Bert Bakker, 2000.

Parks, George Bruner. *Richard Hakluyt and the English Voyages*. New York: American Geographical Society, 1928.

Parr, Charles McKew. *The Voyages of David de Vries, Navigator and Adventurer*. New York: Thomas Y. Crowell Co., 1969.

Patterson, Jerry E. *The City of New York: A History Illustrated from the Collections of the Museum of the City of New York*. New York: Harry N. Abrams, 1978.

Phipps, Geraldine M. *Sir John Merrick: English Merchant-Diplomat in Seventeenth Century Russia*. Newtonville, Mass.: Oriental Research Partners, 1983.

Powys, Llewelyn. *Henry Hudson*. New York: Harper & Brothers, 1928.

Price, J. L. *Holland and the Dutch Republic in the Seventeenth Century: The Politics of Particularism*. Oxford: Clarendon Press, 1994.

Quinn, Arthur. *A New World: An Epic of Colonial America from the Founding of Jamestown to the Fall of Quebec*. Winchester, Mass.: Faber and Faber, 1994.

Quinn, David B., and A. N. Ryan. *England's Sea Empire, 1550–1642*. London: Allen & Unwin, 1983.

Read, Conyers. *Mr. Secretary Walsingham and the Policy of Queen Elizabeth*. 3 vols. Cambridge: Harvard University Press, 1925.

Read, John Meredith, Jr. *A Historical Inquiry Concerning Henry Hudson, His Friends, Relatives, and Early Life, His Connection with the Muscovy Company, and Discovery of Delaware Bay.* Albany, N.Y.: John Munsell, 1866.

Regin, Deric. *Traders, Artists, Burghers: A Cultural History of Amsterdam in the 17th-Century.* Amsterdam: Van Gorcum & Comp. B. V., 1976.

Reich, Jerome R. *Leisler's Rebellion: A Study of Democracy in New York, 1664–1720.* Chicago: Chicago University Press, 1953.

Renaud, J. G. N. *Het Huis en de Heren van Heemstede Tijdens de Middeleeuwen.* Heemstede: Vereniging Oud-Heemstede-Bennebroek, 1952.

Ricciardi, Christopher. "From Private to Public: The Changing Landscape of Van Cortlandt Park; Bronx, New York, in the Nineteenth Century." Masters thesis, Syracuse University, 1997.

Reitbergen, P. J. A. N. *A Short History of the Netherlands.* Amersfoort, Netherlands: Bekking, 1998.

Riker, James. *Revised History of Harlem: Its Origin and Early Annals.* New York: New Harlem Publishing Co., 1904.

Rink, Oliver. *Holland on the Hudson: An Economic and Social History of Dutch New York.* Ithaca: Cornell University Press, 1986.

Ritchie, Robert C. *The Duke's Province: A Study of New York Politics and Society, 1664–1691.* Chapel Hill: University of North Carolina Press, 1977.

Rogers, P. G. *The Dutch in the Medway.* London: Oxford University Press, 1970.

Rose, Peter G. *The Sensible Cook: Dutch Foodways in the Old and New World.* Syracuse, N.Y.: Syracuse University Press, 1989.

Rothschild, Nan. *New York City Neighborhoods: The 18th Century.* San Diego: Academic Press, 1990.

Rowen, Herbert H. *John de Witt, Grand Pensionary of Holland, 1625–1672.* Princeton, N.J.: Princeton University Press, 1978.

———. *John de Witt: Statesman of the "True Freedom."* Cambridge: Cambridge University Press, 1986.

———. *The Princes of Orange: The Stadholders in the Dutch Republic.* Cambridge: Cambridge University Press, 1988.

Royal Netherlands Academy of Arts and Sciences. *The World of Hugo Grotius (1583–1645). Proceedings of the International Colloquium Organized by the Grotius Committee.* Amsterdam: APA-Holland University Press, 1984.

Russell, Bertrand. *A History of Western Philosophy.* London: George Allen and Unwin, 1946.

Rutkow, Ira M. *Surgery: An Illustrated History.* St. Louis: Mosby, 1993.

Ruttenber, E. M. *Indian Tribes of Hudson's River to 1700.* 1872. Reprint: Saugerties, N.Y.: Hope Farm Press, 1992.

Rybczynski, Witold. *Home: A Short History of an Idea.* New York: Viking, 1986.

Savelle, Max. *The Colonial Origins of American Thought.* Princeton, N. J.: Van Nostrand, 1964.

Schama, Simon. *The Embarrassment of Riches: An Interpretation of Dutch Culture in the Golden Age.* New York: Knopf, 1987.

Scharf, J. Thomas. *The History of Westchester County.* Philadelphia: Preston, 1886.

Schechter, Stephen L., and Richard B. Bernstein, eds. *New York and the Union.* Albany: New York State Commission on the Bicentennial of the United States Constitution, 1990.

Scheurleer, T. H. Lunsingh, and G. H. M. Posthumus Meyjes. *Leiden University in the Seventeenth Century.* Leiden: Universitaire Pers Leiden, 1975.

Schmidt, Benjamin. "Innocence Abroad: The Dutch Imagination and the Representation of the New World, c. 1570–1670." Doctoral dissertation, Harvard University, 1994.

Shattuck, Martha. "A Civil Society: Court and Community in Beverwijck, New Netherland, 1652–1664." Doctoral dissertation, Boston University, 1993.

Shonnard, Frederic. *History of Westchester County, New York, from its earliest settlement to the year 1900.* Harrison, N.Y.: Harbor Hill, 1974.

Siefker, Phyllis. *Santa Claus, Last of the Wild Men.* Jefferson, N.C.: McFarland, 1997.

Simmons, Amelia. *American Cookery.* Albany, N.Y.: Charles & George Webster, 1796.

Sobel, Dava. *Galileo's Daughter: A Historical Memoir of Science, Faith, and Love.* New York: Walker, 1999.

Spencer, Hazelton. *The Art and Life of William Shakespeare.* New York: Harcourt, Brace, 1940.

Sprunger, Keith L. *Trumpets from the Tower: English Puritan Printing in the Netherlands, 1600–1640.* Leiden: E. J. Brill, 1994.

Stephanson, Anders. *Manifest Destiny: American Expansion and the Empire of Right.* New York: Hill and Wang, 1995.

Sweetman, Jack. *The Great Admirals: Command at Sea, 1587–1945.* Annapolis, Md.: Naval Institute Press, 1997.

Sykes, Bryan. *The Seven Daughters of Eve: The Science That Reveals Our Genetic Ancestry.* New York: Norton, 2001.

Tantillo, L. F. *Visions of New York State: The Historical Paintings of L. F. Tantillo.* Wappingers Falls, N.Y.: The Shawangunk Press, 1996.

Taylor, E. G. R. *Tudor Geography.* New York: Octagon, 1968.

Thompson, Benjamin F. *History of Long Island: From Its Discovery and Settlement to the Present Time.* 3 vols. New York: Dodd, 1918.

Thornton, Russell. *American Indian Holocaust and Survival: Population History Since 1492.* Norman: University of Oklahoma, 1987.

Tieck, William. *Riverdale, Kingsbridge, Spuyten Duyvil: New York City; a Historical Epitome of the Northwest Bronx.* Old Tappan, N.J.: F. H. Revell Co., 1968.

Trudel, Marcel. *The Beginnings of New France 1524–1663.* Toronto, Ontario: McClelland and Stewart, 1973.

Tuchman, Barbara W. *The First Salute.* New York: Knopf, 1988.

Tuck, Richard. *Philosophy and Government, 1572–1651.* Cambridge: Cambridge University Press, 1993.

Tuckerman, Bayard. *Peter Stuyvesant, Director-General for the West India Company in New Netherland.* New York: Dodd, Mead, 1893.

Vaille, F. O., and H. A. Clarke, eds. *The Harvard Book, A Series of Historical, Biographical, and Descriptive Sketches, by Various Authors.* Cambridge, Mass.: Welch, Bigelow, 1875.

Van den Boogaart, E., ed. *Johan Maurits Van Nassau-Siegen, 1604–1679: A Humanist Prince in Europe and Brazil.* The Hague: The Johan Maurits van Nassau Stichting, 1979.

Van Den Brink, Herman. *The Charm of Legal History.* Amsterdam: Adolf M. Hakkert, 1974.

Van Deursen, A. T. *Plain Lives in a Golden Age: Popular Culture, Religion and Society in Seventeenth-Century Holland.* Cambridge: Cambridge University Press, 1991.

Van Gastel, Ada Louise. "Adriaen Van der Donck, New Netherland, and America." Doctoral dissertation, University of Pennsylvania, 1985.

Van Gelder, H. E. *'S-Gravenhage in Zeven Eeuwen.* Amsterdam: Meulenhoff, 1937.

Van Nierop, H. F. K. *The Nobility of Holland: From Knights to Regents, 1500–1650.* Cambridge: Cambridge University Press, 1993.

Van Rensselaer, Mariana G. *History of the City of New York in the Seventeenth Century*. 2 vols. New York: Macmillan Company, 1909.

Venema, Janny. "Beverwijck: A Dutch Village on the American Frontier, 1652–1664." Doctoral dissertation, Vrije Universiteit Amsterdam, 2003.

Vigne, Randolph, and Charles Littleton, eds. *From Strangers to Citizens: The Integration of Immigrant Communities in Britain, Ireland and Colonial America, 1550–1750*. Portland, Ore.: Sussex Academic Press, 2001.

Vinckeboons, Joan, Gunter Schilder, and Jan van Bracht. *The Origins of New York*. Zurich: Edition Seefeld, 1988.

Voorhees, David William. *The Holland Society: A Centennial History 1885–1985*. New York: The Holland Society, 1985.

Wagman, Morton. "The Struggle for Representative Government in New Netherland." Doctoral dissertation, Columbia University, 1969.

Wedgwood, C. V. *The Political Career of Peter Paul Rubens*. London: Thames and Hudson, 1975.

Wertenbaker, Thomas Jefferson. *The Puritan Oligarchy: The Founding of American Civilization*. New York: Scribner's, 1947.

Weslager, C. A., *A Man and His Ship: Peter Minuit and the Kalmar Nyckel*. Wilmington, Del.: Kalmar Nyckel Foundation, 1989.

Weslager, C. A., with A. R. Dunlap. *Dutch Explorers, Traders and Settlers in the Delaware Valley, 1609–1664*. Philadelphia: University of Pennsylvania Press, 1961.

Wessels, J. W. *History of the Roman-Dutch Law*. Grahamstown, Cape Colony: African Book Company, 1908.

White, Christopher. *Rembrandt*. London: Thames and Hudson, 1984.

Willan, T. S. *The Muscovy Merchants of 1555*. Manchester, Eng.: Manchester University Press, 1953.

Williams, Bernard. *Descartes: The Project of Pure Enquiry*. New York: Penguin, 1978.

Williams, Selma R. *Divine Rebel: The Life of Anne Marbury Hutchinson*. New York: Holt, Rinehart and Winston, 1981.

Williamson, James A. *The Age of Drake*. 5th ed. London: Adam & Charles Black, 1965.

Wilstach, Paul. *Hudson River Landings*. New York: Tudor Publishing, 1933.

Zandvliet, Kees. *Mapping for Money: Maps, Plans, and Topographic Paintings and their Role in Dutch Overseas Expansion During the 16th and 17th Centuries*. Amsterdam: Batavian Lion International, 1998.

Zuckert, Michael P. *Natural Rights and the New Republicanism*. Princeton, N.J.: Princeton University Press, 1994.

Zumthor, Paul. *Daily Life in Rembrandt's Holland*. New York: Macmillan, 1963.

ARTICLES, TALKS, ADDRESSES, REPORTS

Atkins, T. Astley. "Adriaen Van der Donck: An Address Delivered Before the Westchester Historical Society," Yonkers, New York, 1888.

Andrade, Manuel Correia de. "The Socio-Economic Geography of Dutch Brazil." In E. Van den Boogaart, ed. *Johan Maurits Van Nassau-Siegen, 1604–1679: A Humanist Prince in Europe and Brazil*. The Hague: The Johan Maurits van Nassau Stichting, 1979.

Bankoff, H. Arthur, Frederick A. Winter, and Christopher Ricciardi. "Archaeological Excavations at Van Cortlandt Park, the Bronx, 1990–1992." Report on file with the New York City Landmarks Preservation Commission.

Banner, Stuart. "Manhattan for $24: American Indian Land Sales, 1607–1763." Paper presented to the Law and Economics Workshop, John M. Olin Center for Law and Economics, University of Michigan Law School, October 25, 2001.

Barry, Dave. "A Certified Wacko Rewrites History's Greatest Hits." *Milwaukee Journal-Sentinel,* December 26, 1999.

Becker, Alfred. "Mr. Adriaen Van der Donck, the Earliest Lawyer in New York." *New York State Bar Association Report* 27 (1904).

Beier, A. L. "Vagrants and the Social Order in Elizabethan England" *Past and Present* 64 (August 1974).

Berlin, Ira. "From Creole to African: Atlantic Creoles and the Origins of African-American Society in Mainland North America." *William and Mary Quarterly* 53 (April 1996).

Bodle, Wayne. "Themes and Directions in Middle Colonies Historiography, 1980–1994." *William and Mary Quarterly* 51 (July 1994).

Bonomi, Patricia U. "The Middle Colonies: Embryo of the New Political Order." In Alden T. Vaughan and George Athan Billias, eds., *Perspectives on Early American History.* New York: Harper & Row, 1973.

Browner, Jessica A. "Wrong Side of the River: London's disreputable South Bank in the sixteenth and seventeenth century." *Essays in History* 36 (1994).

Christoph, Peter R. "The Freedmen of New Amsterdam." *Journal of the Afro-American Historical Society* 5, nos. 3 and 4 (1984).

———. "Story of the New Netherland Project." *de Halve Maen* (September 1988).

Cohen, David. "How Dutch Were the Dutch of New Netherland?" *New York History* 62 (1981): 43–60.

Cohen, Ronald D. "The Hartford Treaty of 1650: Anglo-Dutch Cooperation in the Seventeenth Century." *New-York Historical Society Quarterly* (October 1969).

de Koning, Joep. "From Van der Donck to Visscher." *Mercator's World* 5, no. 4 (July/August 2000).

———. "Make Governors Island a Beacon of History." *New York Newsday,* May 24, 2001.

Dunn, Shirley, "Enlarging Rensselaerswijck: 17th Century Land Acquisition on the East Side of the River." In Nancy Anne McClure Zeller, ed. *A Beautiful and Fruitful Place: Selected Rensselaerswijck Seminar Papers.* Albany, N.Y.: New Netherland Publishing, 1991.

Fabend, Firth Haring. "The Pro-Leislerian Dutch Farmers in New York: A 'Mad Rabble,' or 'Gentlemen Standing Up for Their Rights'?" *de Halve Maen,* 63 (March 1990).

———. "What Historians Really Know About New York's History." Talk prepared for the Annual Meeting, Friends of New Netherland, January 22, 2000.

———. "Church and State, Hand in Hand: Compassionate Calvinism in New Netherland." *de Halve Maen* 75 (Spring 2002).

Finkelman, Paul. "The Soul and the State: Religious Freedom in New York and the Origin of the First Amendment." In Stephen L. Schechter and Richard B. Bernstein, eds. *New York and the Union.* Albany: New York State Commission on the Bicentennial of the United States Constitution, 1990.

Fockema Andreae, S. J. "Data on the Dutch Background of Peter Stuyvesant." *de Halve Maen* 39 (January 1964).

Freyre, G. "Johan Maurits Van Nassau-Siegen from a Brazilian Viewpoint." In E. Van den Boogaart, ed. *Johan Maurits Van Nassau-Siegen, 1604–1679: A Humanist Prince in Europe and Brazil.* The Hague: The Johan Maurits van Nassau Stichting, 1979.

Frijhoff, Willem. "Dominee Bogardus als Nieuw-Nederlander," *Jaarboek van het Central Bureau voor Genealogie.* Den Haag: Central Bureau voor Genealogie, 1996.

———. "Identity Achievement, Education, and Social Legitimation in Early Modern Dutch Society: The Case of Evert Willemsz (1622–23)." International Symposium in Europe, Netherlands, 1999.

———. "Neglected Networks: New Netherlanders and Their Old Fatherland—The Kieft Case." Paper delivered at the 2001 Rensselaerswijck Seminar in New York City.

———. "New Views on the Dutch Period of New York," *de Halve Maen* 70 (Fall 1997).

Gehrhardt, Volcker. "On the Historical Significance of the Peace of Westphalia: Twelve Theses." In Klaus Bussman and Heinz Schilling. *1648: War and Peace in Europe*. 3 vols. Münster: Westfälisches Landesmuseum, 1998.

Gehring, Charles. "The Founding of Beverwijck, a Dutch Village on the Upper Hudson." *Dutch Settlers Society of Albany Yearbook* 51 (1989–1993).

———. *"Hodie Mihi, Cras Tibi:* Swedish-Dutch Relations in the Delaware Valley." In Carol E. Hoffecker, Richard Waldron, Lorraine E. Williams, and Barbara E. Benson, *New Sweden in America*. Newark: University of Delaware, 1995.

———. "New Netherland—Translating New York's Dutch Past." *Humanities* 14 (November-December 1993).

———. "New Netherland Manuscripts in United States Repositories." *de Halve Maen* 57 (August 1983).

———. "Totidem Verbis." *De Nieu Nederlanse Marcurius* 4 (1988).

———. "Wringing Information from a Drowned Princess." Paper presented to the Rensselaerswijck Seminar, Albany, New York, 1994.

Goodfriend, Joyce D. "The Dutch in 17th-Century New York City: Minority or Majority?" In Randolph Vigne and Charles Littleton, eds. *From Strangers to Citizens: The Integration of Immigrant Communities in Britain, Ireland and Colonial America, 1550–1750*. Portland, Ore.: Sussex Academic Press, 2001.

———. "New Netherland in the Atlantic World: Comments and Reflections." *de Halve Maen* 70 (Winter 1997).

———. "The Sabbath Keeper." *Seaport* (Fall 2001).

———. "Writing/Righting Dutch Colonial History," *New York History* (January 1999).

Goosens, Eymert-Jan. "Monuments to Peace in the Netherlands." In Klaus Bussman and Heinz Schilling. *1648: War and Peace in Europe*. 3 vols. Münster: Westfälisches Landesmuseum, 1998.

Gray, Albert. "An Address on the Occasion of the Tercentenary of the Death of Richard Hakluyt." London: The Hakluyt Society, 1917.

Groenveld, Simon. "New Light on a Drowned Princess—Information from London." *de Halve Maen* 74 (Summer 2001).

Grumet, Robert S. "Hunting Indian History," "Trade, War and Diplomacy," "The English Imprint," "Survival of the Fittest," "The Diaspora." Series published in *Hudson Valley* (January-June 1991).

Guerra, F. "Medicine in Dutch Brazil." In E. Van den Boogaart, ed. *Johan Maurits Van Nassau-Siegen, 1604–1679: A Humanist Prince in Europe and Brazil*. The Hague: The Johan Maurits van Nassau Stichting, 1979.

Heck, Earl Leon. "A Sketch of Adriaen Van der Donck: Colonizer, Statesman and First Historian of Early New York." Unpublished typescript presented to the New York State Library, Albany, 1960.

Hershkowitz, Leo. "New Amsterdam's Twenty-Three Jews—Myth or Reality?" In Shalom Goldman, ed., *Hebrew and the Bible in America: The First Two Centuries*. Hanover, N.H.: Brandeis University Press, 1993.

————. "The New York City Charter, 1686." In *Roots of the Republic: American Founding Documents Interpreted*. Madison, Wis.: Madison House, 1990.

————. "The Troublesome Turk: An Illustration of Judicial Process in New Amsterdam." *New York History* vol. 46, no. 4 (October 1965).

Hoetink, H. R. "Some Remarks on the Modernity of Johan Maurits." in E. Van den Boogaart, ed. *Johan Maurits Van Nassau-Siegen, 1604–1679: A Humanist Prince in Europe and Brazil*. The Hague: The Johan Maurits van Nassau Stichting, 1979.

Hoffman, William. "Van der Donck-Van Bergen." *New York Genealogical and Biographical Record* 67. New York: New York Genealogical and Biographical Society, 1936.

Hopkins, Vivian C. "The Dutch Records of New York: Francis Adrian Van Der Kemp and De Witt Clinton." *New York History* (October 1962).

Howard, Ronald. "John Romeyn Brodhead." *Dictionary of Literary Biography* 30 (1984).

Hutchinson, William R. "Diversity and the Pluralist Ideal." In William Peter, ed., *Perspectives on American Religion and Culture*. Malden, Mass.: Blackwell, 1999.

Israel, Jonathan I. "Art and Diplomacy: Gerard Ter Borch and the Münster Peace Negotiations, 1646–8." In Jonathan I. Israel, *Conflicts of Empires: Spain, the Low Countries and the Struggle for World Supremacy, 1585–1713*. London: The Hambledon Press, 1997.

————. "The Dutch Role in the Glorious Revolution." In Jonathan I. Israel, ed., *The Anglo-Dutch Moment*. Cambridge: Cambridge University Press, 1991.

————. "The Intellectual Debate About Toleration in the Dutch Republic." In C. Berkvens-Stevelinck, J. Israel, and G. H. M. Posthumus Meyjes, eds., *The Emergence of Tolerance in the Dutch Republic*. Leiden: Brill, 1997.

————. "Toleration in Seventeenth-Century Dutch and English Thought." In Jonathan I. Israel, *Conflicts of Empires: Spain, the Low Countries and the Struggle for World Supremacy, 1585–1713*. London: The Hambledon Press, 1997.

Jacobs, Jaap. "Between Repression and Approval: Connivance and Tolerance in the Dutch Republic and in New Netherland." *de Halve Maen* 71 (Fall 1998).

————. "The Hartford Treaty: A European Perspective on a New World Conflict." *de Halve Maen* 68 (Winter 1995).

————. "A Hitherto Unknown Letter of Adriaen van der Donck." *de Halve Maen* 71 (Spring 1998).

————. "A Troubled Man: Director Wouter van Twiller and the Affairs of New Netherland in 1635." Paper presented at the Conference on New York State History, Bard College, Annandale-on-Hudson, New York, June 6, 2001.

Jordan, Terry G. "The Material Cultural Legacy of New Sweden on the American Frontier." In Carol E. Hoffecker, Richard Waldron, Lorraine E. Williams, and Barbara E. Benson, *New Sweden in America*. Newark: University of Delaware, 1995.

Kielty, Bernardine. "The Sidewalks of New York." Pamphlet published for the Bowman Hotels by the Little Leather Library Corporation, New York, 1923.

Klein, Milton M. "Origins of the Bill of Rights in Colonial New York," *New York History* (October 1991).

Klever, Wim. "Conflicting 'Considerations of State'. Van den Enden's Opposition Against de la Court's Aristocratic Republicanism and Its Follow-Up in Spinoza's Work," *Foglio Spinoziano* (online journal), no. 17 (2001).

Klooster, Wim. "Winds of Change: Colonization, Commerce, and Consolidation in the Seventeenth-Century Atlantic World." *de Halve Maen* 70, no. 3 (Fall 1997).

Koot, Christian. "In Pursuit of Profit: The Netherlands' Trade in Colonial New York, 1664–1688. Paper presented at the Conference on New York City History, CUNY Graduate Center, October 2001.

Kress, Jack. "Progress and Prosecution." *Annals of the American Academy of Political and Social Sciences* 423 (1976).

Kross, Jessica. "The Dutch and the English in New York," *Journal of Urban History* 21 (1994).

Kupp, Jan. "Dutch Notarial Acts Relating to the Tobacco Trade of Virginia, 1608–1653." *William and Mary Quarterly* 30 (October 1973).

Kupperman, Karen Ordahl. "Early American History with the Dutch Put In." *Reviews in American History* 21 (1993).

Lovejoy, David S. "Equality and Empire: The New York Charter of Libertyes, 1683." *William and Mary Quarterly* 21 (1964).

Lucas, Stephen E. "The *Plakkaat van Verlatinge:* A Neglected Model for the American Declaration of Independence." In Rosemarijn Hoefte and Johanna C. Kardux, *Connecting Cultures: The Netherlands in Five Centuries of Translatlantic Exchange.* Amsterdam: VU University Press, 1994.

Macdonald, Robert R. "The City of New Amsterdam Located on the Island of Manhattan in New Netherland." Museum of the City of New York website (www.mcny.org), n.d.

McNaughton, Douglas. "The Ghost of Henry Hudson." *Mercator's World* (May–June 1999).

Martinez, Andrès. "Editorial Observer—Translating New York's History into English." Editorial, *New York Times,* August 7, 2001.

Martinez, Jeanette. "New Netherland Documentary Projects." *de Halve Maen* 66 (Spring 1993).

Matson, Cathy. "Damned Scoundrels' and 'Libertisme of Trade': Freedom and Regulation in Colonial New York's Fur and Grain Trades." *William and Mary Quarterly* 51 (July 1994).

Middleton, Simon. "Artisans and Trade Privileges in New Amsterdam." Paper presented at the Rensselaerswijck Seminar, New York City, 2001.

———. "How it came that the bakers bake no bread: A Struggle for Trade Privileges in Seventeenth-Century New Amsterdam." *William and Mary Quarterly* 58 (April 2001).

Mout, M. E. H. N. "Limits and Debates: A Comparative View of Dutch Toleration in the Sixteenth and Early Seventeenth Centuries." In C. Berkvens-Stevelinck, J. Israel, and G. H. M. Posthumus Meyjes, eds., *The Emergence of Tolerance in the Dutch Republic.* Leiden: Brill, 1997.

Mowat, Barbara. "Prospero's Book." *Shakespeare Quarterly* 52, no. 1 (2001).

Murrin, John. "English Rights as Ethnic Aggression: The English Conquest, the Charter of Liberties of 1683, and Leisler's Rebellion in New York." In William Pencak and Conrad Wright, eds., *Authority and Resistance in Early New York.* New York: New-York Historical Society, 1988.

———. "The New York Charter of Liberties, 1683 and 1691." In Stephen Schechter, ed., *Roots of the Republic: American Founding Documents Interpreted.* Madison, Wis.: Madison House, 1990.

New York City Landmarks Preservation Commission. "Street Plan of New Amsterdam and Colonial New York." Report number LP-1235, June 14, 1983.

———. "Van Cortlandt Mansion." Report number LP-0890, July 22, 1975.

Newark *Daily Advertiser,* December 6, 1850.

Page, Willie F. "By Reason of Their Colour: Africans in New Netherland, 1626–1674." *de Halve Maen* 71 (Winter 1998).

Pennington, John. "An Examination of Beauchamp Plantagenet's Description of the Province of New Albion." In *Memoirs of the Historical Society of Pennsylvania* 4, Part I. Philadelphia: McArty & Davis, 1840.

Pentikainen, Juha. "The Forest Finns as Transmitters of Finnish Culture from Savo Via Central Scandinavia to Delaware." In Carol E. Hoffecker, Richard Waldron, Lorraine E. Williams, and Barbara E. Benson, *New Sweden in America*. Newark: University of Delaware, 1995.

Plantenga, Bart, "The Mystery of the Plockhoy Settlement in the Valley of Swans," *Mennonite Historical Bulletin* (April 2001).

Postma, Johannes. "A Monopoly Relinquished: The West India Company and the Atlantic Slave Trade." *de Halve Maen* 70 (Winter 1997).

Quinn, Doris C. "Theft of the Manhattans." *de Halve Maen* 66 (Summer 1993).

Reiss, A. J. "Public Prosecutors and Criminal Prosecution in the United States of America." *Juridical Review* (April 1975).

Riker, David M. "Govert Loockermans: Free Merchant of New Amsterdam." *de Halve Maen* 62 (September 1989).

Rink, Oliver A. "Unraveling a Secret Colonialism." *de Halve Maen* 59, 60 (Spring and Summer 1987).

Rosenblatt, Betsy L. "New York State's Role in the Creation and Adoption of the Bill of Rights." *New York History* (October 1991).

Rothschild, Nan A., and Arnold Pickman. *The Archaeological Excavations on the Seven Hanover Square Block.* Report on file with the New York City Landmarks Preservation Commission, 1990.

Rothschild, Nan A., Diana diZerega Wall, and Eugene Boesch. *The Archaeological Investigation of the Stadt Huys Block: A Final Report.* Report on file at the New York City Landmarks Preservation Commission, 1987.

Rothschild, Nan A., and Christopher N. Matthews. *Phase 1A–1B Archaeological Investigation of the Proposed Area for the Construction of Six Tennis Courts on the Parade Grounds of Van Cortlandt Park, the Bronx, New York.* Report submitted to the City of New York Department of Parks and Recreation, n.d.

Rowen, Herbert. "The Revolution that Wasn't: The *Coup d'Etat* of 1650 in Holland." In Craig E. Harline, ed., *The Rhyme and Reason of Politics in Early Modern Europe: Collected Essays of Herbert H. Rowen.* Kluwer Academic Publishers, Dordrecht, the Netherlands, 1992.

Rozell, Ned. "Sea Ice Reduction May Be Another Climate Change Clue." *Alaska Science Forum,* Article 1255 (October 5, 1995).

Schmidt, Benjamin. "Mapping an Empire: Cartographic and Colonial Rivalry in Seventeenth-Century Dutch and English North America." *William and Mary Quarterly* 54 (1997).

Shattuck, Martha Dickinson. "The Dutch and the English on Long Island: An Uneasy Alliance." *de Halve Maen* 68 (Winter 1995).

Sieber, Harry. "The Magnificent Fountain: Literary Patronage in the Court of Philip III." *Cervantes: Bulletin of the Cervantes Society of America* 18.2 (1998).

Swan, Robert J. "The Black Presence in Seventeenth-Century Brooklyn." *de Halve Maen* 63 (Winter 1990).

Tanis, James R. "The Dutch-American Connection: The Impact of 'The Dutch Example' on American Constitutional Beginnings." In Stephen L. Schechter and Richard B. Bernstein, eds. *New York and the Union.* Albany: New York State Commission on the Bicentennial of the United States Constitution, 1990.

Trebor, Haynes. "The Flushing Remonstrance." Pamphlet commissioned by Bowne House, Flushing, New York, 1957.

Tvengsberg, Per Martin. "Finns in Seventeenth-Century Sweden and Their Contributions to the New Sweden Colony." In Carol E. Hoffecker, Richard Waldron, Lorraine E.

Williams, and Barbara E. Benson, *New Sweden in America*. Newark: University of Delaware, 1995.

Uhlenbeck, J. D. "Genealogie van het geslacht Farret." *De Nederlandsche Leeuw* 55 (1937).

United States Fish and Wildlife Service, Southern New England–New York Bight Coastal Ecosystems Program. "Significant Habitats and Habitat Complexes of the New York Bight Watershed." Charlestown, R.I., 1997.

Van Alstyne, Jr., W. Scott. "The District Attorney—An Historical Puzzle." *Wisconsin Law Review* (January 1952).

Van den Boogaart, Ernst. "The Servant Migration to New Netherland, 1624–1664." In P. C. Emmer, ed., *Colonialism and Migration; Indentured Labour Before and After Slavery*. Dordrecht: Martinus Nijhoff, 1986.

Van Gastel, Ada. "Adriaen van der Donck als woordvoerder van de Nieuw-Nederlandse bevolking," *Jaarboek van het Central Bureau voor Genealogie*. Den Haag: Central Bureau voor Genealogie, 1996.

———. "Adriaen van der Donck in Rensselaerswyck: 1641–1643." *de Halve Maen* 60 (Winter 1987).

———. "Van der Donck's Description of the Indians: Additions and Corrections." *William and Mary Quarterly* (July 1990).

Van Hoevenberg, Alma R. "The Stuyvesants in the Netherlands and New Netherland." *The New-York Historical Society Quarterly Bulletin* 10 (April 1926).

Van Laer, A. J. F. "Annals of New Netherland: The Essays of A. J. F. Van Laer," edited and annotated by Charles Gehring. Pamphlet published in Albany, New York: New Netherland Project, 1999.

———. "The Translation and Publication of the Manuscript Dutch Records of New Netherland, with an Account of Previous Attempts at Translation." Pamphlet printed in Albany: University of the State of New York, 1910.

Van Winkle, Edward. "The Stuyvesant Family Bible." *The New-York Historical Society Quarterly Bulletin* 18 (April 1934).

Van Zandt, Cynthia J. " '. . . our river savages . . . betook themselves (unknown to us) and went to Manhattan City, in New Holland, to exact revenge on our behalf': Cross-Cultural and Multi-Ethnic Alliances in the 17th Century Mid-Atlantic." Paper presented to the American Historical Association Annual Meeting, January 10, 1998.

Van Zwieten, Adriana. "On Her Woman's Troth: Tolerance, Custom, and the Women of New Netherland." *de Halve Maen* 72 (Spring 1999).

Venema, Janny. "The Court Case of Brant Aertsz van Slichtenhorst Against Jan van Rensselaer." *de Halve Maen*, 74 (Spring 2001).

Voorhees, David William. "The 1657 Flushing Remonstrance in Historical Perspective." Remarks delivered at the Unveiling Ceremonies of the Flushing Remonstrance Queens Borough Public Library, Flushing, New York, November 19, 1999.

———. "First Families." *Seaport* (Fall 2001).

———. "The 'fervent Zeale' of Jacob Leisler." *William and Mary Quarterly* 51 (July 1994).

———. "In the Republic's Tradition: The Persistence of Dutch Culture in the Mid-Atlantic Colonies after the 1664 English Conquest." *de Halve Maen* 74 (Fall 2001).

Wagman, Morton. "The Origin of New York City's Government: From Proprietary Control to Representative Democracy." *de Halve Maen* 57 (February 1983).

Ward, Harry M. "The Search for American Identity: Early Historians of New England." In Alden T. Vaughan and George Athan Billias, eds., *Perspectives on Early American History*. New York: Harper & Row, 1973.

White, Philip. "Municipal Government Comes to Manhattan." *New-York Historical Society Quarterly* 37, no. 2 (April 1953).

Williams, James Homer. " 'Abominable Religion' and Dutch (In)tolerance: The Jews and Petrus Stuyvesant." *de Halve Maen* 71 (Winter 1998).

Wright, Langdon G. "Local Government and Central Authority in New Netherland." *New-York Historical Society Quarterly* 57, no. 1 (January 1973).

Zabriskie, George Olin. "The Founding Families of New Netherland, No. 4—The Rapalje-Rapelje Family." *de Halve Maen* 46 (January 1972), 7–8, 16; 47 (April 1972), 11–13; 47 (July 1972), 11–14.

Zabriskie, George Olin, and Alice P. Kenney. "The Founding of New Amsterdam: Fact and Fiction." *de Halve Maen* 50, 51, 52 (1976 and 1977).

Zeller, Nancy Anne McClure, ed. *A Beautiful and Fruitful Place: Selected Rensselaerswijck Seminar Papers*. Albany, N.Y.: New Netherland Publishing, 1991.

INDEX

Abraham's Sacrifice (ship), 37
Adams, John, 28, 301
Adriaensen, Willem, 127
Allerton, Isaac, 126, 140
Amboyna (Ambon), 72–73, 248, 260–61
Amboyna: A Tragedy (Dryden), 73
America: Anglocentrism of history, 220,
302–3, 311–12, 339n. 196, 344n. 263,
349–50n. 314; anti-Dutch bias, 311,
319, 349–50n. 314; Articles of
Capitulation and Bill of Rights, 304–5,
315; democratic government, Dutch
influence, 28, 100, 198–208, 220–21,
244–45; as divinely anointed, 302;
Dutch colonies and settlers (*see*
Manhattan; New Netherland); Dutch
linguistic and cultural legacy, 2,
269–71, 310–18, 349–50n. 314;
English colonies and settlers, 35,
71–72, 87, 115, 157–61; English land
grants and bogus claims, 185–87;
English roots, 2, 157, 284; first bounty
hunter, 188; first district attorney or
public prosecutor, 313–14, 349–50n.
314; first permanent European
settlement, 23; first New World
settlement founded by a woman, 160;
Flushing Remonstrance and First
Amendment, 276; "forest Finns,"
277–79, 279n., 316; fur trade, 33, 35,
75–81, 126, 179, 182, 194;
homosexuality, 187–89; ideas of liberty,
284–85, 304–5; immigration,
seventeenth-century, 37–38, 40–49, 61;
Jansson-Visscher map, 217, 224–25;
log cabin building, 279, 279n.;
Manifest Destiny, 302, 317; melting

pot, Dutch colony and, 312, 313;
merchant and trade groups (*see* West
India Company); multiculturalism and
revival of interest in Dutch colonial
history, 312; myth of origin, 301,
302–3, 317; national character, Dutch
influence, 28; "natural law," 264, 345n.
264; religious freedom, Dutch
influence, 96–97, 274–76; religious
pluralism, 276–77, 312–13; slavery and
Royal African Company, 293; Swedish
colony, 88–89, 114–17; tobacco,
194–95; transatlantic crossing, 37;
utopian community, 220. *See also*
Manhattan; New England; New
Netherland
American Cookery (Simmons), 270
American Revolution, 80, 100, 156, 320
amputation, 147
Amsterdam: amenities, 40, 212–13; art and
printing, 214; creation of American
colony, New Amstel, 282–83; Descartes
in, 97, 213; discovery of Van Rappard
documents, 53, 53n.; Free University
of, 142; fur trading and, 35;
harborfront, 33; inn of Pieter de Winter,
85, 110; Jewish community, 275; letter
by Van der Donck to Dr. La Montagne,
in Municipal Archives, 231; liberality
and tolerance, 2–3, 26, 61; Netherlands
Maritime Museum, 149; populace,
melting pot, 213; prosperity and
Golden Age, 212–13; prostitution, 214;
seventeenth-century, 25; tobacco trade
and, 194–95, 195n.; Town Hall,
214–15, 215n.; Walloon Church, 41;
West India House, 48, 75, 154

Amundsen, Roald, 34n.
Anatomy Lesson of Dr. Tulp, The
	(Rembrandt), 40, 328n. 35
Arminius, 96, 97
Arms of Amsterdam, 54
Articles of Capitulation, 304–5, 307, 315
Austrian National Library, 217–18

Bacon, Nathaniel, 120
Barents, Willem, 28–29
Barsimon, Jacob, 275
Baxter, George, 181, 237, 264
Baxter, Thomas, 260, 263
Bayard, Judith, 153–54, 154n., 168, 169,
	176, 208, 233, 234
Beck, Matthais, 274
Beech, Nan, 111, 127
Belgium, 16, 40, 70, 232n.
Bentyn, Jacques, 122
Bermuda, 37–38
Blaeu, Johannes, 225
Blake, Robert, 248
Blauvelt, Willem, 83, 187, 194, 207–8
Block, Adriaen, 34, 225
Blommaert, Samuel, 88
Bogardus, Everadus, 140, 141, 165, 179,
	191, 335n. 141
Bol, Jan Claesen, 179
Bonomi, Patricia, 312
Bout, Jan Evertsen, 111, 197, 207, 212, 213,
	231
Bradford, William, 95, 136
Brazil, 144, 149, 150–52, 277
Breda, Holland, 93, 94–95, 153, 154n., 176,
	225–26
"Broad Advice," 124, 336n. 148
Brodhead, John Romeyn, 52, 263, 311
Bronck, Jonas, 140, 290
Bronx (Bronck), 140; Anne Hutchinson in
	Pelham Bay, 160; River, 163
Brooklyn (Breuckelen), 127, 192, 262; Ferry,
	263, 296; Flatbush (Vlackebos), 262;
	Lady Deborah Moody's Gravesend,
	160, 262
Brown, William, 126
Browne, Robert, 45
Burr, Aaron, 5, 321

Cabot, John, 15–16, 18–19, 74
Calvin, John, 156
Calvinism, 61, 68, 85, 96, 153, 168, 169,
	170, 187, 274–75
Camden, New Jersey, 181

Cape Henlopen, 88, 115
Cape May, 40, 88, 115, 277
Castellio, Sebastian, 96–97
Catskill Mountains, 134, 138–39
Chambers, Thomas, 126
Chancellor, Richard, 18
Charles I, 45, 67–74, 96, 219, 222; art and
	artists and, 69–70; Civil War and,
	155–58, 219; daughter's marriage to
	Willem II, 222
Charles II, King of England, 3, 219, 286;
	takeover of Dutch colonies, 289,
	291–300, 307
Christina, Queen of Sweden, 88, 115,
	213
Christoph, Peter, 4, 323
Coen, Jan Pieterszoon, 63
Congo, Antony, 83, 165
Connecticut, 158, 164, 180, 237–38, 260,
	286–90
Connecticut River (Fresh River), 34, 43, 87,
	237
Coorn, Nicolaes, 188
Coriolanus (Shakespeare), 15
Cornelissen, Gelain, 108
Crèvecoeur, J. Hector St. John de, 313, 321,
	351n. 321
Cromwell, Oliver, 164, 219, 245–47; Anglo-
	Dutch Wars and, 247–50, 261, 265;
	capture of Jamaica, 247; George
	Downing and, 285–86; Western
	Design, 261, 265
Croon, Lysbeth, 241
Crossed Heart, The (ship), 306
Cunaeus (Piet van der Cun), 100
Curaçao, 146, 149, 150, 151, 152, 168, 179,
	274, 288, 306
Curaçao Papers, 221

Dandrada, Salvador, 275
Dee, John, 16–17
De Forest, Isaac, 107
De Graaf, Reinier, 98
De Hondt, Joost, 29
De Jure Belli ac Pacis (Grotius), 210
Dela Croix, Jeronimus, 77
Delaware Bay, 31, 88–89, 183
Delaware Indians, 32, 42, 184
Delaware River (South River), 34, 43, 44, 58,
	88; English threat to Dutch control,
	183; New Amstel settlement, 282–83;
	New Sweden and, 114–17, 164–65,
	181–184, 277–79
De Lucena, Abraham, 275

democracy, 100; American Revolution and, 156; English Civil War and, 156–57, 219; forerunner, Peace of Westphalia, 210; Manhattan and representative government, 198–208, 229, 244–45; political activism, seventeenth-century and, 219; Van den Enden's coterie, 220

De Rasière, Isaack, 54, 55, 58, 59, 62–63, 64

De Ruyter, Michiel, 299

Descartes, René, 97–98, 100, 101–2, 154, 171, 213, 310

Description of New Netherland, A (Van der Donck), 136–38, 137n., 251–52; second edition, 281–82

Description of the Province of New Albion, A (Plantagenet), 187

De Sille, Nicasius, 297

De Truy, Philip, 200

De Vernuis, Jacque, 106–7

De Vries, David, 81–82, 83, 107, 119–20, 121–22, 123–24, 125, 173, 173n, 333n. 108

De Wale, Johannes, 98

De Winter, Jacob, 253

De Witt, Jan, 241, 248, 265, 286, 291

De Wolff, Dirck, 268

Dijckman, Johannes, 325, 351n. 325

Dircksen, Willem, 126

Discourse on Method (Descartes), 98, 102

Discourses and Mathematical Demonstrations Concerning Two Sciences (Galileo), 97

Documents Relating to New Netherland, 1624–1626, in the Henry E. Huntington Library, 53n.

Dokkum, Netherlands, 148

Dongan, Thomas, 276–77

Doughty, Francis, 160–61, 164, 165, 264, 281

Doughty, Mary, 161, 166, 176, 195–96, 207, 245, 281

Downing, George, 285–88, 290, 291, 295, 299

Drake, Sir Francis, 18

Dryden, John, 73

Dutch Antilles, 146

Dutch East India Company (VOC), 24, 26, 29–30, 52, 102

Dutch Republic. *See* Netherlands

Dutch West India Company, 39–40, 47, 48, 52, 53, 55, 56, 61, 62, 63, 75, 81, 87, 88, 100, 102, 105, 106, 108, 113, 117, 122, 140, 141, 144–45, 151, 189, 193, 228, 275; American appeal to be

separate from, 165, 193–98, 206–8, 216–31, 240–45; Anglo-Dutch Wars and resurgence of power, 249, 259–60; English takeover of American colonies and, 288, 299–300; failure of, 224, 242; Long Island towns and, 264; Manhattan focus of (1655), 277; Manhattan purchased for, 3, 49–50, 53, 54, 56, 57, 58, 65, 329–30n. 49; peace treaty with Indians ordered, 161; Peter Stuyvesant and, 146–55, 161, 165, 306, 324, 341–42n. 228; reversal of ruling against, 245, 249; slave trade, 273–74, 291; soldier's pay, 57, 330n. 57

D'Wys, Gulyam, 259

East Indies, 25–26, 63, 68, 71, 72–73, 248

Eaton, Theophilus, 236, 236n., 237, 238

Eighty Years' War, 210

Elizabeth I, Queen of England, 16, 18, 68

Encyclopedia of the North American Colonies, 312

Endecott, John, 160, 237–38

England: American colonies and settlers, 2, 3, 35, 87, 115; Anglo-Dutch Wars, 247–50, 259–61, 265, 307–8; Charles I and Personal Rule, 67–74; Church of England, 156; Civil War, 155–58, 164, 246–47, 337n. 164; as colonial power, 113; Cromwell's Western Design, 261, 265; defeat of the Spanish Armada, 18, 29; disputation of Dutch claims to New York, 73–75, 81–82, 115, 181; Dutch alliance, 45, 67–74; Dutch Republic, contrast with, 26, 27; Dutch Republic, politics and, 30; economy and trade, 15, 17, 18, 34, 247; East Indies and, 71, 72–73; exploration, 13–14, 15–16, 17–24; Glorious Revolution, 308–9; Henry Hudson, desire for return of, 30, 33–34; India and, 73, 113; invasion of New Netherland, aborted, 261, 265; land grants in colonies, 186; merchant and shipping companies, 13–15, 23–24, 35–36; Navigation Act, 247; Protestantism and Cromwell, 155–58, 246; religious persecution, 158–59; Restoration, 286, 289; seizure of *Unity,* 71–72, 73–74; Spain and, 69–70; takeover of Manhattan and New Netherlands, 3, 8, 216, 284–300; Whitehall Palace, 70

Episcopius, Simon, 97

Erasmus, Desiderius, 171

Erie Canal, 8, 81, 316–17

Exercitatio Anatomica De Motu Cordis et Sanguinis in Animalibus (Harvey), 63

exploration: America and Canada, by Henry Hudson, 31–35; Arctic, 17–22, 327n. 21; circumnavigation of the globe, 18; Dutch, 28–30; English, 15–24; "established theory," 20, 327n. 21; maps and mapmakers, 16, 17, 29; search for a northern passage to Asia, 17–24, 28–30, 34–35, 34n.; Spanish, 17; Strait of the Three Brothers, 17. *See also* Hudson, Henry.

Eyckenboom, Den ("The Oak Tree"), 103, 108, 333n. 108

Farret, John, 149–50, 152–53, 154, 179

Fernando de Noronha Island, 149

Finns, 277–79, 279n., 316

Fishkill, New York, 41–42

Flipsen (Philipse), Frederick, 269

Flushing (Vlissingen), New York, 207, 262, 264

Flushing Remonstrance, 276

Forrester, Andrew, 185–86

Fort Orange (Albany), 46–47, 49, 52, 58, 59, 65, 75–76, 87, 102, 109, 139, 162, 188, 190, 295, 308, 316; Beverwyck, 267–68, 308; Dutch legacy in place names, 310; as Willemstad, 308

Fortune (ship), 37

Fox, Dixon Ryan, 344n. 263

France: fur trade in America and Indian alliances, 76, 79; Henry Hudson and, 30

Franklin, Benjamin, 321, 351n. 321

Frederik Hendrik, Prince of Orange, 45, 222

Frijhoff, Willem, 142–43, 143n.

Frisius, Gemma, 16, 17

fur trade, 33, 35, 39, 44–45, 75–81, 126, 182; beaver hats, 76; beaver pelts per year passing through Manhattan, 194; wreck of the *Princess* and, 179, 191

Galileo, 97, 99

Geddes, Jenny, 155, 157

Gehring, Charles, 1, 4–6, 7, 52, 53n., 142–43, 151, 271, 323–25, 351n. 322

Geraerdy, Philip, 107

Gerrit, Manuel "The Giant," 84, 300

Gerritsen, Philip, 141

Gerritson, William, 161

Goderis, Joost, 259

Goedhuys, Diederik Willem, 137n.

Gomarus, 96

Gorges, Sir Ferdinando, 186

Grotius, Hugo, 99–100, 137, 154, 171, 178, 210, 264, 310, 345n. 264

Gustavus Adolphus, King of Sweden, 61, 88, 210

Hackensack Indians, 119, 164

Hakluyt, Richard, 19–20

Hall, Thomas, 171, 185, 197

Halve Maen (ship), 31, 206

Hartford, Connecticut, 82, 87, 237, 287, 290; Hartford Treaty, 237–38, 243; Huyshope Avenue and Dutch origins, 238, 238n.

Harvard, John, 285

Harvey, William, 63, 67, 98

Heckewelder, John, 32

Hempstead (Heemsteede), New York, 262–63

Hendricksz, Jeuriaen, 126

Henrietta, Duchess of Orleans, 307

Henri IV, King of France, 30

Herman, Augustin, 171, 185, 197, 198, 201, 207, 219, 235, 242; Jansson-Visscher map, 217, 224–25

Heyn, Piet, 63

Hoboken, New Jersey, 241

Holland, 93, 93n. *See also* Netherlands

Holmers, Willem, 126

Holmes, Robert, 295

homosexuality, 187–89

Hooglandt, Cornelis, 127

Hooker, Thomas, 87

Hopewell (ship), 20, 21–22

Hopkins, Edward, 237, 238

Hudde, Andries, 127

Hudson, Henry, 5, 9; American exploration, 31–35, 96, 206, 225; background, 19; crew mutinies, 22, 35, 328n. 35; death, 35, 328n. 35; discovery of Manhattan and Hudson River, 32–33; Dutch sponsorship, 24, 26, 29, 81, 96, 206, 328n. 29; first voyage, 20–21; Indian encounters, 32, 33; influence, 35; lack of historical recognition, 18–19; London house, 326–27n. 13; Muscovy Company and, 13–14, 19–24, 327n. 14; political intrigue, 29–30; search for northern passage, 19–22, 34–35, 34n.; second voyage, 21–22; ships, 20, 21–22, 31

Hudson, John, 21, 35
Hudson Bay and Hudson Strait, 34, 35
Hudson River, 5, 8, 32–33, 34, 38; Dutch
    settlements on, 46–47, 58, 75–81,
    102–4; Indians of, 38; as North River,
    43; as River Mauritius, 38. *See also*
    Manhattan
Huguenots, 153
Huntington, Henry E., 53
Huron Indians, 79
Hutchinson, Anne, 160

India, 73, 113
Indians. *See* Native Americans
Iroquois League, 80
Irving, Washington, 3
Ivan the Terrible, 18

Jacobs, Jaap, 82
James I, King of England, 30, 35, 45, 186
James II, Duke of York, 3, 292–93, 294;
    American land grant, 294; as King
    James II, 308, 320; Manhattanites'
    freedoms and, 305
Jansen, Hendric, 108, 127
Jansen, Tonis, 108
Janszen, Michael, 185, 197, 198, 200
Japan, 291
Java, 63
Jeannin, Pierre, 30
Jefferson, Thomas, 98
Jersey City, New Jersey, 123, 241
Jews: in America, 9, 275; in Dutch Republic,
    26, 95, 275; Stuyvesant and, 275
Joachimi, Albert, 70–71, 87, 157–58, 192
Jogues, Isaac, 333n. 107
Johnson, Jeremiah, 136
Juet, Robert, 32, 33

Kalmar Nyckel (ship), 88, 115
Kidd, William, 106
Kieft, Willem, 108, 112–28, 181, 207; case
    against, 170–71, 172–79, 180; currency
    crisis and directive, 117–18; death in
    shipwreck, 179, 191, 192; directive on
    Indian tax, 118–19, 173, 177; edict
    against Raritan Indians, 120, 173;
    English refugees to Manhattan and,
    159–60; letter to Minuit, 116;
    opposition to, 139–45, 151, 154, 161,
    168, 170–71, 172–79; peace treaty with
    Indians, 161–64; replacement, 154–55,

165–66, 167; tax on beavers and beer,
    140–41; Van der Donck and, 134; War
    against the Indians and Pavonia
    massacre, 121–28, 151, 152, 172
"Knickerbocker" history (Irving), 3
Kremer, Gerhard (Mercator), 16, 17
Kress, Jack, 349–50n. 314
Krol, Bastiaen, 37, 59, 65, 87
Kuyter, Jochem, 139–40; banishment and
    exile, 178–79; case against Kieft,
    140–41, 165, 167, 168, 170–71,
    172–79; return to Manhattan and
    decision against Kieft, 197–203; wreck
    of the *Princess,* survival, 179, 191–92

Lake Ontario, 80
La Montagne, Johannes, 114, 118, 162,
    184–85, 204; Van der Donck's letter to,
    231
Lampe, Jan, 62, 62n.
law: first district attorney (*schout*) or public
    prosecutor, 313–14, 349–50n. 314;
    Grotius and international, 99;
    Manhattan, legal system and
    punishment, 61–63, 84; "natural law,"
    concept of, 264, 345n. 264; Van der
    Donck and American, 99–100, 103–4
Leete, William, 287, 289
Leiden, Holland, 45, 93–102; University of,
    94, 95, 97–100, 135, 178, 250
Leisler's Rebellion, 309
Le Maire, Isaac, 30
Lenni Lenape Indians, 38, 54
Letters from an American Farmer
    (Crèvecoeur), 313
Levy, Asser, 275, 300
Locke, John, 100
London: Downing Street, 286; Great Fire,
    23; Henry Hudson house, 326–27n.
    13; Muscovy House, 15, 23;
    seventeenth-century, 13–15, 21
Long Island, 127; division between Dutch
    and English, 238; English takeover,
    290; Gravesend, 160, 262–63; New
    Albion and claims of Plowden, 186–87,
    338n. 186; "Remonstrance and Petition
    of the Colonies and Villages in this New
    Netherland Province," and breach with
    Stuyvesant, 262–64
Loockermans, Govert, 106, 113, 144, 170,
    184, 185, 197, 198, 219
Loper, Jacob, 207
Lupoldt, Ulrich, 111
Luther, Martin, 156

Mahican Indians, 38, 46, 52, 57–58, 87, 135–36, 141, 161

Maine, 186; Fort Gorges, 186

Manhattan (New Amsterdam, New York City), 2; African settlers and slaves, 83, 84, 165, 233, 273–74, 346n. 273; as American beginning, 3, 303; archaeological excavations, 196, 196n., 337n. 172, 339n. 196; Battery Park, 60; beaver on seal, 76; "birth certificate," 55–56; Board of Nine, 185, 190, 193, 193n., 194, 196, 198, 199, 201, 204, 207, 229, 235; Brewer's Bridge, 107; British invasion, aborted, 261, 265; Broadway, 60, 60n.; burgher status, 268, 271; canal, 266; case of Kieft vs. Kuyter, Melyn, *et al.*, 172–79, 191–92; chosen as capital of New Netherlands, 49, 58, 81; City Tavern (City Hall), 192, 196, 257, 258n., 297; claims of Andrew Forrester, 185–86; as company town (West India Company), 61–62, 81, 105, 108, 113, 143–45, 233; Corlaer's Hook (Lower East Side), 123; cost of living, 227; culture, society, lawlessness, prostitution, 61, 62, 64–65, 83–85, 89, 106, 111, 167; currencies, 64, 65, 76, 117–18; Customs Building, 60; decision-making, people's demand for representative government, 171, 172, 197–208, 221, 229, 244–45, 257–64, 265, 305; decline (1640), 89; deed to, 54, 55, 58; Deutel Bay (Turtle Bay), 111, 111n.; 121; disputation of Dutch claims to by English, 73–75, 81–82; Dutch linguistic and cultural legacy, 269–71, 310–18; Dutch retaking (1673) and subsequent to return to British, 308, 309; early construction, 59–60, 82–83, 104–5, 107, 126, 171; Ellis Island, 259; English religious refugees in, 158–61; English takeover, 3, 8, 284–300; first kosher butcher shop, 300; first minister, 64; flag of United Provinces, colors and New York sports teams, 183; Fort Amsterdam, 59–60, 62, 122, 124, 126, 127–28, 132, 140, 159, 168–69, 184, 193; fortification, Anglo-Dutch Wars, 260, 287–88; as free port, 64, 105–6, 107, 110, 117, 194; government, post-incorporation, 257–64, 265–66; Greenwich Village, 56–57, 233–34; growth, 61, 82, 149–60, 171, 266, 269–70; harbor, 104–5, 107; Harlem,

110, 271–72; Harlem River, 196; Henry Hudson and, 33; immigrants, as landing for, 61, 309–10, 316, 317; incorporation as city (1653), 257–58, 258n., 345n. 265; inhabitants, 2, 5, 8, 58, 61, 83–85, 86, 107, 165, 234, 333n. 107; as international port and shipping hub, 151, 194, 195, 266, 268, 303–4, 339n. 196; Jews in, 275, 300; Kieft's directive on taxing Indians, 118–19, 173, 177; Kieft's War against the Indians, 121–28, 151, 152; legal disputes and land transfers, 126–27, 259, 271; legal system and punishment, 61–63, 84, 132, 169–70, 258, 264; Leisler's Rebellion, 309; lifestyle and rise in comfort, 106–8, 266, 337n. 172; location and topography, 8, 9–10, 42, 60; merchant class, rise of, 105–6, 108, 126; Mohawk name, *Gänóno,* 42; multiethnic society, melting pot, 107, 125, 258, 272, 300, 302, 305, 309–10, 312, 313; murder of Claes Swits, 110–12, 121, 122; Museum of the American Indian, 60, 258n.; Native Americans on, 54, 58, 60, 110–12, 118–19; New Albion and claims of Plowden, 186–87, 338n. 186; New York City Charter, 304–5, 315; Noten (Nut) Island (Governor's Island), 47, 49; opposition to Kieft and Indian policies, 124–25, 126, 139–45, 151, 154, 161, 167–68, 170–71, 172–79; origins of name, 33, 42; paths, roads, thoroughfares, 60, 60n., 107, 192–93, 233; peace treaty with Indians, 161–64; Peach War, 279–81; people's grievances about rule of West India Company, 198–99; petition for political status to The Hague, 142–45, 143n., 154, 170, 175, 206–8, 216–31; political structure, city council, 107, 114, 118, 121–22, 139–45, 176, 178–79, 193, 201, 257–64 (*see also* Board of Nine, above); portrait (Van der Donck's), 217–18, 225; post-English takeover, 303; as prototype for America, 3, 6, 258–59, 272; publicity in Europe and immigration, 228, 229–30, 235, 341–42n. 228; purchase of, 3, 49–50, 53, 54, 56, 57, 58, 65, 329–30n. 49; renamed New York, 300; St. Mark's-in-the-Bowery, 6–7, 234n.; "Stuyvesant's Bouwerie," 233–34, 266, 346n. 273; Stuyvesant's directives and laws, 169;

taverns and breweries, 83, 106, 107, 110, 111, 121, 126, 127, 141, 169, 172, 192, 337n. 172; tax on beavers and beer, 140–41; tobacco trade, 194–95; tolerance, policy of, 125, 159, 258–59, 273, 317; transfer of colony, 304–5; uniqueness of peoples, culture, and structure, 2, 6, 8, 113, 258; upward mobility and entrepreneurs, 268–69; Van der Donck as father of, 143; Van Rappard documents, 53–54; Wall Street, 260; wildlife of, 42, 43. *See also* Stuyvesant, Peter

Manifest Destiny, 302, 317

maps and mapmakers, 16, 17, 29; Jansson-Visscher map of colonial America, 217, 224–25; Mercator projection, 16; view of Manhattan, 217–18

Maryland, 186, 187n.

Mason, John, 120

Mau, Sijmen Lambertsz, 36

Maurits, Prince of Orange, 45, 101–2

May, Cornelis, 40

Mayflower (ship), 140

Melting Pot, The (Zangwill), 317–18

Melyn, Cornelius, 107, 139–40, 207, 219, 262; banishment and exile, 178–79; case against Kieft, 165, 167, 168, 170–71, 172–79; return to Manhattan and Prince of Orange's decision, 197–203; wreck of the *Princess*, survival, 179, 191–92

Mercator. *See* Kremer, Gerhard

Michaelius, Jonas, 64, 65, 66, 71, 273

Milkmaid, The (ship), 153

Milton, John, 249

Minqua Indians (Susquehannocks), 182, 184, 280

Minuit, Peter, 48–50, 53, 54, 58–59, 62, 64, 65–66, 71, 75, 81, 112, 114, 157; death, 117; letter from Willem Kieft, 116; New Sweden and, 88–89, 114–17, 164, 181; purchase of land, Atlantic coast, 65–66; purchase of Manhattan, 49–50, 53, 54, 56, 57, 58, 65, 329–30n. 49; purchase of Staten Island, 56, 65

Mohawk Indians, 46, 57, 65, 75–81, 135–36, 141, 188–89, 295; Agheroense and Kieft's peace treaty, 162–63; lawsuit against West India Company, 189; Van der Bogaert's journey and, 80, 331n. 80

Mohawk River, 8, 43, 75, 76

Moody, Lady Deborah, 159–60, 165

Muscovy Company, 13–15, 18, 19, 23–24, 29, 327n. 14

Native Americans: alliances with Dutch, 46–47, 59, 75–81; alliances with French, 76, 79; British prejudice against, 261; burial of dead, 77; cannibalism, 47; canoes, 196, 196n.; Dutch language and, 310; encounters with European settlers, 42–43, 44, 75–81, 85, 106; encounters with Henry Hudson, 32, 33; fur and other trade items, 44–45, 75–81, 126, 179, 182, 280; Kieft's directive on taxing, 118–19, 173, 177; Kieft's peace treaty with, 161–64; Kieft's War, 121–28, 173; languages, character, culture, 50–51, 57–58, 76–81, 119, 135–36, 331n. 80; Manhatesen (or Manhattan) Indians, 54, 58, 60; Mahican and Mohawk conflicts, 46–47, 52; massacres by, 160; massacres of, 85, 120, 123–24, 172, 177; murder of Claes Swits, 110–12, 121, 122; Peach War, 279–81; purchase of Manhattan from, 3–4, 49–50, 53, 54, 56, 57, 58, 329–30n. 49; real estate transactions, 49–50, 51–52, 57–58, 65–66, 87, 115, 119, 137–38, 184; "River Indians," 38; shaman healing ceremony, 78–79; smallpox and other diseases, 78; stereotypes, 135; unification of, 127; Van der Donck and, 131, 135–36, 137–38, 141, 162–63; violence against and retaliation, 112, 120, 123–28, 173; wampum (*sewant*), 64, 76, 79, 117–18, 163. *See also specific tribes*

Negro, Jan, 83, 165

Netherlands (United Provinces): Act of Abjuration, 245; American appeal to take over New Netherland from West India Company, 193–98, 206–8, 216–31, 240–45; American colony (*see* New Netherland); Anglo-Dutch Wars, 247–50, 259–61, 265, 307–8; "Batavianized" names, 125; Binnenhof, 145, 215, 239; Catholic provinces, 69; child-raising, 94; colonies, empire builders, merchant princes, 113, 124–25, 144, 145, 146–55, 171, 212, 268; communication system, 63–64; coup attempt by Willem II, 238–40; cultural innovations, 25; domination of trade, 291; dress, 27, 211, 211n.; Dutch National Archives, Van Twiller letter, 82; Dutch Republic, 6, 26, 27–28, 70, 93, 93n., 232n.; economic and political power, 25–26; East Indies and, 25–26,

63, 68, 71–72, 291; England, alliance with, 45, 67–74; England contrasted with, 26, 27; English disputation of Dutch claims to North America, 73–75, 81–82; English political intrigue in, 29–30; English seizure of Dutch vessel, 71–72, 73–74; English takeover of American colonies, 294–300; English takeover of slave-trading posts, 291–94, 299; exploration and discovery, 16; flag of United Provinces, 183; fur trade, 34, 35, 65, 179; geography, 26; Gevangenpoort, 224, 224n.; Golden Age, 101, 211–13, 284, 291, 310; government, 215–16, 218–19, 221–22, 244–45; The Hague, 29, 56, 73, 141, 145, 157, 179, 215, 221, 227, 230, 239; home as personal space, coziness, 101; House of Orange and Nassau, 222; Indian policy, 46–47; inheritance laws, 226n.; intellectual and political ideas, 171, 210, 219–21; Jewish community in, 26, 95, 275; language, seventeenth-century, 4–5, 323; lifestyle, 101, 212–13; loss of archives of Dutch East and West India Companies, 52, 55; as melting pot, 125; merchant and trade groups (*see* Dutch East India Company; West India Company); merchant support of Henry Hudson, 24; national character, 28, 126, 171; peace treaty with Spain (Münster Treaty, Peace of Westphalia), 193, 194, 207, 209–12, 340n. 209; policy of tolerance, 6, 26, 95, 96–97, 125–26, 274, 310; political and religious refugees, 6, 26, 35, 45–46, 95, 125; Protestantism of, 45, 61, 69; religious freedom, 96–97, 245, 274–75; royalist crisis, 221–23; settlers for New Netherland from, 223, 226, 228, 341–42n. 228; slave trade, 273–74, 291, 293; social class and upward mobility, 27–28; Spain and Spanish wars, 27, 29, 38–39, 45, 63, 68, 94–95, 125, 144; tulip frenzy, 99, 99n.; Union of Utrecht (de facto constitution), 245; voyage and report of Henry Hudson, 31–33; waning of Empire and British takeover, 284–300. *See also* Amsterdam

New Albion, 186–87

New Amsterdam. *See* Manhattan

Newark, New Jersey (Achter Col), 127

New Castle, Delaware, 282–83

New England: anti-Dutch propaganda in, 260–61; Boston as capital, 180, 181;

Brownists, 45; emigration from, to Manhattan, 158–61; Hartford Treaty, 237–38, 243, 290; Massachusetts, 158, 160, 260, 286; New Plymouth, 158, 260, 289; Pilgrims and Puritans, 3, 61, 64, 85, 96, 140; population growth, 158; religious persecution and persecution of witches, 159–60; Restoration and Winthrop's charter for Connecticut, 286–90; Stuyvesant and, 179–81, 206, 235–38, 290; United Colonies, 158

Newfoundland, 17, 31, 74

New Haven, 158, 164, 180, 183, 236, 236n., 260, 286–87, 289–90

New Jersey, 38, 115, 269n., 303

New Netherland: accounts of, 3–4; Catskills, 134, 138–39; description, Van der Donck, 129–31; Dutch claims to settlement, 35, 40, 43, 96; Dutch retaking (1673) and subsequent to return to British, 308; early contact with Pilgrims, 64; early leaders of, 47–50, 53, 54, 58–59, 62, 64, 81–82, 108, 112–27 (*see also* Manhattan; Stuyvesant, Peter); English takeover, 284–300; English threat to, 216; first European child born in, 41; fur and timber trade, 33, 34, 35, 39, 44–45, 75–81, 126, 179, 182, 191; 194; geography, 8; Hartford Treaty, 237–38, 243, 290; history, recap by Van der Donck, 205–6, 328n. 29; Indian attacks, 127–28, 160; law and order, 103–4; linguistic and cultural legacy, 269–71; Mohawk River Valley, 8, 43, 75; populace, 2; Rensselaerswyck, 102–4, 106, 108–9, 127, 129, 132, 139, 189–90, 267, 310, 335n. 139; settlement, 38, 40–49, 58, 75; size, 2, 303; transfer of colony to English, 304–5. *See also* Fort Orange; Manhattan; *specific governors*

New Netherland Project, 7, 52, 312, 322–25

New Sweden, 88–89, 114–17, 164–65; flag colors, 183; "forest Finns," 277–79, 279n., 316; Fort Christina, 116, 117, 182; Fort Mosquito, 182; Fort Nassau, 182; fur trade and, 182; Johan Printz leadership, 182–84; Peach War and, 279–81; Stuyvesant and, 181–84; Stuyvesant and recapture of, 277–79

Newton, Brian, 149, 174, 201, 204

Newton, Isaac, 97

Newtown (Middelburgh), New York, 262

New York, 3; archives on Dutch New Netherland, 1, 4, 5–6, 9, 151, 300, 319–25, 351n. 321; Dutch trade under English rule, 303; loss of early records, 52–53, 55, 300, 319–20; named after Duke of York, 300; Netherlands Center, 137n.; origins, uniqueness, 7–8, 300; religious pluralism, 276–77; Saw River Parkway, 163; State Library, Albany, 1; Van Rappard documents, 53–54, 53n.
New York Harbor, 32, 104, 303
Nicolls, Richard, 8, 294–300, 303, 306, 313
Night Watch, The (Rembrant), 76, 112
Nyack Indians, 164, 206

O'Callaghan, Edmund, 49, 311
O'Donnell, Thomas, 136
Of Plymouth Plantation (Bradford), 136
Ogden, John and Richard, 126
Oneida Lake, 80
Op Dyck, Gysbert, 237
O'Sullivan, John, 302
Oxenstierna, Axel, 88

Pauw, Adriaen, 209–11, 211n., 241, 248, 340n. 209, 343n. 248
Pavonia, 241; massacre, 123–24, 125, 172, 177
Peace of Westphalia, 193, 194, 207, 209–11
Penn, William, 41, 181
Pepys, Samuel, 76, 286, 291
Pequot Indians, 85, 120
Peterszen, Claes (Dr. Nicolaes Pietersen Tulp), 40, 328n. 35
Philadelphia, 181, 220
Philip II, King of Spain, 18
Philip III, King of Spain, 29
Philip IV, King of Spain, 69
Pia, Pierre, 127
Pilgrims, 3, 61, 85, 140, 301; Brownists, 45; early contact with Dutch in Manhattan, 64; in Leiden, 45–46, 95–96; *See also* Connecticut; New England; New Haven
Plancius, Peter, 18, 29
Plockhoy, Pieter, 220
Plowden, Sir Edmund, 186–87, 187n., 189, 338n. 186
Portugal: Brazil and, 152, 277; exploration and colonization, 17, 25; loss of East Indies to the Dutch, 26; slave trade, 61
Princess Amelia (ship), 179, 191–92

Principle Navigations Voyages Traffiques and Discoveries of the English Nation, The (Hakluyt), 19
Printz, Johan, 182
privateering and piracy, 39, 63, 83, 86, 106, 183, 187, 194, 263; Anglo-Dutch Wars and, 259–60; *La Garce* (ship), 187, 207; outlawing of privateering, 207–8
Purchas, Samuel, 23
Puritans, 3, 61, 85, 94; America's myth of origin and, 301–3, 317; English Civil War and, 156–58; incursions into Dutch territory, 158, 164; massacre of the Pequots, 85; Oliver Cromwell and, 246; theocracy and intolerance, 301–2. *See also* Connecticut; New England; New Haven

Quakers, 275–76
Queens, New York, 160

Raleigh, Sir Walter, 23, 34
Rapalje, John, 41
Rapalje, Joris, 37, 40–41, 43, 44, 46, 48, 58, 75, 87, 105–6, 113, 121, 136, 165, 299
Rapalje, Sarah, 41, 127
Raritan Indians, 106, 119, 120, 173, 206
Reagan, Ronald, 157
Rechgawawanck Indians, 164
Reformed Dutch Church, 275, 310
Reiss, A. J., 314
religious freedom, 96–97, 245, 274–75;
Rembrandt, 40, 76, 112, 328n. 35
Remonstrance of New Netherland (Van der Donck), 205–6, 216, 223–25, 227–28, 263, 341–42n. 228
republicanism, 27, 100. *See also* democracy
Reyniers, Griet, 85–86, 113, 165, 299
Rockefeller, Nelson, 4, 322
Roman Catholicism, 156. *See also* Netherlands; Spain
Rubens, Peter Paul, 69–70, 157
Russell, Bertrand, 6
Russia, English trade, 18, 34. *See also* Muscovy Company

St. Beninio (ship), 236
St. Germain, Jean, 127
St. Martin (island), 146–47, 151, 152
Santa Claus, 270–71, 314–15
Santorio, Santorio, 63
Schaghen, Pieter, 55–56

Schepmoes, Jan, 126

Schuyler, Cortlandt van Rensselaer, 4

Schuylkill River, 115, 182, 182n.

Scotland, 157

Sea-Mew (ship), 48

Sears, Isaac, 320

Sedgwicke, Robert, 265

Shakespeare, William, 15, 18, 37

Simmons, Amelia, 270

slavery and slave trade, 61, 83, 84, 151, 165, 273–74; English takeover of, 293; Royal African Company, 293

Smith, Dirck, 277

Smith, James, 126

Smith, John, 22–23, 31

Snediger, Jan, 127

South America, 25, 61, 63, 83; Spanish, Portuguese, and Dutch fight for, 144, 150–52, 277

Spain: colonial empires, 25, 65, 146–47, 150–51, 277; decline of empire, 63; Duke of Alva, attack on Dutch Protestants, 125; English-Dutch alliance against, 45; English peace treaty with, 69–70; exploration by, 17; invasion fleet against England (Spanish Armada), 18, 29; Netherlands and, 27, 29, 38–39, 63, 68, 69, 94–95, 125, 146–47; peace treaty with Dutch Republic (Münster Treaty), 193, 194, 207, 340n. 209; Roman Catholicism and, 18, 27; Spanish Main, 83, 183; treasure fleet, 63

Spinoza, Baruch, 26, 171, 220, 310

Springsteen, Bruce, 269, 269n.

Stael, Michiel, 223–24, 227, 239, 341–42n. 228

Stam, Arent Corssen, 108

Staten Island (*Staten Eylandt*), 32, 48–49; David de Vries farm, 119–20, 173, 173n.; purchase, 56

Steen, Jan, 94

Stow, John, 14

Stuyvesant, Balthasar, 208, 234, 298, 306

Stuyvesant, Peter, 3, 8, 9, 60; arrival in Manhattan, 165–66, 167–68; Articles of Capitulation and individual freedoms, 305–6, 307; aviary, 288; Board of Nine and, 185, 190, 193, 193n., 194, 195, 199–200, 201, 207, 235; breach with Long Island towns, 262–63; Calvinism and religious intolerance, 153, 168, 169, 170, 275–76; change of city

government and, 257; charges of homosexuality against Van den Bogaert, 187–89; children, 208, 234, 298; claims of Andrew Forrester, 185–86; claims of Plowden and New Albion, 186–87, 338n. 186; death, 306; English comrades, 149, 174, 181, 201; English takeover and, 287–88, 295–300, 304–5, 324; English threat to Dutch colony and, 183; estate in Greenwich Village, 233–34; family and background, Friesland, 147, 148, 171–72, 233; Farret and poetry exchanged, 149–50, 152–53, 154, 336n. 149; Flushing Remonstrance, 276; governor of Manhattan, 154–55, 168–90, 199–208, 235–38, 257, 258, 265, 273–74, 275–76, 287–88, 295–300, 324; handwriting, 324; Indians, negotiations with, 206; justice administered by, 169–70, 178–79; Kieft vs. Melyn, Kuyter, *et al.*, 170–71, 172–79, 208; loss of leg, 146–48, 152–53; mandamus served on, 202–3, 206; New England and, 180–81, 206, 235–38; New Sweden and, 181–84, 277–79; ordered back to Dutch Republic and return to America, 306; ordinance against depositions, 205; political acumen, 170, 180, 184, 235–38; political scandal, sale of guns to Indians, 203; Rensselaerswyck and, 189–90; representative (popular) government, position on, 174, 199–208, 258, 265; return of Melyn and Kuyter and case against rule of, 197–203; return to Netherlands, recuperation, and marriage, 153–55, 154n.; *St. Beninio* affair, 236; slavery and freed Africans, 273–74, 346n. 273; States General reversal of ruling against, 245, 249; States General ruling against, 230, 234–35, 243–45; tomb, 7, 234, 234n.; transformation after loss of colony, 306; Van der Donck and, 166, 175–76, 185, 189, 190, 199–204, 208, 234, 243–45, 338n. 176; West India Company, service in Caribbean and South America, 146–55, 168; wife, 153–54, 154n., 168, 169, 176, 208, 233, 234; Winthrop (younger) and, 287–88, 297; wooden leg, 154, 166

Sweden, 61, 87–89; claims in America, 88–89, 114–17

Swits, Adriaen, 126
Swits, Claes, 110–12, 113, 121, 122, 126, 165
Swits, Cornelis, 165

Tappan Indians, 56, 119, 123, 164
*Tekel or Balance of the great monarchy of
    Spain . . .* , 63
Tempest, The (Shakespeare), 37
Tenner, Nicolaes, 126
Thirty Years' War, 88, 125–26, 181, 210
Thomassen (Tomassen), Willem, 77, 79, 127
Thorne, Robert, 20
tobacco trade and markets, 194; Amsterdam
    and, 194–95, 195n.
Treasure of Health (Van Beverwijck), 94
Trenton, New Jersey, 181
Trico, Catalina, 37, 40–41, 43, 44, 46, 48,
    58, 75, 87, 113, 121, 127, 136, 165,
    299–300
Tromp, Maarten, 248
*True Relation of the Unjust, Cruel, and
    Barbarous Proceedings against the
    English at Amboyna, A,* 72, 260–61
Tryon, William, 320–21
Turner, John, 126

United States Constitution and Bill of
    Rights, 315–16; Flushing
    Remonstrance and First Amendment,
    276;
Unity (ship), 65, 71, 72, 73–74, 88, 157
Usselincx, Willem, 38, 75
utopian community, 220

Van Angola, Anna, 165
Van Bergen, Adriaen, 95, 226
Van Bergen, Agatha, 226, 226n., 262
Van Beverwijck, Johan, 94
Van Brugge, Carel (Charles Bridges), 149
Van Campen, Jan Claeszoon, 150
Van Couwenhoven, Jacob, 197, 207, 212,
    213, 231
Van Crieckenbeeck, Daniel, 46–47, 52, 54,
    59, 65, 87
Van Curler, Arent, 108, 133, 134, 138
Van Curler, Jacob, 110–11
Van den Bogaert, Harmen, 75, 76–81, 87,
    111, 126–27, 187–89, 316, 331n. 80
Van den Enden, Franciscus, 220
Van der Cappellen, Alexander, 228
Van der Donck, Adriaen, 9; American

democratic cause of, 131, 142–45,
    143n., 165, 198–208, 216–31, 243–45,
    258, 259, 305, 309; *American,* use of
    word, 143n.; 172; arrival in America,
    104–9, 112; background and
    education, intellectual mentors,
    94–102, 210; beaver expertise, 194;
    Board of Nine and, 190, 195, 196, 199,
    201, 204, 207; case of Kieft vs. Kuyter,
    Melyn, *et al.,* 170, 172–79; Catskill
    purchase attempted, 138; claims of
    Andrew Forrester and, 185–86; death,
    281; defeat and return to Manhattan
    (1653), 252–54; depositions written by,
    and Stuyvesant response, 204–5;
Description of New Netherland,
    136–38, 137n., 251–52, 281–82; family
    in Breda, and immigration of, 225–26,
    245, 245n., 262; as father of New York,
    143; in Holland presenting case to The
    Hague, 209–32; house excavated, 196,
    196n., 339n. 196; imprisonment,
    200–4; Indians and, 131, 135–38, 141,
    162–63; on Indian women, 119;
    Jansson-Visscher map, 217, 224–25;
    land grant (Colen Donck), saw mill, title
    of *Jonker,* and naming of Yonkers,
    163–64, 176, 195–96, 245, 290; as
    lawman (*schout*) and lawyer, 109, 110,
    112, 131–32, 178, 188n., 207, 250,
    253, 314, 333n. 109; letter to Dr. La
    Montagne, 231; Manhattan activists
    and, 140, 141–45, 143n., 335n. 140;
    marries Mary Doughty, 161, 176, 337n.
    161; Melyn's return and decision
    against Kieft and Stuyvesant, 197–203;
    politics and, 176, 185, 190, 195, 199,
    231, 264; portrait of New Amsterdam
    and, 217–18, 225; as "President of the
    Commonalty," 190; as promoter of
    immigration to Manhattan, 226–29,
    253–54, 341–42n. 228; release from
    prison, 204; *Remonstrance of New
    Netherland,* 205–6, 216, 223–25,
    227–28, 263, 341–42n. 228; return to
    Manhattan and final years, 261–65;
    ship's manifest listing supplies for,
    245n.; States General presentations,
    216–18, 240–45; States General
    reversal of ruling and detention in
    Holland, 245, 249, 250–53; States
    General victory and recall of Stuyvesant
    letter, 243–45; Stuyvesant and, 166,
    175–76, 185, 189, 190, 199–204, 208,

262, 338n. 176; Van Rensselaer and, 102–3, 129, 131–34, 138–39, 141, 204; writings, 129–31, 136–38, 137n., 159, 163, 165–66, 167, 244, 263, 281–82, 335n. 141

Van der Donck, Gysbert, 262

Van der Kemp, Francis Adrian, 321–22, 351n. 322

Van Dinklagen, Lubbert, 200–1, 204, 216, 235, 253

Van Dyck, Anthony, 70, 157

Van Dyck, Hendrick, 172

Van Gastel, Ada Louise, 137, 137n.

Van Heemskerck, Jacob, 29

Van Laer, A. J. F., 53n., 322

Van Leeuwenhoek, Antoni, 98–99

Van Meteren, Emanuel, 24, 33

Van Oldenbarnevelt, Jan, 45

Van Rappard, Alexander Ridder, 53

Van Rappard, Frans Alexander Ridder, 53, 53n.

Van Rensselaer, Jeremias, 139

Van Rensselaer, Kiliaen, 87, 88, 102–3, 108, 129, 131–34, 138–39, 141, 189, 204

Van Rensselaer family, 57

Van Ruytenburch, Willem, 112

Van Salee, Anthony "The Turk," 86, 113, 126, 127, 165, 299

Van Slichtenhorst, Brant, 57, 189–90

Van Tienhoven, Cornelis, 140, 143, 166, 169, 170, 173, 233; disappearance, 266–67; representative to States General, 206, 227, 230–32, 240–41; sex scandal, 241

Van Twiller, Wouter, 82, 85, 108, 113

Van Wassenaer, Nicolaes, 43

Varlo, Charles, 187n.

Veenendaal, Hanny, 137n.

Venema, Janny, 57, 323–25

Verbrugge, Seth, 286

Verbrugge family, 106, 144

Verhulst, Willem, 46, 47, 49, 52, 53, 54–55, 329–30n. 49

Virginia colony, 23, 31, 34, 35, 72, 108, 120; Jamestown settlement, 195; Manhattan and, 195

Vogels, Arnout, 36

Vos, Hans, 188, 188n.

Walloons, 40, 45, 95, 114

Waltingen, Jacob, 122

Westchester County, 269, 290

West Indies, 35

Weymouth, George, 29, 31, 34

whaling, 21

Wickquasgeck Indians, 60, 111, 119, 196, 196n.; account of death of Adriaen van der Donck, 281; murder of, by Europeans, 112, 123; murder of Claes Swits, 110–12, 121; peace treaty with, 164; trail, 60n., 111

Willem I, Prince of Orange (William the Silent), 27, 45, 94, 95, 222

Willem II, Prince of Orange, 198, 222–23, 238–40, 274

Willem Frederik, 239, 240

Willett, Thomas, 237

William and Mary, King and Queen of England, 308–9, 320

Wilmington, Delaware, 181; Swede's Landing, 89

Wilson, Woodrow, 302

Winslow, Josiah, 289

Winthrop, John (elder), 180, 181, 236, 246, 285

Winthrop, John (younger), 287–90, 295, 297, 304, 307

Yonkers, New York, 163

Zangwill, Israel, 318

Zoutberg ("Salt Mountain"), 85